THE

NINE

ALSO BY JEFFREY TOOBIN

*Opening Arguments: A Young Lawyer's First Case—
United States v. Oliver North*

The Run of His Life: The People v. O. J. Simpson

*A Vast Conspiracy: The Real Story of the Sex Scandal That
Nearly Brought Down a President*

*Too Close to Call: The Thirty-Six-Day Battle
to Decide the 2000 Election*

THE

NINE

Inside the Secret World of the Supreme Court

Jeffrey Toobin

DOUBLEDAY

New York   London   Toronto
Sydney   Auckland

PUBLISHED BY DOUBLEDAY

Copyright © 2007 by Jeffrey Toobin

All Rights Reserved

Published in the United States by Doubleday, an imprint of
The Doubleday Broadway Publishing Group, a division of
Random House, Inc., New York.
www.doubleday.com

DOUBLEDAY and the portrayal of an anchor with a dolphin are
registered trademarks of Random House, Inc.

Book design by Michael Collica

Photo research by Photosearch, Inc. NY

Library of Congress Cataloging-in-Publication Data
Toobin, Jeffrey.
The nine : inside the secret world of the Supreme Court /
Jeffrey Toobin.
p.   cm.
Includes bibliographical references and index.
1. United States, Supreme Court. 2. Political questions and judicial
power—United States. 3. Judicial review—United States.
4. Conservatism—United States. 5. Law–Political aspects. I. Title.
KF8748. T66 2007
347.73'26—dc22
2007020287

ISBN 978-0-385-51640-2

PRINTED IN THE UNITED STATES OF AMERICA

5   7   9   10   8   6   4

To Adam

CONTENTS

THE STEPS

The architect Cass Gilbert had grand ambitions for his design of a new home for the Supreme Court—what he called "the greatest tribunal in the world, one of the three great elements of our national government." Gilbert knew that the approach to the Court, as much as the structure itself, would define the experience of the building, but the site presented a challenge. Other exalted Washington edifices—the Capitol, the Washington Monument, the Lincoln Memorial—inspired awe with their processional approaches. But in 1928 Congress had designated for the Court a cramped and asymmetrical plot of land, wedged tightly between the Capitol and the Library of Congress. How could Gilbert convey to visitors the magnitude and importance of the judicial process taking place within the Court's walls?

The answer, he decided, was steps. Gilbert pushed back the wings of the building, so that the public face of the building would be a portico with a massive and imposing stairway. Visitors would not have to walk a long distance to enter, but few would forget the experience of mounting those forty-four steps to the double row of eight massive columns supporting the roof. The walk up the stairs would be the central symbolic experience of the Supreme Court, a physical manifestation of the American march to justice. The stairs separated the Court from the everyday world—and especially from the earthly concerns of the politicians in the Capitol—and announced that the justices would operate, literally, on a higher plane.

That, in any event, was the theory. The truth about the Court has always been more complicated.

For more than two hundred years, the Supreme Court has confronted the same political issues as the other branches of government—with a similar mixed record of success and failure. During his long tenure as chief justice, John Marshall did as much as the framers of the Constitution themselves to shape an enduring structure for the government of the United States. In the decades that followed, however, the Court fared no better than presidents or the Congress in ameliorating the horror of slavery or avoiding civil war. Likewise, during the period of territorial and economic expansion before World War I, the Court again shrank from a position of leadership, mostly preferring to accommodate the business interests and their political allies, who also dominated the other branches of government. It was not until the 1950s and 1960s, and the tenure of Chief Justice Earl Warren, that the Court consistently asserted itself as an independent and aggressive guarantor of constitutional rights.

For the next thirty years, through the tenures of Chief Justices Warren E. Burger and William H. Rehnquist, the Court stood nearly evenly divided on the most pressing issues before it. On race, sex, religion, and the power of the federal government, the subjects that produced the enduring controversies, control of the Court generally belonged to the moderate swing justices, first Lewis F. Powell and then Sandra Day O'Connor, who steered the Court in line with their own cautious instincts—which were remarkably similar to those of the American people. The result was a paradox. Like all their predecessors, the justices belonged to a fundamentally antidemocratic institution. They were not elected; they were not accountable to the public in any meaningful way; their life tenure gave them no reason to cater to the will of the people. Yet the touchstones of the years 1992 to 2005 on the Supreme Court were decisions that reflected public opinion with great precision. The opinions were issued in the Court's customary language of legal certainty—announced as if the constitutional text and precedents alone mandated their conclusions—but the decisions in these cases probably would have been the same if they had simply been put up for a popular vote.

That, now, may be about to change. Through the tense standoff of the Burger and Rehnquist years, a powerful conservative rebellion against the Court was building. It has been, in many respects, a remarkable ideological offensive, nurtured at various times in such locales as elite law schools, evangelical churches, and, most importantly and most recently, the White House. Its agenda has remained largely the same over the decades. Reverse *Roe v. Wade* and allow states to ban abortion. Expand executive power. End racial preferences intended to assist African Americans. Speed executions. Welcome religion into the public sphere. Because the Court has been so closely divided for so long, conservatives have made only halting progress on implementing this agenda. Now, with great suddenness (as speed is judged by the Court's usual stately pace), they are very close to total control. Within one vote, to be precise.

The Court by design keeps its operations largely secret from the outside world, but there are occasions when its rituals offer a window into its soul. One such day was September 6, 2005, when the justices gathered to say good-bye to William Rehnquist, who had died three days earlier.

Rehnquist had had 105 law clerks in his thirty-three years on the Court, and they all knew him as a stickler for form, efficiency, and promptness. So well before the appointed hour, the group gathered in one of the Court's elegant conference rooms. Seven former clerks and a former administrative assistant had been chosen to carry Rehnquist's casket into the building, and they wanted to make sure they did it right. The eight of them gathered around the representatives from the funeral home and asked questions with the kind of intensity and precision that the chief used to demand of lawyers arguing in front of him. Who would stand where? Should they pause between steps or not? Two feet on each step or just one? Only one of them had been a pallbearer before, and he had words of warning for his colleagues. "Be careful," said John G. Roberts Jr., who had clerked for then associate justice Rehnquist from 1980 to 1981. "It's harder than you think."

At precisely ten the pallbearers and the hearse met on First Street, in front of Cass Gilbert's processional steps. The casket was like Rehnquist himself—plain and unadorned. The seven men and one woman grabbed the handles on the pine casket and turned to bring the chief inside the building for a final time. The soft sun of a perfect late-summer morning lit the steps, but the glare off the marble was harsh, nearly oppressive.

As the pallbearers shuffled toward the Court, an honor guard of the other law clerks stood in silence to the left. On the right were the justices themselves. It had been eleven years since there was a new justice, the longest period that the same nine individuals had served together in the history of the Supreme Court. (It had been five decades, since the death of Robert H. Jackson, in 1954, that a sitting justice had died.) The justices lined up according to the Court's iron law of seniority, with the junior member toward the bottom of the stairs and the senior survivor at the top.

The casket first passed Stephen G. Breyer, appointed in 1994 by President Bill Clinton. Such ceremonial duty ill suited Breyer, who still had the gregarious good nature of a Capitol Hill insider rather than the grim circumspection of a stereotypical judge. He had just turned sixty-seven but looked a decade younger, with his bald head nicely tanned from long bike rides and bird-watching expeditions. Few justices had ever taken to the job with more enthusiasm or enjoyed it more.

Breyer's twitchy exuberance posed a contrast to the demeanor of his fellow Clinton nominee, from 1993, Ruth Bader Ginsburg, standing three steps above him. At seventy-two, she was tiny and frail—she clasped Breyer's arm on the way down. Elegantly and expensively turned out as usual, on this day in widow's weeds, she was genuinely bereft to see Rehnquist go. Their backgrounds and politics could scarcely have differed more—the Lutheran conservative from the Milwaukee suburbs and the Jewish liberal from Brooklyn—but they shared a love of legal procedure. Always a shy outsider, Ginsburg knew that the chief's death would send her even farther from the Court's mainstream.

The casket next passed what was once the most recognizable face among the justices—that of Clarence Thomas. His unforgettable confirmation hearings in 1991 had seared his visage into the national consciousness, but the justice on the steps scarcely resembled the strapping young person who had transfixed the nation. Although only fifty-seven, Thomas had turned into an old man. His hair, jet black and full during the hearings, was now white and wispy. Injuries had taken him off the basketball court for good, and a sedentary life had added as much as a hundred pounds to his frame. The shutter of a photographer or the gaze of a video camera drew a scornful glare. Thomas openly, even fervently, despised the press.

David H. Souter should have been next on the stairs. When Rehnquist died, Souter had been at his home in Weare, New Hampshire, but he hadn't received word until it was too late to get to the morning's procession. It was hard to reach him when he was in New Hampshire, because Souter had a telephone and a fountain pen but no answering machine, fax, cell phone, or e-mail. (He was once given a television but never plugged it in.) He was sixty-five years old, but he belonged to a different age altogether, more like the eighteenth century. Souter detested Washington, enjoyed the job less than any of his colleagues, and cared little what others thought of him. He would be back for the funeral the following day.

Anthony M. Kennedy was absent as well, and for equally revealing reasons. He had been in China when Rehnquist died, and he, too, couldn't make it back until the funeral on Wednesday. Nominated by Ronald Reagan in 1987, Kennedy had initially seemed the most conventional, even boring, of men, the Sacramento burgher who still lived in the house where he grew up. But it turned out the prototypical country club Republican possessed a powerful wanderlust, a passion for international travel and law that ultimately wound up transforming his tenure as a justice.

Three steps higher was Antonin Scalia, his famously pugnacious mien softened by grief. He had taken the position on the Court that Rehnquist left in 1986, when Reagan made him chief, and the two men had been judicial soul mates for a generation. An opera lover, Scalia was not afraid of powerful emotions, and he wept openly at the loss of his friend. Scalia had always been the rhetorical force of their counterrevolutionary guard, but Rehnquist had been the leader. At sixty-nine, Scalia too looked lost and lonely.

Sandra Day O'Connor wept as well. O'Connor and Rehnquist had enjoyed one of the more extraordinary friendships in the history of the Court, a relationship that traversed more than fifty years, since she watched the handsome young law student heft trays in the cafeteria at Stanford Law School. (She would later join his class there and graduate in just two years, finishing just behind him, the valedictorian.) They both settled in Phoenix and shared backyard barbecues, even family vacations, until Rehnquist moved to Washington in 1969, joining the Court in 1972.

Nine years later, Ronald Reagan made O'Connor the first woman justice. Her long history with Rehnquist might have suggested that she would turn into his loyal deputy, but that never happened. Indeed, more than anyone else on the Court, it was O'Connor who frustrated Rehnquist's hopes of an ideological transformation in the law and who came, even more than the chief, to dominate the Court.

And though her grief for Rehnquist was real, she may have been weeping for herself, too. She was seventy-five and her blond bob had turned white, but she loved being on the Supreme Court even more than Breyer did, and she was leaving as well. She had announced her resignation two months earlier, to care for her husband, who was slipping further into the grip of Alzheimer's disease. Losses enveloped O'Connor—a dear old friend, her treasured seat on the Court, and, worst of all, her beloved husband's health.

And there was something else that drew O'Connor's wrath, if not her tears: the presidency of George W. Bush, whom she found arrogant, lawless, incompetent, and extreme. O'Connor herself had been a Republican politician—the only former elected official on the Court—and she had watched in horror as Bush led her party, and the nation, in directions that she abhorred. Five years earlier, she had cast the decisive vote to put Bush into the White House, and now, to her dismay, she was handing over her precious seat on the Court for him to fill.

Finally, at the top of the stairs, was John Paul Stevens, then as ever slightly removed from his colleagues. Gerald R. Ford's only appointee to the Court looked much as he did when he was named in 1975, with his thick glasses, white hair, and ever-present bow tie. Now eighty-five, he had charted an independent course from the beginning, moving left as the Court moved right but mostly moving according to his own distinctive view of the Constitution. Respected by his colleagues, if not really known to them, Stevens always stood apart.

The strain from the march up the forty-four steps showed on all the pallbearers except one. The day before carrying Rehnquist into the Supreme Court for a final time, John Roberts had been nominated by President Bush to succeed Rehnquist as chief justice. He was only fifty years old, with an unlined face and unworried countenance. Even with his new burdens, Roberts looked more secure with each step, especially compared with his future colleagues.

The ceremony on the steps represented a transition from an old Court to a new one.

Any change would have been momentous after such a long period of stability in membership, but Rehnquist's and O'Connor's nearly simultaneous departures suggested a particularly dramatic one—generational, ideological, and personal. Conservative frustration with the Court had been mounting for years, even though the Court had long been solidly, even overwhelmingly, Republican. Since 1991, it had consisted of either seven or eight nominees of Republican presidents and just one or two Democratic nominees. But as the core of the Republican Party moved to the right, the Court, in time, went the other way. Conservatives could elect presidents, but they could not change the Court.

Three justices in particular doomed the counterrevolution. Souter, drawing inspiration from icons of judicial moderation like John Marshall Harlan II and Learned Hand, almost immediately turned into a lost cause for the conservatives. Like travelers throughout history, Kennedy was himself transformed by his journeys; his internationalism translated into a more liberal approach to legal issues. Above all, though, it was O'Connor who shaped the Court's jurisprudence and, with it, the nation.

Few associate justices in history dominated a time so thoroughly or cast as many deciding votes as O'Connor—on important issues ranging from abortion to affirmative action, from executive war powers to the election of a president. Some might believe Cass Gilbert's marble steps really did protect the justices from the gritty world of the Capitol. But the Rehnquist Court—the Court of *Bush v. Gore*—dwelled in the center of American political life.

In these years, the Court preserved the right to abortion but allowed restrictions on the practice; the justices permitted the use of affirmative action in higher education, but only in limited circumstances; they sanctioned the continued application of the death penalty but also applied new restrictions on executions. Through one series of cases, the justices allowed for greater expression of public piety in American life, but in a handful of others, they gave a cautious embrace to the cause of gay rights.

These decisions—the legacy of the Rehnquist Court—came about largely because for O'Connor there was little difference between a judicial and a political philosophy. She had an uncanny ear for American public opinion, and she kept her rulings closely tethered to what most people wanted or at least would accept. No one ever pursued centrism and moderation, those passionless creeds, with greater passion than O'Connor. No justice ever succeeded more in putting her stamp on the law of a generation. But the unchanging facade of Cass Gilbert's palace offers only the illusion of permanence. O'Connor's legacy is vast but tenuous, due mostly to her role in 5–4 decisions, which are the most vulnerable to revision or even reversal with each new case.

That process—the counterrevolution that had been stymied for twenty years—has now begun.

PART
ONE

PART ONE

1

THE FEDERALIST
WAR OF IDEAS

For a long time, during the middle of the twentieth century, it wasn't even clear what it meant to be a judicial conservative. Then, with great suddenness, during the presidency of Ronald Reagan, judges and lawyers on the right found a voice and an agenda. Their goals reflected and reinforced the political goals of the conservative wing of the Republican Party.

Earl Warren, who served as chief justice of the United States from 1953 to 1969, exerted a powerful and lasting influence over American law. The former California governor, who was appointed by Dwight D. Eisenhower, put the fight against state-sponsored racism at the heart of his agenda. Starting in 1954, with *Brown v. Board of Education*, which outlawed segregation in public education, the justices began more than a dozen years of sustained, and usually unanimous, pressure against the forces of official segregation. Within the legal profession in particular, Warren's record on civil rights gave him tremendous moral authority. Warren and his colleagues, especially William J. Brennan Jr., his close friend and strategist, used that capital to push the law in more liberal directions in countless other areas as well. On freedom of speech, on the rights of criminal suspects, on the emerging field of privacy, the Warren Court transformed American law.

To be sure, Warren faced opposition, but many of his Court's decisions quickly worked their way into the permanent substructure of American law. *New York Times Co. v. Sullivan*, which protected newspapers that published controversial speech; *Miranda v. Arizona*, which established new rules for interrogating criminal suspects; even *Griswold v. Connecticut*, which announced a right of married people to buy birth control, under the broader heading of privacy—all these cases, along with the Warren Court's many pronouncements on race, became unassailable precedents.

Richard M. Nixon won the presidency in part by promising to rein in the liberalism of the Court, but even though he had the good fortune to name four justices in three years, the law itself wound up little changed. Under Warren E. Burger, whom Nixon named to succeed Warren, the Court in some respects became more liberal than ever. It was under Burger that the court approved the use of school busing, expanded free speech well beyond *Sullivan*, forced Nixon himself to turn over the Watergate tapes, and even, for a time, ended all executions in the United States. *Roe v. Wade*, the abortion rights decision that still defines judicial liberalism, passed by a 7–2 vote in 1973, with three of the four Nixon nominees (Burger, Lewis F. Powell, and Harry A. Blackmun) in the majority. Only Rehnquist, joined by Byron R. White, appointed by John F. Kennedy, dissented.

Through all these years—from the 1950s through the 1970s—the conservatives on the Court like White and Potter Stewart did not differ greatly from their liberal colleagues. The conservatives were less willing to second-guess the work of police officers and to reverse criminal convictions; they were more willing to limit remedies for past racial discrimination; they deferred somewhat more to elected officials about how to organize and run the government. But on the big legal questions, the war was over, and the liberals had won. And their victories went beyond the judgments of the Supreme Court. The Warren Court transformed virtually the entire legal culture, especially law schools.

It was not surprising, then, that on the day after Ronald Reagan defeated Jimmy Carter in 1980, Yale Law School went into mourning. On that day, Steven Calabresi's torts professor canceled class to talk about what was happening in the country. The mood in the room was one of bewilderment and hurt. At the end, the teacher asked for a show of hands among the ninety first-year students before him. How many had voted for Carter and how many for Reagan? Only Calabresi and one other student had supported the Republican.

The informal poll revealed a larger truth about law schools at the time. Most professors at these institutions were liberal, a fact that reflected changes that had taken place in the profession as a whole. The left-leaning decisions of the Warren and Burger Courts had become a reigning orthodoxy, and support among faculty for such causes as affirmative action and abortion rights was overwhelming.

But even law schools were not totally immune from the trends that were pushing the nation's politics to the right, and a small group of students like Calabresi decided to turn these inchoate tendencies into something more enduring. Along with Lee Liberman and David McIntosh, two friends from Yale College who had gone on to law school at the University of Chicago, Calabresi decided to start an organization that would serve as a platform to discuss and advocate conservative ideas in legal thought. They considered several names that would showcase their erudition—"The Ludwig von Mises Society," and "The Alexander Bickel Society"—but they settled on a more elegant choice. They called themselves the Federalist Society, after the early American patriots who fought for the ratification of the Constitution in 1787. Calabresi's guide on the Yale Law School faculty was Professor Robert Bork. Liberman and McIntosh started a Federalist branch at Chicago and recruited as their first faculty adviser a professor named Antonin Scalia.

The idea for a conservative legal organization was perfectly timed, and not just because of the Republican ascendancy in electoral politics. In this period, liberalism may have been supreme at law schools, but it was hardly an intellectually dynamic force. In the 1960s, liberal scholars at Yale and elsewhere were writing the law review articles that gave intellectual heft to the decisions of the Warren Court, but by the eighties, the failures of the Carter administration turned many traditional Democrats away from the practical realities of law to a more exotic passion—advocating (or decrying) a movement known as Critical Legal Studies. Drawing heavily on the work of thinkers like the Italian Marxist Antonio Gramsci and the French poststructuralist Jacques Derrida, CLS devotees attacked the idea that law could be a system of neutral principles, or even one that could create a fairer and more just society. Rather, they viewed law mainly as a tool of oppression that the powerful used against the weak. Whatever its ultimate merits, CLS was singularly inconsequential outside the confines of law schools, its nihilism and extremism rendering it largely irrelevant to the work of judges and lawmakers. At law schools, then, the field was largely open for a vigorous conservative insurgency.

So the Federalist Society both reflected and propelled the growth of the conservative movement. It held its first national conference in 1982, and by the following year there were chapters in more than a dozen law schools. Recognizing the intellectual potential of the society, conservative organizations like the John M. Olin and Scaife foundations made important early grants that allowed the Federalists to establish a full-time office in Washington. The Reagan administration began hiring Federalist members as staffers and, of course, appointing them as judicial nominees, with Bork and Scalia as the most famous examples. (Bork and Scalia both went on the D.C. Circuit in 1982. Calabresi himself went on to be a professor of law at Northwestern.)

The young Federalists who started organizing in the early eighties did not merely strive to recapitulate the tactics of their conservative elders. The prior generation, those who waged their decorous battle against the extremes of the Warren Court, preferred "judicial restraint" to "judicial activism." For conservatives like Justices Stewart or John Marshall Harlan II, who were two frequent dissenters from Warren Court decisions, the core idea was that judges should defer to the democratic branches of government and thus resist the temptation to overturn statutes or veto the actions of government officials. But the new generation of conservatives had more audacious goals. Indeed, they did not believe in judicial restraint, and they represented a new kind of judicial activism themselves. They believed that constitutional law had taken some profoundly wrong turns, and they were not shy about demanding that the courts take the lead in restoring the rightful order.

With the election of Ronald Reagan, conservative ideas suddenly had important new sponsors in Washington. Reagan was elected on promises of shrinking the federal government, which he proposed to do by cutting the budgets for social programs. Many in the Federalist Society sought a legal route to the same goal. Back in 1905, the Supreme Court had said in *Lochner v. New York* that a law that set a maximum number of hours for bakers was unconstitutional because it violated the bakers' freedom of contract under the Fourteenth Amendment's protection of "liberty" and "property." By the 1940s, the Roosevelt appointees to the Supreme Court had repudiated the "*Lochner* era," and for decades no one had seriously suggested that there might be constitutional limits on the scope of the federal government's power. Then, suddenly, in the Reagan years, some conservatives started questioning that wisdom and asserting that much of what the federal government did was unconstitutional. (The second event ever sponsored by the Federalist Society was a speech at Yale in 1982 by Professor Richard Epstein of the University of Chicago Law School in favor of *Lochner v. New York*.) While Reagan was arguing that Congress *should not* pass regulations, the Federalists were saying that, under the Constitution, Congress *could not*.

Edwin Meese III, Reagan's attorney general in his second term, provided a framework for the emerging conservative critique of the Warren and Burger era when he called for a "jurisprudence of original intention." The words of the Constitution, he said, meant only what the authors of the document thought they meant. Or, as the leading "originalist," Robert Bork, put it, "The framers' intentions with respect to freedoms are the sole legitimate premise from which constitutional analysis may proceed." According to Bork, the meaning of the words did not evolve over time. This was an unprecedented view of the Constitution in modern times. Even before the Warren Court, most justices thought that the words of the Constitution were to be interpreted in light of a variety of factors, beyond just the intentions of the framers. As the originalists' greatest adversary, William Brennan, observed in 1985, "the genius of the Constitution rests not in any static meaning it might have had in a world that is dead and gone, but in the adaptability of its great principles to cope with current problems and current needs."

In large measure, the debate over original intent amounted to a proxy for the legal struggle over legalized abortion. No one argued that the authors of the Constitution intended for their words to prohibit states from regulating a woman's reproductive choices; to Bork and Scalia, that ended the debate over whether the Supreme Court should protect a woman's right to choose. If the framers did not believe that the Constitution protected a woman's right to an abortion, then the Supreme Court should never recognize any such right either. In the *Roe* decision itself, Harry Blackmun had acknowledged that the words of the Constitution did not compel his decision. "The Constitution does not explicitly mention any right of privacy," Blackmun had written, but the Court had over time "recognized that a right of personal privacy, or a guarantee of certain areas or zones of privacy, does exist under the Constitution." The interpretive leap of *Roe* was Blackmun's conclusion for the Court that "this right of privacy . . . is broad enough to encompass a woman's decision whether or not to terminate her pregnancy." And it was this conclusion above all that the new generation of conservatives in Washington during the Reagan years began trying to persuade the Court to reverse.

One of those young lawyers was Samuel A. Alito Jr., who was just six years out of law school when he joined the staff of the Justice Department shortly after Reagan was inaugurated in 1981. Four years later, he was presented with a classic dilemma for a committed legal conservative: how best to persuade the Court to overturn *Roe v. Wade*—all at once or a little bit at a time?

In 1982, Pennsylvania had tightened its restrictions on abortion, including requiring that women be prevented from undergoing the procedure without first hearing a detailed series of announcements about its risks. The Court of Appeals for the Third Circuit had declared most of the new rules unconstitutional—as violations of the right to privacy and the rule of *Roe v. Wade*. Alito had joined the staff of the solicitor general, the president's chief advocate before the Supreme Court, and he was assigned the job of suggesting how best to attack the Third Circuit's decision and persuade the Supreme Court to preserve the Pennsylvania law. Around that time, over the Reagan administration's objection, a majority of the justices had reaffirmed their support of *Roe*. The question for Alito was what to do in light of the justices' intransigence. In a memo to his boss on May 30, 1985, Alito wrote, "No one seriously believes that the Court is about to overrule *Roe*. But the Court's decision to review [the Pennsylvania case] may be a positive sign." He continued, "By taking these cases, the Court may be signaling an inclination to cut back. What can be made of this opportunity to advance the goals of bringing about the eventual overruling of *Roe v. Wade* and, in the meantime, of mitigating its effects?" Alito wound up recommending an aggressive line of attack against *Roe*. "We should make clear that we disagree with *Roe v. Wade* and would welcome the opportunity to brief the issue of whether, and if so to what extent, that decision should be overruled," he wrote; at the same time, the Justice Department should defend the Pennsylvania law as consistent with *Roe* and the Court's other abortion decisions.

The solicitor general filed a brief much in line with what Alito recommended, but the case, *Thornburgh v. American College of Obstetricians and Gynecologists*, turned out to be a clear defeat for the Reagan administration. In a stinging, almost contemptuous opinion, written by Blackmun, the Court rejected the Pennsylvania law, declaring, "The States are not free, under the guise of protecting maternal health or potential life, to intimidate women into continuing pregnancies." In a plain message to the conservative activists now in charge at the Justice Department, he wrote, "The constitutional principles that led this Court to its decisions in 1973 still provide the compelling reason for recognizing the constitutional dimensions of a woman's right to decide whether to end her pregnancy." Raising the rhetorical stakes, Blackmun went on to quote Earl Warren's words for the Court in *Brown v. Board of Education*: "It should go without saying that the vitality of these constitutional principles cannot be allowed to yield simply because of disagreement with them." To Blackmun, the war on *Roe* was morally little different from the "massive resistance" that met the Court's desegregation decisions a generation earlier.

But while *Roe* commanded a majority of seven justices in 1973, the decision in *Thornburgh* was supported by only a bare majority of five in 1986. So within the Reagan administration, the lesson of the case was obvious—and one that conservatives took to heart. They didn't need better arguments; they just needed new justices.

Reagan himself had little interest in the legal theories spun by his Justice Department. He had long been on record as opposed to legalized abortion, but the president was manifestly uncomfortable with the subject as well as with the most zealous advocates in the prolife cause. So when, early in his first term, he received the unexpected resignation of Potter Stewart, the president's first reaction was less ideological than political. He wanted above all to fulfill his campaign promise to appoint the first woman to the Court, with her precise stands on the issues a distinctly secondary concern. After searching the small pool of Republican women judges, Reagan selected the thoroughly obscure Sandra Day O'Connor in 1981. O'Connor's ambiguous record on abortion meant that the evangelical wing of the Republican Party regarded her with hostility; Jerry Falwell, then the leader of the Moral Majority and a key figure in Reagan's election, said "good Christians" should be concerned about O'Connor. But at this point, Falwell and his colleagues did not yet control the Republican Party, much less the presidency, so Reagan ignored their complaints. And true to form, O'Connor in her first abortion cases, like *Thornburgh*, tread cautiously, voting to uphold restrictions but never committing to an outright reversal of *Roe*.

Reagan's reelection emboldened the hard-core conservatives in his administration, especially when it came to selecting judges. This was largely because William French Smith, the bland corporate lawyer who was attorney general in Reagan's first term, was replaced by Meese, who put transformation of the Supreme Court at the top of his agenda. Soon, Meese had his chance. In 1986, just days after the decision in *Thornburgh*, Burger resigned as chief justice. Reagan's first move was an obvious one. During his fourteen years on the Court, William Rehnquist had grown from being an often solitary voice of dissent to the leader of the Court's ascendant conservative wing. Just sixty-one years old, and popular with his colleagues, he was the clear choice to replace Burger as chief. But who, then, to put in Rehnquist's seat?

Meese considered only two possibilities—Scalia or Bork, both waiting impatiently for the call in their nearby chambers at the D.C. Circuit. Both were real conservatives, not "squishes," as young Federalist Society lawyers referred to Harlan, Stewart, and the other moderate conservatives. Bork had virtually invented originalism as an intellectual force, and he had been a vocal spokesman against almost every Supreme Court landmark of the past two decades—especially, of course, *Roe v. Wade*. Nine years younger, Scalia had a nearly identical ideological profile, if not quite as distinguished an intellectual pedigree. For his part, Reagan was taken by Scalia's gruff charm and liked the fact that Scalia would be the first Italian American on the Court. The Democrats, who were a minority in the Senate, decided to concentrate on stopping Rehnquist from becoming chief justice and so gave Scalia a pass. He was confirmed unanimously, while Rehnquist won anyway by a 65–33 vote. At the same time, Bork was all but promised the next seat to come open.

Less than a year later, on June 26, 1987, Lewis Powell resigned, and Reagan promptly named Bork as his replacement. A great deal had changed, however, including the Senate itself, which was now led by a Democratic majority. Reagan's popularity had slipped, thanks largely to the Iran-Contra affair, which had become public at the end of 1986. There was no Rehnquist nomination to distract from a fight over a new justice. And the seat at stake was not that of Burger, who had become a reliable conservative vote, but that of Powell, who was the swing justice of his day and the fifth vote for the majority in *Thornburgh* and other abortion rights cases. Bork himself was an ornery intellectual, with a scraggly beard and without any natural ethnic or religious political base. For Democrats, in short, he was an inviting target.

More than anything, the fight over Bork's nomination illustrated that Meese and his allies had done a better job of persuading themselves of the new conservative agenda than they had of convincing the country at large. In truth, many of the Warren Court precedents—the ones Bork had attacked for so long—remained popular with the public and, consequently, in the Senate. By 1987, the *Miranda* warnings were deeply ingrained in the culture, not least because of their endless repetition on television police dramas; the word *privacy* may not have appeared in the Constitution but Bork's criticism of that right—and his defense of Connecticut's right to ban the sale of birth control—sounded extreme to modern ears.

Most of all, though, racial equality (if not affirmative action) had become a bedrock American principle, and Bork had simply backed the wrong side during the civil rights era. In 1963, he had written a notorious article for the *New Republic* in which he had assailed the pending Civil Rights Act. Forcing white barbers to accept black customers, Bork wrote, reflected "a principle of unsurpassed ugliness." More than his views about privacy and abortion, it was Bork's history on race that doomed his nomination. The key block of voters in the Senate were moderate Democrats from the South like Howell Heflin of Alabama, who were actually sympathetic to Bork's cultural conservatism. But these senators were all elected with overwhelming black support—and they would not abide views that, fairly or not, sounded racist. Bork ultimately lost by a vote of 58–42.

Enraged by the attacks on Bork, Reagan had said he would nominate a replacement for Bork that the senators would "object to as much as the last one." So Meese and his allies tried to foist a potentially even more conservative, and a much younger, nominee on the Senate, Douglas H. Ginsburg, a recent Reagan appointee to the D.C. Circuit. But Ginsburg's nomination collapsed over a few tragicomic days, following revelations that the law-and-order judge had smoked marijuana as a professor at Harvard Law School.

Howard Baker now stepped into the process. A former senator who had been brought in as chief of staff to steady the White House after the Iran-Contra revelations, Baker had little interest in the ideological groundbreaking that Meese was leading at the Justice Department. Baker was an old-fashioned conservative who wanted a justice in his own mold, a believer in judicial restraint. With the White House reeling from multiple fiascos, Baker just wanted to pick someone who would be confirmed—a conservative, to be sure, but not necessarily someone who would please Meese and the other true believers. The call went out to Anthony M. Kennedy, a thoughtful and earnest judge on the Ninth Circuit from Sacramento. He was confirmed quickly and without incident.

George H. W. Bush served as a transitional figure between the old Republican Party and the new. He was born to the country club GOP of his father, the cautious and corporate senator from Connecticut, but the forty-first president was elected in 1988 courtesy of the evangelical and other hard-core conservatives who were increasingly dominating the party. In the Reagan years, figures like Jerry Falwell, Pat Robertson, and, later, James C. Dobson were content to be heard by the White House; but in the first Bush presidency, they wanted more. And the issues that meant the most to them—abortion, above all—were decided by the Supreme Court. They wanted their own justices.

On the Court, and in much else, Bush tried to finesse the demands of the far right. To win their support in the first place, Bush had sworn fealty to the new conservative orthodoxies, including opposition to *Roe v. Wade*, but it was clear that his heart was never in the cause. For this reason, then, Brennan's resignation in July 1990 was for Bush more an annoyance than an opportunity. He was preoccupied with the sudden fall of Communism and had no stomach for a fight in the Democratic Senate over a Supreme Court nominee—especially about issues that meant little to him personally. A Yankee aristocrat, Bush surrounded himself with men in the same mold, like his White House counsel, C. Boyden Gray, and attorney general, Richard Thornburgh (who as governor of Pennsylvania was the defendant in the 1986 abortion case).

As his first choice for the Supreme Court, Bush chose yet another man with a background and temperament similar to his own—David H. Souter. The appointee had spent virtually his entire career in New

Hampshire state government, where he had a nearly invisible public profile. (Thurgood Marshall, in his final cranky years on the Court, still spoke for many when he greeted the news with "Never heard of him.") John Sununu, the White House chief of staff, promised conservatives that the appointment would be "a home run" for them, but Souter's moderate testimony at his confirmation hearing suggested otherwise. Democrats, grateful that Bush had avoided a confrontational choice, raised few objections, and Souter was confirmed by a vote of 90–9.

Even before Souter's record refuted Sununu's prediction (as it surely did), conservatives registered their outrage at his appointment—and their demands for Bush's next choice. Sununu promised that the president would fill the next vacancy with a nominee so conservative that there would be "a knock-down, drag-out, bloody-knuckles, grassroots fight." Thus, a year later, Clarence Thomas.

Marshall resigned on June 27, 1991, almost a year to the day after Brennan, and this time conservatives insisted that Bush appoint one of their own. By this point, with Brennan also gone, Marshall was the last full-throated liberal on the Court. His seat was especially precious to his political opponents, since only two members of the *Thornburgh* majority from 1986—Blackmun and Stevens—remained; the replacements for the other three would all be selected by presidents who publicly opposed *Roe v. Wade*. The decision appeared as good as overruled.

Thomas's confirmation hearings, of course, turned into a malign carnival of accusation and counterclaim between the nominee and his one-time aide Anita Hill. But that sideshow obscured the larger significance of Thomas's appointment. Even though the nominee was unusually reticent in answering the senators' questions, it was easy to infer that the forty-three-year-old judge believed in what might be called the full Federalist Society agenda: that the justices should interpret the Constitution according to the original intent of the framers, that Congress had repeatedly passed laws that infringed on executive power and violated the Constitution, and that the crown jewels of liberal jurisprudence—from *Miranda* to *Roe*—should be overruled.

The scope and speed of the conservative success was remarkable. In just about a decade, conservatives had taken ideas from the fringes of intellectual respectability to an apparent majority on the Supreme Court. Thomas's confirmation, on October 15, 1991, by a vote of

52–48, meant that Republican presidents had appointed eight of the nine justices—and Byron White, the lone Democrat, was more conservative, and a stronger opponent of *Roe*, than most of his colleagues. With Rehnquist, O'Connor, Scalia, Kennedy, Souter, and Thomas completing the roster, how could the conservative cause lose?

2

GOOD VERSUS EVIL

lections impose rituals of transition on the executive and legislative branches, but the judiciary, especially the Supreme Court, glides uninterrupted into the future. The justices who take their places from behind the red curtain on the first Monday in October are usually the same ones who appeared the year before, and they are likely to be there the following October as well. The Court is defined more by continuity than by change. But still, at some moments, even the hushed corridors of the Court crackle with anticipation of a new order. The fall of 1991 was such a moment.

The signs of transition at the Court were physical as well as ideological. It was one of the rare times in Court history when four retired justices were alive. Warren E. Burger, Lewis F. Powell, William J. Brennan Jr., and Thurgood Marshall were still making occasional visits to the Court, all of them walking embodiments of both the sweep of the Court's history and its relentless retreat into the past.

Burger, the white-maned former chief justice, who had left the bench in 1986, maintained a surpassing ability to annoy his colleagues, even in retirement. He had departed the Supreme Court to lead a commission on the bicentennial of the Constitution, feeding, perhaps, his taste for pomp, which was always stronger than his interest in jurisprudence. (The celebration in 1987 was widely ignored, even in legal circles.) Worse, Burger's taste for bureaucratic empire building had led to the construction of a huge structure for the Federal Judicial Center on a desolate plot of land near Union Station. Retired justices of the Court traditionally maintained chambers in the Supreme Court building, but among the hazy justifications for the FJC was that it would provide a new home for retired justices.

Characteristically, Burger neglected to check with the justices themselves to see if they had any interest in uprooting themselves from Cass Gilbert's marvelous structure. None had.

Powell, the Virginia gentleman and centrist who controlled the outcome of so many important decisions, remained as popular as ever and even, in one way, influential. In 1986, the year before he retired, he had cast the deciding vote in *Bowers v. Hardwick*, which upheld Georgia's right to criminalize consensual gay sodomy. Byron R. White's opinion for the Court was brusquely dismissive of the very notion of a constitutional protection for gay sex. But in 1990, Powell told a law school audience that he "probably made a mistake" in joining the majority in that case. Powell's admission kept the controversy about *Bowers* alive and signaled that his favored disciple, O'Connor, might also have doubts about having voted the same way.

Burger and Powell passed without much notice on their visits to the Court, but Brennan always drew a crowd. The history of the Court abounds with long tenures, but even three decades does not guarantee that a justice will leave much of a legacy. Forgotten justices like James M. Wayne (thirty-two years on the Court), Samuel Nelson (twenty-seven), and Robert Grier (twenty-four) illustrate that longevity and obscurity can coexist. But Brennan's thirty-four years ranked among the most consequential tenures the Court had ever seen. His opinion in *Baker v. Carr* led to the rule of one person, one vote; *New York Times Co. v. Sullivan* transformed the law of libel to expand First Amendment protections for the press; his opinion in *Eisenstadt v. Baird* made the result in *Roe v. Wade* almost inevitable. But even more than the opinions he wrote himself, there was his role as the Court's master vote counter, first with his great friend Earl Warren and then as the wily leader of the Court's shrinking but still influential liberal wing.

Brennan's influence didn't end with retirement, either, and not just because hundreds of his opinions remained precedents of the Court. He grew especially close to his successor, David Souter. "I'd stick my head in his chamber door, and he'd look up and say, 'Get in here, pal,' and when I was ready to go he'd call me pal again," Souter said at Brennan's funeral in 1997. "He wouldn't just shake my hand; he'd grab it in both of his and squeeze it and look me right in the eye and repeat my name. If he thought I'd stayed away too long, he'd give me one of his bear hugs to let me know that I'd been missed. . . . And he might tell me a few things that were patently false, which he thought

I might like to hear anyway. He'd bring up some pedestrian opinion that I'd delivered, and he'd tell me it was not just a very good opinion but a truly great one, and then he'd go on and tell me it wasn't just great but a genuine classic of the judge's art. And I'd listen to him, and I'd start to think that maybe he was right." Brennan's seven years with Souter put a stamp on the younger man's career.

Thurgood Marshall was the least seen of the retirees. He was the only member of the Court since Warren who would have held a place in American history even if he had never become a justice. As an architect of the NAACP Legal Defense and Education Fund's assault on segregation, he had argued and won many of the civil rights landmarks of the 1940s and 1950s, including *Brown v. Board of Education* in 1954. Lyndon Johnson had put him on the Court in 1967, but Marshall's tenure had been unhappy. The causes he cared about were in eclipse for most of those years, and he spent his last years fighting ill health and trying to hang on until a Democratic president could appoint his successor. "If I die, just prop me up!" he would instruct his law clerks.

So Marshall's resignation in 1991, a week before his eighty-third birthday, came as a surprise. "I'm getting old, and coming apart," he explained at a freewheeling press conference the next day, where he sat slumped over in a chair, looking disheveled. He was asked whether he thought President George H. W. Bush had an obligation to appoint another minority justice in his place. "I don't think that should be a ploy," he answered, "and I don't think it should be used as an excuse, one way or the other." A reporter followed up, "An excuse for what?" Marshall's answer seemed directed at his most likely successor. "Doing wrong," he said. "Picking the wrong Negro. . . . My dad told me way back . . . there's no difference between a white snake and a black snake. They'll both bite."

Unwritten Supreme Court protocol called for a wall of separation between the sitting justices and the confirmation process. Nominees were never so presumptuous as to make contact with the Court before they were confirmed, and justices generally refrained from commenting, even in private, about their possible new colleagues. So it was, at first, with the confirmation hearings of Clarence Thomas, which began on September 10, 1991.

There was never much doubt that Thomas would be the nominee. A year earlier he had been confirmed for the United States Court of Appeals for the D.C. Circuit, and the prospect of his replacing Marshall had been much discussed then. The dilemma facing Bush and the Republicans was clear. If Marshall left, they could not leave the Supreme Court an all-white institution; at the same time, they had to choose a nominee who would stay true to the conservative cause. The list of plausible candidates who fit both qualifications pretty much began and ended with Clarence Thomas.

On July 1, 1991, President George H. W. Bush introduced Thomas as his nominee at a press conference at his vacation home in Kennebunkport, Maine. There was awkwardness about the selection from the start. "The fact that he is black and a minority has nothing to do with this," Bush said. "He is the best qualified at this time." The statement was self-evidently preposterous; Thomas had served as a judge for only a year and, before that, displayed few of the customary signs of professional distinction that are the rule for future justices. For example, he had never argued a single case in any federal appeals court, much less in the Supreme Court; he had never written a book, an article, or even a legal brief of any consequence. Worse, Bush's endorsement raised themes that would haunt not only Thomas's confirmation hearings but also his tenure as a justice. Like the contemporary Republican Party as a whole, Bush and Thomas opposed preferential treatment on account of race—and Bush had chosen Thomas in large part because of his race. The contradiction rankled.

Still, there was much to admire in Thomas, as the early days of his confirmation hearings showed. Thomas began his testimony with a personal story that was extraordinary by any measure. He had grown up in poverty in Pin Point, Georgia, without a father and with a mother who earned twenty dollars every two weeks as a maid. She was so poor, in fact, that she had to send her two boys to live with their grandparents. "Imagine, if you will, two little boys with all their belongings in two grocery bags." Hard work put him through Holy Cross College and Yale Law School, and he had thrived during his career in government, as an ever-rising official in the federal bureaucracy during the Reagan administration.

Still, as soon as Thomas began answering questions, problems emerged. Four years earlier, Robert Bork's nomination had been defeated because he expounded broadly about his well-established, and very conservative, judicial philosophy. Consequently, the conventional wisdom had become that nominees should avoid taking substantive stands on most legal issues. But Thomas took the approach to an extreme. In awkward, wooden answers, he gave the impression that he had no views, not simply that he was declining to express them. In one infamous exchange, he told Senator Patrick Leahy that he had never even discussed *Roe v. Wade.*

Still, there was little organized opposition to Thomas, and his confirmation looked assured. On Friday, September 27, the Judiciary Committee split 7–7 on Thomas, but even that tepid nonendorsement meant that the full Senate would give him an up-or-down vote. There was little reason to think he might lose.

Then, on Saturday, October 6, the name Anita Hill leaked to the press, and the rest of the Thomas confirmation battle became a tawdry national obsession. Hill had been a young lawyer on Thomas's staff, first at the Department of Education and then at the Equal Employment Opportunity Commission. During those years, she had confided to friends that her boss had made a series of bizarre sexual comments and overtures to her. In the summer leading up to Thomas's confirmation hearings, Hill had discussed with some of those friends whether she should come forward with what she knew about the nominee. Through these conversations, Hill's name reached Democratic staffers on the Judiciary Committee and then several reporters. Once her name became public, the committee decided that she should tell her story in public.

Over seven surreal hours on Friday, October 11, Hill gave testimony that soon became part of American folklore. She said Thomas had talked about his large penis, about his skill at giving oral sex, and about pornographic films starring Long Dong Silver. There was "one of the oddest episodes," when Thomas looked at a soda can in his office and asked, "Who has put pubic hair on my Coke?" Later that night, after Hill's marathon testimony, in a confrontation that would become equally famous, Thomas returned to the hearing room. He denied Hill's allegations in their entirety and denounced the proceeding as a "high-tech lynching for uppity blacks." Thomas rejected Hill's allegations of mistreatment, but otherwise refused to answer any questions about his relationship with Hill or his personal life.

The nation watched as the hearings continued through the weekend, with Republican senators accusing Hill of "erotomania" and perjury, and of making up her testimony from her reading of *The Exorcist.*

There were supporting witnesses for both sides, and the hearings didn't end until 2:03 a.m. on Monday, October 14, less than forty-eight hours before the Senate was scheduled to vote.

At the Supreme Court, a handful of clerks had caught parts of the hearing on the few televisions that were scattered in offices on the second floor of the Court. But it wasn't just custom that led the Court to ignore the circus on the other side of First Street. There was more important news, closer to home. Nan Rehnquist, the chief's wife, was dying.

When he became chief justice in 1986, Rehnquist arrived with one great advantage. He wasn't Warren Burger.

In his seventeen years as chief, Burger had managed to alienate all of his colleagues. The greatest breach, and the most surprising, was with Harry Blackmun. No closer friends had ever served together on the Court. They had met in kindergarten in St. Paul, Minnesota, and grown up together. In 1933, Blackmun was best man at Burger's wedding. Burger made his name first in national politics, serving in a senior post in the Eisenhower Justice Department, and he engineered both his own and then Blackmun's appointment to the federal court of appeals. Burger became chief justice in 1969, and a year later, after the nominations of Clement Haynsworth and G. Harrold Carswell failed, Burger inveigled President Nixon to name Blackmun in their place. In their early days on the Court, the two men were known as the Minnesota Twins.

The relationship soon soured. In part, the differences between the two men were simply ideological, as Blackmun moved closer to Brennan and Marshall on the left. But it was more the way Burger ran the Court that came to madden Blackmun and his colleagues. The main duty of a chief justice is to chair the Court's conference every Friday when it is in session. At those secret meetings, held in the chief's conference room, the nine justices review the argued cases and cast their votes. When he is in the majority, the chief justice assigns who will write the opinion for the Court; when the chief is in dissent, the senior associate justice in the majority makes the assignment.

The problem, it seemed, was that Burger could not run the conference. Discussions meandered aimlessly and ended inconclusively. Justices sometimes thought that Burger would switch his vote to keep control of opinions or even try to assign cases where he was not in the majority. (William O. Douglas, then the senior associate justice, thought that was how Burger assigned Blackmun to write *Roe v. Wade*.) Potter Stewart, who was appointed by Eisenhower in 1958, grew so frustrated with Burger that he took an unprecedented form of revenge. Stewart responded eagerly to an approach from Bob Woodward, who had just become famous for his work on Watergate, letting the journalist know that he would cooperate with an extended investigation of the Burger Court. Stewart's interviews provided a basis for *The Brethren*, written by Woodward and Scott Armstrong and published in 1979. The book, full of vivid inside detail that had never before been divulged to the public, portrayed Burger as a pompous, egomaniacal bumbler. (Stewart wound up resigning in 1981, at the unusually young age of sixty-six, opening the seat that went to O'Connor.)

Rehnquist never went public with his distress about Burger, but he also seethed. In the Burger years, opinions came out late or not at all, forcing cases to be "put over," or reargued, in subsequent years. Once, when Lewis Powell was ill, Rehnquist wrote him about his frustration with Burger. Powell, who joined the Court at the age of sixty-four, served as a kind of older brother to all the justices, and Rehnquist felt comfortable unburdening himself in alternately brusque and whimsical ways.

"Sometimes when [Burger] runs out of things to say, but he doesn't want to give up the floor, he gives the impression of a Southern Senator conducting a filibuster. I sometimes wish that neither the Chief nor Bill Brennan would write out all their remarks beforehand and deliver them verbatim from the written page," Rehnquist wrote. "Bill is usually thorough, but as often as not he sounds like someone reading aloud a rather long and uninteresting recipe. Then of course Harry Blackmun can usually find two or three sinister aspects of every case which 'disturb' him, although they have nothing to do with the merits of the question. And John Stevens, today, as always felt very strongly about every case, and mirabile dictu had found just the right solution to every one. As you might imagine, my conference discussion was, as always, perfectly suited to the occasion: well-researched, cogently presented, and right on target!"

So when Rehnquist became chief in 1986, Burger had provided him with a clear picture of how not to run a conference. Rehnquist set out to do it differently, and he led by example. He would begin by briefly summarizing the case, giving his own view of the proper result, then going around the table in order of seniority. (The tradition had been for discussion in seniority order, then votes in reverse seniority order. Rehnquist thought that was a waste of time and combined the two rounds into one.)

The other justices followed his example. Their comments were shorter, the resolution of the cases was clearer. No one spoke twice before everyone had a chance to speak once. In time, the brevity of the conferences would come to have a large and unexpected impact on the workings of the Court, but for the moment everyone was pleased with the efficiency.

Case assignments changed, too. Every chief justice wields power through assigning big cases to his favorites (or, especially, to himself), but Rehnquist made the system as fair as possible. No one received a new assignment until he (or she) had finished the previous one. As with speaking at conference, every justice was assigned one case before anyone was assigned two. Rehnquist didn't interfere with assignments when he was in the minority. Everyone on the Court, liberals and conservatives alike, welcomed the changes.

One of the signatures of the Burger years was that the Court decided more and more cases every year. The number of filings increased, but the number of cases the justices accepted jumped even faster. By the mid-1980s, they were hearing as many as 150 cases a year—double the number from the 1950s. Like the chaotic conferences, the ever-rising number of lawsuits contributed to an atmosphere of chaos. In those jumbled final days of the term each year, Burger often couldn't corral five justices to agree on a majority opinion. The splintered justices would thus fail to settle the issue before them and therefore offer little guidance to the lower courts addressing similar questions. At a basic level of competence, the Court wasn't doing its job.

For the most part, the justices controlled their calendar; they could decide how many cases to hear simply by granting or refusing writs of certiorari. (Four votes are needed to grant a writ to hear a case.) As it happened, White and Blackmun had idiosyncratic views of the certiorari process. White thought the Court should grant cert whenever there was even a suggestion that two circuit courts of appeals viewed an issue differently; other justices thought it necessary to resolve only significant circuit splits. Blackmun regarded a denial of cert as tantamount to a decision on the merits, so he wanted to grant whenever he disagreed with a lower court's view. White and Blackmun's approaches, plus various combinations of others, meant the caseload was becoming close to unmanageable.

By the time Burger resigned, all of the remaining justices wanted to reduce the number of cases. But how to do it in a way that wouldn't also take away their opportunity to advocate their own quirky view of the cert process? In a little-noticed development, Rehnquist figured out a solution. One area the justices all wanted to pare was so-called mandatory appeals. Certain federal laws, mostly in obscure areas, gave the parties the absolute right to have their cases heard by the Supreme Court. These cases, which amounted to a dozen or more every year, absorbed a lot of the Court's time on trivial issues. So Rehnquist lobbied Congress to change the law. The task required just the kind of Washington savvy that Burger claimed to have but didn't. Rehnquist accomplished his mission in just two years. In 1988, Congress passed a law that essentially gave the Supreme Court complete control of its docket. To a person, the justices were extremely grateful to the chief.

Rehnquist's personality also changed the atmosphere on the Court. Burger was an Anglophile who collected antiques and fine wines. (When Blackmun joined the Court, Burger gave him a top hat as a gift.) Such was Burger's vanity that he placed a large cushion on his center seat on the bench, so he would appear taller than his colleagues. Rehnquist had none of those pretensions, at least in his early years as chief. He had a single beer and one cigarette at lunch every day. (Later, he struggled, with intermittent success, to quit smoking and switched to what he would always call a "Miller's Lite.") By the time he became chief, Rehnquist had pared his long sideburns and dropped the wide ties that were his concessions to 1970s fashion, but he still cut a shambling figure when he took his lunchtime strolls around the neighborhood.

John Dean, Nixon's White House counsel, remembered that when he first introduced Rehnquist to the president, the then–assistant attorney general "was wearing a pink shirt that clashed with an awful psychedelic necktie, and Hush Puppies." According to the White House tapes, after Rehnquist left, Nixon asked Dean, "Is he Jewish? He looks it. . . . That's a hell of a costume he's wearing, just like a clown." As chief, Rehnquist, a Lutheran of Swedish ancestry, disposed of the worst of the ties but kept the Hush Puppies.

For a large, strapping man, Rehnquist had a delicate constitution. He had a chronically bad back, from an injury he sustained while gardening, and the pain would sometimes cause him to stand up during oral arguments at the Court and take a few steps behind his chair. In the early 1980s, he was even hospitalized for the back problems, and the treatment created new issues. The painkillers caused him to slur his words, and the problem became embarrassingly noticeable when he asked questions in Court. The FBI investigation in connection with his promotion to chief justice revealed that Rehnquist's medical problems were more serious than the public was led to believe. He had been addicted to the sedative Placidyl for at least four years, and when he was hospitalized during his withdrawal from the medication in 1981, he suffered hallucinations. On one occasion, he told a nurse that "Voices outside the room are saying they're going to kill the president." Still, by the time he became chief, in 1986, his condition appears to have stabilized, in part because he took up tennis. Even though he was entitled to hire four law clerks, he generally took only three, which suited his weekly doubles game.

Rehnquist had married his wife, Natalie Cornell, known as Nan, after his service in World War II. A native of Wisconsin, Rehnquist had developed a taste for desert heat during his time as a weather spotter in North Africa, and the newlyweds settled in Phoenix. (The chief's military service also instilled in him a lifelong curiosity about the weather that matched his interest in low-stakes gambling. He'd often bet his law clerks how much snow had fallen in the plaza in front of the Court.) Nan matched her husband in a mutual absence of pretensions, and their marriage was long and happy. But shortly after Rehnquist became chief, Nan was diagnosed with cancer. Their struggle with her illness, combined with the markedly improved atmosphere at the Court, only deepened the affection of Rehnquist's colleagues for him. She died on October 17, 1991.

That was just two days after Thomas, at long last, won confirmation in the Senate. But the tally of votes on October 15 didn't conclude the drama surrounding Thomas's nomination. Hill's testimony had set off a furious scramble among many journalists and Democratic activists to corroborate or refute her charges. (Records of Thomas's videotape rentals were of particular interest.) Rumors abounded that other women were going to come forward with evidence of objectionable behavior by Thomas. Even though he had been confirmed, Thomas would not actually become a justice—and thus removable only by impeachment by the House and conviction by the Senate—until he took the oath of office. And before the furor over Hill erupted, the White House and Rehnquist had tentatively planned for Thomas to take it from the chief justice on November 1.

But that was seventeen full days after the Senate vote—a period of time when anything could happen. Thomas's supporters wanted him sworn in immediately. But with Nan Rehnquist's death on October 17, the White House faced the delicate problem of intruding on the chief justice's grief for a final act of damage control on Thomas's nomination.

At first the administration tried to finesse the problem, by holding an unofficial swearing in—a party, in effect—on the White House lawn on Friday, October 18. The ceremony would have no legal significance, but it would contribute to an atmosphere of finality around the confirmation. Hundreds of guests, including many members of Thomas's family (including his father, from whom he had been long estranged until shortly before his nomination) and celebrities like Sylvester Stallone and Reggie Jackson, joined the president to salute the new justice.

Still, Thomas was not yet an actual member of the Court, and investigative reporters were still hard at work. White House officials decided the stakes were high enough to risk offending Rehnquist, so they asked him to administer the oath to Thomas only days after Nan Rehnquist's death. The chief agreed, and the swearing in took place on October 23 in a conference room at the Court, the first such private ceremony in fifty years. The official explanation for the speeded-up procedure was to allow Thomas's secretaries and clerks to get on the Supreme Court payroll—a transparent rationalization since his employees were already on the federal payroll at the D.C. Circuit.

The rushed oath turned out to be a wise move. That same day, according to Jane Mayer and Jill Abramson, three reporters for the *Washington Post* "burst into the newsroom almost simultaneously with information confirming that Thomas' involvement with pornography far exceeded what the public had been led to believe." They had testimony from eyewitnesses and the manager of a video store where Thomas rented such fare. But since Thomas had been sworn in, the *Post* decided not to pursue the issue and dropped the story.

The whole Thomas confirmation could scarcely have been a greater assault on the Court's sense of seemliness. The crudity of the accusations, the brutality of Thomas's response, the vindictive discourse on all sides made for a perfectly awful combination. That the White House, if not Thomas himself, had intruded on Rehnquist's grieving for political purposes made it even worse.

O'Connor, who was considered the social as well as the political center of the Court, had a habit of dividing the world—people, buildings, controversies, issues—into two categories: attractive and unattractive. The words referred not so much to what was or wasn't pleasing to the eye but rather to an overall level of decency and likability. To her, and her colleagues at the Court, the Thomas hearings *defined* unattractive.

Then, it got worse. The November 11, 1991, issue of *People* magazine featured a seven-page spread on Clarence and Virginia Thomas and their view of the confirmation ordeal. Ginny Thomas was a political force in her own right, a Labor Department lawyer at the time and later a senior official with the Republican congressional leadership and with conservative foundations. She said that after Hill made her claims, "the Clarence Thomas I had married was nowhere to be found. He was just debilitated beyond anything I had seen in my life. About 12:45 a.m., he said, 'I need you to call your two friends from your Bible-study group, and their husbands, and get them here with me in the morning to pray.' Clarence knew the next round of hearings to begin that day was not the normal political battle. It was spiritual warfare. Good versus evil. We were fighting something we didn't understand, and we needed prayerful people in our lives. We needed God." The couple posed for photographs—grinning cheek to cheek, holding hands on the plush carpet, curled up on the sofa reading the Bible. Thomas told the reporter, "It's been brutal, just brutal. I don't know if it's over, but we found a way to survive. And we have each other."

The interview came at a time when the justices rarely said anything to the press, much less engaged in soul baring for *People* magazine. Thomas's cooperation with the magazine was especially inappropriate because, just a month earlier, he had refused to answer exactly these kinds of questions about his personal life before the Judiciary

Committee. The *People* spread compounded the Court's sense of bewilderment about him.

Thomas moved into his chambers and heard . . . nothing from his new colleagues. In part, this was just the style of the Rehnquist Court. The justices did not casually drop by one another's offices. At the D.C. Circuit and in his other government jobs, Thomas liked to wander the halls, shoot the breeze, or make spur-of-the-moment lunch plans, but that simply wasn't done at the Court. He met his new colleagues at conference, where they greeted him cordially, but their interaction stopped there. For Thomas, the silence in his chambers was deafening.

So Thomas retreated. Two of the first decorating touches on the bare walls of his office were telling. In the entrance foyer he posted an admonition to respect the confidentiality of all Supreme Court business. On the door to his private office, he put the words "Do Not Disturb." He used to enjoy taking lunchtime walks around the D.C. Circuit courthouse, but his notoriety made anonymity impossible. He even stopped driving his beloved black Corvette to work. ("REZ IPSA," the vanity license plate said, a play on the Latin legal phrase that means "The thing speaks for itself.") The car was too recognizable. "I used to love to walk out with my clerks and walk down to the Old Post Office and have barbecue or something like that or walk over to Union Station and have cheese fries or something," Thomas told the *Docket Sheet*, the Supreme Court's internal newsletter, in the only interview he gave after *People*. "My total loss of anonymity has been the big change in that regard." In one respect, it was fortunate that Thomas almost never left the Supreme Court building by foot in his first year, because it meant that he probably never saw the boldly lettered graffito on a Capitol Hill sidewalk across the street. It said, "Anita Told the Truth."

Unlike most of his fellow justices, Thomas made an effort to learn the names of the people who worked at the Court—the cafeteria workers, clerks, and cops. Despite his friendly demeanor, the Court employees saw how devastated he was by the confirmation battle. Years later, Thomas recalled that one of the Supreme Court police officers who noticed how "battered and beaten" he looked took to welcoming him each day with the words "Don't let them take your joy."

Just weeks after joining the Court, Thomas had a chance to strike back at the "them" who had tormented him in the hearings. The question before him: Should *Roe v. Wade* be overruled?

QUESTIONS PRESENTED

There were two kinds of cases before the Supreme Court. There were abortion cases—and there were all the others.

Abortion was (and remains) the central legal issue before the Court. It defined the judicial philosophies of the justices. It dominated the nomination and confirmation process. It nearly delineated the difference between the national Democratic and Republican parties. And in 1992, the issue—and the Court—appeared to be at a turning point.

For the first time since *Roe v. Wade* was decided nineteen years earlier, eight of the nine justices on the Court had been appointed by Republicans, whose party was publicly and officially committed to ending legalized abortion. (And the single Democratic appointee, Byron White, who was named by John F. Kennedy in 1962, had dissented in *Roe* and voted against abortion rights in every subsequent case.) If there was ever a perfect opportunity to overturn *Roe* once and for all, the spring of 1992 was it.

Unlike the other branches of government, the courts, even the justices of the Supreme Court, cannot simply decide to take action on an issue of importance to them. They must wait until a case happens to move through the lower courts in a way that raises the issue. Savvy lawyers can shape the process. Indeed, as the Court became more conservative in the Burger years, certain liberal civil rights groups would sometimes actually put up money to pay off plaintiffs in controversial cases, so that the justices would not decide the case and create a "bad" precedent. But sometimes the interests aligned so that a major issue landed in the Court at the most dramatic possible time. That was what happened right after Thomas joined the Court.

In the years since *Roe*, states with antiabortion majorities had tried in different ways to pass restrictive laws that the Supreme Court would approve. The laws tracked the evolution of the Court. As the Court became more conservative, the states became bolder in tightening the restrictions. Anticipating the Court's move to the right on abortion—and hoping to push it further in that direction—Pennsylvania had passed one of the nation's most restrictive laws in 1989. The law forced women who wanted an abortion to wait twenty-four hours after contacting a clinic before getting one, and mandated that the women be given a lecture about fetal development and alternatives to abortion. Minors seeking abortions would have to get permission from a parent (or a judge), and married women would have to inform their husbands of their plans.

On October 21, 1991—six days after Thomas was confirmed and two days before he was sworn in—a three-judge panel of the United States Court of Appeals for the Third Circuit upheld the Pennsylvania law almost in its entirety. The majority in *Planned Parenthood of Southeastern Pennsylvania v. Gov. Robert P. Casey* rejected only one part of the law, the provision mandating that married women first inform their husbands if they sought an abortion. "Most married women will discuss the abortion decision with their husbands," the majority said. But some married women would not, because "many husbands are capable of violence in circumstances of this kind and will use physical force and the threat thereof to keep the wife from access to the clinic." The third judge on the Third Circuit panel disagreed, arguing that he would have upheld the spousal notification requirement along with the rest of the law.

That third judge, Samuel A. Alito Jr., had just been appointed to the bench a year earlier by President George H. W. Bush, and this was his first major opinion. He was only forty-one years old, a former federal prosecutor and Justice Department official who could expect serious scrutiny as a possible Supreme Court candidate down the line. Like all such judges, Alito knew that he would be in great measure defined by how he ruled on abortion. So the case was of no small consequence, and unlike the other judges on his panel, Alito didn't split the difference. He supported all of Pennsylvania's restrictions—including the requirement that women notify their spouses in advance before obtaining an abortion.

Spousal notification would affect very few women in Pennsylvania, Alito said. The evidence in the case showed that between 70 and 80 percent of women who sought abortions were unmarried, he noted, and 95 percent of married women who sought abortions did tell their husbands. "Thus, it is immediately apparent," Alito wrote, that the law "cannot affect more than about 5 percent of married women seeking abortions or an even smaller percentage of all women desiring abortions." In light of these small numbers, there was no "broad practical impact needed to establish an 'undue burden.' "

In one important respect, the three Third Circuit judges agreed. By 1992, *Roe v. Wade* was still nominally the leading Supreme Court case on abortion rights, but the Third Circuit scarcely paid any attention to Harry Blackmun's venerable landmark. Rather, its judges concluded that the views of a different justice represented the true center of the Court; their opinions represented their best efforts at speculating how this justice—Sandra O'Connor—would view the case. When it came to abortion rights, even at the start of the 1990s, the Rehnquist Court was in fact the O'Connor Court.

After blazing through Stanford Law School and graduating in 1952, O'Connor did not receive a single job offer as a lawyer. (The major Los Angeles law firm of Gibson, Dunn & Crutcher said she could come to work as a legal secretary.) But O'Connor ignored the slights, as became her custom, and concentrated instead on building a life with her new husband, John. He graduated from Stanford Law a year after she did, and following his army stint in Germany, they settled in the booming but still very small city of Phoenix.

The next years passed in a blur, which was the pace of life O'Connor preferred. She had three boys in six years. She worked first at a small law firm, then as an assistant attorney general. She volunteered for local hospitals and the Salvation Army and worked her way up the hierarchy at the Junior League. She and John, who became a successful lawyer himself, hosted lively barbecues for dozens of people (often including Bill and Nan Rehnquist) at their adobe home in Paradise Valley. Once, according to her biographer Joan Biskupic, the O'Connors staged a campy dedication party for a bridge they had built over their backyard pool. Men wore top hats and tails, with white shorts and sneakers, and women sported gowns and pith helmets. Boiled beef, potatoes, and English muffins were served, and bagpipes provided accompaniment.

Much later, in her chambers at the Supreme Court, O'Connor would demand that her law clerks replicate her own headlong style of living. Marriage, children, career, exercise, culture, politics, volunteer work—she had done it all and everyone else should, too. Female clerks were required to join in her three-mornings-a-week exercise class at the Court gym. (Late in her tenure, she added salsa dancing to the workouts.) Male clerks planning weddings were ordered to get in shape. (One stuffed an ice cream cone in his desk drawer so she wouldn't see it.) Clerks dozing from exhaustion would be instructed to join her at special private showings at the National Gallery. An annual clerks' picnic by the cherry blossoms in the Tidal Basin would (and often did) take place even in the rain. For O'Connor, even holidays were occasions for exertion. For Halloween, she demanded that her clerks decorate a pumpkin with a newsy theme. After 9/11, there was "Osama Bin Pumpkin"; a year later, a Martha Stewart pumpkin—wearing prison garb.

The formative political event of O'Connor's years in Phoenix took place in 1969, when her local state senator moved to Washington to take a job in the Nixon administration. Though she had been an assistant attorney general for only four years—and women politicians were still a novelty—she persuaded the governor, Jack Williams, to appoint her to fill the seat. O'Connor took to legislative work immediately, building coalitions, making deals, pushing bills through the process. The job suited her personality. She got along with people and liked to get things done. O'Connor came of age when Barry Goldwater dominated the Arizona Republican Party—and she supported him for president in 1964—but her work in politics never had a particularly ideological edge. Fittingly, one of the first bills she sponsored was to repeal a 1913 law that prohibited women from working more than eight hours a day. To O'Connor, this was paternalism, not protection.

O'Connor took the same pragmatic approach to the subject of abortion, displaying the kind of artful political tacking on the issue that she would show on the Court. She had taken office when a drive was on to change abortion laws in the state legislatures, and Arizona was no exception. At the time she became a senator, Arizona law prohibited abortions except to save a woman's life, and the following year, 1970, a liberalization bill came before a committee where O'Connor served. On April 29, 1970, according to local newspapers, she voted to end criminal prohibitions on abortions in Arizona. The measure passed the committee but never came up for a vote of the full senate. While she supported that prochoice measure, she also backed a restriction on abortion rights, in the form of a law that would have allowed only licensed physicians to perform abortions. Shortly after O'Connor became majority leader of the senate, *Roe v. Wade* made these initial rounds of legislative approaches moot; abortion would be legal regardless of what the state legislatures did. In Arizona at least, since the right to choose abortion was now protected by the U.S. Constitution, the issue faded from the state's immediate political agenda.

In a curious postscript, O'Connor's record on abortion rights was a focus of the vetting process when Reagan was considering naming her to the Court in 1981. O'Connor told the vetter, a young Justice Department aide named Kenneth Starr, that she had never cast a vote on the abortion liberalization measure. Starr took her word for it, and no one else thought to check the Phoenix papers for a record of her vote. (The scrutiny of Supreme Court nominees became much closer in later years.) The omission allowed O'Connor to assure the Reagan team that she "personally" opposed abortion at the same time as she left a studied ambiguity about how she felt about the legal status of abortion rights. In truth, it seemed, O'Connor never gave abortion rights a great deal of attention as a legislator. To the extent she thought about abortion, she tried to steer a middle course between extremes on the issue—an approach that would remain her touchstone in the infinitely higher-stakes setting of the Supreme Court.

As the lawyers in the *Casey* case turned their attention from the Third Circuit to the Supreme Court, the counsel for the plaintiffs had politics as much as law on her mind. Like all other Supreme Court practitioners, Kathryn Kolbert, the ACLU attorney who had shepherded the litigation through the Third Circuit, knew O'Connor's penchant for the middle ground, but the lawyer wanted to take that option away. Kolbert thought it was time to challenge the Supreme Court— and the American electorate. So she devised one of the most audacious litigation tactics in Supreme Court history.

By the time the Third Circuit decided *Casey*, Kolbert and her colleagues thought that the protections of *Roe v. Wade* had been whittled away for so long that it was better for their cause to have the precedent reversed once and for all. Kolbert wanted the Supreme Court to decide *Casey*—and presumably overturn *Roe*—before the 1992 election. That way, there would be no doubt about the stakes for future Supreme Court appointments.

Kolbert had to move fast. After the decision by the three-judge panel of the Third Circuit on October 21, 1991, the ACLU could have petitioned all of the judges on that court to rehear the case en banc. That would have taken months. Alternatively, the Supreme Court rules gave her side ninety days, until mid-January 1992, to file a petition for a writ of certiorari. A petition submitted at that time probably would not have been acted upon until late spring, so the case would not have been argued until the fall of 1992 and the decision handed down in 1993, too late. To place the fate of *Roe* before the voters in time for the next election, Kolbert had to figure out a way to have the case argued and decided by the end of the 1991 term—that is, by June 1992.

It took Kolbert just three weeks, until November 7, to file her cert petition. According to the Supreme Court rules, the party seeking review in the Court begins its brief with a section called "Questions Presented." The art in writing these questions is to frame the issue in a way that will make at least four justices inclined to take the case. But Kolbert was writing for a broader audience than the Court itself, so she crafted the single question in the most provocative way she could: "Has the Supreme Court overruled *Roe v. Wade*, holding that a woman's right to choose abortion is a fundamental right protected by the United States Constitution?" It didn't take a law degree to understand that on the eve of the 1992 election, the future of *Roe* was now squarely before the Court.

Kolbert's strategy of forcing the Court to rule before the election was so transparent that it offended Chief Justice Rehnquist. He didn't like the idea of the Court's being used as a pawn in a political debate, and he didn't care for litigants trying to game the Court's schedule, either. So, the liberals on the Court believed, Rehnquist struck back. Using the powers of the chief justice, he simply kept *Planned Parenthood v. Casey* off the list of cert petitions that the justices would consider in their weekly conference. Rehnquist saw that the case was "relisted" and thus unresolved. Rehnquist was running out the clock. Harry Blackmun, whose entire tenure on the Court was coming down to a defense of his opinion in *Roe*, was furious as were his law clerks. In an unusual joint memorandum, they wrote, "We feel strongly that the case should be heard this spring. . . . If you believe that there are enough votes on the Court now to overrule Roe, it would be better to do it this year before the election and give women the opportunity to vote their outrage."

But how to do it? How could Blackmun and the prochoice justices force *Casey* onto the Court's calendar? John Paul Stevens figured out the answer. Stevens's reserved manner and penchant for writing solo dissents and concurrences sometimes gave the impression that his iconoclasm equaled a lack of influence. But his raw intelligence and knowledge of the Court's rules—along with his willingness to stroke the bigger egos of his colleagues—gave him a crucial advantage. To break the logjam on *Casey*, Stevens threatened to write a dissenting opinion on Rehnquist's decision to relist the case. (Blackmun said he would join Stevens in the public protest.) Relisting was usually a purely procedural matter utterly unfamiliar to the general public. As far as anyone could tell, no justice had ever written an opinion dissenting from a relisting. That was the point. Stevens knew that to write one now—and to accuse Rehnquist of stalling because of abortion politics in a presidential election—would create a sensation. Rehnquist, ever mindful of protecting the Court's reputation as well as his own, backed down. He agreed to put the case on the calendar, and on January 21, 1992, the Court announced that it would hear the *Casey* appeal on April 22—the final day of argument for the term and the last chance to have the case decided by Election Day.

At the conference where the justices agreed to take *Casey*, David Souter pointed out that there was still one more matter to settle. The Court often adopted the "Questions Presented" in the brief of the appealing party, but Souter didn't like the provocative one that Kolbert had submitted. In a memo to his colleagues, Souter said, "I suggested that the question be rephrased." Souter did not want to acknowledge that the only choice in *Casey* was to make an up-or-down judgment on *Roe*. He wanted the flexibility to rule on the specifics of the Pennsylvania statute, without necessarily passing on the ultimate issue of *Roe v. Wade*. In his memo, Souter proposed "that a question be added specifically addressing the issue of precedent: What weight is due to considerations of stare decisis in evaluating the constitutional right to abortion?" Stare decisis, which means "to stand by that which is decided," is the Latin term for the rule of precedent. Souter's colleagues ultimately decided not to use his question, preferring instead to list each provision of the Pennsylvania law and ask whether each was constitutional. But Souter's question still turned out to be the most important one in the case.

Few justices had rockier debuts than David Souter. He was sworn in on October 8, 1990, a week after the Court's term started, and he never managed to catch up with the work his first year. By the spring of 1991, months had passed without an opinion from him. Finally, he delivered six opinions in the final month, but overall his performance had been embarrassing. At least, in that first term, the Republicans who supported Souter had reason to be pleased, for his record was decidedly conservative. He had joined Rehnquist and Scalia in most of the big cases that year, including one that touched on abortion. In *Rust v. Sullivan*, he cast the key vote in a 5–4 decision that upheld the so-called abortion gag rule, which forbade doctors who received federal funds from even mentioning abortion to their patients.

At first, Souter's eccentricities drew more notice around the Court than his jurisprudence. Fifty-two years old and a lifelong bachelor, he had the habits of a gentleman from another century. During the day, he would leave the lights off in his office and maneuver his chair around the room, reading briefs by the sun. He ate the same thing for lunch every day: an entire apple, including the core and seeds, with a cup of yogurt. When the justices sat together in their dining room, the two items would be delivered to Souter on the same fine china that served his colleagues; Souter was familiar with Coca-Cola, but he had never heard of a beverage that several of the other justices favored—Diet Coke. Souter did all his writing by fountain pen. Perhaps the best-known fact about the new justice was that when Warren Rudman, the New Hampshire senator who was Souter's friend and patron, gave Souter his first television set, he apparently never plugged it in. By the end of Souter's first term, there was some sentiment around the Court that he was overwhelmed by his new job. Souter almost said as much in his customary first interview with the Court's in-house publication, the *Docket Sheet*. "I really see myself less as working than as trying to keep from being inundated by the flow of things to be done," he said. "Somebody used the phrase that coming here is like walking through a tidal wave, and it is."

When the term ended in June 1991, Souter did not so much leave Washington as flee. He returned to the converted farmhouse in

Weare, New Hampshire, that had been his grandparents' home and where he had grown up. (Contrary to rumor, Souter did not live with his mother; she had moved elsewhere.) The swirl of events leading to his appointment had deprived him of the time to think about the magnitude of the task before him. In a letter declining an invitation from Blackmun to join him on his annual summer trip to Aspen, Souter wrote, "I have wanted as much as possible to be alone to come to terms in my own heart with what has been happening to me. . . . I have also felt the need to engage in some reading and thinking about matters that will be coming before the Court." He wanted his summers, he wrote later, "wholly free for . . . self-education. I need some period of the year when I can make a close approach to solitude."

When Souter returned the following fall for his second term—the year of *Casey*—it became clear both that he had been underestimated in Washington and that he brought a distinctive judicial philosophy to the bench. For most of the twentieth century, the political left and right had their clear judicial analogues on the Supreme Court. In rough terms, William Brennan and his allies used the Constitution as a vehicle for liberal change—to build a society with greater freedom and equality. On the other side, Rehnquist and Scalia generally put forth the view that courts should defer to political majorities and legislators and interpret the Constitution in line with the original intent of the framers. There was, however, a third tradition in American law, which was less familiar to the public because, unlike the others, it did not neatly reflect the division between the Democratic and Republican parties. But it was to this third tradition that David Souter belonged.

At his confirmation hearings in 1990, Souter made his affiliation plain. At the time, Souter was widely regarded as a "stealth" candidate because even though he had been attorney general of New Hampshire and a justice of the state supreme court, he had not taken public stands on the most controversial judicial issues of the day, like abortion. Prochoice advocacy groups assumed that as a justice Souter would simply do the bidding of the contemporary Republican Party. As the National Organization for Women said in a leaflet distributed during his hearings, STOP SOUTER OR WOMEN WILL DIE.

In those hearings, Souter did not so much take sides in the great legal debate of the day as puzzle the partisans on both sides. The hearings revealed that Souter had given deep thought to the Constitution and embraced a philosophy most closely associated with John

Marshall Harlan II, who served on the Supreme Court from 1955 to 1971. Harlan, whose grandfather and namesake served on the Court from 1877 to 1911, was hardly a radical liberal; indeed, he dissented from many of the Warren Court's most celebrated rulings. But neither was Harlan exactly a conservative, at least in modern terms. He believed that law existed to preserve the stability of society and that adherence to precedent best guaranteed a limited and predictable role for the judiciary. Above all, he believed in the rule of stare decisis. Like Harlan, Souter put his faith in the common law, the accumulated wisdom of judges and courts going back to the Middle Ages.

Also like Harlan, Souter believed that the Constitution expressed a libertarian ideal—that freedom from the restrictions of government counted as much as, or more than, the right of legislators to pass laws limiting individual freedom. And the people's rights were not limited by the precise language of the Constitution, either. One of the strongest arguments against so-called unenumerated rights in the Constitution is that a written document should be limited in meaning to its precise terms.

In a famous dissenting opinion from 1961, Harlan rejected that view, stating that "the full scope of the liberty guaranteed by the Due Process Clause cannot be found in or limited by the precise terms of the specific guarantees elsewhere provided in the Constitution. This 'liberty' is not a series of isolated points pricked out in terms of the taking of property; the freedom of speech, press, and religion, . . . and so on. It is a rational continuum which, broadly speaking, includes a freedom from all substantial arbitrary impositions and purposeless restraints." Harlan's view on unenumerated rights had become a crucial intellectual building block in the Court's future decisions recognizing the right to privacy and, later, the right to abortion.

For David Souter, in 1992, the question then was whether restrictions on the right to choose abortion were the kind of "arbitrary imposition" prohibited by the Constitution. The way that Souter addressed that kind of question was to look at the common law and precedent. Thus, his proposed question, the key issue in the case: "What weight is due to considerations of stare decisis in evaluating the constitutional right to abortion?" For Souter, the answer wouldn't just resolve *Casey* but define his judicial worldview.

Even early in Rehnquist's tenure as chief justice, the Court's oral arguments were transformed from the Burger years. Throughout the eighties, it was a quiet bench. Brennan, Marshall, and Blackmun asked hardly any questions, and Burger, White, and Powell only a few more. The change began when Scalia joined the Court in 1986. His pugnacious wit and open partisanship raised the energy level in the courtroom, and lawyers could soon expect a hot bench on even the most arcane issues. One way O'Connor prepared for oral argument was to plan questions with her clerks, and she began a tradition of asking the first question of most lawyers. Rehnquist and Kennedy liked to talk, too, and the overall level of volubility on the Court made what happened on April 22, 1992, so extraordinary.

"We'll hear argument next in No. 91–744, *Planned Parenthood of Southeastern Pennsylvania v. Robert P. Casey*," Rehnquist said in his familiar long-voweled midwestern drawl. "Ms. Kolbert?"

"Mr. Chief Justice, and may it please the Court. Whether our Constitution endows government with the power to force a woman to continue or to end a pregnancy against her will is the central question in this case," Kolbert began. "Since this Court's decision in *Roe v. Wade*, a generation of American women have come of age secure in the knowledge that the Constitution provides the highest level of protection for their child-bearing decisions."

That was as long as the Court allowed most advocates to speak without jumping in with questions. But there was only silence from the justices, so Kolbert kept going. "This landmark decision, which necessarily and logically flows from a century of this Court's jurisprudence, not only protects rights of bodily integrity and autonomy but has enabled millions of women to participate fully and equally in society. The genius of *Roe* and the Constitution is that it fully protects rights of fundamental importance. Government may not chip away at fundamental rights, nor make them selectively available only to the most privileged women."

More silence from the bench. A murmur began in the audience, a very knowledgeable group, especially in a big case like this one. Why weren't they asking any questions? Why were they paralyzed?

Three minutes, four minutes, still no questions from the justices, and no retreat from Kolbert. Her strategy was the same as the one in her brief—go for broke, all or nothing, overturn the Pennsylvania regulations in their entirety or overturn *Roe v. Wade*. "Our nation's history and tradition also respects the autonomy of individuals to make life choices consistent with their own moral and conscientious beliefs," Kolbert said. "Our Constitution has long recognized an individual's right to make private and intimate decisions about marriage and family life, the upbringing of children, the ability to use contraception. The decision to terminate a pregnancy or to carry it to term is no different in kind." Finally, after eight minutes, O'Connor spoke up, in her characteristic singsong earnestness, reminiscent of a nursery school teacher.

"Ms. Kolbert, you're arguing the case as though all we have before us is whether to apply stare decisis and preserve *Roe* [*v.*] *Wade* in all its aspects," she said. "Nevertheless, we granted certiorari on some specific questions in this case. Do you plan to address any of those in your argument?"

Kolbert replied, in so many words, no. She was not going to concede that the individual restrictions could be separated from the larger question of preserving *Roe*. Kennedy tried, too—"You have a number of specific provisions here that I think you should address"— but Kolbert wouldn't yield. To her, ruling on *Casey* meant ruling on *Roe*.

At the conference of the justices that week, the result was muddled. Seven justices—Rehnquist, White, O'Connor, Scalia, Kennedy, Souter, and Thomas—wanted to uphold most of Pennsylvania's restrictions on abortion. Only Stevens and Blackmun wanted to strike them down. But there were tensions within the majority. Rehnquist, White, and Scalia were on record wanting to overrule *Roe*, and Thomas (his confirmation uncertainty notwithstanding) wanted to join them. But there was not yet a fifth vote to overturn *Roe* outright. Neither O'Connor, Kennedy, nor Souter was ready to go that far. So at the end of the conference, Rehnquist assigned *Casey* to himself, intending to write an opinion that allowed states almost a free hand in regulating abortion. As a practical matter, *Roe* would be overturned, but not in so many words.

Then, early the following week, Souter decided to pay a visit to O'Connor.

COLLISION COURSE

Outsiders tend to be surprised by how rarely Supreme Court justices speak to each other, one on one. Under Rehnquist, the nine spent a good deal of time together as a group. Argument days, most Mondays and Wednesdays when they were in session, were preceded by the traditional thirty-six handshakes, each justice with every other, and they had lunch together most of these days as well. There were also conference discussions every Friday during these weeks. After the conference, however, the justices tended to communicate with one another through memos, which were often drafted by their law clerks. (After e-mail became ubiquitous, the memos also circulated electronically, but always with paper copies as well; among the justices, only Thomas and Breyer, and eventually Stevens, were fully comfortable communicating by e-mail.)

There was, in short, very little of the informal contact of normal office life, just a few phone calls and even fewer visits to one another's chambers. Some justices had substantive discussions with individual colleagues as rarely as once or twice a year. So Souter's walk down the hall to visit O'Connor had more significance than it would have in another law office. It was meaningful, too, that Souter went to see O'Connor, not the other way around. All of the justices, not just Souter, went to O'Connor. The way to win a majority in the Rehnquist Court was to earn O'Connor's support, so her colleagues invariably came to her as supplicants.

In his second year on the Court, Souter sought nothing less than to undermine the central tenet of the conservative revolution which his appointment was supposed to advance. Souter was appointed to overturn *Roe v. Wade*; instead, he was going to try to save it.

In his gentle manner, Souter told O'Connor he was uncomfortable with the chief's approach in *Casey*. Couldn't they find a way to preserve the core of *Roe* while upholding most of the specific provisions of the Pennsylvania law at issue? Indeed, Souter said, O'Connor's own opinions pointed the way.

O'Connor's views on the right to abortion grew out of the original decision in *Roe*. There, in 1973, Blackmun had written that the "fundamental" right to privacy "is broad enough to encompass a woman's decision whether or not to terminate her pregnancy," but the right to abortion was not absolute. Where a state could show that there was a "compelling state interest" in limiting the right to choose abortion, the Court would approve the restriction. To discern the state's interest in regulating abortion, Blackmun devised a framework that relied on pregnancy's trimester calendar. The justice canvassed the medical literature and determined that in the first trimester the prospect of carrying a pregnancy through to childbirth was clearly more risky for a woman than an early-term abortion. Thus, he wrote, the state could not restrict abortion during this period, and the decision "must be left to the medical judgment of the pregnant woman's attending physician." (Much of the opinion in *Roe* was expressed in terms of the rights of the physician, rather than those of the woman; as a former general counsel for the Mayo Clinic, in Minnesota, Blackmun had a high regard for the medical profession.)

But as the pregnancy continued, Blackmun wrote, laws could reflect the government's interest in protecting the fetus, not just the woman's rights. After the first trimester, the state could regulate abortions, but only in "ways that are reasonably related to maternal health." Finally, "subsequent to viability," the state could restrict or even ban abortion, except when it is necessary "for the preservation of the life or health of the mother." In essence, *Roe* introduced a sliding scale on which a woman's right to abortion was greatest early in her pregnancy and could be limited as the fetus grew. Even so, Blackmun insisted, any law restricting abortion, even late in a pregnancy, would have to ensure protection of not only a woman's life but also her health. Blackmun elaborated on this point in his lesser known but still important opinion in *Doe v. Bolton*, a challenge to Georgia's abortion law, which was decided by the Court on the same day as *Roe*. Again expressing the right to abortion as a doctor's choice, Blackmun wrote that the decision to perform the procedure "may be exercised in the light of all factors—physical, emotional, psychological, familial, and the woman's age—relevant to the well-being of the patient." In other words, when a woman's health was at stake, at whatever stage of the pregnancy, she and her doctor should be able to choose an abortion.

O'Connor took an independent tack on abortion from the beginning of her tenure on the Court. In her first important case on the subject, in 1983, the majority struck down a set of rules in Akron, Ohio, that were clearly designed to discourage women from having abortions, including a regulation requiring that all abortions occurring after the first trimester take place in hospitals and another calling for a twenty-four-hour waiting period for women seeking abortions. O'Connor wrote a dissenting opinion, in which she defended the regulations and attacked part of Blackmun's logic in *Roe v. Wade*. Improvements in medical technology, O'Connor declared, would render the trimester analysis obsolete. Increasing numbers of premature infants would be able to survive birth at ever-earlier stages of pregnancy, she argued, and women would be able to have safer abortions later in pregnancy. "The *Roe* framework, then, is clearly on a collision course with itself," she continued, in what became her most famous sentence as a justice. "As the medical risks of various abortion procedures decrease, the point at which the State may regulate for reasons of maternal health is moved further forward to actual childbirth. As medical science becomes better able to provide for the separate existence of the fetus, the point of viability is moved further back toward conception."

O'Connor proposed a new legal framework to replace *Roe*. Adopting a phrase contained in a brief filed in the case by President Reagan's Justice Department, she wrote that abortion regulations should be upheld unless they created an "undue burden" on a woman seeking to have the procedure. O'Connor didn't define exactly what she meant by an "undue burden," but she argued that, according to such a standard, the Akron restrictions should be upheld. In fact, when it came to medical science, Blackmun turned out to be more prescient than O'Connor. She was wrong to conclude that the point of viability would shift in any meaningful way. In *Roe*, Blackmun had written, "Viability is usually placed at about seven months (28 weeks) but may occur earlier, even at 24 weeks." Early in the twenty-first century, more than three decades after *Roe*, it is still rare for a fetus younger than twenty-three or twenty-four weeks to survive. (The term of a normal pregnancy is thirty-eight to forty weeks.)

As usual when it came to controversial issues, O'Connor's preference was for the matter to be settled in the political arena rather than in the courts. As a former state legislator herself, she always had a predisposition to favor the judgments of these officials. Quoting an opinion by Justice Oliver Wendell Holmes Jr. from 1904, O'Connor wrote, "In determining whether the State imposes an 'undue burden,' we must keep in mind that, when we are concerned with extremely sensitive issues, such as the one involved here, 'the appropriate forum for their resolution in a democracy is the legislature.' "

But through her first decade on the Court, even as O'Connor criticized *Roe*, she never called for its outright rejection. In 1989, the Court came close to overturning *Roe* when it approved a Missouri law prohibiting most abortions in public hospitals. In *Webster v. Reproductive Health Services*, Rehnquist, joined by White, Scalia, and (for the most part) Kennedy, all but called for the end of *Roe*. But O'Connor, characteristically, held back, writing, "When the constitutional invalidity of a State's abortion statute actually turns upon the constitutional validity of *Roe*, there will be time enough to reexamine *Roe*, and to do so carefully."

This, then, was the state of O'Connor's thinking when Souter paid her his visit. Opposed to Blackmun's reasoning in *Roe*. Supportive of efforts by state legislators to limit abortion. Cautious—as always—about getting out of step with public opinion. But "time enough" had passed. She had to take a stand on *Roe*.

Even though the conference in *Casey* resulted in Rehnquist's assigning himself the majority opinion, that didn't end the matter as far as Souter was concerned. He hated to see the Court drawn so directly into a contested political issue. He believed, perhaps naively, that there was an island of "law" that could be insulated from the daily rush of events. It had been almost twenty years since *Roe*, and while the Court had allowed states to regulate and limit abortion during that time, there had been little doubt that the Constitution forbade a complete prohibition on abortion. Yet Rehnquist's position at conference, and the opinion he was writing, would clearly permit a total ban.

O'Connor agreed with Souter. She had a less mystical attachment to the idea of precedent than Souter did, but her more political instincts led her in the same direction. The country had come to terms with *Roe.*

Something else was bothering O'Connor, too. She was appalled by the provision of the Pennsylvania law that required married women who were seeking abortions to inform their husbands. The court of appeals had struck down this provision, but Rehnquist proposed to uphold the view of the dissenting judge from the lower court. But that opinion—the one by Judge Samuel Alito—outraged O'Connor. She saw this provision as paternalism at best and sexism at worst. O'Connor had finely tuned radar for discrimination against women (something she sometimes lacked for bias against, say, African Americans), and she couldn't abide the notion that the Court would uphold such a law.

So Souter and O'Connor were aligned on the idea that the Court should uphold what they came to call the "essence" of *Roe,* and they agreed that they should try to strike down the spousal notification provision. But they had only four votes for these positions—their own, plus those of Blackmun and Stevens, who were ready to reject the whole Pennsylvania law. They knew that there was only one place to go for a possible fifth vote—the chambers of Tony Kennedy.

Souter and Kennedy could hardly have approached the job of Supreme Court justice more differently. Souter avoided attention, loathed controversy, and disliked high-profile cases. Kennedy relished his public role and sought out the opinions that would make the newspapers. Seated at his keyboard typing furiously, Kennedy always labored most closely on the sections of opinions that might be quoted in the *New York Times.*

If Souter thought the proper role for a judge was as the (nearly) silent steward of judicial tradition, Kennedy had a much more romantic notion of a robed crusader for the rule of law. He liked to talk about the "poetry" of law and of great "teaching cases," that is, opinions that instructed law students on timeless principles. Kennedy had been a judge for close to his whole professional life, since Gerald Ford made him the nation's youngest member of the court of appeals in 1975, when he was thirty-nine. Through his twelve years on the Ninth Circuit, and even in summers while he was a justice, Kennedy continued teaching at the McGeorge School of Law in his hometown of Sacramento. He saw law as not just a collection of cases but a system that ought to be explainable to, and understood by, the next generation of lawyers.

Kennedy was also a serious Catholic, of pre–Vatican II vintage, who went to Mass every Sunday and prayed in the old-fashioned manner, hands clasped before him. Abortion repelled him. He fully adopted his church's teachings on the subject. Once, before he joined the Court, he had called *Roe* the "*Dred Scott* of our time," a reference to the infamous 1857 ruling that sanctioned slavery and helped spark the Civil War. But Kennedy knew the difference between his duties as a judge and his convictions as a Catholic. As he once wrote, "The hard fact is that sometimes we must make decisions we do not like." Even though he and his church opposed abortion, that did not answer the question of whether the Constitution protected it.

Kennedy's peculiar combination of traits—his earnestness and his ambition, his naiveté and his grandiosity, his reverence for the law and his regard for his own talents—made him receptive to Souter's appeal. Kennedy thought there was nobility in judging; saving *Roe* would show the world that the justices were something more than mere pols. A statesmanlike compromise suited both Kennedy's politics and his conception of the role of the judge.

So Kennedy signed on with Souter and O'Connor. His was the most dramatic switch of the three, because it had been only three years since he voted with Rehnquist in *Webster*, an opinion that advocated overruling *Roe*. Even more dramatically, Kennedy had clearly supported Rehnquist at the conference in *Casey*. No vote is ever final on the Court until an opinion is announced, but changes from conference votes are still unusual, especially when, as in *Casey*, it was Kennedy's vote that allowed Rehnquist to start drafting his majority opinion. Nonetheless, in early May, Souter, O'Connor, and Kennedy decided to work together secretly on *Casey*, each of the justices telling only a single law clerk in their chambers that they were planning a joint opinion.

Unaware of these machinations, the chief justice continued drafting what he expected would be the majority opinion. Writing with typical dispatch, Rehnquist circulated a draft on May 27, just a little more than a month after the argument. According to the chief, the

Court would uphold all of the provisions of the Pennsylvania law. Rehnquist wrote, "The Court was mistaken in *Roe* when it classified a woman's decision to terminate her pregnancy as a 'fundamental right.' " If the chief's opinion won the support of a majority of justices, states would be free to regulate or even ban abortion altogether. As Blackmun wrote in the margin of the first page of Rehnquist's draft: "Wow! Pretty extreme!"

The "troika," as they would later become known, agreed with Blackmun's view of the chief's draft opinion. The way Rehnquist summarily dismissed *Roe* eliminated any chance that he might draw Souter, O'Connor, or Kennedy back into a majority with him. In their secret collaboration, Kennedy had agreed to write the opening section of the opinion, where they announced that they would preserve *Roe.* Souter would write next, about the importance of stare decisis, and O'Connor would write the final section, explaining why the spousal notification provision of the Pennsylvania law had to be struck down. On May 29, two days after Rehnquist circulated his draft, Kennedy sent a handwritten note to Blackmun:

> Dear Harry,
>
> I need to see you as soon as you have a few free minutes. I want to tell you about some developments in *Planned Parenthood v. Casey,* and at least part of what I say should come as welcome news.
>
> If today is not convenient, I will be here tomorrow. Please give me a call when you are free.
>
> Yours, Tony

At their meeting the following day, Blackmun saw how anguished Kennedy was about his role in preserving the right to choose abortion. Because of *Roe,* no justice had received more death threats than Blackmun, and he comforted Kennedy by telling him the mail sometimes brought pleasant surprises, too. Blackmun showed his junior colleague a letter from a nun, of all people, praising him for allowing a desperate woman to get an abortion. After Kennedy left, the always meticulous Blackmun wrote himself a simple note on a piece of pink Supreme Court memo paper: "Roe sound." As Linda Greenhouse observed in her book about Blackmun, "The choice of this slightly old-fashioned word was significant. To a lawyer, 'sound' conveys not just survival but correctness and legitimacy." *Roe*—the right to choose—was sound.

Souter, O'Connor, and Kennedy circulated the result of their secret collaboration—a draft opinion of sixty-one pages—on June 3. Rehnquist took the news with equanimity. Antonin Scalia did not.

Roe represented everything Scalia most despised, and still despises, about modern jurisprudence—and the modern world. He had defined his career as a justice by his insistent and unwavering demand that the case be overturned.

Scalia was fifty-six years old in 1992, a veteran of six years on the Court, at the height of his intellectual and physical powers. He was squat and neckless, with a five o'clock shadow that was almost as pronounced as Souter's. He dominated the Court's oral arguments with barbed questions and jokes, and his opinions were forceful, oratorical, and a pleasure to read. He was the dominant personality on the Court, and he had the clearest, most identifiable judicial philosophy among the justices. But by the time of *Casey* it was clear that Scalia's zest, passion, and intelligence did not translate into the most important thing one member of a court of nine could have—influence.

O'Connor, still in her uncertain early years as a justice when Scalia joined the Court, was the first to be alienated by him. In the *Webster* case, Scalia had written that her opinion declining to address *Roe* "cannot be taken seriously." Later, as she became more confident, O'Connor would ignore Scalia's taunts—"That's just Nino," she would say—but at first his contempt burned her. Scalia's breach with Kennedy was even more surprising. Both men were born in 1936, observant Catholics, contemporaries at Harvard Law School, and appointed to the Court a year apart; Kennedy bought a home in the same Virginia suburb as Scalia. For a time, the portly New Yorker and rangy Californian were even unlikely jogging partners. But Kennedy, a politically as well as temperamentally moderate person, came to be repelled by Scalia's dogmatism.

In time, Scalia would revel in his isolation and wear it almost as a badge of honor. His judicial philosophy was so clear and consistent, and his obligation to follow it so principled, that he could not bring himself to bargain with his colleagues. "Originalists have nothing to trade!" he would say. "We can't do horse-trading. Our view is what it is, and we write our dissents."

But originalism never caught on with anyone else on the Court, except Thomas. Justices like O'Connor, Souter, and Kennedy believed there was more to constitutional interpretation than just divining the intent of the framers, including such factors as subsequent decisions of the Court, the expectations of the public, and the underlying values in the Bill of Rights, not just its text. In short, these justices believed in a "living Constitution," a concept for which Scalia had nothing but contempt. "A 'living Constitution' judge," Scalia once explained, is a "happy fellow who comes home at night to his wife and says, 'The Constitution means exactly what I think it ought to mean!' "

Scalia thought *Roe* was the worst example of the living Constitution run amok—until he read Kennedy's section of the joint opinion in *Casey*. Kennedy had a weakness for high-flown, sometimes rather meaningless rhetoric, and he was at his airy best (or worst) in *Casey*. "Liberty finds no refuge in a jurisprudence of doubt," he began. In plain English, Kennedy meant that law had to be consistent and predictable, but there was in fact a noble lineage to "a jurisprudence of doubt." Theorists like Oliver Wendell Holmes Jr. and Learned Hand thought it was critical for judges to reflect doubt that their conclusions were correct for all time. Worse, from Scalia's perspective, was Kennedy's defense of the right to privacy: "At the heart of liberty is the right to define one's own concept of existence, of meaning, of the universe, and of the mystery of human life." Even many supporters of *Roe* would have trouble defining "the mystery of human life," much less asserting that it was protected by the Constitution, but such phrases sent Scalia into a genuine rage. In the last days before *Casey* was announced, traditional notions of Court etiquette were tossed aside in the heat of the battle. Scalia visited Kennedy at home to try to talk him out of his position; one of Scalia's law clerks waylaid Souter in the hallway to lobby him to change his mind. Nothing worked.

Indeed, the exclamation point to the troika's victory in *Casey* came after a typically astute behind-the-scenes maneuver by Stevens. Through its many drafts, the troika's opinion had become somewhat disorganized and confusing. On June 18, Stevens wrote to the three authors, "You have indicated that you would welcome suggestions that will enable Harry and me to join as much of your opinion as possible." So Stevens proposed an artful reorganization of the troika's work, thereby making it possible for the two liberals to join the opinion from the beginning. "In my view," Stevens went on, "an opinion that begins as an opinion of the Court"—that is, for a majority of justices—"and continues to speak for a Court for 25 pages would be far more powerful than one that starts out as a plurality opinion and shifts back and forth between a Court opinion and a plurality opinion." Kennedy accepted Stevens's idea with alacrity, and the historical significance of the opinion was immediately enhanced.

As he often did, Scalia had to content himself with writing an alternately weary and angry dissent, where he would "respond to a few of the more outrageous arguments in today's opinion, which it is beyond human nature to leave unanswered." The issue in the case, he wrote, is "whether the power of a woman to abort her unborn child is a 'liberty' . . . protected by the Constitution of the United States. I am sure it is not. I reach that conclusion not because of anything so exalted as my views concerning the 'concept of existence, of meaning, of the universe, and of the mystery of human life.' Rather, I reach it for the same reason I reach the conclusion that bigamy is not constitutionally protected—because of two simple facts: (1) the Constitution says absolutely nothing about it, and (2) the longstanding traditions of American society have permitted it to be legally proscribed." (Clarence Thomas, who in his confirmation hearings just months earlier professed an open mind about *Roe*, joined in Scalia's view that "*Roe* should undoubtedly be overruled.")

On the morning of June 29, the last day of the term and the day the decision was to be announced, Kennedy was at his melodramatic best. He had invited Terry Carter, a reporter for *California Lawyer* magazine, to join him in his chambers before the justices took the bench. Kennedy has a coveted suite overlooking the Court's marble staircase and plaza, and he stood staring down at the demonstrators who had gathered, waiting for the judgment in *Casey* to be rendered. "Sometimes you don't know if you're Caesar about to cross the Rubicon or Captain Queeg cutting your own tow line," Kennedy mused, and then he asked the reporter to leave. He needed to "brood" before Court convened.

In the end, there was no doubt about the real winner on the Court in *Casey*. In a little more than a decade, O'Connor had succeeded in recasting *Roe v. Wade* on her own terms. Moreover, she had triumphed with a position that was shared by virtually none of her colleagues over that time. The liberals—like Brennan, Marshall, Blackmun, and Stevens—had wanted to preserve the original rule of *Roe*. The conservatives—like Rehnquist, White, Scalia, and Thomas—had wanted to do away with *Roe* altogether. Even O'Connor's allies in *Casey*, Kennedy and Souter, had embraced her position more out of expediency to build a majority than out of enthusiasm for her view. But the point remained: her view was the law.

In practical terms, O'Connor's victory meant the "trimester framework" was out, but she did adopt Blackmun's recognition that the key point in pregnancy was viability. "We conclude the line should be drawn at viability, so that, before that time, the woman has a right to choose to terminate her pregnancy," the troika wrote. "The concept of viability, as we noted in *Roe*, is the time at which there is a realistic possibility of maintaining and nourishing a life outside the womb." Then, in the sentence that sealed O'Connor's triumph, they wrote, "In our view, the undue burden standard is the appropriate means of reconciling the State's interest with the woman's constitutionally protected liberty." A stray observation from a separate opinion by O'Connor had become the law of the land on the most contentious constitutional issue of her time. "A finding of an undue burden is a shorthand for the conclusion that a state regulation has the purpose or effect of placing a substantial obstacle in the path of a woman seeking an abortion of a nonviable fetus." In practical terms, the new rule meant that states could not prohibit early-term abortions, which were by far the most common. Not coincidentally, O'Connor's solution to the problem of abortion closely reflected public opinion on the issue.

The final section of the joint opinion, the one drafted by O'Connor alone, drew the least attention but offered the greatest clues about the future of the Court. The Pennsylvania law provided that "no physician shall perform an abortion on a married woman without receiving a signed statement from the woman that she has notified her spouse that she is about to undergo an abortion." In his opinion on the Third Circuit, Alito approved this provision, but O'Connor laid into it, sounding more like a women's studies professor than a Goldwater Republican. She wrote that "common sense" suggested that "in well functioning marriages, spouses discuss important intimate decisions such as whether to bear a child. But there are millions of women in this country who are the victims of regular physical and psychological abuse at the hands of their husbands. Should these women become pregnant, they may have very good reasons for not wishing to inform their husbands of their decision to obtain an abortion. . . . We must not blind ourselves to the fact that the significant number of women who fear for their safety and the safety of their children are likely to be deterred from procuring an abortion as surely as if the Commonwealth had outlawed abortion in all cases."

To O'Connor, in this case and henceforth, the crucial issue was women's autonomy and health. She said that Alito's view was "repugnant to our present understanding of marriage and of the nature of the rights secured by the Constitution. Women do not lose their constitutionally protected liberty when they marry." It was O'Connor's Court now, responsive above all to the legal philosophy and political savvy of the former state senator from Arizona.

BIG HEART

Early in the third week in March of 1993, Byron White called to invite Ron Klain to breakfast at the Court on Friday, the nineteenth. On the surface, there was nothing especially unusual about White's summons. Klain had clerked for White for two years in the late 1980s and gone on to start a career in law and politics—as chief counsel for the Democrats on the Senate Judiciary Committee and then as an associate counsel for the new president, Bill Clinton. As it happened, Klain's portfolio included Clinton's judicial appointments.

White liked talking to Klain because the justice still fancied himself a political insider—and a Democrat, even if few others did. Long ago, White had been a dashing figure of John F. Kennedy's New Frontier. When he was appointed to the Court in 1962, the Senate was giving little scrutiny to Supreme Court nominees, and his hearing before the Judiciary Committee lasted fifteen minutes and consisted of eight questions. He had never been a judge, had spent most of his career in private law practice in Colorado, and was far better known for his exploits as a college and professional football star than for his brief tenure as Kennedy's deputy attorney general. By far the best-known fact about White was his nickname, Whizzer, which he hated. At the time of his appointment, White's views on constitutional issues were a mystery.

In three decades on the Court, White established himself as a thoroughgoing conservative. He dissented from most of the last round of famous decisions in the Warren Court—like *Miranda v. Arizona*—and he became a leading voice on the right through the Burger and Rehnquist years. He had dissented from *Roe* in 1973, wrote a scathingly dismissive opinion about gay rights in *Bowers v. Hardwick* in 1986, and generally voted for the government over the individual. (On race and the scope of federal power—the issues that most engaged him in the Kennedy Justice Department—he inclined toward a more liberal view.) To Klain and others, White would insist that it was the Democratic Party that had changed, not him, and that he remained true to the spirit of JFK, but he had few takers for that view.

As the week progressed, Klain started to have suspicions about the real purpose of the breakfast. He checked with some other former law clerks who sometimes joined him for breakfast with White, and he learned that none of them had been invited. Still, Klain told no one from the White House about his appointment.

No breakfast was served. At 9:00 a.m. on March 19, White's secretary ushered Klain into chambers, and the justice was seated at his big partner's desk by the window. As usual with White, who was gruff and dour even before he turned seventy-five, there was little small talk.

White slid a sealed envelope across the table to Klain. "I'd like you to bring that back to your boss," he said.

Klain nodded.

"And I have a copy for you if you would like to see it."

The letter said White was resigning. Bill Clinton would have the first appointment to the Court by a Democrat since Lyndon Johnson named Thurgood Marshall in 1967.

Why now? Klain asked. The timing was a little unusual, as there was something of a tradition of justices resigning at the end of the term, in June. White spun an elaborate theory, which Klain had trouble following, about how the Court had now accepted all its cases for the year and that made it a good time to leave. Besides, White added, "I've done this job long enough." Despite everything, White said, he remained a Democrat, and he wanted a Democrat to appoint his successor.

Before Klain got up to leave, he asked when White planned to release the news to the press.

"Ten a.m."

Klain blanched. It was already past 9:15, and he wanted to make sure his colleagues in the White House weren't blindsided by the news. Klain had walked to the Court from his home on Capitol Hill, so he had no car to race across town. Should he go back and get it? Catch a cab? He borrowed the phone in White's secretary's office and tried to reach Bernie Nussbaum, the White House counsel, or his deputy, Vince Foster. No one was available. And he couldn't call when he was en route, because cell phones did not yet exist. His panic rising, Klain started dialing any White House number he could remember and finally passed the news to Ricki Seidman, a colleague. He then ran into the plaza in front of the Court and waved down a taxi.

At 9:45 a.m., Betty Currie, the president's secretary, was waiting outside the Oval Office for Klain's arrival. Moments later, slightly out of breath, Klain handed the letter to Clinton, who had already been told its gist.

"Strange," Clinton said. "He was just here. He looked good." The previous week, White had come to the Oval Office to swear in Janet Reno as attorney general.

"Okay," Clinton said, handing White's letter back to Klain. "Let's talk about this tomorrow."

If Byron White wasn't a typical Democrat, neither was Bill Clinton. That was especially true when it came to the defining subject before the Supreme Court, abortion.

In 1992, a fiery Texas politico had opened the Democratic Convention with the words, "My name is Ann Richards. I'm pro-choice, and I vote." The remark was a testament to the centrality of abortion rights in Democratic Party orthodoxy. The issue marked perhaps the clearest difference between the two parties, one prochoice and the other prolife. Indeed, Robert P. Casey, the governor of Pennsylvania (and the defendant in *Casey*), had been denied the chance to speak at that convention in part because of his prolife views. Clinton himself was prochoice; he could never have been nominated otherwise. But Clinton's view of abortion reflected his centrist New Democrat approach. He recognized that the subject of abortion made many people, especially swing voters, uncomfortable, and he wanted at least to reassure them that he recognized the difficulty of the issue. On the campaign trail, Clinton always used the same formulation when talking about abortion, saying that he believed it should be "safe, legal—and rare."

During the campaign, when Clinton discussed the kind of individuals he would appoint to the Court, he expressed himself with characteristic political dexterity—or, seen in a different light, typical doublespeak. He would have no litmus test for his justices—but he would appoint only those who shared his prochoice views. In fact, Clinton had given the subject more thought than most other future presidents.

On Saturday afternoon, March 20, 1993, the president began to spell out specifically what he wanted in a future justice. In the small dining room adjacent to his private study—later infamous as the site of his trysts with Monica Lewinsky—Clinton met with Vice President Al Gore and White House lawyers Nussbaum, Foster, Klain, and Bruce Lindsey to discuss White's replacement. Almost as a lark, a couple of weeks earlier, Klain and Walter Dellinger, a Duke law professor temporarily on the White House staff before becoming assistant attorney general, had drawn up a list of fifty possible Supreme Court appointees. There were appeals court judges (mostly Jimmy Carter appointees to the federal bench), law professors, a few politicians and private lawyers. The list didn't amount to much—just a row of names and their current affiliations—but it constituted, at that moment, the full extent of Clinton administration research on Supreme Court nominees. So Klain passed it around.

Clinton glanced at it. "Look," he said, "the Court is totally fragmented and it's dominated by Republican appointees." (Indeed, White was the only Democratic appointee on the Court.) "It's not enough for someone to vote the right way," he said. "We've got to get someone who will move people, who will persuade the others to join them. It's what Warren did. I want someone like that."

Clinton thought it was unhealthy that the Court was dominated by former judges, few of whom had what he regarded as adequate real-world experience. Clinton's term for these judges was "footnote people," who were caught up in the minutia of law rather than its implications for people. The names of several nonjudges came up, but it quickly became clear that Clinton was most interested in one of them—Mario Cuomo, then governor of New York.

Clinton and Cuomo had a complicated relationship. Clinton admired the New Yorker's way with words but found his indecisiveness maddening. Midway through his third term as governor, Cuomo expected a degree of deference from Clinton that the president did not always display. When Clinton first called Cuomo to discuss the Supreme Court, the governor ducked his call. His secretary told Betty

Currie that Cuomo was in budget negotiations with the state legislature and couldn't be disturbed.

Several members of Clinton's staff—notably George Stephanopoulos and Gene Sperling, a top economic aide who once worked for Cuomo—loved the idea of putting Cuomo on the Court. To them, it was just the kind of bold gesture that could transform the Court and burnish Clinton's own record as well. When Stephanopoulos spoke to the governor by phone, on March 30, Cuomo wouldn't commit himself, saying, half jokingly, "I can't believe you've descended to this level of groveling exploitation."

The back-and-forth lasted several days. Clinton reached Cuomo from Air Force One, and Cuomo said he was leaning against accepting the nomination but would continue to think about it. Clinton left for a summit with Boris Yeltsin with the matter unresolved. As was customary in the Clinton White House, news of the negotiations with Cuomo leaked to the press, embarrassing the president. By April 7, after Clinton had returned to the United States, Stephanopoulos was badgering Andrew Cuomo, the governor's son and chief adviser, on the phone. *We need an answer.*

According to Stephanopoulos, Andrew said he had spoken to his father for two and a half hours that day, and the governor ultimately said, "If you want me to, I'll call Clinton and take it." Word flashed around the White House that Cuomo was the choice, to be announced the following day. Klain stopped his search and started preparing for the ceremony. But an hour later, Cuomo faxed Clinton a letter that said his duty to New Yorkers outweighed his desire to serve on the Supreme Court. The Cuomo nomination was dead—or so it appeared.

Meanwhile, even with Cuomo out of the running, Clinton was still infatuated with the idea of naming a politician. Important decisions are a form of autobiography, and Clinton believed his skills with people and his "big heart" were more important than mere legal expertise. He was determined to appoint someone in his own image. Clinton also had a politician's conviction that legislation, rather than litigation, was the best way to solve society's problems, so he didn't want to waste a great deal of political capital pushing a controversial choice through the Senate. Clinton had built his campaign on economic issues, and he didn't want to divert his focus in Congress. His economic program, with health care next on the agenda, was simply more important to him than taking a risk on a novel choice for the Supreme Court.

Clinton turned next to George Mitchell, the Senate majority leader and a former federal district judge in Maine. He had the same kind of skills as Cuomo, but without the governor's need for psychodrama. True to form, Mitchell didn't agonize when Clinton offered him the job. He declined on the spot, preferring his job in the Senate and his mission of passing Clinton's legislative program. Next came Richard Riley, the former governor of South Carolina who was Clinton's secretary of education. He, too, declined, with winning self-awareness. "I was a mediocre country lawyer," Riley told the president. "This isn't my thing."

What about Bruce Babbitt? Clinton asked. Like Riley, Babbitt had been a Democratic governor in a largely Republican state, and he now served in Clinton's cabinet, as secretary of the interior. And as the former attorney general of Arizona, Babbitt would have none of Riley's qualms about his own fitness for the job. Let's do Babbitt, subject to a background check, Clinton told his team.

So Vince Foster and Klain spent an entire night in Babbitt's office in the Interior Department, a vast sprawling space that is sometimes described as the best office in Washington. They pored over tax returns, especially payments to household help. (This was just weeks after Clinton's nomination of Zoe Baird for attorney general had foundered because she had hired illegal immigrants as a family nanny and a chauffeur. Worries about a "Zoe Baird problem" became an enduring preoccupation for public figures of all kinds.) The all-night vetting session turned up no problems. The White House lawyers told Babbitt to prepare for an announcement in the Rose Garden the following day.

In the morning, though, Clinton had misgivings. First, the *Washington Times*, a conservative paper owned by the Reverend Sun Myung Moon, reported that Babbitt had gambling debts in Las Vegas casinos that were paid off by the mob. More important, Clinton had spoken to Orrin Hatch, the ranking Republican on the Judiciary Committee, and Hatch had said Babbitt would have a hard time getting confirmed. Babbitt's strong pro-environmental views had alienated a group of Republican senators from the West, and they might take revenge—either on Babbitt's nomination or on Clinton's choice for his replacement at Interior. Several western Democrats were pushing New Mexico congressman Bill Richardson for the Interior post, but Vice President Gore didn't think Richardson was "green" enough for the job.

So Clinton dropped Babbitt, with perhaps greater alacrity than the situation warranted. None of the problems with a Babbitt nomination were likely insurmountable. (The *Washington Times* story turned out to be completely bogus.) Both Babbitt and a successor at Interior would likely have been confirmed eventually. In truth, Clinton always had some ambivalence about Babbitt, because the two men were almost too similar, down to their accomplished and ambitious wives. (Clinton had chosen Hattie Babbitt as the U.S. representative to the Organization of American States.) There was a thread of competition in the relationship between the Clintons and the Babbitts, and Clinton might have wanted to remind Babbitt which one of them was the president.

More than a month had passed since White's letter, and Clinton still had no nominee, not even a front-runner. Perhaps, Clinton conceded, after four politicians it was time to look at some judges. There was no question about Clinton's favorite judge. It was Richard Arnold, who sat on the federal court of appeals in Arkansas. Arnold was a leading ornament of the federal judiciary—a scholarly moderate respected by colleagues across the political spectrum—but the Arkansas connection was troubling. Clinton had already named a number of allies from his home state to top jobs in his administration, and an Arnold selection might have looked like cronyism, especially since Arnold's wife had served as Governor Clinton's director of cultural affairs. In truth, the Arnolds and the Clintons traveled in different social circles in Little Rock and were not close friends, but the taint would have been hard to avoid. So Clinton passed on Arnold.

Al Gore had an idea—Gilbert S. Merritt Jr., another Carter appointee to the federal court of appeals, if less well known than Arnold, and a friend of the Gore family from Tennessee. Merritt had appeal on another score. At that moment, Clinton was struggling with the nomination of Lani Guinier as assistant attorney general for civil rights. During her confirmation battle, it emerged that she had written some provocative articles about voting rights that led opponents to deride her as a "quota queen." The appointment of a white male Southerner like Merritt would reestablish Clinton's centrist credentials. Clinton sent his vetters to work, and they came back with a possible problem relating to Merritt's tenure as U.S. attorney, back in the

1960s. It might not have been disabling by itself, but the issue allowed the general lack of enthusiasm surrounding Merritt to turn it into a disqualification.

By this point, Clinton had taken to reading the ever-growing amount of background material on possible nominees himself. Some of the write-ups came from his administration, some from volunteer lawyers who were helping from the outside, and some were simply sent over the transom—from members of Congress or the vast network known as the Friends of Bill (and Hillary). In the meantime, the Guinier nomination blew up, with Clinton withdrawing her nomination after deciding her writings were indefensible. Clinton and his staff's handling of the Guinier situation was so abysmal that it changed the dynamic surrounding the Supreme Court choice. Now Clinton thought naming a woman was a *good* idea—to mend fences after the Guinier fiasco.

Clinton plucked a name from one of the lists—Janie Shores. What about her? Clinton asked. So Klain faxed her the vetting forms that all possible appointees had to complete.

Shores was the first woman to serve on the Alabama Supreme Court, but she was utterly unknown in Washington legal circles, and no one—not Clinton or anyone on his staff—had any idea where she stood on constitutional issues or much of anything else.

Bernie Nussbaum, the White House counsel, who was growing increasingly embarrassed as the names came and went, decided to make a stand: "You are not nominating Janie Shores to the Supreme Court. No one knows who she is. This is insane." Clinton relented. (Inside the White House, the blameless Shores became a symbol of the chaotic process; years later, the mere mention of her name would reduce some staffers to helpless laughter.)

From the day White resigned, Ted Kennedy, the Senate veteran from Massachusetts, had been pushing Stephen Breyer. A former Kennedy staffer and professor at Harvard Law School, Breyer was chief judge of the federal court of appeals based in Boston. Clinton had a real reverence for Kennedy (without the edge of competition that colored his relationship with others, like Cuomo and Babbitt). The president also respected Kennedy's political instincts, which the venerable old pol now deployed. Instead of calling Clinton again in support of Breyer, Kennedy prevailed upon Orrin Hatch to tell Clinton that Breyer would be a fine choice. Hatch had liked Breyer since he took a leave from Harvard to work for Kennedy on the

Judiciary Committee in the late seventies. Clinton was impressed by Hatch's call. Let's dig in on Breyer, he told his staff.

So Foster, Klain, and Seidman flew up to Massachusetts. Unfortunately, just a few days earlier, Breyer had taken a bad spill from his bicycle near his home in Cambridge, and he was still a patient at Mount Auburn Hospital. (In keeping with the quasi-public nature of the search, local reporters learned that the vetting team was in the hospital, and the White House aides had to slip out a side door to avoid them.) But the interview had gone well. Breyer was told to come to Washington for a talk with Clinton and then, probably, a formal announcement.

Breyer had broken ribs and punctured a lung in his accident. He wasn't allowed to fly, so the judge took a bone-jarring train ride to Washington, where Foster met him at the station and took him to the Oval Office. The meeting between Breyer and Clinton went badly. Normally a friendly, almost garrulous man, Breyer was short of breath from his injury and still in pain. Afterward, Clinton told his staff Breyer seemed "heartless"—when a big heart seemed to be the president's main criterion. Breyer's background in administrative law suggested an unduly conservative bent. "I don't see enough humanity," Clinton said. "I want a judge with a soul." (Breyer, who was told none of this, had been instructed to wait by the phone.)

The annual picnic for members of Congress on the South Lawn of the White House happened to be scheduled the night of Breyer's interview with Clinton. The president called a meeting for 11:00 p.m. to hash out a decision. The meeting featured all of the flaws for which Clinton's early decision-making process was known. There were too many people (twelve staffers) talking for too long (ninety minutes) at a time of day more suited for a college bull session. Rather than make a decision, Clinton concluded by asking everyone in the room for their votes on Breyer, which revealed a majority, but not unanimity, in his favor. "Let's get him over here tomorrow," Clinton said at the end. "I'm going to do it. We'll announce it tomorrow."

But first thing the following morning, Foster and Klain were back in the Oval Office. Foster had been going over the Breyer family records for household help and the like, and the papers were a mess. Maybe it was fixable, but maybe it wasn't. Clinton sagged into his chair. Searching as ever for more options, he said no one had asked Janet Reno for her ideas. (It might seem obvious to include the attorney general in deliberations about a Supreme Court nomination, but

Clinton barely knew Reno. She was newly installed in office after a different nomination debacle, which saw Baird and then Kimba Wood rise and fall as candidates.)

Clinton told Klain to go to the desk of his personal assistant Nancy Hernreich, who sat with Betty Currie outside the Oval Office, and call Reno for her suggestions.

Reno came right to the phone, and the first thing she said was, "Why aren't you people looking at Ruth Bader Ginsburg?"

For one of the most accomplished lawyers and judges of her generation, Ruth Ginsburg had an astonishing ability to disappear in a crowd. She was tiny, for one thing, barely five feet tall and a hundred pounds, with the bearing of a little bird. But Ginsburg's presence was small, too. She had a shy, almost timid smile, and her eyes were hidden behind enormous glasses. Ginsburg's conversations were famous for long silences that sometimes left admirers (or clerkship applicants) babbling incoherently to fill the vacuum. She was sixty years old in 1993, older than most recent Supreme Court nominees, and the grooves in her personality were set, for better or worse.

At the time of the Clinton presidency, Ginsburg led a cosseted life in her apartment at the Watergate, but her voice still bore traces of her hardscrabble upbringing in Brooklyn. Ruth Bader's sister died in childhood, and she lost her mother to cancer when she was seventeen, the day before she graduated from high school. She went to Cornell, where she met her husband, Martin, and they both went on to Harvard Law School, where she was one of nine women in a class of more than five hundred students. There, shortly after the birth of their daughter, Martin was struck by testicular cancer. Through his long and difficult treatment, Ruth cared simultaneously for him and their child, attended class and took notes for both of them, typed his papers, and made law review herself. Perhaps as a consequence, in later years Ginsburg had less sympathy than some judges for complaints of overwork from her clerks.

Martin and Ruth Ginsburg settled in New York, where Martin practiced tax law and Ruth began a career teaching law, first at Rutgers and then, in 1972, as the first tenured woman at Columbia. She joined the American Civil Liberties Union and led its early efforts in what was then known as the women's liberation movement.

Ginsburg was hardly a radical, and she became famous for canny strategy by litigation jujitsu. Her goal, of course, was to end the discrimination that was then pervasive against women, but she needed a way to dramatize the issue in front of judges who were invariably male.

So Ginsburg looked for cases where laws reflecting gender stereotypes actually penalized men, not women. In one, husbands of military officers had to prove that they were "dependent" spouses to receive certain benefits. In another, Oklahoma law allowed young women between the ages of eighteen and twenty to buy near beer, while men of the same age could not. The Supreme Court struck down the provisions in both cases, ruling that laws could not survive if they were based solely on stereotypes and assumptions about gender differences. These cases, which nominally benefited men, led to the downfall of many more laws that penalized women. In all, Ginsburg won five out of the six cases she argued before the justices. In 1980, President Carter named her to the D.C. Circuit, the second most important court in the nation.

In light of this background—and Clinton's commitment to diversity on the bench—it is surprising that Ginsburg's name came to the fore so late in the process. She had been on Klain and Dellinger's original list of fifty, but Ginsburg's tenure on the court of appeals had earned her some skepticism among the more liberal members of the administration. Ginsburg had been a moderate-to-conservative judge, especially on criminal matters, and she often found herself aligned with one-time colleagues Robert Bork and Antonin Scalia. (Scalia and Ginsburg struck up a friendship on the appeals court, based in part on their shared love of opera, and their families celebrated New Year's Eve together for many years.) In her academic writing, Ginsburg had even criticized *Roe v. Wade*, which won her even greater suspicion.

But Clinton was intrigued when Klain came back with Reno's endorsement of Ginsburg. "Pat Moynihan has been calling me every day saying we should nominate her," Clinton said. That Moynihan, a New York Democrat, was also chairman of the Senate Finance Committee, which had primary jurisdiction over Clinton's health care plan, made a gesture to him doubly appealing. Nussbaum added that he had been similarly lobbied by Marty Ginsburg, an old friend of his from New York legal circles, who was as voluble as his wife was reserved. (It was no coincidence that the first two women on the Supreme Court were both married to successful lawyers who were secure in their own careers and enthusiastic backers of their wives' ambitions.)

Klain had one caution for Clinton—Ginsburg's position on *Roe*. "She's not where most of the groups are on the issue," he said. With the Guinier nomination, Clinton had felt his staff did not accurately characterize her law review articles, so the president demanded that Klain produce Ginsburg's speeches and articles about *Roe*. He would read them himself. In them, Clinton found that Ginsburg did believe that the Constitution protected a woman's right to choose abortion, just under a different theory than *Roe*. She felt laws banning abortion were a form of sex discrimination—a violation of equal protection of the laws—rather than an affront to the right to privacy, as Blackmun's opinion had held. This was good enough for Clinton. He called Orrin Hatch and ran Ginsburg's name by him. Impressed by her moderate record on the D.C. Circuit, Hatch said she would have no problem in the Senate. Breyer was told to return to Cambridge, his chances fading.

Over the weekend, Foster, Klain, and Jim Hamilton, a private lawyer, went to the Ginsburgs' apartment at the Watergate. Characteristically, for a tax lawyer and a man dedicated to smoothing his wife's way to the Court, Marty Ginsburg had their records in meticulous order. (The contrast to the Breyers' messy accounts was stark.) Typically also, in the meeting at the Watergate, Ruth said almost nothing. If Clinton didn't like Breyer, it was hard to see how he would bond with an icy character like Ginsburg. Still, she would have her interview the following day, on Sunday morning. On Saturday night, the nomination still looked like an open contest.

That was when Andrew Cuomo called George Stephanopoulos and asked if there was a done deal.

Andrew said that his father's thinking about the seat on the Court had evolved. The governor believed that Clinton was about to name Breyer, and he thought that there was no chance that Clinton would name two white males in a row. So Cuomo thought his own chances were now or never.

Stephanopoulos was skeptical. "Are you sure your father will accept if the president calls?" he asked Andrew. "We can't go down this road again. Before the president even thinks about picking up the phone, we have to be absolutely certain that the answer will be nothing but yes."

"Let me check," Andrew said, then put Stephanopoulos on hold. "I just asked him. The answer is yes."

Stephanopoulos called upstairs to Clinton, who was in the White House residence, and asked if he could come up and see him. Clinton gave a bemused smile at Cuomo's latest peregrination. The idea of a dramatic, transformative choice like Cuomo still appealed to the president. "Mario will sing the song of America," he told Stephanopoulos. "It'll be like watching Pavarotti at Christmastime." At a party at the British Embassy that night, Clinton told Stephanopoulos that he still wanted to see Ginsburg in the morning, but Cuomo was his first choice. Close to midnight, Andrew and Stephanopoulos spoke again, and they arranged for Cuomo to await a call around six on Sunday evening.

Clinton and Ginsburg met that morning. Earlier, Nussbaum had passed along an observation from Erwin Griswold, the venerable former dean of Harvard Law School and solicitor general. He said that as Thurgood Marshall had been to civil rights, Ruth Bader Ginsburg had been to women's rights. That kind of symbolism appealed to Clinton, and he felt more favorably toward her than ever. In their meeting, Ginsburg talked about the early loss of her mother, followed by the near loss of her husband, and her identification with the underdog throughout her life. What Clinton saw—and his aides missed— was that beneath Ginsburg's reserved exterior was a heroic American woman. To be sure, this was a woman with a big heart.

Clinton called a final meeting of his selection team for 5:00 p.m. The president was a half hour late, and almost as soon as he arrived, Stephanopoulos was called away to the phone: it was Mario Cuomo. The governor had changed his mind again. "I surrender so many opportunities if I take the Court," he said, "I feel that I would abandon what I have to do." Stephanopoulos sheepishly returned to the Oval Office to say that he had been misled once more and Cuomo was definitively out of the running. The following afternoon, Clinton announced the choice of Ruth Bader Ginsburg—arguably his seventh choice—to be the 107th justice of the Supreme Court.

The ceremony, in the brilliant June sunshine of the Rose Garden, featured Ruth Ginsburg's tribute to her late mother, "the bravest and strongest person I have known, who was taken from me much too soon. I pray that I may be all that she would have been had she lived in an age when women could aspire and achieve and daughters are cherished as much as sons." Clinton was weeping as he walked

Ginsburg back inside the White House, but Brit Hume, then of ABC News, asked him about "a certain zigzag quality of the decision-making process here"—which was, if anything, an understatement.

Clinton all but snarled a response: "I have long since given up the thought that I could disabuse some of you from turning any substantive decision into anything but a political process. How you could ask a question like that after the statement she just made is beyond me." The president's outburst dominated the following day's news, but Ginsburg's appointment received good reviews. As Hatch promised, there was no confirmation controversy. Her hearings lasted three quiet days in July, and Ginsburg was confirmed by a vote of 96 to 3.

The Ginsburg nomination turned out to be an apt metaphor for the Clinton presidency as a whole. The process that led to her selection was chaotic, but the result was admirable—the selection of a universally respected justice who reflected, with great precision, the moderate-to-liberal politics of the president who chose her. Indeed, more than any recent president since Johnson, Clinton was able to use his appointments to shape the Court in line with his own views. Still, even years later, he seemed embarrassed by the events leading up to Ginsburg's selection. Clinton devoted less than 2 of the 957 pages of his memoir to her nomination—one of the most consequential acts of his presidency.

As for Mario Cuomo, he gave varying explanations over the years for why he turned down the appointment in 1993. He would have lost his right to speak out; he cared too much about economic issues that wouldn't come before the Court. Mostly, Cuomo said, he felt that he was the only person who could hold on to the New York governorship for the Democrats. But, of course, he didn't, losing to George Pataki in 1994. After a failed stint as a radio talk show host, Cuomo returned to law practice in New York City.

EXILES RETURN?

O n July 20, 1993, the first day of Ginsburg's confirmation hearing, Vince Foster killed himself. The deputy White House counsel, a close friend of both Clintons from Little Rock and a key figure in the Supreme Court selection process, never acclimated himself to the rough-and-tumble of political Washington. There, for the first time in his life, he had faced public criticism, and the pain of this experience exacerbated an apparently long-standing inclination toward depression. In the White House, the sadness over Foster's death to some extent overshadowed the triumph of Ginsburg's nomination.

Clinton's entire first year was characterized by similarly vertiginous swings of good and bad fortune. Politically and otherwise, this president lived on the edge. In August, Congress passed Clinton's economic plan—by a 218–216 vote in the House and 50–50 in the Senate, with Vice President Gore breaking the tie. The following month, Clinton hosted the historic handshake between Israeli prime minister Yitzhak Rabin and Chairman Yasir Arafat of the PLO on the South Lawn of the White House. But the Clintons' health care plan, the ostensible reason George Mitchell turned down the nomination, went nowhere. And the controversy over the Clintons' 1979 investment in an Arkansas land deal known as Whitewater escalated. In January 1994, Clinton asked for an independent counsel to examine his conduct and determine if there were any grounds for prosecution. That investigation, of course, would mutate through the remaining seven years of Clinton's presidency and lead to his impeachment.

The year 1994 amounted to a slow-motion disaster for Clinton. Ethical controversies, none major in themselves, kept popping up—

among them the disclosure of Hillary Clinton's windfall profit in commodities trading, the resignation of Associate Attorney General Webster Hubbell, and the prolonged investigation of Foster's suicide. On February 11, a former Arkansas state employee named Paula Jones held a raucous press conference at a conservative political event, claiming unspecified misconduct by Clinton in a Little Rock hotel room. Health care reform, the centerpiece of Clinton's presidency, continued its march toward irrelevancy, then death, in Congress.

In the midst of this dismal year, on April 6, Harry Blackmun announced his resignation. Unlike White's departure the previous year, this change did not come as a surprise. In his separate opinion in *Casey*, Blackmun had all but announced his plans to leave the Court. "I am 83 years old," he had written in June 1992. "I cannot remain on this Court forever." The election of a prochoice president, and then White's replacement by Ginsburg, told Blackmun that his monument, *Roe v. Wade*, was safe for the foreseeable future. (With Ginsburg, the 5–4 margin in *Casey* had become a 6–3 prochoice majority.) At Renaissance Weekend in December 1993, Blackmun had given Clinton a strong hint that he would retire the following year, and that is what he did.

The transformed political environment of 1994 changed the selection process—and the Court itself. The constitutional right to choose abortion may have been safe, but a conservative movement was cresting. Democrats still controlled the White House and both houses of Congress, but the momentum was with their adversaries. To some extent, the shift reflected the immediate political problems of a new administration, but there were deeper trends at work, too. The judicial counterrevolution had been in the making for a long time.

In April 1994, Clinton began the search for Blackmun's replacement much the way he did for White's thirteen months earlier. Again, Clinton wanted a politician instead of a judge, and again he asked George Mitchell to take the seat. The Maine senator had already announced that he would not run for reelection in November, so there appeared to be few obstacles to his accepting. But Mitchell told Clinton that he wanted to make one last push for health care as majority leader. Taking the appointment would doom the legislation, he said. In the end, Mitchell just didn't want to be a Supreme Court justice. After a period of agonizing, Bruce Babbitt also took himself out of the running.

Clinton's search for a Supreme Court justice returned to its customary location—square one. This time, though, there was a seriousness and discipline that had been lacking the previous year. Clinton had already thought about most of the likely candidates. His own deteriorating political status made a consensus choice virtually a necessity. And there was, finally, the recognition that Blackmun's replacement would likely be the last appointment that Clinton would get to make. By Supreme Court standards, the remaining justices were relatively young in 1994. For a generation of putative Democratic appointees, it was now or never.

Senator Kennedy resumed pushing for Stephen Breyer. Like many other things about the earlier selection process, news of Clinton's dismal interview with Breyer had leaked. So Kennedy, ever resourceful, sent the president a videotape of a witty speech Breyer had given to a group of visiting judges from Russia. See, the Massachusetts senator was saying, he's not such a stuffed shirt. Breyer was fortunate, too, that Nussbaum had been replaced as White House counsel by Lloyd Cutler, a Washington corporate lawyer with a great fondness for Breyer.

For Clinton, though, the real issue was Richard Arnold, the federal appeals court judge from Little Rock.

Arnold belonged to frontier aristocracy. In the early part of the century, his maternal grandfather, Morris Sheppard, had served as a senator from Texas for almost three decades. His daughter married into the Arnolds of Texarkana, where the men had been practicing law for generations. Born in 1936, Richard received a classical education, studying Latin and Greek first at Phillips Exeter Academy and then at Yale, where he graduated first in his class. In a debate with students from Oxford and Cambridge who quoted Cicero in Latin, Arnold clinched the argument by replying from memory with the next passage of the work. Arnold was likewise valedictorian at Harvard Law School, class of 1960, ahead of his classmate Nino Scalia. He clerked for Justice Brennan on the Supreme Court. Such were his intellect and charisma that Arnold was nearly a legend before he even began practicing law.

Arnold settled in Arkansas, working alternately in private practice and government service, mostly for Governor and then Senator Dale Bumpers. He wrote a new constitution for the state. In 1978,

President Carter nominated him to the district court and, two years later, to the Court of Appeals for the Eighth Circuit. In a remarkable testament to the esteem in which the Arnold family was held, the first President Bush named Richard's younger brother Morris to the same court in 1991. They were the only brothers in American history to serve on the same federal court of appeals.

In the legal profession, an Arnold nomination would have been greeted with something close to acclamation. Richard's politics were moderate; in his best-known ruling, in 1979, he forbade the state of Arkansas from limiting high school girls to half-court basketball while allowing boys to play full court. More than any ideology, Arnold was better known for his eloquence and fairness, and he was admired across the political spectrum. After Blackmun stepped down, more than a hundred federal judges wrote a joint letter to Clinton asking that he nominate Arnold—their action remains unprecedented. Scalia, his law school classmate, called Arnold and asked, "Would it help if I screamed how awful you are?" Clinton himself adored, even looked up to Arnold. They were occasional golfing partners, and as with everything else, Arnold excelled at the game.

There was only one problem. Arnold, who was fifty-eight, had been diagnosed with cancer almost two decades earlier. In blunt terms, Clinton didn't want to nominate Arnold if he thought the judge was soon going to die.

Steven Umin, a Washington lawyer and close friend of Arnold's since their days at Yale College, understood that Arnold's health would be the major issue in his candidacy for the Court. He thought the only way to address the issue was head-on. Two of Umin's former law partners, Edward Bennett Williams, and Larry Lucchino, later a prominent baseball executive, had been treated for lymphoma by Lee Nadler, a professor at the Dana-Farber Cancer Institute at Harvard Medical School. Nadler was among the world's foremost authorities on Arnold's disease. Most relevantly, Nadler had helped push Paul Tsongas out of the race for president in 1992, saying that the former senator's cancer remained life-threatening. (Tsongas died of the disease in 1997.) Umin thought if Nadler would offer a positive prognosis for Arnold, who had a similar illness to Tsongas's, Clinton would surely appoint him to the Court.

Through Mack McLarty, the White House chief of staff (and himself a great fan of Arnold's), Umin arranged for Clinton himself to call Nadler and ask him to review Arnold's medical file. A pugnacious character with abundant self-confidence, Nadler turned Clinton down. "Mr. President, you can ask me to do anything you want," Nadler said. "But if somebody is going to ask me to look at this guy's records, it's got to be him. Then I would report to him, and he could share the report with you."

Amused by the doctor's moxie, Clinton said he was sure Arnold would approve and he would see that the records were sent to Nadler promptly. In their one telephone conversation during this period, a follow-up to Clinton's call, Arnold told Nadler, "Just do the right thing, doctor. Tell the truth."

A few days later, Arnold's records arrived at Nadler's home, outside Boston. The first clue to the seriousness of Arnold's condition was the size of the file—thousands of pages, which stacked ten feet high. The judge had been diagnosed in 1976, eighteen years earlier, with low-grade non-Hodgkin's lymphoma. He was treated immediately and suffered few ill effects. But Arnold's disease did not follow a usual course. In 1991, a lymphoma was found in his colon. In 1993, he had radiation to eliminate tumors in his sinuses. Also that year, Arnold received chemotherapy to eliminate malignant cells in his blood and bone marrow.

The paradox was that Arnold had continued to function more or less normally. The disease was not debilitating. Some people lived with these kinds of recurrences for many years. But Nadler saw that the tumors were changing biologically, making them harder to treat. At the least, years of difficult chemotherapy were in Arnold's future. On the morning of Friday, May 13, Nadler called Arnold, who was sitting on an appeal in Minneapolis, and told him his conclusions. "Lee, you have no choice," Arnold said. "You have to say no."

At 1:00 p.m. that day, Nadler reached Clinton, who was on a speakerphone in the Oval Office. The conversation began in a light-hearted vein, when Nadler said he could hear that Clinton was eating lunch.

"What are you eating, Mr. President?"

"A Big Mac and fries," Clinton said.

"As an oncologist, I don't think that's so smart."

Nadler said there was no way he could say that Arnold's disease "would not interfere" with his duties as a Supreme Court justice. He had cancer all through his body. What Arnold needed was skilled, continuing care.

"Any way we can turn you around on this?" Clinton asked. There wasn't, said Nadler.

At 3:45, Clinton asked his staff to leave him alone to think about what to do. A half hour later, he reached Arnold at the Memphis airport, where he was changing planes on the way home to Little Rock. Clinton was weeping when he said he wasn't going to appoint him.

Far from holding a grudge against Nadler, Arnold asked to become his patient. His distinguished service on the judiciary continued, as did his cancer treatments. In time, though, chemotherapy became less effective, and he died on September 23, 2004, at the age of sixty-eight. Eight Supreme Court justices, including Stephen Breyer, issued statements mourning Arnold's passing, an unprecedented set of tributes to a lower-court judge.

At 6:15 p.m. on May 13, Clinton went on television to nominate Breyer. The announcement was peculiar, because the White House, eager to make the evening news, didn't even bother to wait for Breyer to come down from Boston, so the president stood alone in the Rose Garden. This search had taken just thirty-seven days, compared with the eighty-seven-day marathon to pick Ginsburg, but this selection, too, ended with a kind of disappointment for Clinton. His words were perfunctory as he talked about Breyer, and the president's face bore traces of the sadness he felt in learning the severity of Arnold's illness. Still, with Breyer as with Ginsburg, the nomination would come to be seen as a great success. Clinton had again selected a justice who won close to universal praise and reflected the president's own values and views with great precision.

When Breyer finally did make it to the White House the following Monday, he made a subtle allusion to the disaster of his previous visit. "I'm glad I didn't bring my bicycle down," he said. At fifty-five, Breyer had an almost childlike glee at being nominated. Clinton remembered that even though Breyer had been all but publicly humiliated in the contest for White's seat, he still came to Ginsburg's swearing-in.

The gesture was characteristic. Breyer was the sunniest individual to serve on the Supreme Court in a great many years. Optimism was the core of his character. He had a résumé that was almost as dazzling as Arnold's—Stanford, Marshall Scholar at Oxford, Harvard Law School, clerkship for Justice Arthur J. Goldberg, then tenure at a young age at Harvard Law—but the biggest influence on him came at a less exalted institution.

Breyer was a product of a specific place and time—San Francisco in the 1950s. When he became famous, much later, the only one of his alma maters that he would invariably mention in speeches was Lowell High School. "That doesn't mean a lot to you, but it means a lot to me," he would say, to puzzled audiences. Lowell was the most elite public school in the city, with competitive admissions, and the place sizzled with the ambitions and smarts of recent immigrant offspring. This was not the San Francisco of the following decade, of Haight-Ashbury and the Summer of Love, but rather a growing metropolis that was both cozy and booming. In summers, Breyer worked as a "hasher" (a slinger of hash) in a city-owned camp in the Sierras where the families of firemen, policemen, doctors, and lawyers mingled happily. Few places, before or since, matched San Francisco of that era for civic harmony and commitment to community. (As Breyer would always note of this period, the options were not quite as open for blacks and women.) For forty years, Breyer's father worked as a lawyer for the San Francisco school system. His mother was a homemaker who volunteered with the Democratic Party and the League of Women Voters.

For all his degrees, the most important part of Stephen Breyer's education began in the midseventies when he commuted from Harvard to Washington to work as a counsel for the Senate Judiciary Committee, then chaired by Edward Kennedy. There, Breyer eventually became chief counsel and encouraged Kennedy to embrace a cause that moderated his image as a doctrinaire liberal: deregulation—of the airlines, of trucking, and of the natural gas industry. It was an unusually harmonious and productive time for the committee, and Breyer won the admiration of senators across the political spectrum.

This turned out to be especially important in 1980, when Jimmy Carter nominated Breyer to the First Circuit. Ronald Reagan had already won the election when Breyer came before the committee, and the Republican chairman, Strom Thurmond, had no reason to let the lame duck president fill a precious seat on the court of appeals. But Kennedy prevailed upon Orrin Hatch to ask Thurmond to let Breyer through. Calling Breyer "a member of the family," for his work on the committee, Hatch won over the venerable chairman. Breyer was the last judge confirmed before Carter left office. Amid similar good feelings, the Senate confirmed his nomination to the Supreme Court by an 87–9 vote on July 29, 1994.

Breyer arrived at the Court bearing an uncynical love of government. He believed that government existed to serve people and solve problems, and to a great extent, that it did. More to the point, Breyer admired and trusted Congress and thought that the people's representatives generally worked in the people's interest. After the first or second time, most justices wearied of attending the president's State of the Union address, fretting about the question of when to applaud and generally disdaining their awkward status at the occasion. But Breyer felt his attendance was a gesture of solidarity with the other branches of government, and he never missed it—even when he was the only justice there.

In other words, as Stephen Breyer began his first full term on the Court, he was profoundly out of step—with the country, with the Congress, and even, to some extent, with his new colleagues. The country, it seemed, had turned on the very idea of government and especially on its personification, the members of Congress. On November 8, 1994, voters unseated the Democratic majority in both the House and the Senate. That same day, as it happened, the Court heard arguments in a case that threatened everything Breyer believed in—*United States v. Lopez*.

The members of the Federalist Society and others who wanted the Court to undermine the constitutional basis for a strong federal government needed a case where the issue was raised. So in the strange serendipity that often yields important cases, the matter of Alfonso Lopez Jr. appeared with exquisite timing.

On March 10, 1992, Lopez, a twelfth grader, arrived at Edison High School in San Antonio carrying a concealed .38 caliber handgun and five bullets. Acting on an anonymous tip, school authorities confronted him, and Lopez disclosed the weapon. He was arrested and charged under Texas law with possession of a firearm on school premises. But the state charges were dismissed the next day when federal agents accused him of violating the Gun-Free School Zones Act of 1990, which prohibited possession of a gun at or near a school. Lopez would have walked quietly away from the case if he had been sentenced to probation. But the judge gave him six months, which interfered with Lopez's plans to join the Marine Corps, so he asked his public defender to appeal. The facts of the case were simple; the law, it turned out, was not.

By the time Lopez's case began working its way through the courts, the ideas championed by the Federalist Society had coalesced. The society itself had grown to forty thousand members, with an annual budget of more than $3 million. The movement even got a name, courtesy of Judge Douglas H. Ginsburg, who was once briefly famous. After Robert Bork's nomination failed in the Senate, Reagan named Ginsburg, then a forty-one-year-old judge on the D.C. Circuit, as his replacement. Ginsburg's nomination quickly collapsed, however, following news reports that he had smoked marijuana while he was a law professor. Ginsburg soldiered on as a fervently conservative appeals court judge, and he later published an article in *Regulation*, a libertarian magazine published by the Cato Institute. Ginsburg wrote in an admiring tone about the state of constitutional law before 1937, when the Supreme Court struck down virtually all efforts to regulate the economy. The Court had relied on doctrines like the Commerce Clause, which now represented what Ginsburg called the "Constitution in Exile." "The memory of these ancient exiles," he wrote, "banished for standing in opposition to unlimited government, is kept alive by a few scholars who labor on in the hope of a restoration, a second coming of the Constitution of liberty—even if perhaps not in their own lifetimes."

In short, the Constitution in Exile movement represented a direct threat to the modern welfare state, and the *United States v. Lopez* case loomed as its first major test in the Supreme Court.

As usual, O'Connor had an early question for Drew S. Days III, the solicitor general, who was defending the constitutionality of the guns-in-schools law.

"Is the simple possession of something at or near a school 'commerce' at all? Is it?"

"I think the answer to that is that it is," Days answered.

"I would have thought that it wasn't," O'Connor replied in her direct way, "and I would have thought that it, moreover, is not inter-state."

It was an inauspicious start to Days's argument, which went down-hill from there. O'Connor, Kennedy, Rehnquist, and Scalia demanded to know how Congress could presume to regulate mere gun posses-sion, near a school or otherwise.

But the subtext of the questions was almost as significant as the words themselves. The justices oozed contempt for Congress, which they clearly regarded as a bumbling, only quasi-respectable institu-tion.

"Can you tell me, Mr. Days," Scalia said, with a smirk, "has there been anything in our recent history in the last twenty years where it appears that Congress made a considered judgment that it could *not* reach a particular subject?"

Laughter drowned out the beginning of Days's answer.

At another point, Days said that Congress had a "rational basis" for connecting school violence to commerce.

In response, Souter quipped, "Benjamin Franklin said, 'It is so wonderful to be a rational animal, that there is a reason for everything that one does.'" Again, laughter filled the courtroom.

Through most of its history, the Supreme Court had close ties to Congress. Many justices were ex-senators. But the Rehnquist Court had no such connections. Rehnquist and Scalia had worked only in the executive branch, O'Connor and Souter in state government, Kennedy, Stevens, and Ginsburg in private practice and law schools. Thomas, who observed his customary silence during the *Lopez* argu-ment, had worked briefly on the staff of Senator John Danforth of Missouri, but the searing experience of his confirmation hearings per-manently soured him on Congress. Breyer alone felt any sort of kin-ship with this coordinate branch of government.

It was still early in Breyer's career on the Court, so he had not yet asserted himself as the powerful presence in oral arguments that he would become. But finally, frustrated at both Days and his colleagues, Breyer unloaded on the public defender who was representing Lopez. "So what would you say about the obvious argument, the simple ar-gument against your position, that this isn't a borderline case?

"The guns move in interstate commerce, likely, the books do, the desks do, the teachers might," Breyer said. "People will not move to places in this country where children are being killed in schools by guns, and in fact, if the Federal Government can't do something about it, maybe the whole economy will go down the drain in a thousand obvious ways." Breyer referred to a case from 1942 where the Court said that homegrown wheat was sufficiently connected to interstate commerce to be regulated under the Commerce Clause. "If some homegrown wheat affects interstate commerce, which I guess is a borderline question economically, certainly guns in schools do really affect commerce." All Breyer had done was summon the unquestioned state of constitutional law for more than a half-century.

But Breyer's advocacy (in the form of his questions) did not persuade a majority of his colleagues. On April 26, 1995, the Court ruled 5–4 that Congress had violated the Commerce Clause in passing the Gun-Free School Zones Act. Rehnquist's opinion (joined by O'Connor, Scalia, Kennedy, and Thomas) represented the first time since 1935 that the justices had invalidated a law on the grounds that Congress exceeded its authority under the Commerce Clause. The rhetoric of the opinion meshed with that of Newt Gingrich, the newly installed Speaker of the House. Quoting James Madison in *Federalist No. 45*, Rehnquist wrote, "The powers delegated by the proposed Constitution to the federal government are few and defined. Those which are to remain in the State governments are numerous and indefinite." The scope of "big government" was officially under assault from both sides of First Street.

The decision prompted the first full-throated dissent of Breyer's career. "In my view, the statute falls well within the scope of the commerce power as this Court has understood that power over the last half century," he wrote. Worse, he said, the majority's decision represented a major threat to many other laws on the books. "Congress has enacted many statutes (more than 100 sections of the United States Code), including criminal statutes (at least 25 sections), that use the words 'affecting commerce' to define their scope," Breyer wrote. "The Court's holding . . . threatens legal uncertainty in an area of law that, until this case, seemed reasonably well settled." But that, of course, was the point. The seeds sown by the Federalist Society and its allies were starting to bear fruit.

Like the other justices, Breyer knew the famous question that William Brennan used to ask his law clerks. What's the most important law at the Supreme Court? The clerks would puzzle for some time. Freedom of speech? . . . Equal protection? . . . Separation of powers? . . . until the justice would raise his tiny hand and say, "Five!

The law of five! With five votes, you can do anything around here!" Breyer, who clerked on the Court in its liberal heyday, would remark when the Brennan story was told, "Easy for him to say. He *started* with *seven* votes." But Justice Stephen Breyer served on a very different Court. In the summer after *Lopez*, a friend praised him for his opinion in the case. Breyer gave a wistful smile and waved four fingers in the air. "Four votes," he said. "Only four votes."

WHAT SHALL BE ORTHODOX

I t wasn't just the Federalist Society leading the conservative offensive in the Supreme Court during the 1990s. The law professors and their students could come up with theories and write learned articles and op-ed pieces, but the movement needed the legal equivalent of foot soldiers, too—the lawyers who would actually bring and argue the cases before the Court. In law, as in politics, the best troops came from the most passionate and engaged part of the conservative coalition—evangelical Christians.

Evangelicals joined the fight at the Supreme Court because they, even more than academic critics on the right, were the most outraged by the state of America. While conservative scholars spun theories about the scope of the Commerce Clause, evangelical activists witnessed the actual impact of Supreme Court decisions. In front of abortion clinics. At school board meetings. At high school football games. And the activists were right: the Court had long lined up against their interests. For more than a generation, the justices had engaged in a more-or-less explicit initiative to secularize the Constitution.

When it came to religion in public life, the framers of the Constitution espoused two potentially contradictory ideas. The First Amendment states, "Congress shall make no law respecting an establishment of religion, or prohibiting the free exercise thereof." For more than a century after the founding of the republic, the courts tolerated a great deal of religion in the public sphere—like prayer and Bible reading in schools, frequent invocations of God and evocations of the Ten Commandments in government buildings (and on currency). At the time, this kind of "free exercise" of religion did not amount to an "establishment" thereof. Indeed, the government was free to *require* some degree of piety, or patriotism, from its citizens.

This was especially true in the late 1930s, when public schools around the country insisted that students salute and pledge allegiance to the flag at the beginning of each school day. Many Jehovah's Witnesses objected to the practice, believing that it violated the commandment "Thou shalt have no other gods before me." As World War II grew closer, the Witnesses faced a vicious response. Students were expelled from school. Protests were held outside their homes. When they asked the Supreme Court for protection, in the 1940 case of *Minersville School District v. Gobitis*, they lost. The majority asserted that schools had the right to insist that students participate in rituals designed to "secur[e] effective loyalty to the traditional ideals of democracy."

Within months of that decision, though, the Supreme Court, along with the rest of the nation, saw what could happen in a society where loyalty was coerced and nonconformism punished. The chilling example of fascism in Europe reminded Americans, including judges, of the importance of freedom of speech and worship. In this way, the example of Nazism shaped what the American Constitution would become. The transition was fast, too. Just three years after *Gobitis*, in 1943, the Witnesses brought a nearly identical challenge, and this time they won, in a case that may represent the Supreme Court's quickest reversal of one of its own precedents.

Justice Robert H. Jackson's opinion for the majority in *West Virginia Board of Education v. Barnette*, one of the most eloquent in the Court's history, set down principles that would become lodestars of the American creed. "To believe that patriotism will not flourish if patriotic ceremonies are voluntary and spontaneous instead of a compulsory routine is to make an unflattering estimate of the appeal of our institutions to free minds," he wrote, before concluding with one of the most famous passages in the annals of the Court: "If there is any fixed star in our constitutional constellation, it is that no official, high or petty, can prescribe what shall be orthodox in politics, nationalism, religion, or other matters of opinion or force citizens to confess by word or act their faith therein. If there are any circumstances which permit an exception, they do not now occur to us."

From this ruling, it was just a short jump for the Court to impose ever-greater limits on mandatory observances of any kind in public settings. The next key moment came in 1962, when the Court banned prayer in public schools, even when children were given the right not to participate. In *Engle v. Vitale*, Justice Hugo Black employed the same reasoning as Jackson did in prohibiting mandatory salutes of the flag. "When the power, prestige and financial support of government is placed behind a particular religious belief, the indirect coercive pressure upon religious minorities to conform to the prevailing officially approved religion is plain," he wrote. A year later, the justices banned mandatory Bible reading in public schools as well.

The backlash to these rulings was not long in coming. Prayer and Bible reading had been staples of American public education for generations. The court-ordered end to such religious observance in public schools was soon followed by the chaotic late 1960s. The cause-and-effect was debatable, but for many Christians there was a clear connection between the increased secularization of public life and the licentiousness and disorder that followed. In this period, Rev. Billy Graham, in an indirect way, and then Rev. Pat Robertson, in explicit terms, merged their religious messages with a conservative political agenda. In the election of 1980, Rev. Jerry Falwell mobilized what he called the Moral Majority to defeat a Democratic president and a generation of liberal senators. By the time Bill Clinton was elected president, the evangelical movement represented the core of his conservative opposition. The twin pillars of their agenda were clear—one against legalized abortion, the other for public religious expression, especially prayer in schools.

By the midnineties, after *Casey*, there was no point in pushing an antiabortion agenda on a Court that had made up its mind on the issue. But the issue of religious expression was wide open. Curiously, although the evangelical movement had amassed enormous political clout, it had not cultivated comparable leadership in the legal arena. But all social movements in America eventually find a strategist who sets their course in the courts—their Thurgood Marshall or Ruth Bader Ginsburg—and this was the moment when the evangelicals discovered theirs. Oddly enough, their savior, Jay Sekulow, turned out to be a nice Jewish boy from Brooklyn.

Sekulow's mother went to high school with Ruth Bader Ginsburg, but Jay didn't just come from a different generation than the new justice—he chose to live in a different world. He was born on June 10, 1956. His family tracked the migration pattern of the country as a whole—city to suburb to Sun Belt, in his case, Brooklyn to Long Island to Atlanta. An indifferent student, unmotivated rather than unintelligent, Sekulow initially planned only to attend a two-year college and then get a job. But junior college ignited a desire, if not exactly a roaring bonfire, for more education. Too lazy to look elsewhere, Sekulow settled on a college close to his home, Atlanta Baptist College. He worried what his parents, moderately observant Jews, might say about his choice, but his father encouraged him. "Baptist-shmaptist," the senior Sekulow said. "Go ahead. Get yourself a good education."

Sekulow was drifting through the mandatory Bible classes when a friend, whom he regarded at the time as a "Jesus freak," challenged him to study the Book of Isaiah. Sekulow knew that Jews were supposed to believe that someday the Messiah would come—but that he hadn't come yet. Still, in reading the passages about the Messiah, Sekulow thought he recognized the description—it was Jesus Christ. Sekulow still considered himself a Jew, but one who believed that Jesus was the savior. In time, Sekulow learned that there were other Jews who shared his belief, and they were called "Jews for Jesus." At a ceremony in February 1976, Sekulow marched to the front of a Jews for Jesus church service and announced that he had committed his life to Jesus Christ.

Still, he had to make a living. Sekulow went to law school at Mercer University, in Georgia, found a job with the Internal Revenue Service, and then started a private practice with a friend. His firm set up tax shelters for renovations of historic buildings in Atlanta. Soon Sekulow and his partner were prospering. As Sekulow later related in speeches, he was amazed that clients were paying him retainers of $25,000 or more, and he was just twenty-six years old! "Both my family and my business life were flourishing," he said. "In addition to the law practice, I began a real estate development firm which grossed over $20 million after the first year." Sekulow generally omitted what happened next. The deals turned sour. His law firm declared bankruptcy. A new chapter in his life hovered somewhere between a good idea and a necessity.

Fortunately, about a year earlier, Sekulow had signed on as the general legal counsel for the national Jews for Jesus organization, and it turned out that the group had a case that was heading to the Supreme

Court. Sekulow decided to argue it himself and wound up changing American constitutional law.

Jews for Jesus believes its members should engage in missionary work to seek out converts. Their best-known (or notorious) form of proselytizing consists of aggressive leafleting, especially in public places like airports. In response to this practice, which was frequently annoying to passengers, the governing board of Los Angeles International Airport banned all "First Amendment activities" on its grounds. On July 6, 1984, pursuant to the policy, airport police evicted Alan Howard Snyder, "a minister of the Gospel" in Jews for Jesus, for distributing religious literature. Before Sekulow became involved in the matter, his colleagues in California sued to invalidate the airport rule.

The original theory of the case was straightforward. Proselytizing was a form of religious activity among Jews for Jesus followers. A blanket ban on the practice thus interfered with their First Amendment right to the "free exercise" of their religion. That was how these cases had customarily been argued. Religious expression was always defended under the Free Exercise Clause.

But Sekulow's relative ignorance about the Constitution turned out to be his best weapon. Sure, cases involving religion were always argued under the Free Exercise Clause. But Sekulow came up with a different theory. The First Amendment, after the religion clauses, goes on to say that Congress shall make no law "abridging the freedom of speech." (In a series of cases after World War II, the Court said that the First Amendment was binding against states and localities as well as Congress.) Sekulow thought the eviction of the Jews for Jesus minister was a speech case, not a religion case. What the airport was doing was censoring free speech—and it didn't matter whether the speech concerned religion or politics, which was the more familiar basis for free speech claims. What made Sekulow's idea so appealing was that the Court had been far more generous in extending protection to controversial speech than to intrusive religious activities. Sekulow could draw on a legion of cases where the justices protected all sorts of obnoxious expression, including distributing obscenity, waving picket signs, even, in one famous case, wearing a jacket bearing the words "Fuck the Draft" in the Los Angeles County Courthouse.

Sekulow wondered how these activities could be permitted but not the polite distribution of pamphlets.

So did the justices. At the oral argument on March 3, 1987, Sekulow later recalled in a speech, "I had walked into the courtroom thinking about Jesus and how he overturned the moneychangers' tables at the Temple. Jesus was an activist. He stood up for what he knew was right. I drew strength from his example." But in front of the justices, Sekulow didn't even mention religion. He said the case was solely about free speech. Sekulow knew he was on to something when he heard his adversary list all the supposed reasons that the airport banned the Jews for Jesus leafleters. At one point, Thurgood Marshall, who was by then ailing, crotchety, and usually silent on the bench, roused himself and growled, "Can I ask you a question? What is wrong with what these people do?"

"Nothing is wrong with what they do," the lawyer said.

"Well, how can you prohibit something that doesn't do anything wrong?"

Marshall had gone to the heart of the matter. For all the airport's rationalizations, the case was about the censorship of an unpopular group—exactly what the speech clause of the First Amendment was designed to prevent. The vote in *Board of Airport Commissioners of the City of Los Angeles v. Jews for Jesus, Inc.* was unanimous, with O'Connor writing for the Court that the ordinance violated the First Amendment.

Sekulow immediately began putting his insight to work for the broader evangelical movement. A group of students at Westside High School in Omaha wanted to start a Christian club, to read the Bible and pray together after class. The principal and local board of education turned the group down, saying that to permit a Christian student group in a public school would amount to an "establishment" of religion, in violation of the First Amendment. Sekulow took the appeal to the Supreme Court.

Again, Sekulow steered away from the religion arguments under the First Amendment. To him, the case was about the free speech rights of the students. If other youth groups could use the school facilities, why not the Christian kids? Once more, Sekulow won overwhelmingly, with O'Connor again writing the opinion and only Stevens in dissent. More importantly, O'Connor essentially gave Sekulow and his allies a road map for expanding the place of religion in public schools. In the key passage in *Board of Education of Westside Community Schools v. Mergens*, O'Connor wrote, "There is a crucial difference between government speech endorsing religion, which the Establishment Clause forbids, and private speech endorsing religion, which the Free Speech and Free Exercise Clauses protect. We think that secondary school students are mature enough and are likely to understand that a school does not endorse or support student speech that it merely permits on a nondiscriminatory basis." The Court was saying that religious activity was welcome at public schools, as long as it was students and not teachers or administrators who initiated it. Evangelical students and their parents were only too happy to accept the invitation.

Sekulow's victory in the *Mergens* case in 1990 drew Pat Robertson's attention. The son of a senator and a graduate of Yale Law School himself, Robertson had established himself as a political, financial, and religious powerhouse. He had started the Christian Broadcasting Network in 1960 and soon found that he needed $7,000 per month to keep it on the air. So he ran a telethon seeking seven hundred people to give $10 apiece, and he called the program *The 700 Club*. Based in Virginia Beach, the network and its signature program launched Robertson's vast empire, which included, by the 1980s, broadcast, real estate, cable operations, and even a university, Regent, with more than a thousand students. (Later, he sold just one part of his operation to ABC for $1.9 billion.) In 1988, Robertson ran a respectable race for the Republican presidential nomination, which included besting Vice President George H. W. Bush in the Iowa caucuses, but he had never figured out a reliable way to bring his fight to the courts.

So in 1990, he asked Sekulow to join him in starting a conservative counterpart to the American Civil Liberties Union. Like the ACLU, the new entity would not limit itself to a single issue—such as abortion or school prayer—but instead represent a complete political agenda. Even the name of the new operation would announce an institutional rival to the ACLU; it was called the American Center for Law and Justice, the ACLJ. (The idea also addressed Sekulow's personal financial problems, because Robertson put his enormous direct-response fund-raising expertise at the disposal of the ACLJ.)

Robertson's money and clout turned Sekulow from a freelance operative with an interesting idea into a major player in shaping the agenda of the Supreme Court. But he needed cases that would give the justices the opportunity to rule in his favor.

Sekulow's mission wasn't easy, at least at first. For one thing, he didn't look the part. His New York accent never faded, and his sharp suits, loud ties, and monogrammed shirts suggested a Seventh Avenue garment executive more than an evangelical activist. Once, at a hearing where he was defending Operation Rescue's antiabortion protesters, clinic workers assumed the fast-talking lawyer represented them. "Wrong table," he said.

But the evangelical community was growing so fast, and bumping up against government regulation so often, that cases flooded the ACLJ. In many of them, the question was how much of a Christian message the evangelicals could get into the schools. Organized prayer was out; Christian student groups were in. What, then, about non-student evangelical groups using school property after hours?

That was Sekulow's first major case under Robertson's auspices. New York state law allowed community groups to use school property for "social, civic, and recreational meetings" that were "nonexclusive and open to the general public." Lamb's Chapel, a small evangelical church on Long Island, asked to use the Center Moriches school district's facilities to show a series of six films featuring lectures by James Dobson, a central figure in the national evangelical movement. Dobson had founded Focus on the Family, in Colorado Springs, and turned it into a sprawling enterprise with a broad (and very conservative) political and religious agenda. The lectures were a guide to "the undermining influences of the media that could only be counter-balanced by returning to traditional, Christian family values instilled at an early stage." In Focus on the Family's description of one lecture, for example, " 'The Family Under Fire' views the family in the context of today's society, where a 'civil war of values' is being waged. Dr. Dobson urges parents to look at the effects of governmental interference, abortion and pornography, and to get involved." (This disclaimer followed: "Note: This film contains explicit information regarding the pornography industry. Not recommended for young audiences.") The school district rejected the request to show the films, because they "appear to be church related." Sekulow took the case to the Supreme Court.

There, from the start, Sekulow stuck with his trademark argument. "Mr. Chief Justice and may it please the Court," he began. "This case is about censorship of Lamb's Chapel's speech, which was entertained for the purpose of having a film series at the school facilities to show and discuss contemporary family issues. The direct targeting of religious purpose as an exclusion under the access policy of the school district is both content based and viewpoint based, and does not meet constitutional scrutiny." Like the Jews for Jesus leafleters in L.A. and the Christian students in Omaha, the Lamb's Chapel evangelicals were victims of government repression, not the advance agents of a state religion.

"So what provision of the Constitution are you relying on?" O'Connor asked.

"First Amendment, as applied to the states through the Fourteenth, freedom of speech."

"Which part of it?"

"Free speech."

Religion couldn't be privileged under the Constitution, Sekulow insisted, but it couldn't be penalized, either. "The way I understand the respondents' argument, the atheists are in, the agnostics are in, the communists are in, the religion is not in," Sekulow told the justices. "This is the type of viewpoint discrimination that this Court has not sanctioned." The result, in *Lamb's Chapel v. Center Moriches Union Free School District*, was another unanimous victory for Sekulow. In 1995, under the same theory, the court ruled that the University of Virginia could not subsidize some student publications but at the same time refuse to fund one called *Wide Awake: A Christian Perspective at the University of Virginia*. As Justice Kennedy wrote for the Court, "For the University, by regulation, to cast disapproval on particular viewpoints of its students risks the suppression of free speech and creative inquiry in one of the vital centers for the nation's intellectual life, its college and university campuses."

By the midnineties, the issue was settled. According to the standards of Supreme Court litigation, Sekulow had emerged out of nowhere to revolutionize an important rule of law. As a result of his efforts, it was clear that if a school, airport, or other public forum was going to open up its facilities to some individuals or groups, the authorities couldn't exclude religious speakers from the list. This was an important victory, but the evangelical agenda extended a great deal further. With Republicans now in control of both the House and the Senate (and many state houses), there was suddenly a real possibility that governments might begin subsidizing religious activities. Gingrich and others made plain that they believed churches did a better job of delivering all kinds of government services—from job training to running schools and prisons—than traditional official bureaucracies. They wanted the federal government not merely to permit these activities but, if possible, to encourage and pay for them as well. The question, then, was whether these ever-closer ties between church and state would be approved by the Supreme Court.

The answer would likely turn on a bland phrase that blossomed into one of the most controversial issues of the Rehnquist years—"the *Lemon* test." The phrase dated to *Lemon v. Kurtzman*, a 1971 opinion by Chief Justice Burger. As the term evolved through the years, it meant that any law that involved church and state functions had to meet three criteria to be constitutional. The law had to (1) have a secular purpose, (2) neither advance nor inhibit religion, and (3) avoid excessive "entanglement" of government and religion. Over the years, the Court has proposed many such "tests," which usually prove easier to announce than apply. That was true for *Lemon* as well. When it came to church and state, the real rule on the Rehnquist Court was simpler. As with so many other areas of the law, like abortion, it was O'Connor's vote that made the difference. If she thought a law was constitutional, it was; if not, it wasn't.

For Scalia, the *Lemon* test epitomized everything he loathed about modern constitutional law, and about O'Connor's jurisprudence in particular. "Like some ghoul in a late-night horror movie that repeatedly sits up in its grave and shuffles abroad after being repeatedly killed and buried, *Lemon* stalks our Establishment Clause jurisprudence once again, frightening the little children and school attorneys of Center Moriches Union Free School District," he wrote memorably in a concurring opinion in *Lamb's Chapel*. In Scalia's view, *Lemon* gave judges virtually unlimited discretion to resolve cases according to what seemed fair to them. In contrast, Scalia wanted judges to apply clear rules, dictated by the intent of the framers, and the long history of entanglement between religion and American public life gave him a rich lode of material for his originalism. Prayer in schools, religious displays like crèches on government land, public celebrations of God and his works—all had been present at the time of the framers and should be allowed today, according to Scalia. He believed that the framers meant the Establishment Clause merely to prohibit the creation of a single state religion or government action that favored one religion over another; as for other government activities that endorsed religion generally or aided all religions equally, that was entirely appropriate. In the words of the dreaded *Lemon* test, Scalia believed that the Constitution not only permitted but encouraged entanglement between church and state.

In at least one respect, Scalia had a point. As many as six justices had criticized the *Lemon* test, but it still haunted the Court, mostly because O'Connor upheld it. On church-state issues, like so many others, O'Connor had the swing vote, but not because she had trouble making up her mind about whether she was a liberal or a conservative. For O'Connor, centrism *was* a judicial philosophy in itself. When she gave tours of the Court, O'Connor would always point out the beautiful cast-iron lampposts in the courtyards. "Look at the bottom of the lampposts," she'd say. "They've got turtles around the bottom, holding up the rest of it. That's like us on the Court. We're slow and steady, and we don't move too fast in any direction." O'Connor believed that steadiness was a virtue, and it was O'Connor who, like the turtles, carried the opinions of the Court on her back.

A case toward the end of Clinton's first term illustrated the difference in Scalia's and O'Connor's approaches to church-state issues. As had often happened before, simple facts led the Court to a complex result. In the fall of 1993, various civic groups in Ohio began seeking space for their holiday displays on the ten-acre plaza near the statehouse in Columbus. The local authorities gave permission for the state to put up a Christmas tree, for a local synagogue to erect a menorah, and for the United Way to post a sign about the progress of a fund-raising campaign. But the city denied a request from the local branch of the Ku Klux Klan to place a Latin cross on the plaza, on the ground that such a cross on public property would represent the "establishment" of a state religion, in violation of the First Amendment. Vincent Pinette, the head of the KKK in Ohio, sued to win the right to raise the cross.

In 1995, the Court ruled 7–2 that the KKK should have the right to display the cross on Capitol Square. The case produced a bewildering six different opinions, with various justices affiliating themselves with all or parts of several of them. Scalia and O'Connor both supported the KKK's legal position, but their rationales heightened the differences between them. (Stevens and Ginsburg were the dissenters; they believed that allowing the KKK to put up the cross did violate the Establishment Clause.)

For Scalia, as always, the issue was clear. To him, speech by and about religion received precisely the same protection under the First Amendment as any other kind of speech. "Our precedent establishes that private religious speech, far from being a First Amendment orphan, is as fully protected under the Free Speech Clause as secular private expression," he wrote. "Indeed, in Anglo American history, at least, government suppression of speech has so commonly been directed *precisely* at religious speech that a free speech clause without religion would be *Hamlet* without the prince." True, the government itself might not be able to erect religious symbols, but if that government allowed Democrats and Republicans to give speeches on a public square, it had to permit Christians, Jews, and even the KKK to put up any symbols they wished as well. To Scalia, the Establishment Clause "applies only to the words and acts of *government*. It was never meant, and has never been read by this Court, to serve as an impediment to purely *private* religious speech."

O'Connor disagreed completely. In her view, a private religious display *could* violate the Establishment Clause if a "reasonable, informed observer . . . would think that the State was endorsing religion or any particular creed." In Columbus, no reasonable person could think that the state was endorsing the KKK's cross, so the group had a right to display it. O'Connor's solution to the problem was a flexible balancing test, like the one in *Lemon*. The problem with such an approach, of course, was that it would not always be clear what the justices themselves, much less the mythical "reasonable, informed observer," would conclude about a given religious display. With characteristic vitriol (especially where O'Connor was concerned), Scalia said her opinion was "perverse" and "bizarre," and "invited chaos." And this was in a case where the two justices *agreed* on the result.

By 1995, O'Connor could slough off Scalia's tirades. After fourteen years on the Court, she had come to feel great self-confidence in her judgments, and if her views didn't always give perfect guidance to the lower courts, she thought it was better to be right than consistent. "We're a common law court," she would say, without a trace of defensiveness. "Of course, we 'make' law as we go along." O'Connor was perfectly content each year to watch the parade of crèches, crosses, menorahs, and the like passing through the Court's docket, awaiting her thumbs up or thumbs down.

The next subject on the horizon was what would become known as faith-based initiatives—government programs handed over to be run by private and religious organizations. As Sekulow and other litigators planned their litigation strategies, the question would usually come down simply to: "What will Sandra do?"

8

WRITING SEPARATELY

Few lawyers anticipating their appearances before the Supreme Court spent much time asking, "What will Clarence do?" As O'Connor relished her place at the center of the Court's decisions, Thomas embraced an alternative model of judging, one where he viewed himself as a principled outsider who cared little whether his opinions commanded a majority or even a single additional vote. He was a justice neither influenced by nor with influence upon his colleagues.

Thomas rarely spoke in oral arguments. He was the only justice who suffered through a brutal confirmation fight. He was the only African American. He was more than a decade younger than most of his colleagues. He traveled in an entirely different milieu, socializing at recreational vehicle campgrounds and NASCAR tracks (where few people recognized him) and in the salons of right-wing activists (where he was revered). He was the friendliest, warmest justice, and he was full of rage. He denounced self-pity and pitied himself. There was no one on the Court remotely like him—philosophically, jurisprudentially, or personally.

As Thomas approached the completion of his first decade on the Court, he had established the most distinctive judicial perspective among the justices. He was by far the most conservative member of the Rehnquist Court, probably the most conservative justice since the Four Horsemen, FDR's nemeses, retired during the New Deal. Thomas's opinions, if they ultimately commanded a majority, would create not only new precedents—*Roe* overturned, virtually all religious displays allowed, virtually no executions stopped—but a transformed nation. His opinion in *Lopez*, the Commerce Clause case, offered a clue to the shape of that possible new world. Thomas joined Rehnquist's majority opinion striking down the Gun-Free School Zones Act, but in a concurring opinion he said he thought the Court should have gone much further.

"I write separately to observe that our case law has drifted far from the original understanding of the Commerce Clause," Thomas stated, before beginning a lengthy analysis of what the term "commerce" meant in 1789, noting, for example, his view that "manufacturing and agriculture" were outside the eighteenth-century understanding of that word. Accordingly, Thomas said, he thought any federal regulation of manufacturing or agriculture was unconstitutional. To Thomas, the change in the nation over two centuries mattered less than honoring the intent of the framers. "Even though the boundary between commerce and other matters may ignore 'economic reality' and thus seem arbitrary or artificial to some, we must nevertheless respect a constitutional line that does not grant Congress power over all that substantially affects interstate commerce." That no justice had expressed views like his for decades—and that his approach would invalidate much of the work of the contemporary federal government— disturbed Thomas not at all. As he said, "Although I might be willing to return to the original understanding, I recognize that many believe that it is too late in the day to undertake a fundamental reexamination of the past 60 years."

Thomas was engaged in a lonely, often solo, effort to restore the Constitution in Exile, the world of Supreme Court precedent before 1937. Even if he was rarely joined by his fellow justices, his chambers at least remained a controversy-free zone. Of all the justices, Thomas imposed the tightest ideological screen in the hiring of law clerks, deputizing a small group of former clerks to determine the views of prospective hires. Other justices hired clerks who generally shared their opinions; only Thomas imposed specific ideological litmus tests. Prospective clerks ran a three-stage gauntlet, which generally began with a first interview with Jack Goldsmith, a law professor, then a round with either John Yoo, also a professor, or Christopher Landau, a Washington lawyer and one of Thomas's first clerks. (Both Goldsmith and Yoo went on to work for President George W. Bush and helped to set administration policy regarding executive authority to conduct the war on terror.) Finally, the current group of clerks would interrogate the applicant. They asked about ideology—abortion, federalism, Commerce Clause, death penalty, search and seizure—to make sure that the putative clerk shared Thomas's (and their own) extreme views. Only after these interviewers reached a consensus on the applicant's suitability did they permit an interview with Thomas, who generally limited himself to a low-key chat about the applicant's family and interests. Asked about his ideological approach to the hiring of clerks at the National Center for Policy Analysis, a conservative think tank, Thomas said, "I won't hire clerks who have profound disagreements with me. It's like trying to train a pig. It wastes your time and aggravates the pig." Of Thomas's first forty clerks on the Supreme Court, one was black.

Thomas's extreme views extended well beyond the Commerce Clause. Throughout the 1990s, Rehnquist, Kennedy, and (as ever) O'Connor tried to revitalize the doctrine of states' rights, ruling that several federal laws impinged on aspects of state sovereignty. These developments were sometimes called a "federalism revolution," but that now seems an exaggeration. The changes the Court imposed on federal-state relations were, on the whole, rather modest. For example, the Court limited Congress's right to pass laws that gave citizens the opportunity to sue state officials; similarly, they interpreted federal statutes so that they did not give citizens the right to sue states. These were important, but hardly revolutionary, limitations on federal power, with little practical impact on the lives of most people.

Thomas always joined these states' rights rulings but often wrote concurring opinions urging the Court to cut back even more on federal authority. He asserted, for example, that he thought Congress had no right to make a federal crime of bribing state or local government officials—a kind of case that local U.S. attorneys had been bringing for decades. In 1997, the Court struck down part of the Brady Bill, the federal gun control law that directed state officials to conduct background checks on prospective handgun purchasers. Thomas signed on to Scalia's majority opinion, of course, but in a brief concurrence suggested an even broader point, that all gun control was unconstitutional. He wrote, "Marshaling an impressive array of historical evidence, a growing body of scholarly commentary indicates that the 'right to keep and bear arms' is, as the Amendment's text suggests, a personal right." Thomas's libertarian view of the original intent of the framers sometimes led him to broad definitions of freedom of speech—the one area where he tended to join the Court's moderates—but his jurisprudence overall hewed predictably to a consistent conservative line. To prepare his law clerks for their chambers' lonely crusade, Thomas required the new ones to watch the 1949 movie version of Ayn Rand's classic homage to individualism, *The Fountainhead*, which concerns an architect's struggle to maintain his integrity in a world of conformity.

Rehnquist rarely assigned important majority opinions to Thomas, because his extreme views made it difficult for him to persuade a majority of his colleagues to join him. In late 1999, the justices agreed to uphold a federal program that passed government funds to state and local agencies, which in turn lent educational equipment to public, private, and religious schools. The Court agreed that the law did not violate the Establishment Clause, and Rehnquist assigned the case to Thomas, who couldn't even muster four other justices. Thus, Thomas's opinion began with the embarrassing opening (under the circumstances) that he "announced the judgment of the Court," rather than the customary "delivered the opinion of the Court." In her separate opinion explaining why she could not join Thomas, O'Connor said she rejected his attempt to approve the "diversion of government aid to religious indoctrination."

Indeed, it is difficult to point to a single truly significant majority opinion Thomas had written. Many of his assignments were unanimous opinions on minor subjects—"dogs," in the Court's parlance. When asked which of his opinions was his favorite, Thomas would usually cite a 1996 case where the Court unanimously overturned an award to a railroad worker who had sustained injuries after trying to manipulate a "knuckle" between two cars. "It was a little case that didn't matter to anyone," Thomas said in a speech. "It's almost inconsequential. It was a fun little opinion. I went back into the history of trains." (In fact, as the journalist Tony Mauro first reported, the case was not inconsequential. Thomas's opinion made it much harder for railroad workers to recover for the horrific accidents that can take place when they climb between two railcars in the process of coupling. Years after the decision, the plaintiff in the case, William Hiles, was still bedridden most of the time.)

Probably the greatest contrast between Thomas and his colleagues was that he fundamentally did not believe in stare decisis, the law of precedent. If a decision was wrong, Thomas thought it should be overturned, however long the case may have been on the books. As he wrote once, "When faced with a clash of constitutional principle and a line of unreasoned cases wholly divorced from the text, history, and structure of our founding document, we should not hesitate to resolve

the tension in favor of the Constitution's original meaning." All justices of the Supreme Court, from Brennan on the left to Scalia on the
right, develop something close to reverence for the Court's precedents; no one besides Thomas would have dismissed two hundred
years of stare decisis in such a cavalier way. At an appearance at a New
York synagogue in 2005, Scalia was asked to compare his own judicial philosophy with that of Thomas. "I am an originalist," Scalia said,
"but I am not a nut."

So Thomas was ideologically isolated, strategically marginal, and, in
oral argument, embarrassingly silent. He was also universally adored.

Fellow justices, law clerks, police officers, cafeteria workers, jani-
tors—all basked in Thomas's effusive good nature. His rolling basso
laughter frequently pierced the silence of the Court's hushed corridors.
Unlike the rest of his colleagues, Thomas learned the names of all the
new clerks every year, including those of his ideological adversaries,
and he frequently invited the young lawyers into his chambers to
chat, often for two or three hours. One year Thomas became friendly
with a Stevens clerk, a lesbian whose partner was a professional snowboarder; Thomas liked the two of them so much that for a while he
kept a photograph of the snowboarder on his desk. When the wife of
one of his former law clerks lay dying in the hospital, Thomas and his
wife spent several nights comforting the couple through the ordeal.

Thomas didn't treat just law clerks this way. He would meet law
students at moot courts, or people at ball games and auto races, and
invite them to visit him at the Supreme Court. When they did, the
conversations would also sometimes last into the evening. If there was
a football game on television (especially Thomas's beloved Dallas
Cowboys), he would pass out cigars to anyone who wanted to watch
with him. When he joined the Court, Thomas played basketball with
clerks in the Court's top-floor gym, the famous "highest court in the
land." But within a year the justice injured his knee and rarely played
again.

Although Thomas asked almost no questions of the lawyers at oral
argument, he wasn't silent on the bench. Thomas sat to Breyer's right,
and the two of them often whispered and joked to each other, barely
muffling their frequent laughter. Things sometimes got so raucous
between them that Kennedy, who sat on the other side of Thomas,

would lean forward, trying to get away from the noise. Breyer and Thomas passed notes, too, often mocking each other's positions in good-natured ways. "States' rights über alles," Breyer might write, and Thomas, in another case, would jot, "Always for the criminal, eh?" This wasn't feigned fellowship. It was a portrait of colleagues who genuinely cared for each other.

There was a new measure of joy in Thomas's personal life as well in this period. In the midnineties, his son from his first marriage, Jamal, went off to college at the Virginia Military Institute. (For this reason, Thomas recused himself in 1996 when, in an especially satisfying moment for Ginsburg, she wrote the opinion holding that the state-funded school could no longer refuse to admit women.) The following year, Thomas's six-year-old grandnephew, Mark Martin Jr., came to live with him. Mark's father was in prison on cocaine trafficking charges, and his mother was struggling to raise four children on her own. Thomas was roughly the same age when his grandfather adopted him, saving him from similarly chaotic circumstances. New fatherhood, when he was close to fifty, invigorated Thomas and filled his home life with happiness.

It also changed Thomas's approach to transportation. The justice had a long-standing obsession with Corvettes, the great American sports cars, and he often drove one on the twenty-four-mile trip to the Court from his home in remote Fairfax Station, Virginia. But shortly after Mark Junior's arrival, Thomas purchased a custom-made forty-foot Prevost motor coach, with leather furniture, satellite television, and onboard galley—a "condo on wheels," as he once called it. Thomas adored the vehicle, which he called "the bus," and kept a photograph of it by his desk, near the portraits of Booker T. Washington, Frederick Douglass, and Winston Churchill. For vacations, even on many weekends, Thomas would pack up his wife and young Mark and simply take off. They would stay at campgrounds or parking lots near NASCAR races. Often, the justice would take advantage of Wal-Mart's policy (well known in the RV world) of allowing such vehicles to remain overnight in their parking lots. In all these places, Thomas mixed easily with other "RVers," some of whom would recognize him, many of whom would not. In 2004, Thomas received the "Spirit of America" award from the Recreation Vehicle Industry Association. "Being an RVer helps me do my job better," he said in his speech to the group. "The world I live in is very cloistered. The bulk of my adult life has been spent in Washington, D.C. RVing allows me to get out and see the real America. In RV campgrounds, you wave at everybody and they wave back."

Yet even in the friendly confines of his chambers, Thomas carefully tended the grudges held since his confirmation hearings. For years, he kept a list in his desk of the roll-call vote in his 52–48 confirmation. But his targets weren't only the senators who voted against him. "When I left Georgia over twenty-five years ago, a familiar source of the unkind treatment and incivility were just bigots," he said at a speech in Macon in 1993. "Today, ironically, a new brand of stereo-types and ad hominem assaults are surfacing across the nation's col-lege campuses, in the national media, in Hollywood, and among the involuntarily ordained 'cultural elite.' Who are the target? Those who dare to question current social and cultural gimmicks, those who in-sist that we embrace the values that have worked and reject those that have failed us, those who dare to disagree with the latest ideological fad." This would become the theme of Thomas's speeches over the fol-lowing decade—his own courageous fight against the "elites" who were out to get him. Friends and associates would often claim that Thomas's rage had mellowed, but that seems unlikely. In 2007 he told *BusinessWeek*, in a rare interview, that he thought the news media were "universally untrustworthy because they have their own notions of what I should think or I should do."

Thomas never identified his enemies by name—the "smart-aleck commentators and self-professed know-it-alls," as he once described them—but it was usually clear whom he meant. The list began, of course, with the senators who opposed his confirmation. Thomas also regarded most of the press as part of the elite, and a friend quoted him as saying the happiest day of his life was when he canceled his sub-scription to the *Washington Post*. Likewise, Thomas detested Yale Law School, his alma mater, and he had a "Yale Sucks" bumper sticker on the mantel of his chambers for a time. He believed that he was treated paternalistically while he was on campus and that the school aban-doned him (in favor of another Yale law graduate, Anita Hill) during his confirmation hearings. Sneering references to Yale were a standard part of his speeches. As Thomas put it in a talk for *Headway* maga-zine, a now-defunct conservative publication, in 1998, "I couldn't get a job out of Yale Law School. That's how much good it did me. I think I'll send the degree back, while I'm at it." Six years later, as the com-mencement speaker at Ave Maria School of Law, a new institution grounded in Catholic legal principles, he accepted an honorary degree with the quip, "As the rift from my alma mater remains, I will need a degree from a law school." Thomas frequently did moot courts and commencement addresses at small law schools and Catholic and evangelical colleges, but he never returned to Yale. For speaking engagements, he described his rule as "I don't do Ivies."

It was possible to interpret Thomas's refusal to ask questions at oral argument as a sign of simmering resentment. Even as recently as the 1980s, such silence might have drawn little attention because several justices of that era—among them Brennan, Marshall, and Blackmun—asked relatively few questions. But the Court in the 1990s featured eight active interrogators, making the contrast all the greater. In his public appearances, Thomas was often asked about his reluctance to participate. His answers varied. Sometimes he said he asked questions only if other justices had not covered the subject of interest to him. Other times, he said he gained more from listening than he did by speaking. In private, he would sometimes express frustration with his colleagues for interrupting too much and showing off. In 2000, Thomas explained his silence to a student group by saying that as a youth he was self-conscious about speaking Gullah, a regional dialect of coastal Georgia, and so he "developed the habit of listening." This last explanation was especially peculiar. It is possible that Thomas spoke some Gullah when he lived in Pin Point, Georgia. But from the age of six, Thomas lived with his English-speaking grandfather in Savannah, where Gullah was rarely spoken, and attended rigorous parochial schools, where he spoke only English and received excellent grades.

One reason Thomas maintained his silence may simply be because the media called so much attention to it—and he wasn't going to give his critics the satisfaction of seeing him change his ways. Among friends, he would mock the way the liberal press described justices who moved to the left as "evolving" and "growing" on the Court. "I ain't evolvin'," he would say.

In public, Thomas would discuss over and over again the way anger has shaped his life. At a commencement speech in 1996 at Liberty University, which was founded by Rev. Jerry Falwell, Thomas departed from the usual pablum offered on such occasions to give an extraordinary self-portrait. He recalled his own graduation from college, at Holy Cross, twenty-five years earlier. He was something close to a radical in those days, an overall-wearing Black Power devotee with inchoate dreams of changing the world. "I thought I knew all the answers," he said. "It was all so clear. I was just relieved to have completed my college education. I had often thought of giving up and going home. To my core, I was a swirling combination of frustration, of anger, of disappointment, of anxiety and perhaps there was a glimmer of hope, but it was well hidden. Mostly I was just confused. I had alienated my grandfather, and the dreams of my youth to become a Catholic priest had evaporated. It was indeed a dark night of my soul." (In a lighter vein, he would sometimes recall that his Afrocentric worldview in those days inspired the name of his son. "We called him Jamal, so you can see where my head was in those days.")

Always, when recounting the pain in his life, Thomas would return to the subject of his confirmation hearings: "And it is only by God's grace and on his mighty shoulders that my wife and I endured the unpleasantness of my confirmation. In the end, our strategy was to rely on him, to endure the agony and then transcend the aftermath of bitterness, and we as a team, an inseparable team, are so grateful to you who lifted us up in prayer."

Thomas appeared in public about as often as the other justices, but he picked his audiences with greater care. Only once in his first decade on the Court did he venture away from safe, sympathetic crowds where he could be guaranteed a warm reception. On that occasion, he decided to take on the most incendiary subject of all—race.

Thomas's views on the subject were clear. Like Scalia and Rehnquist, he believed in a "color-blind Constitution," that is, that the Constitution forbade any consideration of race. Most notably, of course, he thought any kind of affirmative action or preferential treatment for blacks should be banned under the Equal Protection Clause. He was a proud heir to the civil rights tradition of Booker T. Washington, which focused less on government assistance to blacks than on self-help and up-by-the-bootstraps individual initiative. To the extent Thomas discussed discrimination at all, it was usually in the context of the vanished South of his youth—or of contemporary bias against Thomas himself. He had an understandable sensitivity to the common (and false) notion that he functioned as Scalia's pawn on the Court. This idea was absurd not least because the two justices' voting records were different, with Thomas well to the right of his senior colleague. What was notable, though, was that Thomas attributed this canard to racial, not political, bias. As he put it in a speech in Louisville, "Because I'm black, it is said that Justice Scalia does my work for me. I understand how that works. But I rarely see him, so he must have a chip in my brain that tells me what to do."

To say that Thomas opposed affirmative action is not to say that he fought all efforts to help poor people, especially blacks. He thought the traditional civil rights movement bred a culture of victimization in blacks and paternalism in whites. He believed that economics, not race, was at the root of poor people's problems, and he opened his chambers to those who shared these views. He would read the names of striving black youngsters in the news and invite them in for pep talks. His friend Tony Welters, an African American health care entrepreneur, started a program at New York University Law School that awarded scholarships—without regard to race—to "outstanding J.D. students who are among the first in their immediate family to pursue a graduate degree." Thomas liked the program so much that he allowed the school to conduct the final interviews each year at the Supreme Court.

As Thomas himself would acknowledge privately, he benefited from affirmative action at every step of his life—in gaining admission to Holy Cross and Yale, in being hired for civil rights jobs in the Reagan administration, and in winning appointment to the Court. But he thought that, ultimately, these kinds of efforts to help people were self-defeating. (He'd always advise young black lawyers to focus on subjects like tax or property law and escape the ghetto of civil rights specialization.) Thomas thought integration was at best a mixed blessing for blacks; he loved the all-black world of the segregated Savannah of his childhood and thought that its replacement did African Americans no favors.

Indeed, Thomas believed virtually all government efforts to help black people wound up backfiring. He liked to point out that the handful of black farmers left in South Carolina were often blocked from selling their land for the best prices by environmental regulations. His favorite quote from his idol Frederick Douglass summed up his view: "The American people have always been anxious to know what they shall do with us. . . . I have had but one answer from the beginning. Do nothing with us! . . . If the Negro cannot stand on his own legs, let him fall."

Once, and only once, Thomas tried out this argument on a skeptical audience. In 1998, he accepted an invitation to speak at the annual meeting of the National Bar Association, the largest organization of black lawyers in the country. A month before his appearance, a group of board members of the NBA wrote to Thomas purporting to withdraw the invitation, but he decided to come anyway. The hotel ballroom was tense when Thomas took the podium in front of about two thousand lawyers and judges, many of whom disagreed with him passionately on issues of civil rights. That the meeting took place in Memphis in the thirtieth-anniversary year of the assassination of Martin Luther King Jr. gave the occasion even greater emotional weight.

Thomas began by recalling King's death and his sense that "the whole world had gone mad." Since that time, though, King's supposed heirs had decided that the "racial divide was a permanent state. . . . Some go so far as to all but define each of us by our race and establish the range of our thinking and our opinions not by our deeds but by our color." In other words, to be black was to share the orthodoxy of the civil rights movement. "I see this in much the same way I saw our denial of rights—as nothing short of a denial of our humanity."

Thomas went on to describe how his despair grew when he was a law student, filling him with "anger, resentment and rage." In time, though, he came to the revelation that "the individual approach, not the group approach, is the better, more acceptable, more supportable and less dangerous one. This approach is also consistent with the underlying principles of the country." As a black man, he was entitled to these views. "I knew who I was and needed no gimmicks to affirm my identity. Nor, might I add, do I need anyone telling me who I am today. This is especially true of the psycho-silliness about forgetting my roots or self-hatred."

Thomas concluded mournfully. "I have come here today not in anger or to anger, though my mere presence has been sufficient, obviously, to anger some. Nor have I come to defend my views, but rather to assert my right to think for myself, to refuse to have my ideas assigned to me as though I was an intellectual slave because I'm black. I come to state that I'm a man, free to think for myself and do as I please. I've come to assert that I am a judge and I will not be consigned the unquestioned opinions of others."

Thomas received a polite reception from the audience, but by this point he and his adversaries were largely talking past one another. Rather than engage his critics, Thomas chose to attack straw men. No one quarreled with Thomas's right to his own views; no one said black people had to speak with one voice; no one asserted that support for causes like affirmative action was obligatory for Thomas or anyone else; Thomas's critics, no less than he, sought "to continue diligently to search for lasting solutions." It was the substance of Thomas's views, not his right to hold them, that his critics attacked. Thomas's speech was a sustained plea for his own victimhood—in support of his antivictimhood philosophy. In any event, the speech turned out to be a one-time-only attempt to talk to his ideological adversaries in public. He quickly resumed circulating in more familiar, and comfortable, territory.

On May 28, 1994, Clarence and Ginni Thomas hosted, and he performed the ceremony for, Rush Limbaugh's third marriage, this one to Marta Fitzgerald, an aerobics instructor whom the radio host met on the Internet. (The couple soon divorced.) Thomas's speaking engagements in Washington were almost exclusively in the world of conservative think tanks and lobbying operations. His first television appearance after his confirmation took place on National Empowerment Television, an offshoot of the Free Congress Foundation, which was run by Thomas's old friend Paul Weyrich, a founding father of the New Right. Thomas visited Weyrich's office several times and spoke at the group's fifteenth anniversary in 1993. Thomas spoke at the Heritage Foundation, another prominent conservative group, and he gave the American Enterprise Institute's Francis Boyer Lecture at the annual black-tie affair that is known around Washington as "the conservative prom."

There, surrounded by many of the most powerful people in the country, Thomas paid tribute to himself for having the courage to agree with them. The theme of his speech was "the question of courage in American life," as reflected in his career on the bench. "In my humble opinion," he said, "those who come to engage in debates of consequence, and who challenge accepted wisdom, should expect to be treated badly. Nonetheless, they must stand undaunted. That is required. And that should be expected. For it is bravery that is required to secure freedom." Rhetorically, Thomas asked whether it was "worth it" to be as courageous as he had been. "If one wants to be popular, it is counterproductive to disagree with the majority. If one just wants to tread water until the next vacation, it isn't worth the agony. If one just wants to muddle through, it is not worth it. In my office, a little sign reads: 'To avoid criticism, say nothing, do nothing, be nothing.' " Never, on these occasions, did Thomas acknowledge that he was not some lonely voice in the wilderness but a Supreme Court justice whose votes, more often than not, were in the majority.

Thomas's status as a conservative hero had tangible, as well as psychic, rewards. Before Thomas became a justice, he was never wealthy; he was already on the Supreme Court when he finished paying off all his student loans. But Thomas made far more financially out of his status as a justice, and a folk hero, than any of his colleagues. He received a $1.5 million book advance from the publishing company owned by Rupert Murdoch, the media entrepreneur who has been a supporter of conservative causes. Rehnquist and Breyer also wrote books, but neither received anything like this kind of money. In touting the book to potential publishers, Thomas told editors that Limbaugh planned to read the book aloud on the air. Thomas said that he would not appear on television morning news shows, fearing attacks from potential interviewers, but he would agree to be interviewed in the more sympathetic environment of Fox News. (More than three years after the contract was announced, and $500,000 paid to him, Thomas had still not delivered a manuscript.)

Thomas received even more direct financial benefits from his job. According to the financial disclosure statements the justices are required to submit, Thomas received $42,200 in gifts over a six-year period. This was more than seven times as much as any of his colleagues, whose gifts tended to consist of crystal figurines and plaques. (Most of the justices accepted all-expenses-paid trips to destinations around the world, where they lectured at universities and met with judges; the only exception was Souter, whose gift and travel disclosure forms, year after year, said: "None.") Most of Thomas's gifts came from conservatives, who had come to admire his work on the bench. For example, Harlan Crow, a Texas businessman, gave Thomas a Bible once owned by Frederick Douglass that was valued at $19,000. (Crow also donated $175,000 for a new Clarence Thomas wing at the local library in Thomas's hometown of Pin Point, Georgia.) Another executive gave Thomas $5,000 to help pay for his grandnephew's education. A Nebraska businessman gave Thomas tires worth $1,200. Under federal law, the justices can accept unlimited gifts from individuals who do not have cases before the Court, as long as the gifts are disclosed.

Thomas's close ties to the conservative political and business worlds were reinforced by his wife, Virginia, who was already a well-known lobbyist for the U.S. Chamber of Commerce when they married in 1987, but who came into her own in the 1990s as a senior aide to Richard Armey, the combative Texas Republican who served as House majority leader. In that role, during the 1996 campaign, she sent a memo to senior Republicans in the House asking for damaging information about President Clinton "as soon as possible." Specifically, she sought any information that would expose "waste, fraud and abuse," the "influence of Washington labor bosses," or "examples of dishonesty." Later, she became director of executive branch relations at the Heritage Foundation.

The best reflection of Thomas's unique status in Washington, and on the Court, may have come at an unusual event in December 1999. Most of the justices attended awards dinners at places like universities and bar associations, but it seems likely that none of his colleagues ever attended an event like this one.

"We are here this evening to acknowledge the remarkable work of some of the more egregious members of the liberal press corps," said M. Stanton Evans to open the festivities at the annual dinner of the Media Research Center, a self-styled conservative watchdog organization, at the Monarch Hotel in Washington. The format for the evening was a mock awards banquet "honoring" what the hosts believed were examples of biased reporting. A procession of conservative luminaries "nominated" journalists for the prizes, and other guests "accepted" the humorously named awards, like the "Presidential Knee Pad Award for Best Journalistic Lewinsky." The tone of the evening was raucous and cheerful. "There is not a vast right-wing conspiracy," said John Fund, of the *Wall Street Journal*'s editorial page. "There's a narrowly focused one—and it's in this room!"

After speeches by Michael Reagan, the president's son and a talk show host, and Oliver North, also at the time a figure in right-wing radio, the climax of the evening came with the presentation of the "I'm-a-Compassionate-Liberal-but-I-Wish-You-Were-Dead Award for Media Hatred of Conservatives." This award was presented to an obscure columnist named Julianne Malveaux, for saying in a cable television interview about Thomas, "I hope his wife feeds him lots of eggs and butter and he dies early like a lot of black men do."

Thomas had been laughing so hard early in the evening that Evans, the MC, said to him, "Justice Thomas, you are a great audience, too." When Thomas stepped up to the microphone to "accept" the award for Malveaux, he received a standing ovation.

"Thank you," the justice said, still laughing. "Normally, we are busy. This is a sitting week, so we have cases to decide tomorrow morning at 9:30, and I usually spend this night working. But we realized that this was such an important occasion that we decided it was time to put aside our personal obligations, the Constitution, the work of the Court, our little nephew, to attend. . . . I am pleased to accept this award on behalf of Suzanne Malveaux." Thomas had mixed up Suzanne, a CNN correspondent, with her distant cousin Julianne; both are African American women.

As always, the confirmation hearings were never far from Thomas's mind. "As I was listening to those awards, I was hoping that Nina Totenberg would also share in it," he said. Totenberg, the NPR legal affairs correspondent, had played an important role in bringing Anita Hill's story to the public. "I have finally had the opportunity to have my surgeon remove her many stilettos from my back, and I'd like to return them."

But Thomas had a larger point to make. It wasn't speeches like this one but his work on the Court that would be the best revenge against his enemies, and he planned on serving for a long time to come. To another rousing ovation, Thomas concluded that anyone hoping for his demise, including Malveaux, should have a great deal of patience. He said, smiling, "My doctor makes it clear that my blood pressure is fine, my cholesterol is normal, and I am in wonderful health."

CARDS TO THE LEFT

The trajectory of the Lewinsky scandal in the Supreme Court reflected its course in the nation at large. The initial disclosures about the president's behavior inspired widespread shock and outrage, and the Court took a harsh initial tack against Clinton. But as the president's enemies ratcheted up the controversy into a constitutional crisis and then initiated the first impeachment proceeding in a generation, the sympathies of the public shifted. So did the Court's. As Clinton rode a wave of popularity into the end of his term, the Court turned sharply in his direction. This happened, in part, because the majority of the Court in these years always tried to remain close to the center of popular opinion. But there was another reason the Court moved left in the late nineties, and it had to do with the changing role of Chief Justice Rehnquist.

The chief was seventy-three years old in 1998, when the Lewinsky story broke, and he didn't have the energy he once did. His back had never fully healed from his long-ago gardening mishap, and his limp had become a permanent shuffle. But it was Rehnquist's intellectual energy that had faded more than his physical strength. He had been a justice for more than a quarter century and chief justice for more than a decade. Rehnquist knew how everyone was going to vote, most of the time. He wasn't going to change anyone's mind—not in conference and not in written opinions. So, subtly but unmistakably, Rehnquist stopped trying. He became, in these years, primarily an administrator, committed more to moving cases efficiently through the pipeline than to shaping their result at the finish. He had reduced the job to its essentials: a morning meeting with his law clerks to talk about the progress of opinions, a meeting with his administrative assistant to address issues affecting the federal judiciary, lunch at his desk, review of paperwork after lunch, and limousine home by 4:00 p.m.

Once a month, there was poker. That didn't change, although, thanks to the Lewinsky scandal, the players in his regular game did.

Bob Bennett and Bill Rehnquist were still raising young children when they met on the grounds of the McLean Swim and Tennis Club in 1972. Nixon had just appointed Rehnquist to the Supreme Court, and Bennett had recently left the United States attorney's office and was beginning a career in private law practice that would make him one of the best-known lawyers in the country. They became friendly, and Bennett invited Rehnquist to join his monthly poker game. For the next thirty-three years, the rest of his life, Rehnquist rarely missed one.

The core group in the poker game remained remarkably stable over the years, though some players did come and go. Besides Bennett and Rehnquist, they included Walter Berns, a professor of constitutional law at Georgetown; Martin Feinstein, the director of the Washington National Opera; Tom Whitehead, a Washington businessman; and eventually Nino Scalia. Other players were Bob's brother Bill Bennett, the former drug czar and conservative activist, and local federal judges David Sentelle, Thomas Hogan, and Royce Lamberth. The game was dealer's choice, usually seven-card high-low, five-card draw, or a Scalia favorite known as choose-'em. After each hand, the cards were "passed to the left"—a phrase that often caused amusement because Bob Bennett was generally the only Democrat at the table. The existence of the game was no secret, but the members avoided attention. After the Washington lawyer Leonard Garment talked about the game to a reporter, he was no longer invited to play.

The location of the poker game rotated among the homes of the players, and Rehnquist always took a turn hosting at his modest town house in suburban Arlington, Virginia. The game unfolded according to a precise ritual. From 7:00 to 7:45 p.m., the players would arrive and eat sandwiches provided by the host. The game would last from 8:00 to 11:00. Small talk was kept to a minimum. (Robert Bork joined the game briefly, but he quit because no one wanted to talk about anything except poker.) For many years, everyone used only first names, but after Rehnquist became chief justice in 1986, the other players started calling him "Chief." They also deferred to him to resolve any disputes that came up during the game. The stakes were low but not penny-ante; a player could win or lose about a hundred dollars in a night. (When Rehnquist was nominated to be chief justice, Bennett discreetly assigned an associate at his firm to research whether the game ran afoul of any gambling ordinances in the District of Columbia, Virginia, or Maryland. The search revealed no problems, and no one ever raised the issue anyway. This was fortunate for Rehnquist, because he also ran the Court's betting pools on NCAA basketball, NFL football, and the Kentucky Derby.)

In May 1994, three months after Paula Jones made her first accusations of improper conduct by Clinton, the president hired Bennett to defend him in the sexual harassment lawsuit she had just filed. The players in the poker game generally avoided the subject of the Supreme Court, but Bennett thought the matter was so high-profile—and so likely to wind up in front of the justices—that he decided to withdraw from the game for the duration of his representation of the president. Scalia in particular tried to talk Bennett out of leaving, but Bennett thought the caution was prudent. He was correct, as on January 13, 1997, he found himself standing before the nine justices to argue the case of *Clinton v. Jones.*

At first the *Jones* case united the justices—against Clinton. The case gave most of them an outlet for their long-standing personal distaste for the president. Shortly after Clinton was first elected, a clerk told Rehnquist that the new president was thinking of nominating his wife as attorney general. "They say Caligula appointed his horse counsel of Rome," the chief replied dryly. O'Connor was almost physically repelled by the sordid nature of Jones's allegations against Clinton; his behavior, as alleged, defined her all-purpose expression of distaste: unattractive. Stevens and Souter likewise found the matter unseemly and would rather have dealt with almost any other subject. Scalia and Thomas were all but openly hostile to Clinton and his agenda. And Clinton's own nominees, Ginsburg and Breyer, had to avoid looking like they were favoring the man who appointed them.

There may have been a high principle at stake in *Clinton v. Jones,* but the facts of the case resembled a trailer-park sitcom more than a Supreme Court case. In brief, Jones alleged that on May 8, 1991, she was sitting at the registration desk for Governor Clinton's Quality Management conference at the Excelsior Hotel in Little Rock. Clinton saw Jones, then named Paula Corbin, and asked one of his state troopers to invite her up to a room he was using in the hotel.

After Corbin went to the room, she asserted, Clinton said, "I love your curves," exposed himself, and asked her to "kiss it." She fled in horror. (For his part, Clinton always said he had no memory of meeting the young woman and denied any misconduct.) Jones sued for sexual harassment, claiming that her superiors in the Arkansas Industrial Development Commission, where she was a secretary, retaliated against her for rebuffing Clinton's advance.

The legal issue before the justices was Bennett's argument that the magnitude of Clinton's duties as president entitled him to a stay of all proceedings in the *Jones* case, including discovery and depositions, until he left office. Or, as Bennett told the justices, "The President of the United States should not be subject to litigation, either at trial or in discovery. Unless there is some compelling necessity, he should not be taken away from his constitutional duties."

At oral argument, the justices were all over Bennett. Rehnquist said the case had nothing to do with Clinton's "official powers as president." Ginsburg made the same point, that the subject of the lawsuit was "conduct unrelated to his office." Souter said he thought that, at a minimum, discovery unrelated to the presidency should proceed.

Stevens asked, "How long do you think it will take to try this case?"

"It's impossible to say," Bennett answered, more prophetically than he knew. "I can tell you the president has spent, personally spent, a substantial amount of time on this case already. The very nature of this case is so personal that it would require his heavy involvement."

Scalia usually embraced expansive claims of executive power, but not this time. There was no way, he asserted, that Clinton was *so* busy. "We see presidents riding horseback, chopping firewood, fishing for stick fish—"

The audience chuckled.

"—playing golf and so forth and so on. Why can't we leave it to the point where, if and when a court tells a president to be there or he's going to lose his case, and if and when a president has the intestinal fortitude to say, I am absolutely too busy—so that he'll never be seen playing golf for the rest of his administration—if and when that happens, we can . . . we can resolve the problem."

For Clinton, the timing of the argument couldn't have been worse. After a desultory campaign by Bob Dole, the Republican nominee, Clinton had just won a solid but hardly overwhelming reelection. In the final days of the campaign, a putative scandal regarding Clinton's fund-raising practices had preempted any postelection honeymoon Clinton might have enjoyed. In January 1997, the *Jones* case looked like a convenient vehicle for the justices to take Clinton down a peg, but the controversy was not yet a major threat to his presidency and a constitutional crisis for the nation. As for Clinton himself, he nursed a measure of paranoia about Rehnquist and his role in the *Jones* case. The swearing-in at his second inauguration took place just seven days after the oral argument in *Clinton v. Jones*. Clinton told friends that the chief justice shook his hand and said, "Good luck—you'll need it." The president took the gesture as vaguely menacing.

A veiled threat hardly seemed like Rehnquist's style, but it was true that the Court at that moment was preparing to demolish Clinton's legal position in the case. As usual for the Rehnquist Court, the tenor of the oral argument turned out to be indicative of the result. On May 27, 1997, the Court ruled unanimously that Clinton could not postpone the lawsuit until he left office. Stevens's opinion for the Court in *Clinton v. Jones* reflected the commendable principle that no man should be above the law, but it also showed a stunning naiveté about contemporary law and politics. Stevens dismissed Clinton's concerns that the *Jones* case would represent much of a burden in the conduct of his presidency. "It appears to us highly unlikely," Stevens wrote in an epically incorrect prediction, "to occupy any substantial amount of [Clinton's] time."

As a result of the Supreme Court's ruling, seven months later, on January 17, 1998, Clinton was forced to answer the questions of Jones's attorneys at a sworn deposition that took place in Bennett's office, a few blocks from the White House. The Court was usually pretty savvy about how its decisions would play out in the real world. But Stevens, who was nearing his eightieth birthday cloistered from the hubbub of life in the age of cable news, had not anticipated that Jones's lawsuit would turn into a magnet for the president's political enemies—a result that may have pleased some of the other justices. Still, Clinton himself made matters immeasurably worse for himself by lying in his deposition, saying, among other things, that he could not remember whether he was ever alone in the White House with Monica Lewinsky.

The events resulting from the Court's decision in *Clinton v. Jones* became landmarks in American history. While Clinton was facing Jones's lawyers in January 1998, Kenneth Starr was expanding his investigation of the Whitewater land deal to include possible misconduct by Clinton in the Jones lawsuit. On August 17, as part of Starr's probe, Clinton was forced to give grand jury testimony at the White House. Four months later, on December 19, 1998, Clinton was impeached by the House of Representatives for perjury and obstruction of justice.

The vote in the House meant that, for the first time in more than a century, there would be a presidential impeachment trial in the Senate, and under the Constitution the chief justice was obligated to preside. As it happened, Rehnquist may have been the best-qualified person in America for the job. Rehnquist used his free summers to produce a series of bland but readable texts, including *Grand Inquests: The Historic Impeachments of Justice Samuel Chase and President Andrew Johnson*, which was published in 1992.

Trent Lott, the Mississippi Republican who was then the majority leader of the Senate, decided to choreograph Clinton's trial to match, as closely as possible, the proceedings against the first President Johnson, in 1868. Rehnquist was a stickler for tradition, too, and he enjoyed reviving those musty rituals. Among these traditions was one that was especially painful for the senators. Under the customs of impeachment trials, all one hundred senators had to watch the entire proceedings in silence from their seats in the Senate chamber; in ordinary circumstances, senators generally visit the floor to vote or speak and then disappear.

As it turned out, Rehnquist had little to do. The Senate heard from no live witnesses, and the "trial" consisted almost entirely of statements by the House "managers"—the members of the Judiciary Committee who served as prosecutors—and Clinton's defense lawyers. Like any other politically savvy observer, Rehnquist could see that there were never anywhere near two-thirds of the Senate prepared to remove Clinton from office, and he wisely chose to stand back and let the trial grind to its preordained conclusion. The dreary proceedings lasted five weeks.

In all that time, Rehnquist made only a single substantive ruling. Throughout the managers' opening statements, they referred to the senators as "jurors." Democrats wanted to emphasize that the Constitution called on the senators to make a broader, political assessment about the propriety of removing the president, not simply the narrow judgment expected of jurors in a criminal case. After several statements from the prosecutors, Senator Tom Harkin of Iowa rose from his chair and said, "Mr. Chief Justice, I object to the use and the continued use of the word 'jurors' when referring to the Senate sitting as triers in the trial of the impeachment of the president of the United States."

In his phlegmatic way, Rehnquist said he saw Harkin's point. "The chair is of the view that the objection of the senator from Iowa is well taken," he said. "Therefore, counsel should refrain from referring to the senators as jurors."

Harkin was delighted. Moments later, he whispered to Senator Daniel Patrick Moynihan of New York, who was seated at the next desk, "I just won my first Supreme Court case!"

At first, the trial generated a flurry of excitement at the Court, and there was a waiting list for the few seats allotted to the justices and their staff. Soon enough, though, the seats went begging. Rehnquist told anyone who asked that he found the experience boring. Still, there was no denying the sense of history in the Senate chamber on February 12, 1999, when the trial came to an end. For the first time in the trial, there was a nervous catch in Rehnquist's voice when he said the words, "Is the respondent, William Jefferson Clinton, guilty or not guilty?"

The outcome had never been in doubt. Impeachment supporters won forty-five votes for the first count and fifty for the second, both well short of the sixty-seven they needed. (Arlen Specter, the crankily independent Republican from Pennsylvania, chose to vote the old Scottish verdict of "Not proven," which was recorded as a no.)

With the senators seated solemnly before him, the chief justice announced, "It is, therefore, ordered and adjudged that the said William Jefferson Clinton be, and he is hereby, acquitted of the charges. . . ."

Later, Rehnquist would sum up his performance in Clinton's impeachment trial with an apt line from one of his favorite Gilbert and Sullivan operettas, *Iolanthe*: "I did nothing in particular, and I did it very well."

Iolanthe also figured in a change in Rehnquist's aesthetics. A few years before the impeachment trial, Rehnquist showed up for an argument at the Court in a new robe, one with four gold stripes on each sleeve.

Evidently, he was copying the costume of the Lord Chancellor from a local production of the operetta. Since coming to the Court, Rehnquist had toned down the wardrobe that had so horrified Richard Nixon, but he had never before shown much interest in his appearance. "We thought it was a joke," O'Connor said of the new robe. The stripes on the robe may have been a bit of whimsy, but his colleagues also knew better than to copy them. The most casual justice had become a chief who zealously guarded his perquisites. Occasionally, a hapless advocate would make the mistake of addressing him as "Justice Rehnquist"—and he would snap, "That's Chief Justice!"

By this point, Rehnquist was devoting more of his energy to the mechanics of the Court—like the need to renovate the Court's deteriorating building—than to the substance of its decisions. He was obsessed with getting through the Court's business. One Sunday around the time of *Clinton v. Jones*, Washington was hit by a freak snowstorm that deposited twenty-one inches of snow. The city deals notoriously badly with even small amounts of snow, so the federal government was shut down the following day. But Rehnquist thought the Court should never concede to the elements. He ordered the Monday arguments to proceed and directed the Court staff to send jeeps to the homes of the justices.

The experience turned out to be a kind of Rorschach test for the justices' characters. Carter Phillips, a prominent advocate before the Court who had to argue on Monday morning, lived near Scalia in the Virginia suburbs and asked if he could catch a lift with him. Scalia agreed and said Kennedy would be coming along as well. The roads were impassable, however, and Scalia had to walk almost a half mile in waist-deep snow just to get to the car. Sweating profusely, wearing a Russian hat and a short-sleeved shirt under his coat, Scalia was livid.

"This is insane," he said. "What is the chief thinking? We're risking our lives out here."

But the justices all respected Rehnquist so much (while also fearing him a little) that no one wanted to be late. Worried that time was growing short, Scalia said to the driver, "By the power invested in me, I authorize you to run these lights!"

"Nino," Kennedy cautioned, "we don't have the power to run a red light." They made it at 9:30, with a half hour to spare. "I even have time to read your brief now, Phillips," Scalia cracked.

Another court car went to fetch Breyer and Ginsburg, who lived near each other—Breyer in Georgetown and Ginsburg at the tony Watergate complex. Elegant as always, if also slightly disengaged from the real world, Ginsburg chose to wear a straight skirt and high heels. Because of the snow on the ground and Ginsburg's outfit, the driver, who usually worked in the clerk's office, had to lift the tiny justice into the air and deposit her in the car. (Later, Ginsburg wrote the fellow a letter of recommendation for law school.) After they arrived, the industrious Breyer directed traffic in the Court's basement garage.

Souter, the self-sufficient New Englander, who had lived with snow for most of his life, rejected all offers of help. He said he would drive himself in his own car—which promptly stalled in a snowbank. Finally rescued by Supreme Court police officers, Souter wound up being the only one late for Court.

Rehnquist made no reference to the weather, and the argument went off as planned. (It happened to be the case about the injured railroad employee, which Phillips won unanimously, with Thomas writing his favorite opinion.)

The biggest change in the chief, though, was in the opinions he produced. As a junior justice, back in the 1970s, he became known for his long and discursive opinions, where he spelled out his conservative philosophy, often in dissent. But his opinions shrank when he became chief justice. In part, Rehnquist was just reflecting his shifting role—from outsider to institutional embodiment of the Court. But fatigue was a factor, too. The chief ran his chambers like an assembly line, with his clerks expected to produce first drafts in ten days or less. Only if they were overburdened would he write a first draft himself. Rehnquist was a brutal editor, stripping his clerks' work down to the essentials, taking out what he called, with some contempt, "the reasoning."

And so in the fall of 1999, the Court reached another turning point. Rehnquist's age started to limit his effectiveness. More important, the country at large had soured on the Gingrich Republicans who had taken over the House in 1994 and then launched the impeachment drama of 1998. Clinton was more popular than ever, and the nation, basking in unprecedented prosperity, had no discernable appetite for a dramatic lurch to the right.

In short, in October 1999 the "Rehnquist revolution," which was never terribly revolutionary in the first place, ground to a halt. On some of the issues that meant the most to him—states' rights, church-state relations, criminal law, and abortion—Rehnquist lost critical cases. The chief even surrendered in one of the causes that had meant the most to him since his days as a young Republican in Arizona.

Rehnquist loved to sing, and he always led the caroling at the Court's annual Christmas party. (Every year or so, a group of law clerks would write the chief justice an earnest letter complaining that the party created an atmosphere of exclusion for non-Christians; Rehnquist, who pointedly never adopted the term "holiday party," would reply by inviting the young lawyers, in effect, to get over it.) In his early years on the Court, Rehnquist even sometimes wrote the sketches for the occasion. In 1975, as Jeffrey Rosen first reported, he wrote a song about his least-favorite Supreme Court opinion, *Miranda v. Arizona*. Sung to the tune of "Angels from the Realms of Glory," it went: "Liberals from the realm of theory should adorn our highest bench / Though to crooks they're always chary / At police misdeeds they blench." The members of the chorus then fell to their knees and sang, "Save *Miranda*, save *Miranda*, save it from the Nixon Four." Nixon's nominees were Warren Burger, Harry Blackmun, Lewis Powell, and, of course, Rehnquist himself.

Miranda embodied everything that Rehnquist detested about the liberal activism of the Warren Court in the 1960s. In the decision, written in 1966 by Earl Warren himself, the Court ruled that any criminal suspect in custody must be read his or her rights. There was no conceivable claim that the framers of the Constitution or Supreme Court justices for a hundred and seventy-five years thought that any such warnings were necessary. Warren and his colleagues had simply invented the requirement to address what they regarded as flaws in the criminal justice system. Rehnquist made clear in opinion after opinion that he didn't think that the warnings were needed, and that they represented a judge-made impediment to the conviction of guilty and likely dangerous criminals. When the case came up in 1999, Rehnquist finally had a chance to drive a dagger into the case, when the Court granted cert on a case addressing whether *Miranda* should still stand.

The real question in the case was, even if *Miranda* had been wrongly decided in the first place, could the Court walk away from such a well-known precedent? At the oral argument of the case, Breyer made just this point in describing *Miranda* as "words that I think probably two billion people throughout the world know. He must be warned, prior to any questioning, that he has the right to remain silent, that anything he says can be used against him in a court of law, that he has the right to the presence of an attorney, and that if he cannot afford an attorney, one will be appointed for him. All right? Now, that's a hallmark of American justice in the last—thirty years?"

The case opened a window on what it meant to be a "conservative" on the Supreme Court—the Rehnquist mode or the Scalia and Thomas approach. To the surprise of many people who followed his career, Rehnquist not only joined the majority in the 7–2 decision upholding *Miranda* but wrote the opinion himself. Rehnquist's words in *Dickerson v. United States* were characteristically terse, and somewhat grudging, with little of his dreaded "reasoning," but his thinking was plain: "*Miranda* has become embedded in routine police practice to the point where the warnings have become part of our national culture," the chief justice wrote. "Whether or not we would agree with *Miranda*'s reasoning and its resulting rule, were we addressing the issue in the first instance, the principles of stare decisis weigh heavily against overruling it now." Scalia, joined by Thomas, wrote one of his classic fire-breathing dissents—and illustrated what a conservative Court, untethered to the rule of precedent, would do to landmarks like *Miranda* (and *Roe v. Wade*).

As usual, Scalia couldn't resist engaging in a little mockery, even of his friend the chief justice. It was true, as Scalia jibed in his dissent, that Rehnquist himself had in the past advocated "an outright rejection of the core premises of *Miranda*." And Scalia concluded with the sort of purple prose that attracts attention more than converts: "Today's judgment converts *Miranda* from a milestone of judicial overreaching into the very Cheops' Pyramid (or perhaps the Sphinx would be a better analogue) of judicial arrogance." It was clear by this point that Scalia didn't need better arguments to win over his colleagues; what he needed was different colleagues.

THE YEAR OF THE ROUT

By the final years of Bill Clinton's presidency, the conservative revolution at the Supreme Court was sputtering. On the issues that mattered most to the members of the Federalist Society and their allies—abortion, federalism, church-state relations, the death penalty, among others—the moderates on the Court held sway.

By this time in Congress, the Republicans, well accustomed to majority status, showed less interest in limiting the size of a federal government that they, to a great extent, now ran. In the sphere of church-state relations, the momentum on the right had also slowed. The career of Jay Sekulow was following a classic Washington trajectory: he came to the capital to do good and stayed to do well.

In one respect, Sekulow did succeed in his goal of creating an American Civil Liberties Union of the right. Like the ACLU, Sekulow's American Center for Law and Justice built a financial empire based largely on direct-mail (and e-mail) contributions from a loyal base of subscribers. But the differences between the ACLU and ACLJ turned out to be more important than the similarities. Sekulow chose not to create an institution like the ACLU but instead to build a monument to himself.

Sekulow drew a salary of more than $600,000 per year, but that was only the beginning of the riches he extracted from the complex financial dealings of the ACLJ and its related organizations. He also turned the nonprofit corporation into a family business. ACLJ raised about $14 million a year, but much of that was funneled into another entity called CASE, whose board of directors consisted of Sekulow, his wife, Pam, and his son Jordan. Jay's brother Gary was chief financial officer for both organizations. Gary, Pam, and Jordan Sekulow all drew salaries for their duties, and Jay's other son, Logan, was given a late-night comedy show on Christian television sponsored by CASE. According to a review of the groups' finances by the journalist Tony Mauro, Sekulow's organizations paid for his full-time chauffeur, leased private planes (one from a company owned by his brother's wife), and bought several homes—all for the benefit of Jay and his family.

The centerpiece of Sekulow's empire was a town house less than a block from the Supreme Court. The ACLJ bought the building for $5 million, then meticulously renovated it, with such features as a hand-painted mural of the Washington skyline in the ground-floor conference room. (The mural cost more than $40,000.) The ACLJ also bought the town house next door to its headquarters for $1.5 million for the use of Sekulow and his family, as well as an $850,000 home in Virginia Beach and a "retreat" in North Carolina. By the late nineties, the convenient D.C. town house allowed Sekulow to become a familiar figure at the Court, whether he was arguing cases or just stopping by to chat up the Supreme Court beat reporters.

Sekulow kept bringing cases to the Court as well, but in the 1999–2000 term, he discovered the limit of his free speech arguments. The case arose out of one of the central rituals of Texas life—the high school football game.

The local school board in Santa Fe, a small town in the southern part of the state (not to be confused with the city in New Mexico), had studied the Court's precedents with care, trying to carve out a role for prayer at the Friday night football games. Following extensive negotiations and litigation, the board established a program where a student elected by his or her peers would give a "nonsectarian, non-proselytizing" prayer before each game. Nevertheless, two students, a Catholic and a Mormon, sued to stop the practice, arguing that the policy violated the Establishment Clause.

Sekulow, representing the school board, went before the justices with what had worked before: "Santa Fe Independent School District has adopted a neutral policy which simply permits student-led, student-initiated speech at football games," he said. The policy "allows for the individual student to determine the content of the message. That message may include a prayer at the student's discretion. . . . The Santa Fe policy creates a venue for student expression. It is neutral as to religious or secular speech."

This time, however, the justices looked behind Sekulow's characterization of what was happening. The record in the case showed that the entire policy was designed by the school to allow students to lead prayers—not just "speech"—at games. "This is not a neutral speech policy," Souter said to Sekulow. "It is not merely religious subject matter. It is religious worship. It is an act of religious practice."

"And if the student decides to engage in a prayer," Sekulow answered, "that is speech protected by the First Amendment, and to then say that a policy—"

"As private speech," Souter shot back. "The question is whether that speech can be, in effect, involuntarily inflicted upon those who may not want it by the power of the state."

Scalia tried to come to the rescue of the school board's policy, but this time his bombastic style hurt his cause. He attempted to trivialize the dispute by pointing out that the two students who brought the case didn't even use their real names, which was why the case was called *Santa Fe Independent School District v. Doe*. "Could I ask you about that? That's just a curiosity I have in this case. I don't even know who the plaintiffs are," Scalia said. "Do people have rights to sue anonymously in federal court? Is anybody who just doesn't want it known that he's bringing a lawsuit, he's ashamed of it for one reason or another, can sue anonymously?"

But it wasn't a question of shame—it was fear. The students who had challenged the policy had been pushed, threatened, and placed in so much danger that the local judge directed that their names be taken off the complaint. That, of course, was precisely the point— that the state had harnessed the power of religious conformity to exclude outsiders.

In an opinion by Stevens, the Court struck down the student-led prayers in Santa Fe by a 6–3 vote, with Rehnquist, Scalia, and Thomas in dissent. The core of Stevens's opinion was a rejection of Sekulow's argument that the prayers were merely "private speech" by the students. "These invocations are authorized by a government policy and take place on government property at government-sponsored school-related events," he wrote. "The expressed purposes of the policy encourage the selection of a religious message, and that is precisely how the students understand the policy." It was no answer, Stevens continued, to say that students who were offended by the prayers could simply choose to avoid the games. The school district could not "exact religious conformity from a student as the price of joining her classmates at a varsity football game."

Sekulow was disappointed, of course, but the defeat in the *Santa Fe* case, combined with his earlier victories before the Court, actually wound up being a model for how the Supreme Court ought to work. The majority of the Court had settled on a reasonable and comprehensible rule for religious observances on government property—that the government had to allow genuinely private religious activity, but at the same time officials could not sponsor or endorse such rituals. After *Santa Fe*, the Court stopped getting so many of these cases because the lower courts generally could apply these rules on their own. The Court's compromise on the issue didn't satisfy everyone, but it didn't offend everyone, either—which made it a classic expression of the style of the Rehnquist Nine at this moment in its history. This was not a Court for the true believers—for Scalia, Thomas, and even Rehnquist himself—but rather a Court for the middle-of-the-road majority.

Mostly, that meant O'Connor. Increasingly, it also meant Stephen Breyer.

Like most other justices, Breyer took a few years to feel fully comfortable on the Court, but by the last years of Clinton's term, he had come into his own. On one level, Breyer made an unlikely power broker. He could be breathtakingly oblivious to his surroundings. One of his law clerks never showed up for work until noon; another lay on the floor for long periods because of a back condition. In neither instance did Breyer inquire or even, apparently, notice, as long as his chambers' work was done. He was also renowned among law clerks for conducting high-volume discussions of Court business in restaurants and other public places. Breyer was so engaged in the work of the Court that he sometimes ignored the exigencies of everyday life.

But Breyer had been paying attention when he watched his former boss Ted Kennedy push legislation through the Senate, building one coalition at a time, often with sometime adversaries. In the same way, Breyer worked his colleagues—decorously, respectfully, but unmistakably—to try to get them to see things his way. This approach was hardly unique in the Court's history—it was a crucial part of the Brennan legend—but the Rehnquist Court had no comparable figure. Souter and Thomas were downright reclusive, and Stevens and

Ginsburg tended that way; Kennedy, sometimes prickly, often mysterious, also kept to himself; Scalia prided himself on never lobbying,
and Rehnquist had no interest in anything that might disrupt the
swift procession of cases from oral argument to conference to opinion.

Once, around this time, the chief read a draft opinion of one of
Scalia's attacks on O'Connor and immediately summoned him to the
phone. "Nino, you're pissing off Sandra again," Rehnquist said. "Stop
it!" For her part, O'Connor was willing to entertain suitors from her
queenly perch at the center of the Court, but she would not deign to
hustle for votes. Breyer would.

Such was the justices' isolation from one another that the best advocacy could be done only in oral argument, when they were a captive audience for one another. For this reason, Breyer planned his questions
with care, not because he was especially interested in the answers but
because his questions were a way of making his case to his colleagues.
Like the law professor he used to be, Breyer favored hypothetical questions. At times, they could be overly long and complex, and Breyer's
point would be lost; once, mysteriously, he asked a question about taking a pet oyster for a walk in the park. But on other occasions Breyer
distilled an issue to its essence. It might be an exaggeration, but not
by much, to say that a single question from Breyer on November 10,
1999, brought the "federalism revolution" to a close.

In the early nineties, several states were making millions of dollars selling the information in their Department of Motor Vehicles
databanks to direct-mail operators, insurance companies, and other
marketers. Citizens began objecting to the practice, and Congress
responded in 1994 by passing the Driver's Privacy Protection Act,
which essentially told states they couldn't make such sales without
the drivers' consent. South Carolina sued to stop enforcement of the
act, asserting that the federal law was a violation of states' rights.

The claim seemed to mesh with the Rehnquist Court's approach to
federalism. Here was Congress dictating to the states how they should
manage a classic function of state government, administering driver's
licenses. In 1997, the Court had struck down part of the Brady Bill
gun control law, saying that the federal government had no right to
force states to conduct background checks on gun buyers. As Scalia
wrote for the Court in that case, "The Federal Government may neither issue directives requiring the States to address particular problems, nor command the States' officers . . . to administer or enforce a

federal regulatory program." Wasn't the law on driver's licenses the same thing—a directive to the states to solve a particular problem?

Breyer thought that the regulation of a massive and complex national economy could only be led by the federal government and that Congress had every right to pass these kinds of laws. But how, he wondered, could he make that point in the context of this case?

South Carolina was represented by its attorney general, Charles Condon, who was also the plaintiff in the case, known as *Reno v. Condon.* One of the immutable laws of oral advocacy in the Supreme Court is that elected officials, like state attorneys general, ought not to do it. Especially in the Rehnquist years, when aggressive questioning from the bench was the rule, nonspecialists generally failed miserably to advance their cause in front of the justices. Politicians generally possessed none of the key attributes of good oral advocacy: intimate knowledge of the Court's precedents, intellectual dexterity with complex concepts, the ability to answer hard questions concisely. (John Ashcroft had a notoriously bad outing in front of the justices when he was attorney general of Missouri; wisely, then, Ashcroft did not follow the informal tradition for each attorney general of the United States to argue a case.) Still, few state attorneys general can set aside their egos long enough to forgo the opportunity to argue themselves. So it was with Charlie Condon.

"This case is not about protecting privacy," Condon began, promisingly enough. "The issue in this case is whether thousands of state officials across the country can be pressed into federal service by the Congress to administer a federal regulatory act. The Driver's Privacy Protection Act is complex, it's burdensome, and it applies only to the states of the United States."

When Condon said, "We're being puppets of the federal government," Breyer decided to spring his trap.

"Isn't that true of every federal prohibition on what a state government does?" Breyer asked. "I mean, suppose you sell hot dogs at the state park. Don't you have to comply with the food and drug laws? I mean, those laws may be complicated, and you may have to say what kind of a hot dog and what kind of a stand, and what about—it's certainly a lot better than the minimum wage, or the—isn't it? I mean, you have to do a lot less than that. In other words, is your argument on this part just going to set aside all federal regulatory programs that tell states what they can't do?"

The question put Condon completely in a box. He could not say that the state could sell inferior hot dogs in its parks. He could not say that the state could pay less than minimum wage. So how did Condon answer?

"Justice Breyer, that again is a good question, but that goes to the heart of this case. We aren't selling hot dogs here." Condon's answer was so inept that some people in the audience started to laugh. But Breyer wasn't finished.

"Well, let me ask you another example," Breyer went on. "Congress passed the Internet Tax Freedom Act, and it told states they couldn't tax these Internet transactions for a period of time, can't do it. I suppose under your theory that's invalid, too. It only dealt with the states and governmental entities. I suppose that's invalid, is that right?"

This question was even more ingenious, because Breyer picked a federal law beloved by conservatives. The federal ban on state taxes on Internet transactions could hardly be characterized as the heavy hand of the liberal federal government. But it was, indeed, a federal restriction on state sovereignty. All Condon could mutter in reply was, "That could raise some concerns."

Through his questions, Breyer had underlined the folly of trying to wall off the states from federal regulation. It couldn't be done, and it shouldn't be done. The case turned into a rout. At the conference, the vote was 8–1 in favor of the federal law. But then Rehnquist, the great patron of states' rights, assigned the opinion to himself and that prompted Scalia, the would-be dissenter, to make the Court unanimous.

The chief had not given up on federalism, of course. In the same term, Rehnquist succeeded in invalidating a part of the federal Violence Against Women Act. The disputed provision allowed women who claimed they had been assaulted because of their gender to sue their attackers in federal court. The provision was the kind of political stunt that generated such contempt for Congress among Rehnquist and his allies. Assault victims could always sue in state court; the federal law was largely symbolic, and rarely invoked, and the Court, 5–4, struck it down as a violation of the Commerce Clause. But the effect of the decision in the real world was almost meaningless; it curtailed lawsuits that weren't being filed anyway. After more than a dozen years as chief justice, Rehnquist had failed to limit the power of the federal government.

In this year of defeat after defeat, Rehnquist also failed to make progress on abortion—in a case where the facts largely favored his side.

The Court had largely stayed away from the subject since *Casey* in 1992. The decision by the *Casey* troika of O'Connor, Kennedy, and Souter had not settled the issue for all time, but they had resolved most of the major controversies. First-trimester abortions could not be banned; parental consent laws were permissible; spousal notification—O'Connor's bête noire—was out. Not coincidentally, public opinion had settled in very much along the lines the Court had devised. President Clinton was pleased with the status quo as well. The law on abortion wasn't broken, so the justices, especially O'Connor, didn't try to fix it.

For a little while after *Casey*, the antiabortion movement floundered, looking for an issue that might restore its momentum in both the political and legal arenas. Then, one day, an anonymous informant slipped an obscure medical paper to Douglas Johnson, a top lobbyist for the National Right to Life Committee. The eight-page work had been prepared for the National Abortion Federation, a group of abortion providers. It was an explicit how-to guide for terminating pregnancies after the twentieth week. The author, Dr. Martin Haskell of Cincinnati, said he had developed a technique where he dilated a woman's cervix over a period of several days and then moved the fetus to a feetfirst breech-birth position. Using surgical scissors to cut into the skull, he vacuumed out the contents and, with the head reduced in size, removed the fetus from the pregnant woman. Haskell called this procedure "dilation and extraction," or D & X. (Previously, late-term abortions had been conducted by removing the fetus in pieces.) Johnson saw to it that the paper received wide circulation in the antiabortion movement, which dubbed the practice described as "partial birth" abortion, because the fetus was alive when the procedure began.

The grisly details had a galvanizing effect both inside and outside the movement. Abortion opponents saw the practice as barbaric and indefensible, nothing less than infanticide. In state legislatures and in Congress, where Republicans now presided, prolife politicians moved quickly to legislate a ban. Supporters of abortion rights were thrown on the defensive. They pointed out that such abortions were extremely rare, amounting to less than one percent of the more than one million abortions performed each year in the United States. And the vast majority of these abortions were done on women who suffered major medical complications or whose fetuses were horribly defective. Still, the images conveyed by the procedure proved to be politically compelling. The Republican Congress passed bans twice in the 1990s, and Clinton vetoed them each time because neither bill had an exception to protect the health of the mother. Abortion opponents had greater success at the state level. Throughout the decade, one state after another passed laws prohibiting the practice. Inevitably, notwithstanding the justices' reluctance to return to the divisive subject, the Supreme Court would have to decide if these laws could stand.

The case came before the justices on April 25, 2000, the second-to-last day of oral arguments for the term that began the previous October. Pushing through a decision of this magnitude before the summer recess at the end of June would clearly be a formidable challenge, given the complexity and contentiousness of the issue. The courtroom was tense when Don Stenberg, the attorney general of Nebraska, stood to defend his state's law, which had been declared unconstitutional by the Court of Appeals for the Eighth Circuit in *Stenberg v. Carhart*. "The issue here today is whether a state may prohibit a little-used form of abortion that borders on infanticide when safe, alternative forms of abortion remain available to women who seek abortions," he said.

Scalia always asked the most questions in oral argument, but the issue in *Stenberg* moved him to a level of hostile garrulousness unprecedented even in his career. He dominated the argument to an almost embarrassing degree. "General Stenberg," he asked at one point, "I took it that what you meant when you said it bordered on infanticide had nothing to do with the viability of the fetus, but that the procedure looks more like infanticide when the child is killed outside the womb than when it is killed inside the womb, and therefore it can coarsen public perception to other forms of killing fetuses or children outside the womb. Is that not what the legislature was concerned about?" (It was, said Stenberg.) To the lawyer for the Nebraska obstetrician who brought the case, Scalia offered this soliloquy: "Neither *Roe* nor *Casey* are written in the Constitution. They may not have mentioned all of the appropriate interests that may be taken into account. Why is it not an appropriate interest that the state is worried about rendering society callous to infanticide? There were very many highly civilized societies, including the ancient Greeks, who permitted infanticide, who said that the right of parents included the right not to be burdened with a child they didn't want, especially a deformed child. And therefore, in order to prevent other societies descending into that degree of callousness, the numerous states have enacted these laws. I don't think it's so much a concern with medical matters. I think it's a concern with the horror of seeing, you know, a live human creature outside the womb dismembered."

Everyone in the courtroom was waiting for O'Connor to tip her hand. Finally, she broke her silence to say: "Mr. Stenberg, let me ask you a question. There is no exception under this statute, as I read it, for exceptions for the health of the woman, is that correct?" He answered, "That is correct, Your Honor, and it's not necessary."

That, of course, was a matter of opinion. The question illustrated O'Connor's priorities when it came to abortion. She was all for limitations and restrictions, but not at the cost of women's health. She didn't care if laws were designed to talk women out of having abortions, but the choice ultimately had to belong to the women themselves.

The issue in *Stenberg* was not simple. The medical testimony about the kinds of procedures outlawed by the Nebraska law, and the effect of the bans on women's health, was closely and inconclusively debated at the oral argument and in the briefs. The result of the conference on Friday, April 28, was similarly ambiguous. Four justices—Rehnquist, Scalia, Kennedy, and Thomas—wanted to uphold the law. Four others—Stevens, Souter, Ginsburg, and Breyer—wanted to strike it down as a violation of *Roe* and *Casey*. O'Connor said she would vote to strike the law down if it did in fact jeopardize women's health.

The result left Stevens as the senior justice in a tenuous majority. The customary route in these circumstances would have been for Stevens to give the opinion to O'Connor, who was the shakiest member of the coalition. But Stevens gave it to Breyer instead. O'Connor was such a reluctant member of the majority that there was a possibility that she might find, as justices sometimes did, that an opinion "wouldn't write"—that is, trying to explain the law's unconstitutionality might push her to an opposite conclusion. Breyer and O'Connor had become close friends, and Breyer had the political skills to keep his senior colleague on board. Moreover, Breyer had the technical expertise to assemble the complex medical evidence in support of invalidating the law. So, with the days in the term slipping away, Breyer set out to save his majority in what would certainly be his most important opinion in six years on the Court.

"Steve," a friend once told Breyer, "you think like an eagle, but you write like a turkey." Yet his plodding, antirhetorical style served Breyer well in the *Stenberg* assignment. He determined to make almost no reference to *Roe*, *Casey*, and the right to privacy; of those two cases, Breyer wrote, "We shall not revisit those legal principles. Rather, we apply them to the circumstances of this case." To do so, he focused on the question O'Connor asked in oral argument. He set out to show that the Nebraska law deprived women of the right to the best medical choices for their health. Or, as Breyer put it in his gnarled prose, "The State fails to demonstrate that banning [this kind of abortion] without a health exception may not create significant health risks for women, because the record shows that significant medical authority supports the proposition that in some circumstances, [it] would be the safest procedure."

Breyer had his law clerk on the case check almost daily with the O'Connor chambers about whether she was with him on the case. At any moment, she might pull out of the majority and write an opinion merely concurring in the judgment; that would make her opinion, not Breyer's, the controlling authority on abortion law. For this reason, in his politically savvy way, Breyer persuaded Stevens and Ginsburg not to circulate their concurring opinions until he had O'Connor's commitment to the majority; Breyer feared that their more liberal views might sour O'Connor on the whole issue. Breyer and O'Connor were both fundamentally more interested in reality than in theory; in complex cases like this one, they both deferred to experts, like the American Medical Association, which opposed the Nebraska law. Finally, just days before the end of the term, the O'Connor clerk on the case called his counterpart in the Breyer chambers and said, "I have something for you that you're going to like." Moments later, a memo from O'Connor to Breyer arrived, saying, "I join your opinion."

Dissenting opinions are not assigned in the same formal way that majority opinions are, but the senior justice in the minority usually coordinates the opinions on his side. In *Stenberg*, Rehnquist deferred to Thomas for the main opinion on their side, giving him a rare opportunity to write in an important case, if only in dissent. Thomas's clerk dueled with Breyer's in pressing the Supreme Court library to track down obscure medical periodicals to bolster their positions. When Thomas was just about finished, Kennedy appeared without warning with a lengthy and passionate dissent of his own. Kennedy felt betrayed by O'Connor and Souter, his fellow members of the *Casey* troika. He thought that case had delineated the outer limits of abortion rights, but now the Court was, in Kennedy's view, going much farther. He wrote that Nebraska "chose to forbid a procedure many decent and civilized people find so abhorrent as to be among the most serious of crimes against human life, while the State still protected the woman's autonomous right of choice as reaffirmed in *Casey*."

Kennedy's dissent set off an uncharacteristic round of pettiness at the Court. His analysis was so much more detailed and thoughtful than Thomas's that Breyer, in responding, referred to Kennedy's opinion as "the dissent." Wait, Thomas objected, Rehnquist had assigned *his* opinion as "the dissent." Which one was "the" dissent? Neither Kennedy nor Thomas would yield. Breyer didn't know what to do. So the three justices—Kennedy, Thomas, and Breyer—visited Rehnquist to resolve the impasse. It was a measure of their respect for the chief that they all deferred to him on a matter like this one, and Rehnquist did come up with a Solomonic solution. Breyer would refer to the "Kennedy dissent" and the "Thomas dissent," and neither one as "the" dissent. Meanwhile, Scalia wrote his own dissent, which surpassed even his own high standards for invective and hysteria. It began, "I am optimistic enough to believe that, one day, *Stenberg v. Carhart* will be assigned its rightful place in the history of this Court's jurisprudence beside *Korematsu* and *Dred Scott*." (*Korematsu* authorized the military exclusion of Japanese American citizens from the West Coast during World War II; *Dred Scott* held that even freed blacks could not become American citizens.)

The extent of the conservative rout in the 1999–2000 term was so great that, in *Stenberg*, O'Connor departed from one of her cardinal principles of jurisprudence. Her position was not supported by public opinion. Indeed, there was nationwide support for bans on "partial birth" abortion. Thirty-one states had banned the practice, and the Nebraska law had passed the state legislature with just a single dissenting vote. In *Stenberg*, O'Connor's reverence for expertise, her suspicion of paternalism, and the deft lobbying of Breyer moved her farther left than she had ever gone in her judicial career.

To be sure, the Court did not suddenly turn into a reincarnation of the liberal Warren Court. The justices had parried conservative legal offensives—on church-state, federalism, and abortion—rather than forging a liberal direction of their own. They had protected the status quo, which was what the country wanted, but that left the conservative movement seething. Even with seven Republican appointees on the Court, and eleven of the last thirteen appointments made by Republican presidents, the justices had not made the sharp turn to the right that conservatives had been seeking for a generation. As the decisions in that year showed, the Court would be sticking to its moderate course.

From the law students and professors in the Federalist Society to the evangelical warriors like Jay Sekulow and James Dobson, there was outrage and frustration. Conservatives still won an occasional case, but they didn't control the Court on the issues that mattered most to them. They had used all their best arguments and come up short. There was only one way to change the Court—by putting their own man in the White House. Control of the presidency was the only route to control of the Court.

In the Court itself, as a new term began in October 2000, a near silence prevailed. Controversial cases seemed to have vanished from the pipeline. For the justices, the sleepy docket was a welcome respite after the dramas of the previous year. Greeting a new group of law clerks that fall, David Souter was smiling when he made a prediction: "This is going to be a very boring year."

PART

TWO

11

TO THE BRINK

andom chance—a freakishly close vote in the single decisive state—gave the Supreme Court the chance to resolve the 2000 presidential election. The character of the justices themselves turned that opportunity into one of the lowest moments in the Court's history. The struggle following the election of 2000 took thirty-six days, and the Court was directly involved for twenty-one of them. Yet over this brief period, the justices displayed all of their worst traits—among them vanity, overconfidence, impatience, arrogance, and simple political partisanship. These three weeks taint an otherwise largely admirable legacy. The justices did almost everything wrong. They embarrassed themselves and the Supreme Court.

The justices never liked to think of themselves as political beings, but all of them except Stevens and Souter maintained a healthy interest in the political scene. It could hardly be otherwise. Winning an appointment to the Supreme Court takes plenty of savvy, and not even total job security can slake a lifelong passion for the business of winning and losing elections.

This was especially true of Sandra O'Connor. She still loved politics and, more to the point, the Republican Party. When Rehnquist ran his occasional betting pools on elections, O'Connor's notes to the chief always referred to the Republicans as "we" and "us." But by 2000, the Republican Party in O'Connor's memory was not necessarily the same as the one in real life. Her personal political trajectory followed that of her first mentor in Arizona politics, Barry Goldwater, whose Senate campaign she worked on in 1958. Where Goldwater had once personified the extreme rightward edge of the Republican

Party, he came in his later years to be a kind of libertarian, uncomfortable with the social agenda of the evangelical conservatives. Goldwater believed in small government and states' rights, but he never signed on for expressions of public piety and regulation of private conduct. Neither, for the most part, did O'Connor. (And she always remembered Goldwater's salty response to Jerry Falwell's assertion that "good Christians" should be wary of O'Connor's nomination. "I think every good Christian ought to kick Falwell's ass," the senator said.)

There was one contemporary politician whom O'Connor really admired—Governor George W. Bush of Texas. She was an old friend of his parents and a tennis partner of the former First Lady's. O'Connor recognized the senior Bush's limitations as a politician, but she thought that his son, the 2000 Republican presidential nominee, had the common touch and a slogan that might have been O'Connor's own— "compassionate conservative." As she tracked Bush's rise to national prominence in the late nineties, O'Connor thought his centrist appeal would win over voters and protect the Republican Party from its extremists. The justice didn't know George W. personally, but she found him very attractive, in every sense of the word.

Sandra and John O'Connor couldn't attend political events, in light of her position, but they still spent a great deal of time out on the town in Washington. Perhaps the best-known story about O'Connor involved her attendance, in 1985, at a black-tie gala sponsored by the Washington Press Club. She was seated at the same table as John Riggins, the hard-living star running back of the Washington Redskins. After far too many drinks, Riggins told her, "Come on, Sandy baby, loosen up. You're too tight." Riggins then proceeded to fall asleep on the floor. Less well known was O'Connor's reaction to the incident. A few weeks later, she showed up at her exercise class wearing a T-shirt that said, "Loosen up at the Supreme Court." And several years later, when Riggins began a short-lived acting career, O'Connor came to his debut at a Washington area community theater with a dozen roses for him.

So it was very much in keeping with the O'Connors' custom that they spent the night of the 2000 election at a party. The couple was especially close to Lee and Juliet Folger, prominent local philanthropists and modern counterparts to the venerable Washington aristocrats known as the "cave dwellers." Mary Ann Stoessel, the widow of the prominent diplomat Walter Stoessel and the O'Connors' host on election night, came from the same milieu. The refined setting of Stoessel's party and the genteel crowd made the events of the evening all the more peculiar.

Everyone knew the election would be close. The polls showed the contest between Vice President Al Gore and Governor Bush coming down to a handful of states, especially Florida. On the night of Tuesday, November 7, Stoessel had placed televisions all over her house, so the seventy or so guests could follow the results as they moved from room to room. Justice O'Connor settled in the small basement den, where one of the televisions was located, and she saw Dan Rather call Michigan and Illinois for the vice president. Then, at 7:49, NBC called Florida for Gore; CBS agreed a minute later; ABC joined the consensus at 7:52.

Hearing Florida called for Gore, Justice O'Connor looked stricken. "This is terrible," she said. "That means it's over." She then walked away in disgust. Later, after her statements at the party became public, O'Connor gave friends a rather implausible explanation for her behavior. She said she was angry not because Gore had apparently won the presidency but because the networks had called the election before voting was complete on the West Coast. But while the meaning of Sandra O'Connor's words may have been debatable, the meaning of what John O'Connor had to say that night was not.

John and Sandra O'Connor were both seventy years old and in their forty-eighth year of marriage in 2000; it was hard to imagine a happier union. Through the years, John's energy had matched Sandra's, but his was coupled with a madcap sense of humor that never failed to delight his more straitlaced wife. As Justice O'Connor's biographer Joan Biskupic learned when John was running for president of the Rotary Club in Phoenix, he listed his qualifications as: "Beautiful wife. Rich father-in-law. Pool hustler." Shortly after Sandra was appointed to the Court, John gave Harry Blackmun a business card that said his skills included "Tigers Tamed, Bars Emptied, Orgies Organized." John became a prominent lawyer in Phoenix but didn't hesitate to give up his career to move to Washington after her appointment. Through the years, he spent time with a couple of different law firms in D.C. but never established himself the way he had in Arizona; the possibilities for conflict with his wife's work were simply too great. But if John worried about living in Sandra's shadow, he never let on.

In the period leading up to the 2000 election, John's health deteriorated. He fainted on a visit to Phoenix, and his heart stopped briefly. He had surgery to install a pacemaker. In the past, John had always been extraordinarily discreet about anything to do with the Court. But on election night, John gave an extended explanation of Sandra's distress. They wanted to retire to Phoenix, but Sandra wouldn't hand her seat to a Democratic president. A Gore victory meant at least four more years for them in Washington, and they wanted to leave. That's why, John said, Sandra was so upset. It was unlike him to talk about their plans in a quasi-public setting. In the end, of course, her mistake in uttering some unduly candid words was trivial; her blunders in the days ahead were not.

The vote count in Florida was fantastically, almost surrealistically, close. (In time, during their coverage on election night, the networks rescinded their projection of the state for Gore, then awarded it to Bush, and finally labeled the state too close to call.) On Wednesday, November 8, the first complete election figures in Florida showed Bush ahead of Gore by 2,909,135 to 2,907,351, or a margin of 1,784 votes. Under Florida law, a result this close required all the counties in the state to do an immediate automatic recount. That process, which essentially meant running all the ballots through the counting machines a second time, took a day. The new results, announced on Thursday, November 9, cut Bush's margin to 327 votes—or .00000056 percent.

Events in the first few days after the election had a hallucinogenic quality. Partisans on both sides had no experience with a controversy like this one. While there were a great many people who were familiar with politics, almost none of them knew anything about how votes were actually cast and counted. And the subject of recounts was even more obscure, familiar only to a tiny band of part-time experts on both sides. (There have never been enough recounts to support even one person's entire career.) No one, of course, had any idea how long the controversy would last, so each side worked with a frantic, sleepless intensity.

The immediate focus of controversy was Palm Beach County, Florida's biggest by area and most Democratic by inclination. Because the local election administrator, Theresa LePore, wanted to make voting easier for the county's many elderly voters, she used 12-point type—rather than the customary 10-point—to lay out the ballot. But with ten candidates, the bigger type meant that there was not enough room to list them all on one page; instead, she spread the names across two pages, with the holes to be punched in the middle, the famous "butterfly ballot." The arrangement left Patrick Buchanan, the rabidly conservative independent candidate, in the second punch-hole position and Gore in the third place. (In Florida, like most other states, the parties are usually listed in order of finish in the most recent governor's race.) As a result, Buchanan received 3,704 votes in Palm Beach—nearly 2,700 more than he'd won in any other county. As Buchanan himself acknowledged, most of the votes were intended not for him but rather for Gore. What, if anything, could be done about these errors after Election Day? It wasn't clear. Still, protesters and news cameras descended on the government center in West Palm Beach.

Scrambling to keep their hopes alive, the members of the Gore team made their first move on November 9, two days after the election. Pursuant to Florida law, they asked four out of the state's sixty-seven counties to conduct manual recounts—ballot-by-ballot reviews to make sure that the votes were correctly recorded. Not coincidentally, Gore asked for recounts in Broward, Miami-Dade, Palm Beach, and Volusia, the four most Democratic-leaning counties in the state. The butterfly ballot controversy applied only in Palm Beach, but the main issue in the other counties concerned the number of so-called undervotes—that is, ballots where the counting machines registered no preference in the presidential race. The Gore team thought a recount was necessary to identify whether any of these undervote ballots had actually been marked with a preference for president. In each county, a little-known entity called the Canvassing Board, made up of three local officials, would vote to determine whether a recount should take place. Gore had not filed a lawsuit, instead asking for manual recounts, which was known under Florida law as filing a protest.

But before any of the boards could even determine whether to conduct a manual recount, the Bush forces struck back in a way that hinted at how the contest would proceed over the following month. They were going to do whatever it took to win this election. Throughout the post–Election Day controversy, the passion to win, fueled in part by the desire to get control of a Supreme Court that had disappointed conservatives for so long, was all on the Republican side. James A. Baker III, the wily former cabinet member who was running the Bush effort, thought that a lawsuit was a terrific idea, and he asked former Missouri senator John Danforth, a part-time clergyman and nationally known figure of rectitude, to represent Bush in the case. Danforth declined, citing the old rule "Candidates don't sue." Undeterred, Baker chose a more zealous advocate, the Washington lawyer Theodore B. Olson, who was only too happy to lead the charge.

In keeping with the frantic pace, Olson filed the lawsuit on Saturday, November 11. Two days later, Olson stood before Judge Donald M. Middlebrooks in federal court in Miami and asked him to stop the recounts before they had even started. His rationale was pretty thin—that Gore's "selective" recounts in only four counties violated the Equal Protection Clause of the Fourteenth Amendment, because they emphasized the votes of some counties over others. (Bush, of course, could have cured this problem by asking for his own recounts anywhere he wanted.) The judge had been working as hard as the lawyers: he was ready with an opinion by the time oral argument was completed on Monday.

Middlebrooks rejected Bush's position and allowed the recounts to proceed. "Under the Constitution of the United States, the responsibility for selection of electors for the office of President rests primarily with the people of Florida, its election officials and, if necessary, its courts," he wrote. "The procedures employed by Florida appear to be neutral. . . . I believe that intervention by a federal district court, particularly on a preliminary basis, is inappropriate." Far from deterred, Baker and the rest of the Bush team had plenty of fight left. The onslaught of litigation prompted by the election had just begun.

The justices and their staffs watched the developments in Florida with the same bewildered fascination as the rest of the country did. But there was one person at the Court who was already thinking several steps ahead in the process. That was Anthony Kennedy.

In part, Kennedy was just doing his job. The justices divide up responsibility for procedural matters by circuit court of appeals, and Kennedy was assigned the Eleventh Circuit, which included Florida. So he had some reason to monitor the developments there. On the day after Judge Middlebrooks's decision, Kennedy circulated a copy to all the other chambers. Just keeping you apprised, the cover memo said. Just filling you in.

In a minor but noticeable way, Kennedy had contravened the rarefied mores of the Court. All of the justices read the newspaper; all of them knew what was happening in Florida; none of them needed Tony Kennedy to give them the latest news. It was amusing, more than offensive, that Kennedy was sniffing around the unfolding controversy. The memo showed just a hint of overeagerness to get in on the action. No one else on the Court would have sent that memo. More than any of the other justices, Kennedy loved drama and what he called "the poetry of the law." Kennedy's vanity was generally harmless, almost charming—sort of like the carpet in his office.

Understatement was the rule for the decor in most justices' chambers. Everyone had a few personal touches—O'Connor employed a southwestern motif, with Native American blankets and curios; Ginsburg had opera mementos; Stevens had the box score from the World Series game in 1932 when Babe Ruth hit his "called shot" home run against the Chicago Cubs. (Stevens had attended the game as a twelve-year-old boy.) Kennedy, in contrast, installed a plush red carpet, more suited to a theater set than a judge's chambers. Worse (or better, depending on one's perspective), the carpet was festooned with gold stars—garish touches that made the office a sort of comic tourist attraction for law clerks and other insiders. All of the justices had the right to borrow paintings from the National Gallery, but Kennedy had taken the fullest advantage, plucking several near-masterpieces from the collection. What was more, he wedged his desk into the far corner of his office, away from the door, so that visitors had to traverse the expanse of his room to shake his hand. It was an office that tried hard, maybe too hard, to impress. (Kennedy even labored on his magnificent view of the east front of the Capitol. When Congress announced plans to build a massive visitors' center between the Court and the Capitol, Kennedy took the lead in lobbying the legislators to make sure it was built entirely belowground, so as not to disrupt the vista. The negotiations turned out to be surprisingly complex, and lasted for years, but Kennedy won this battle, and the view from the Court was largely preserved.)

The first Kennedy memo to his colleagues about the legal machinations in Florida was followed by a second, then another. He was almost providing a legal play-by-play. His hunger for the case was palpable.

Once the Bush lawyers failed in their effort to have the federal court shut down all the recounts at once, they tried to do it one county at a time. By now, both sides had become familiar with the iron law of recounts: the trailing candidate tries to open up the process and recount as many votes as possible in as many places as possible; the leading candidate does just the opposite, fighting to limit the number and locations of any recounts. This wasn't high principle, just political warfare by other means.

The Gore forces had one principal advantage—Florida law—and one major disadvantage—Katherine Harris—in their fight for recounts. State law had a strong presumption in favor of allowing recounts to reach accurate results. As for Harris, she occupied the previously obscure position of secretary of state. An heiress to a real estate fortune, she had an imperious manner and big ambitions. She had vaulted quickly from the state senate to statewide office and had plans to move up the Republican hierarchy. Earlier in the year, she had traveled to New Hampshire to campaign for George W. Bush and later served as cochair of his campaign in Florida. Like many secretaries of state around the country, Harris was both a partisan elected official and the ostensibly neutral arbiter of elections in the state.

Immediately after Election Day, the Bush team placed one of its most trusted legal advisers in Florida, Mac Stipanovich, as its representative in Harris's office. She made no decisions in this period without consulting him. The most important issue for her to decide concerned the recounts. Could the recounts continue longer than seven days after the election, that is, past Tuesday, November 14? The law said both that Harris should certify by the seventh day and that she could also allow recounts to proceed longer. Of course, she did not. If the counties weren't done by then (and three of the four were not finished by then), too bad for them—and Al Gore. But then on Friday, November 17, the Florida Supreme Court, on its own initiative, stepped into the fray to overrule Harris and say that the counties could continue counting votes. The justices of that court scheduled a full argument in the case for Monday, November 20, but in the meantime they ordered the recounts to proceed.

By Monday, Bush's margin in Florida had grown from 300 to 930 votes. (Volusia County had completed its recount, with a net gain of 27 votes for Gore, and the counting of overseas absentee ballots had netted 630 votes for Bush.) The issue before the Florida Supreme

Court was whether the recounts in Palm Beach, Broward, and Miami-Dade would be allowed to proceed. If the Florida Supreme Court stopped those recounts, there was no way that Gore could win.

By 2000, the state supreme court represented a singular part of Florida government. Florida had a Republican governor, Jeb Bush, and Republican majorities in both houses of the state legislature. The only remaining Democratic power center in the state was the supreme court, where all seven members had been appointed by Democratic governors. (One justice was a joint appointment by Bush and his Democratic predecessor, Lawton Chiles.) The court wasn't shy about favoring a progressive—and Democratic—agenda either, as the Bush campaign soon discovered. On Tuesday, November 21, the Florida Supreme Court ruled that the recounts should proceed for the next five days and that Harris could not certify the results until Sunday, November 26. Clearly, the Florida justices felt a great deal of pique toward Harris, whose conduct they described as "unreasonable," "unnecessary," "arbitrary," "contrary to law," and "contrary to the plain meaning of the statute." But the unanimous opinion was not very well reasoned. There was no explanation for why the justices chose to extend the deadline five days—as opposed to four, or six, or any other number. In denouncing Harris for looking too political, the Florida court wound up looking political itself. Still, the Gore forces were suddenly back in business.

The question, then, was whether the U.S. Supreme Court would agree to get involved, and the Bush campaign had a noted authority at close range. About two days before the argument in the Florida Supreme Court, John G. Roberts Jr. came to Tallahassee. Though he was only forty-five at the time, Roberts was already among the top advocates of his generation before the justices. (Eight years earlier, George H. W. Bush had tapped Roberts for a seat on the D.C. Circuit, but Democrats in the Senate stalled the nomination into oblivion.) In Tallahassee, Roberts helped Michael Carvin prepare for his (unsuccessful) representation of Bush before the Florida justices and then advised Baker on how to get the U.S. Supreme Court to take the case. The conventional wisdom was that the justices would want no part of the controversy. But Roberts's gut told him otherwise. They'll take the case, Roberts vowed to Baker, and you'll win it there, too.

It had been two weeks and a day since the election, and until this moment the controversy in Florida still seemed remote from the work of the Court. As Judge Middlebrooks had said, the management of elections is traditionally governed by state law, which is in turn interpreted by state courts. The U.S. Supreme Court had no authority to tell the Florida Supreme Court how to interpret Florida statutes. Not once in the history of their Court had the justices in Washington imposed themselves in the middle of vote counting in one of the states. Why would they do it now?

Roberts had to return to Washington to argue a different case before the Supreme Court, but following his advice, the Bush team filed its petition for certiorari on Wednesday, November 22, the day before Thanksgiving. The Republicans essentially gave the justices a menu of choices. The Republicans claimed that the Florida court violated federal laws on the conduct of elections; that it violated Article II of the Constitution, which suggests that state legislatures, not state courts, make the rules for presidential elections; that the recount process violated the Equal Protection and Due Process Clauses of the Constitution.

The secret to Olson's brief was more in tone than in substance. He played on the justices' collective vanity (not just Kennedy's), saying in essence that they were the only grown-ups in the room. All the others—especially the justices of the Florida court—were just a bunch of partisan hacks. Olson claimed that the Florida court opened the door to "an electoral catastrophe" and that the Supreme Court of the United States had to step in to prevent "the ascension of a president of questionable legitimacy, or a constitutional crisis."

Of course, there were very good arguments in response to Olson's claims. Elections had always been run by states, not the federal courts, and Florida was merely doing what states had done for generations. They were following their own law on recounts. Counting votes had never before been seen as a violation of the U.S. Constitution. Moreover, as a practical matter, the situation in Florida was changing day to day; by the time the justices in Washington heard arguments in this case, the facts on the ground in Florida might be very different—which was why the Supreme Court rarely took a case until it was concluded in all respects. But such arguments never reached the justices, because the Republicans asked for expedited consideration of their case. They wanted the Court to rule on their cert petition before the Democrats even had a chance to defend the ruling of the Florida Supreme Court.

Many litigants before the Supreme Court ask for speedy treatment, but the Court almost never grants it. Particularly during the later Rehnquist years, when the chief put such a premium on efficiency, the Court rarely deviated from its customary schedule. The rhythm of its deliberations on cases seldom varied. The justices rarely even saw a case before all the briefs were submitted by both sides, and then they generally took weeks, if not months, to resolve it.

But in the matter of the election in 2000, the justices departed from their usual rules. There was no order, no regularity, no procedure. The justices decided them on the fly. When an old friend called Stevens to ask for a ticket to the argument of the case, the senior justice answered dryly that he would have to follow the usual procedure on seating. "And I think that's the only procedure that's going to be followed around here," he added.

Most of the justices were not even in the Court building on Wednesday, November 22, so their clerks and the Court staff had to track them down to give them the Republicans' briefs. Many of the law clerks had already left for the Thanksgiving holiday, so the decision on Bush's cert petition went to the justices alone. And they did not wait to hear from the Democrats to issue their decision.

As the justice for the Eleventh Circuit, Kennedy coordinated the rulings, which came in on Thanksgiving Day, November 23, and the following morning, Friday, November 24. The votes were:

Rehnquist—grant
Stevens—deny
O'Connor—grant
Scalia—grant
Kennedy—grant
Souter—deny
Thomas—grant
Ginsburg—deny
Breyer—deny

Since only four votes were needed to grant a petition, the Republicans had one more vote than necessary. The Supreme Court would take the case.

Around midday on Friday, Kennedy summoned one of the lawyers who worked in the clerk's office. These attorneys were career professionals (not to be confused with the individual justices' law clerks, who served for only a year) and tended to be especially wise about the ways of the Court and skillful in predicting what the justices would do. The lawyer Kennedy called was so sure that Kennedy would simply say the Court had denied certiorari that he didn't even bring a pen and paper to the justice's chambers. He could remember a single word: deny.

But Kennedy's first words to the lawyer were, "I hope you brought a pad."

The Court had done more than simply grant the writ of certiorari and the petition for expedited consideration. The justices also accepted two of the three "questions presented" in the Republicans' cert petition. They were willing to hear the Bush team's arguments on whether Florida had violated federal law or Article II of the Constitution. But they did not think the argument that Florida had violated equal protection merited further consideration.

More important, though, as Kennedy dictated the Court's order, which was largely his own work, the five justices in favor of cert had agreed on a schedule that was even faster than the one the Republicans had proposed. This alone was virtually without precedent. The justices rarely agreed to accelerate their schedule at all, but they *never* proposed a timetable that was even quicker than what the parties sought. Olson had asked for oral argument on December 5; Kennedy gave it to him on December 1.

Kennedy was miffed that the lawyer from the clerk's office had not come prepared for their meeting. "E-mail it back to me before you send it out, so I can check it," he said stiffly. The justices—five of them, anyway—*wanted* this case.

By the time of oral argument in *Bush v. Palm Beach County Canvassing Board*, it was clear that the Court should not have taken the case in the first place. The relevant legal issue concerned Gore's "protest" of the election results—his demands for recounts in three remaining counties before Harris certified the election results as final. During the week that the Supreme Court case was pending, only one county of the three actually completed its recount, and in Broward, Gore netted 567 additional votes. In Miami-Dade, Bush supporters staged what became known as the "Brooks Brothers riot," and the canvassing board shut down its recount. In Palm Beach, the canvassing board tried to finish counting its votes but missed Harris's deadline. In any event, on Sunday night, November 26, in a solemn, nationally televised ceremony, Harris did certify the election, with Bush the winner by 537 votes. The Gore forces promptly filed a "contest," which was the next legal procedure, after the precertification "protest," to dispute the result of an election.

So on the morning of Friday, December 1, the justices appeared from behind their massive red curtain to hear an argument about an election "protest" that was, by the standards of this election, ancient history. Simply put, the issue before the justices didn't matter anymore. Still, the mood in the courtroom was chipper, almost giddy. The process in Florida had been so bizarre and unpredictable that there was a sense—a hope—that the Court might put it all right.

In the chair closest to the bench, the seat of honor for spectators, was the stooped figure of Byron White. The former football star looked wizened and unwell, but he, like everyone else who had the chance, didn't want to miss this (apparently) once-in-a-lifetime event.

The argument, however, quickly bogged down into a discussion of minutia. As revealed by their questions to Ted Olson, O'Connor and Kennedy seemed to be having a case of buyer's remorse, regretting that they had ever granted certiorari. As O'Connor put it, "If it were purely a matter of state law, I suppose we normally would leave it alone, where the state supreme court found it, and so you probably have to persuade us there's some issue of federal law here."

Kennedy said, "We're looking for a federal issue." The questions for Gore's lawyer, Harvard Law School professor Laurence Tribe, were also vigorous, but mostly the justices seemed to be looking for a graceful exit.

The justices' conference took place on the same Friday afternoon as the argument. The justices did not take a formal vote, as they customarily did, but instead resolved to try to come up with some unanimous decision. They knew that in such a politically polarizing moment, the Court would send a comforting signal by uniting around a single result. Anyway, the stakes were fairly low. Because the protest was already over, there wasn't a great deal that the Court could do. The conservatives, especially Scalia, were outraged that the Florida Supreme Court seemed to be rewriting the state election code.

He wanted to slap that court down, at least rhetorically. O'Connor, too, didn't like the way the Florida justices appeared to be freelancing—and helping Gore. The more liberal justices, especially Stevens, thought that Florida was merely doing what state courts always did—interpreting state law. Since the "contest" of the election was already under way, Stevens and his allies thought they should just dismiss the appeal and let the process in Florida run its course.

When the conference reached an ambiguous result, Rehnquist often drafted his own opinion and then tried to bring everyone around. Even with a case of this magnitude, the phlegmatic chief didn't actually write this one himself but instead assigned a law clerk, Luke Sobota, to compose the first draft.

Rehnquist resolved to "vacate"—that is, overturn the decision of the Florida Supreme Court—but declined to set out any new rules of law in the decision. "After reviewing the opinion of the Florida Supreme Court, we find that there is considerable uncertainty as to the precise grounds for the decision," the opinion stated. "This is sufficient reason for us to decline at this time to review the federal questions asserted to be present." In other words, the chief was inviting the Florida court to explain itself better but not exactly ruling that it was wrong. This was a shot across the bow of the Florida justices, a warning against further activism in this case, but one with relatively little practical significance at this late date.

The Supreme Court's brief opinion was released on Monday, December 4. It was delivered not by a specific justice but rather per curiam, "by the court," a designation that the Court generally used for minor and uncontroversial opinions. If this had been the Court's only decision in the 2000 presidential contest, the justices' role would be remembered as a modest footnote in the story. As the justices themselves recognized, they never should have involved themselves in the election, but having done so, at least they did no significant harm.

The more important news of December 4 took place in Tallahassee, where a local judge ruled in the Gore team's "contest." He rejected any further recounts and upheld Harris's certification of Bush's victory. That decision now headed to the Florida Supreme Court—and, ultimately, back to the United States Supreme Court.

OVER THE BRINK

No case engaged the justices' law clerks more than the election cases in 2000. Many of them spent the crucial period in December in a frenzy of outrage about the tactics and merits of one party or the other in the controversy. The question, though, is whether the clerks made any real difference in the outcome.

The first person to promote the image of scheming and powerful law clerks was William Rehnquist himself. Forty-three years earlier, shortly after his own clerkship for Justice Robert H. Jackson, Rehnquist wrote an article for *U.S. News & World Report* asserting that "liberal" law clerks were "slanting" the work of the Court to the left. Rehnquist said that a majority of clerks showed "extreme solicitude for the claims of Communists and other criminal defendants, expansion of federal power at the expense of state power, [and] great sympathy toward any government regulation of business." For many years, Rehnquist's picture of the Court as a redoubt of liberal clerks remained the dominant image.

Then in 1998, Edward Lazarus, a former clerk for Harry Blackmun, turned that image around. He saw many clerks operating in support of a conservative agenda. In his book *Closed Chambers*, Lazarus argued that these right-wing clerks "self-consciously styled the Cabal," wielded "very significant power . . . for partisan ends." Reared in Federalist Society cells in law schools, they collaborated for ideological ends in the Court's cafeteria and the cheap Chinese restaurants of Capitol Hill.

The truth about Supreme Court law clerks seems more mundane. Generally in their late twenties, they are top graduates of leading law schools who have first spent a year working as clerks for lower court judges. (The judges who regularly place their clerks on the high court are known as "feeders.") The clerks review cert petitions, helping to winnow the eight thousand or so cases to the eighty or so accepted for review. They discuss the cases with their justices to prepare for oral argument, and, most notably, they write first drafts of opinions. The details of the procedure vary by justice. Thomas appoints a head clerk; O'Connor required clerks to prepare a "bench memo" summarizing the arguments in each case; Kennedy has a classroom-style prep session with his clerks before most oral arguments; and Scalia ignores his clerks for long periods of time. Stevens alone employs a totally different system. He is the only justice who does not participate in the "cert pool," which has one law clerk from the other eight chambers prepare a detailed memo on each cert petition. Stevens also writes his own first drafts. And Stevens, as Rehnquist did, hires only three clerks each year, while the others take four.

The fact that law clerks draft most opinions has given rise to several misimpressions, particularly on the part of the clerks themselves. Because they have this responsibility, many clerks think they are more important than they are. Supreme Court opinions are stylized documents—statements of facts followed by legal analyses—in a format that changes little from case to case. In general, only a small part of each opinion has any lasting significance, and the justices themselves monitor that section with care. Once Rehnquist became a justice, he developed a very different conception of the power of the law clerks. With appealing candor, Rehnquist used to say that he felt bound less by the footnotes than by the texts of prior opinions because the clerks usually wrote the footnotes. Most important, the justices themselves—alone—decide how to vote, and the votes matter more than anything else.

Still, the clerks give the institution a jolt of new energy each year and, in a way, set the tone in the building. O'Connor liked Arizonans, Rehnquist tennis players; Ginsburg favors musicians, Souter quirky intellectuals. Year by year, however, the chemistry varies. In 1999–2000, the term before the election, everyone got along pretty well, though there was one notorious incident when a clerk pushed another into one of the Court's fountains. During the following year—which included the recount controversy—the atmosphere was sour from day one. More than in most years, the justices on the left— especially Stevens, Ginsburg, and Breyer—had very liberal clerks, and across the ideological divide the clerks were similarly fevered in their views. By the time the Court decided the first election case, the mood inside the building was poisonous. Still, once the decision in *Bush v. Palm Beach County Canvassing Board* was rendered, it seemed like the Court had seen the last of the election of 2000; the justices' bland opinion appeared certain to be their final word on the subject.

But the fight in Florida continued. Gore's "contest" of the certified election results had gone before Judge N. Sanders Sauls in Tallahassee. Sauls was known as one of the worst judges in the county—petty, vindictive, and reactionary; in 1998, the Florida Supreme Court had even threatened to demote him because of "the continuing disruption in the administration of justice" on his watch. The assignment of Sauls turned out to be a perverse kind of good luck for Gore.

His conduct of the trial, entitled *Albert Gore, Jr. v. Katherine Harris*, lived up to his reputation. Sauls's opinion, which was rendered in the late afternoon of Monday, December 4, was brief and shoddy. He admitted that "the record shows voter error, and/or less than total accuracy" in the Florida voting machines but found no "reasonable probability that the statewide election result would be different" if the votes had been correctly counted. By nightfall, the Gore lawyers had appealed the case back to the Florida Supreme Court, which had once more become Gore's only hope.

Again, Florida law appeared to be on Gore's side. It was clear that there were major errors in the counting of ballots in Florida; it was clear, too, that a hand recount of the ballots would be more accurate. But Judge Sauls had simply assumed that a recount would make no difference.

The lawyers returned to the Florida Supreme Court on the morning of Thursday, December 7. The Bush forces were projecting an air of inevitability about the result. Baker and other top aides did not even show up for the argument, their absence sending the message that the legal proceedings no longer mattered. But at least some of the justices thought that Sauls had blundered badly—and that the votes still needed to be counted. The key issue from the beginning had involved the undervotes.

At first, one of Bush's strongest arguments had been that checking the undervotes in only four counties—and not the other sixty-three—was inherently unfair. Now, because the election had been certified with Bush in the lead, that argument suddenly helped Gore, who was only asking the court to restart the recounts in Palm Beach and Miami-Dade. But the questions from the justices raised an even more tantalizing prospect—recounting *all* the undervotes in the *entire* state. Surely, as the questions from the justices implied, that would be the fairest way to see if any legitimate ballots had been ignored. There were about 60,000 undervotes in the remaining counties. Why not simply look at them all?

The Democrats could scarcely bring themselves to hope for so sweeping a victory, but at 3:50 p.m. on Friday, December 8, the court spokesman delivered the judgment of the court on the steps of the courthouse in Tallahassee. First, the court agreed that Sauls had erred in certifying the results in two counties—therefore cutting Bush's margin in Florida from 537 to 154 (or 193). It would be up to Sauls, on remand, to determine whether 154 or 193 was correct. But the more astonishing announcement was to come. "By a vote of four to three, the majority of the court has reversed the decision of the trial court," the spokesman, Craig Waters, said. "The circuit court shall order a manual recount of all undervotes in any Florida county where such a recount has not yet occurred. Because time is of the essence, the recount shall commence immediately."

The Florida Supreme Court had resurrected Gore from the political dead.

The entire Gore legal team operated out of a three-lawyer suite in one of Tallahassee's lesser office buildings. (It was actually a branch of a medium-sized Fort Lauderdale law firm; several larger firms in the state declined to take Gore's case, apparently out of fear of offending the Republican power structure in Florida.) Initially, this threadbare operation had no cable-television hookup, no high-speed Internet connection, and no room for the dozen or so lawyers who eventually made their way to town to work for Gore.

The Republicans, in contrast, hired the Tallahassee office of the second-biggest law firm in the state and then rented a sprawling office of their own as well. (Later, they procured still another space in a location that they kept secret from the press, so they could prepare for the contest without being interrupted.) And that was just in the Florida capital. The Bush team was even better situated in Washington, where the center of activity moved as soon as the Florida Supreme Court ordered the expanded recount.

Bush's Supreme Court team, working out of Ted Olson's offices at the firm of Gibson, Dunn & Crutcher, had, under Baker's orders, made preparations for all eventualities. So by Friday afternoon, December 8, it already had the rudiments of a brief asking the Supreme Court to step in and stop the recount ordered by the Florida court. The principal drafting was done by two of Olson's younger partners, Miguel Estrada and Doug Cox, along with Mike Carvin, the Washington lawyer (from another firm) who had argued for Bush in the first case before the Florida Supreme Court. Uppermost in their minds was an observation that their colleague John Roberts had made earlier—that the Court would want this case. And like all other advocates before the Rehnquist Court, the Bush lawyers knew the key vote and their most important audience—Sandra O'Connor.

As always for O'Connor, the practical consequences would matter more than the legal theory, so that's where Olson and company focused their brief. "Few issues could be more important than those presented in this case. At stake is the lawful resolution of a national election for the office of President of the United States," they wrote. The Supreme Court had to intervene, and the justices couldn't just grant cert; rather, they had to issue a stay and stop the recount in Florida before matters went further out of control. "This Court's review is essential in this case in order to protect the integrity of the electoral process for President and Vice President of the United States and in order to correct the serious constitutional errors made by the Florida Supreme Court," Olson's team wrote. "A stay is necessary in order to prevent irreparable harm to [Bush], to the electoral process, and to the Nation as a consequence of the flawed decision below."

The legal basis for Bush's position was incidental and rather weak. The principal argument concerned the obscure provision of Article II of the Constitution that provides that each state shall choose electors "in such manner as the legislature thereof may direct." The Republicans said that it was now the Florida court—and not the legislature—that was "directing" how Florida chose the winner of the state's electoral votes. The sole authority for this claim was a nearly incomprehensible opinion of the Court from 1892. (The Florida court had disposed of this Article II argument by saying that it was simply doing what courts always do—interpreting Florida election law, not making it.) Almost as a throwaway, the Bush team added another claim—that the recounts violated the Equal Protection Clause of the

Fourteenth Amendment. Their casual attention to this argument—just three pages in a forty-two-page brief—was understandable. The Supreme Court, in granting cert in the *Palm Beach* case, had thought the equal protection argument was so weak that it refused even to hear argument on the issue.

Fundamentally, though, the Republicans' appeal to the Court, and especially to O'Connor, was more political than legal. The gist was that a court with a clear Democratic agenda was throwing the election into chaos by making up rules. The Florida Supreme Court's decision had been styled *Gore v. Harris*. But the lawyers in Olson's office changed the caption to the one that would be known to history: *Bush v. Gore*. The brief arrived at the clerk's office of the Supreme Court about five hours after the Florida court's ruling—that is, at 9:18 p.m. on Friday, December 8.

Meanwhile, a little-known trial judge in Tallahassee was disproving the Republican predictions of chaos and disorder in the recount. Just hours after the Florida Supreme Court had ruled, Judge Terry Lewis had called the parties together to work out the mechanics of how the 60,000 undervotes would be counted around the state. (Events were moving so fast that the only available court reporter could not make it into Lewis's court, and so he monitored the hearing from home, listening to the broadcast on C-Span.)

Judge Lewis was as competent a local judge as his colleague Judge Sauls was inept. In Lewis's courtroom, Phil Beck, a renowned Chicago trial lawyer representing Bush, zeroed in on a weakness in the Florida Supreme Court opinion. That court had not laid out a single standard for the counties to use in determining whether a ballot should be included or not. OK, Lewis asked, so what should the standard be? Beck said there couldn't be a single standard, because that would be changing the rules in the middle of the game. The Bush position was a perfect circle. There must be a standard, but there was no way there could be a standard.

Undeterred, Lewis came up with a plan. Shortly before midnight on Friday night, Lewis said that vote counting would commence in the Leon County public library on Saturday morning at eight. (Many of the ballots had already been transferred to Tallahassee.) All other counties were to send him a plan by noon. All counting was to be completed in a little more than a day, by two on Sunday afternoon, December 10. Lewis would remain in his office throughout the weekend to settle any disputes.

By dawn on Saturday, something remarkable was occurring. Working through the night, both the Gore and Bush campaigns had assembled and sent teams to each of the state's counties to monitor the vote counting. Across the state so many judges volunteered that Lewis was able to use them to replace all the county workers who had been planning to supervise the counting. At 9:51 a.m., the chief judge administered an oath to the vote counters in the Tallahassee library. At 10:07 a.m., the counting began. There were four tables, with two judges at each one. Before them were five boxes, each with a different marking: BUSH, GORE, OTHER, NO VOTE, CONTESTED. (Judge Lewis would review the ballots in the last box.) Similar scenes were taking place all over the state.

From the beginning, the core of the Bush argument was that the Florida Supreme Court had created an anarchic mess in an effort to let the Democrats steal the election. But on Saturday morning, judges and county workers of all political persuasions were refuting that proposition. Quietly, efficiently—to be sure, imperfectly—they looked at the ballots and counted the votes. By noon that day, Terry Lewis's deadline of the following afternoon looked like a reasonable target for completing the recount.

As it happened, one of O'Connor's clerks—one of the few who had good relations with both his conservative and his liberal colleagues—was throwing a party on Friday night at a bar in the Adams Morgan neighborhood of Washington. Many law clerks stopped in for a few drinks before returning to work to read Bush's brief, which they knew would be coming.

Back at the Court, alcohol made a contentious environment even more volatile. In the chambers of the conservatives, there was a raw, consuming anger at the Florida Supreme Court. The justices in Tallahassee had never responded to the questions that the justices in Washington had asked in their *Palm Beach* opinion of December 4. Bad enough that they were trying to steal the election for Gore, the clerks on the right were saying, but they were defying the U.S. Supreme Court as well. How dare they jump back into the election without first responding to their superiors on the high court?

Up to this point, the Court had managed to hang on to a strained public unanimity. The only opinion in the case so far had been the brief per curiam in *Palm Beach*. But the veneer of bipartisanship disappeared on Friday night. Scalia was first to respond to the Bush brief, and his anger was searing. He thought the Florida court was contemptuous, defiant, and out of control; it had to be stopped. In a memo to the other justices, he said he didn't just want to grant Bush's request for a stay of the recount. Scalia wanted to issue a stay, grant certiorari on Bush's appeal, and summarily reverse the Florida Supreme Court—all by Saturday morning and all without hearing any oral argument at all. The conservative chambers were coordinating overnight, and each one took a different part of the argument— Article II, statutory, equal protection.

By late on Friday, there were five votes for a stay—Rehnquist, O'Connor, Scalia, Kennedy, and Thomas. For a while that evening, it even looked like the Court might adopt Scalia's view and reverse the Florida decision without an argument, but Stevens, the senior justice in the minority, prevailed upon Rehnquist at least to schedule a conference on the issue for Saturday. Reluctantly, the chief agreed. At first, Rehnquist put the conference down for 1:00 p.m., but Scalia, who was itching to shut down the recount as soon as possible, convinced the chief to move it up to 10:00 a.m.

In a brief, uncomfortable meeting on Saturday, December 9—as the vote counting was beginning in Florida—the justices gathered in the chief's conference room. Scalia still wanted to reverse without argument, and so did Rehnquist and Thomas. O'Connor and Kennedy were willing to hear the parties in the case, but they maintained their vote in favor of a stay. The four others—Stevens, Souter, Ginsburg, and Breyer—dissented. Again, they made the point that had come up in the first case. Why not let the vote count proceed? Maybe Bush would win anyway. But the majority wouldn't budge. Rehnquist drafted an order of just one page. Stay granted. Oral argument on Monday, December 11. Stevens said he would be filing a dissent.

Back in his chambers, the elderly Chicagoan sat in front of the keyboard and tapped out three long paragraphs. Before deciding to make a unanimous Court in *Palm Beach*, Stevens had prepared a dissent in that case, so he was working off a partial draft. In typically rhythmic and elegant prose, Stevens wrote, "To stop the counting of legal votes, the majority today departs from three venerable rules of judicial restraint that have guided the Court throughout its history. On questions of state law, we have consistently respected the opinions of the highest courts of the States. On questions whose resolution is committed at least in large measure to another branch of the Federal Government, we have construed our own jurisdiction narrowly and exercised it cautiously. On federal constitutional questions that were not fairly presented to the court whose judgment is being reviewed, we have prudently declined to express an opinion. The majority has acted unwisely." The counting of legal votes, Stevens insisted, could never constitute an "irreparable harm"—which stays are supposed to prevent.

Scalia had not planned to write anything and to let the stay speak for itself, but he was enraged by Stevens's dissent, so he sat down at his desk to respond. (He was so angry that he delayed the issuance of the stay by taking the time to write, even though he was the one who thought speed was so essential.) His own three-paragraph concurring opinion proved the success of the Republicans' legal strategy—which was far more political than legal. The Republicans had successfully portrayed the Florida court as partisan more than principled, but Scalia betrayed the same bias, albeit in favor of the other side. "The counting of votes that are of questionable legality does in my view threaten irreparable harm to [Bush], and to the country, by casting a cloud upon what he claims to be the legitimacy of his election," Scalia wrote. "Count first, and rule upon legality afterwards, is not a recipe for producing election results that have the public acceptance democratic stability requires."

In normal circumstances—in all other circumstances—the Court would never have considered something so vague as the casting of clouds as amounting to a genuine legal harm, much less one that required the extraordinary step of issuing a stay. Moreover, in the complex tangle of litigation, the Eleventh Circuit Court of Appeals, in a preliminary ruling on the appeal of the federal decision by Judge Middlebrooks in Miami, had prohibited Harris from certifying anyone other than Bush as the winner of the state. So the only *possible* harm was that Florida might count its votes and Gore might pull ahead; as long as the Eleventh Circuit decision stood, Gore could not win the state. But for Scalia, that political problem for Bush—that the vote count might look embarrassing for a while—amounted to "irreparable harm." Scalia was looking at the election entirely through Bush's eyes; by his own words, the justice was clearly more concerned about producing a clean victory for the Republican than about determining the will of Florida's voters. Notably, Scalia's concurring opinion was so extreme that no other justice joined it.

At 2:40 p.m. on Saturday, the public information staff of the Supreme Court summoned the reporters who were keeping vigil and distributed the Court's order. The decision of the Florida Supreme Court was stayed. Cert was granted. Briefs were due the following day. Argument before the justices would take place in less than forty-eight hours, on Monday, December 11, at 11:00 a.m. Never in its history had the Supreme Court worked so fast.

At his home at the Naval Observatory, Gore passed the news to his family and watched the coverage on television. At 3:11 p.m., he sent a BlackBerry message to his chief spokesmen, Mark Fabiani and Chris Lehane: "Please make sure that no one trashes the Supreme Court."

13

PERFECTLY CLEAR

By the morning of Sunday, December 10, when the briefs were due in *Bush v. Gore*, television cameras had already taken up positions on the sidewalk in front of the building. So much news had come out of the Court so fast that every news organization wanted to be ready. The press of media attention was so great that the Court's police warned the justices to keep their curtains drawn because a high-powered lens might be able to read the words on a page.

Inside the building, the clerks were all id—consumed by rage. Each side was thinking the same thing about the other: *They're trying to steal the election*. Bad as relations had been earlier in the year—and earlier in the week—things were far worse now.

As for Stephen Breyer, he was still all superego. Sure, things looked bad now, but logic—his logic—would prevail. He never gave up hope, not on this case or any other. True, a majority of the Court had granted a stay—which meant, under the legal standard, that it was "likely" that they would also rule for Bush on the merits of the case. But that didn't settle the issue, at least not for Breyer. He had an almost messianic belief in the power of reason, and he never despaired about the ability of his colleagues to see the light—or his own ability to persuade them to see it.

Besides, Breyer wasn't so far from the conservatives on *Bush v. Gore*. As a former professor, Breyer could talk the language of legal doctrine and rhetoric as well as anyone, but he also had a bit of the pol in him, too. And Breyer the pol didn't like what the Florida Supreme Court had done. To him, the justices in Tallahassee looked like they were trying too hard to help Gore. Worse, Breyer thought their failure to set a standard for the recount made their motives even more suspect.

He didn't particularly care if one described the problem as one of due process or equal protection or any other legal category. He thought what the Florida justices had done didn't pass the smell test, and that was what mattered to him.

But Breyer had a simple solution: remand the case back to the Florida Supreme Court, order those justices to set a clear standard for the whole state, and then recount the votes. Breyer loved compromise—and he thought this was a good one.

So, on Sunday, Breyer sent his law clerks out on reconnaissance missions to identify potential converts from the majority. There were really only two candidates. Publicly and privately, Rehnquist, Scalia, and Thomas had made their positions clear. They were outraged by what the Florida justices had done, and they wanted to bring the election to a close. There was no chance they would change their minds.

Breyer looked to O'Connor and Kennedy. With O'Connor, on this occasion, Breyer made the same mistake that so many others did about her jurisprudence. Just because she was usually in the middle didn't mean that she had trouble making up her mind. And O'Connor had made up her mind about *Bush v. Gore*—firmly. She thought Bush should win, the case as well as the election. If there was anything O'Connor had learned growing up on a remote ranch, it was self-sufficiency; people had no right to blame anyone else, including the government, for their own mistakes. She had convinced herself that the root of the issue in Florida was simply that some voters hadn't figured out how to cast their ballots the right way. In her view, it wasn't the job of election officials—or the courts—to puzzle over the true meaning of ambiguously marked ballots. If the voters didn't bother to learn how to vote correctly, the state shouldn't try to figure out what these hapless souls meant to do. As for the Florida Supreme Court, those justices just looked like a bunch of Democratic hacks to O'Connor.

Never mind that Florida law called for vote counters to determine the intent of the voters—or that state law also empowered the Florida courts to make that process work. (The Florida courts once ordered a county to count the ballots of voters who used a pen, rather than the required number 2 pencil, to mark their ballots.) Never mind, too, that many ballots were incomplete because of defective voting machines, not incompetent voters. O'Connor had simply run out of patience. In part, she was responding to her perception of the public mood. She thought that the American people were fed up with the whole controversy and, like her, wanted it over. (In fact, polls showed only a slight majority in favor of ending all recounts and considerable support for a complete recount in Florida.) In any case, Breyer's power of persuasion failed. O'Connor was voting to reverse. Later, Souter made an unusual personal appeal for O'Connor's support in the case. O'Connor, like Ginsburg, had a special fondness for the reclusive bachelor justice, but his advocacy didn't work this time, either.

On Sunday, a few liberal clerks thought O'Connor might have to leave the case. As David Margolick first reported, a Ginsburg clerk whose brother worked for the *Wall Street Journal* learned that the paper would be disclosing in Monday's edition the remarks O'Connor had made at the election night party at the Stoessel home. Perhaps, the liberal clerks wondered, she would now recuse herself from the case, because she had indicated so clearly that she wanted Bush to win the election. But the clerks misjudged O'Connor—and the law. O'Connor's comments at the party, while peculiar, hardly displayed a bias in this particular lawsuit, and anyway, there was no way that she was going to walk away from a case of this magnitude.

Kennedy was a different story—perhaps. It had not been an easy term for him. A few weeks before the election, he had been assigned the opinion in *Legal Services Corp. v. Velazquez*, a case where he joined the four liberals—Stevens, Souter, Ginsburg, and Breyer—in striking down a law that barred legal services lawyers from challenging the constitutionality of welfare laws. (Congress had passed the law to halt what it regarded as liberal political activism by government-funded lawyers.) Kennedy had filled his first draft with such flowery language about the First Amendment and the importance of lawyers that he faced a rebellion from his colleagues. They wanted him to tone down his meaningless rhetoric. Kennedy did, reluctantly. Now, in *Bush v. Gore*, the same quartet of liberals needed Kennedy's vote, this time for incalculably higher stakes.

For the justices, Sunday, December 10, was mostly quiet. A few clerks came into the building to wait for the briefs, which were sent by messenger to the justices' homes. The full Court didn't gather again until Monday morning at eleven, when they would hear from the lawyers in the election cases for the final time.

It had been just ten days since the first argument before the justices, but the courtroom seemed like an entirely different place on December 11. The cheerful buzz of December 1 had been replaced by a sullen hum. (Byron White did not return to watch the second argument. A few weeks later, he closed his office in Washington and moved back to Colorado. He died in 2002 at the age of eighty-four.) At the first argument, in the *Palm Beach* case, it had seemed possible that the Supreme Court would rise above the political sniping that had characterized the battle of Florida. But halting the recount made the justices look like another set of partisans. For the Court, any pretense of impartiality, much less nobility, had vanished.

Having won the stay, Ted Olson had now, in effect, to run out the clock. If he could stay out of trouble during oral argument, he would probably win the case (and the election) for his client. But Kennedy surprised him with the first question: "Can you begin by telling us our federal jurisdiction? Where's the federal question here?" This was the point the Gore lawyers had been making all along—that the election was fundamentally a state matter, which should never have wound up before the U.S. Supreme Court. Olson replied evenly that the Florida Supreme Court had violated Article II of the Constitution, which said state legislatures, not state courts, must make the rules for presidential elections. But Kennedy came back with another of Gore's arguments: "To say that the legislature of the state is unmoored from its own constitution and it can't use its courts . . . has grave implications for our republican theory of government."

Was Kennedy switching sides? Not necessarily, because a few moments later, he jumped in with what he apparently regarded as a better argument for Bush, saying, "I thought your point was that the process is being conducted in violation of the Equal Protection Clause and it's standardless." That too, Olson agreed.

Breyer took Kennedy's question as an invitation to make a play for his vote. If the problem was that the Florida Supreme Court didn't set a standard for counting the undervotes, why couldn't they just set a standard now? Or have the Florida courts set one? Or Katherine Harris? Then the recount could begin again, right? Olson grudgingly conceded that a new standard might work. Souter made a similar point. Why not just set a new standard and restart the recount?

Joseph Klock, a prominent Miami lawyer who was representing Harris, went next and gained a measure of immortality for his lack of grace under pressure. In answer to a question from Stevens, Klock called him "Justice Brennan." (Brennan had been gone from the Court for ten years and dead for three.) A moment later, responding to Souter, Klock called him "Justice Breyer." Frustrated, Souter sighed, to much laughter, and quipped, "I'm Justice Souter. You'd better cut that out." Never one to let another justice steal the spotlight, the next voice from the bench said, "Mr. Klock? I'm Scalia!"

Gore had switched lawyers for the second argument, replacing Laurence Tribe, the Harvard law professor, with David Boies, the New York lawyer who had won both cases in the Florida Supreme Court. "I did not find, really, a response by the Florida Supreme Court to this court's remand in the case a week ago," O'Connor said to Boies. "And I found that troublesome." As for the controversy over the standard, O'Connor didn't understand the fuss: "Well, why isn't the standard the one that voters are instructed to follow, for goodness' sake? I mean, it couldn't be clearer. I mean, why don't we go to that standard?" In oral arguments, O'Connor's chaste exclamations—*my goodness!*, *oh dear!*, and the like—were surefire clues to the way she was voting.

In oral argument, Boies didn't have his best day. Souter repeated his concern about the lack of a standard in the Florida decision (and the possibility that different counties might adopt different rules), but he was also looking for a way to restart the count. He said to Boies, "We've got to make the assumption, I think, at this stage, that there may be such variation, and I think we would have a responsibility to tell the Florida courts what to do about it. On that assumption, what would you tell them to do about it?"

Boies hesitated. "Well, I think that's a very hard question"—which produced nervous laughter in the audience. Actually, it wasn't a hard question. The Supreme Court could simply set a standard or instruct the Florida court to set one.

There was a better answer, and Stevens jumped in and provided it. "Does not the procedure that is in place there contemplate that the uniformity will be achieved by having the final results all reviewed by the same judge?" Under the Florida decision, Judge Lewis in Tallahassee was going to monitor all controversies over the ballot counting. The review by a single judge would take care of any disparities. Boies had the wit to grab for Stevens's lifeline, saying, "Yes, that's what I was going to say, Your Honor."

Olson had only a few minutes for his rebuttal, and he did what good oral advocates always do—he shifted his argument in the direction his audience was already going. He had started by focusing on Article II, but he sensed more interest than he expected in equal protection. Several justices—among them O'Connor, Kennedy, Souter, and Breyer—were concerned about the possibility of different standards in different counties. "There is no question, based upon this record, that there are different standards from county to county," Olson said. "And that will happen in a situation where the process is ultimately subjective, completely up to the discretion of the official, and there's no requirement of any uniformity. Now we have something that's worse than that. We have standards that are different throughout 64 different counties. We've got only undercounts being considered where an indentation on a ballot will now be counted as a vote, but other ballots that may have indentations aren't going to be counted at all." With those remarks in their ears, the justices retreated to their conference.

It was not a normal conference. Because of the urgency, the justices had already exchanged several memos on the case, even before oral argument. So by the time they met with one another, it was clear that Rehnquist, Scalia, Thomas, and (almost certainly) O'Connor were committed to reversing the Florida Supreme Court. Stevens and Ginsburg would affirm, and Souter and Breyer were also looking for a way to keep the recount going. Kennedy had circulated a memo earlier that suggested strongly that he agreed with the conservatives, but at the conference he temporized, leading both sides to believe that they might get his vote.

After the conference, on Monday afternoon, Stevens made the first bid for Kennedy's support. Realizing that Kennedy considered the absence of a single standard in the recounts to be a problem, Stevens drafted an order of just a few sentences remanding the case to the Florida Supreme Court for the setting of a statewide standard to continue the recount. He sent his messenger scurrying down the marble hallway to Kennedy and the rest of the justices. He heard nothing back, except from Ginsburg, who said she would join if it was a way of bringing the whole Court together. (The rush of events in *Bush v. Gore* strained the Court's technology, which was, in 2000, still rather primitive. As a security precaution, the e-mail system circulated only within the building. Plus, there was only a single, communal computer from which the justices and clerks could obtain access to the Internet. Because only Thomas and Breyer used computers regularly at the time, there was little pressure from the justices to update. For the most part, the justices communicated with one another by hand-delivered memos, which were typed by their secretaries.)

As he often did, Rehnquist set out to write an opinion for the Court, even without a clear commitment that it would command a majority. He grounded it in Article II, rejecting the Florida court's attempt to change the legislature's plan for the election. But as the chief wrote, he knew he had only four votes for sure—his own, Scalia's, Thomas's, and (almost certainly) O'Connor's.

It all came down to Kennedy, which was as he preferred. The magnitude of the occasion suited Kennedy's taste for self-dramatization. By Monday afternoon, after Rehnquist had circulated his draft of an opinion, Kennedy decided that he would try to write one himself. He thought Rehnquist's reliance on the obscure section of Article II did not comport with the magnitude of the issue at stake. Instead, Kennedy would strike down the Florida court's ruling on equal protection grounds. In a peculiar way, Breyer's advocacy for the middle road turned out to hurt his cause rather than help it. In Kennedy's mind (and, later, O'Connor's), Breyer and Souter's misgivings about the Florida Supreme Court's decision made opposition to it more respectable. O'Connor in particular did not relish the idea of joining with the three conservatives in such a politically charged case. By siding with Kennedy in a position that at least resembled Breyer and Souter's view of the case, O'Connor could convince herself that she was safely in the middle of the Court.

Into Monday night, Kennedy and O'Connor and their clerks collaborated on a draft opinion, drawing largely from the memos they had written in the two election cases over the previous two weeks. (Scalia paid a rare visit to them both that day to encourage their joint effort.) They took the statement of facts from the draft that Rehnquist had circulated and then built their own equal protection argument. By early evening, Kennedy was happy with what he had produced. His vote was now secure. His clerks passed word to the Stevens chambers that Kennedy would not be joining his opinion. With that, Stevens decided he would keep his plane reservation for Florida the following morning, December 12. He could finish his dissent on the telephone with his clerks.

The Equal Protection Clause suited Kennedy's romantic conception of the work of the Supreme Court. The provision was the source of some of the Court's most dramatic and historic rulings, like *Brown v. Board of Education* in 1954 and *Reynolds v. Sims* in 1964, which established the rule of "one person, one vote" in legislative districting. Kennedy's own best-known ruling involved equal protection; in 1996, he had written for a six-justice majority in *Romer v. Evans* that Colorado could not ban its cities from passing laws to protect homosexuals. Kennedy was no liberal, to be sure, but neither was he afraid to use the Constitution as an engine to guarantee equal treatment of all people.

So it wasn't surprising that Kennedy embraced equal protection more than the opaque and technical Article II grounds of Rehnquist's opinion. Taken in its most charitable light, Kennedy's opinion in *Bush v. Gore* could be said to extend the principle of "one person, one vote" from the question of how districts are apportioned before the election to the question of how votes are counted after the election. As Kennedy wrote, "The right to vote . . . is fundamental, and one source of its fundamental nature lies in the equal weight accorded to each vote and the equal dignity owed to each voter." (*Dignity* is a favorite Kennedy word.) Counties had different rules about whether "dimpled chads" should be counted; individual counties sometimes changed the standard in the middle of a recount. "This is not a process with sufficient guarantees of equal treatment," Kennedy wrote starchily.

The problem with Kennedy's analysis, as innumerable commentators subsequently pointed out, was that no court, much less the Supreme Court, had ever before imposed any kind of constitutional rule of uniformity in the counting of ballots. Most states, including Florida, used different voting technologies in a single election. Kennedy was right that the recount might have produced inconsistencies and anomalies. But he was wrong on the larger, far more important point. A recount would have been more accurate than the certified total. The Court's opinion preserved and endorsed a less fair, and less accurate, count of the votes.

O'Connor realized the problems with Kennedy's equal protection analysis. Even at the oral argument, she raised some of them herself in her final questions for Olson, who had emphasized the difficulty of having "different standards from county to county." O'Connor replied, "Well, there are different ballots from county to county, too, Mr. Olson, and that's part of the argument that I don't understand. There are machines; there's the optical scanning. And then there are a whole variety of ballots; there's the butterfly ballot that we've heard about and other kinds of punch card ballots. How can you have one standard when there are so many varieties of ballots?"

Still, in the end, O'Connor discounted her own apt summary of the issue. Notwithstanding her recognition of the problems with the equal protection argument, O'Connor decided to sign on. But she did so in characteristic fashion. Her position was really a version of Breyer's—that the process just didn't sound fair, and it needed to be stopped. To O'Connor, equal protection was a more moderate-sounding way of doing it than Rehnquist's Article II approach. But unlike Kennedy, O'Connor had an aversion to grand pronouncements; she liked opinions narrowly tailored to the facts before the Court, and that was especially true of *Bush v. Gore*. She didn't want to be making a lot of new law that might come back to haunt the Court in future cases. So late on Tuesday morning, December 12, as Kennedy's opinion was starting to be put into final shape, O'Connor told Kennedy she wanted it clear that this opinion would not be creating a whole new set of rights and regulations for elections.

Kennedy responded by adding what became the most notorious sentence in the opinion—indeed, a single sentence that summed up so much of what was wrong with what the Court did. "Our consideration is limited to the present circumstances," Kennedy wrote, "for the problem of equal protection in election processes generally presents many complexities."

In other words, the opinion did not reflect any general legal principles; rather the Court was acting only to assist a single individual—George W. Bush. That was not what Kennedy meant, but that was what he wrote. The sentiment amounted to a natural consequence of the Court's misbegotten encounter with the 2000 election. The business of the Supreme Court is to take cases that establish principles of general application. But as Kennedy's sentence all but conceded, there was no general principle in *Bush v. Gore*—only a specific designation of the winner of one election. More than any other, this sentence invited skepticism about the majority's true motives in the case.

By midafternoon on Tuesday, as the four justices in the minority circulated their dissenting opinions, tempers grew even shorter. Ginsburg had devoted her professional career to the use of the Equal Protection Clause of the Fourteenth Amendment, and it galled her to see that provision perverted by Kennedy's opinion. In a late draft of her dissent, Ginsburg drew on certain early press reports about the black vote in Florida to suggest in a footnote that, if there was any equal protection violation by the state, it was more likely by state and local authorities than by the Florida Supreme Court. The footnote sent Scalia into a rage, and he replied with a memo—in a sealed envelope, to be opened only by Ginsburg herself—accusing her of "fouling our nest" and using "Al Sharpton tactics." Ginsburg backed down and removed the footnote.

Still, the cumulative effects of the dissents worried Kennedy and O'Connor. They needed to show that their views were not as outlandish as the dissenters made them seem. So they decided to seize on the fact that Souter's and Breyer's opinions (which Stevens and Ginsburg joined in substantial part) said the case should be remanded to the Florida Supreme Court for the setting of a standard. Kennedy wrote, "Eight Justices of the Court agree that there are constitutional problems with the recount ordered by the Florida Supreme Court that demand a remedy. The only disagreement is as to the remedy." The statement was borderline disingenuous. In truth, the main point of Stevens's, Souter's, and Breyer's opinions was that the recounts should continue, not that they had "problems."

Stevens was already in Florida, but his clerks screamed at Kennedy's clerk that the sentence distorted Stevens's opinion. (In the confusion of the moment, they actually yelled at the wrong clerk, not the one who had responsibility for *Bush v. Gore.*) In response to the tirade from the Stevens chambers, Kennedy changed the reference to "Seven Justices." Souter and Breyer would have been within their rights to protest as well, but they decided not to bother. That was a mistake. As a result of this sentence, as Kennedy intended, *Bush v. Gore* is often referred to by its supporters as a 7–2 case. In truth, it was never anything but 5–4.

The crisis of *Bush v. Gore* came upon the Court so quickly that the normal flow of business continued unabated, sometimes with comic results. At about nine in the evening on Tuesday, as the last of the opinions were being proofread before being sent to the printer in the basement, a court of appeals law clerk named Anil Kalhan showed up in advance of an interview with O'Connor that was scheduled for the next day. Kalhan thought he would visit friends who were already clerking. But his arrival outraged several other law clerks, who thought that an outsider like Kalhan could not be trusted to keep the result in *Bush v. Gore* secret. Some suggested, in apparent seriousness, that Kalhan be "detained," so he could neither leave nor call outside the building. In any event, no one told Kalhan the result, and he drifted into one of the conference rooms where televisions had been set up to watch the media reports on the announcement. He was not detained, and neither did he get the clerkship.

Over the course of the day, the usual crew of about a dozen regulars in the Supreme Court pressroom had been joined by about fifty other reporters. At 9:40 p.m., Ed Turner, the Court's deputy public information officer, entered the room and announced, "We're going to make a line." He read out the names of the permanent members of the Supreme Court press corps, and they dutifully queued up in the marble hallway. The newcomers stacked up behind them. At 9:52, the large cardboard boxes of opinions appeared, and the line moved at the nervous, half-running pace of paratroopers jumping out of a plane. Members of the public information staff had arranged for reporters to make a quick exit to the street through the door of the Supreme Court gift shop. The television reporters sprinted across the plaza to their camera positions on the First Street sidewalk.

Flipping madly through the pages, the correspondents struggled to make sense of the ruling. Because of the rush, the clerk's office did not prepare a summary, which is customary at the beginning of all Supreme Court opinions. The journalists' confusion was understandable, as the Court's chaotic process was reflected in its finished product. Its opinion, largely written by Kennedy, was again labeled per curiam, "by the court," which was the designation the justices usually used for uncontroversial rulings. Rehnquist insisted on its use here because the final opinion of the Court had been jointly assembled and the phrase would give a pretense of unanimity to the Court's action. The end of the per curiam stated that the case was "remanded for further proceedings not inconsistent with this opinion." That was a familiar phrase in the Court's jurisprudence, but its meaning was, at first, unclear in the context of *Bush v. Gore*. Did it mean the recounts could continue? Foggy thinking by the Court had produced muddy writing, but closer parsing eventually showed that the answer was no.

Inside the Court, televisions had been set up in a pair of nearby conference rooms for the law clerks. The liberals migrated to one gathering, the conservatives to the other. Not surprisingly, the two rooms split close to evenly, like the rest of the country on this night. The liberals had Thai food and beer; the conservatives pizza and

Scotch. They were unanimous only in their hooting derision for the television reporters. None of the justices came to watch; instead they made their way to their cars and drove home.

It had been at least twenty-five years since the nation turned its collective attention to the Supreme Court to resolve a question of such importance. In 1974, the justices had risen to the occasion when, in *United States v. Nixon*, they unanimously ordered the president to turn over the White House tapes and, in a larger sense, comply with the rule of law. Here, in a moment of probably even greater significance, the Court as an institution and the justices as individuals failed. Indeed, their performance on this case amounted to a catalog of their worst flaws as judges.

In one respect, though, the Court received unfair criticism for *Bush v. Gore*—from those who said the justices in the majority "stole the election" for Bush. Rather, what the Court did was remove any uncertainty about the outcome. It is possible that if the Court had ruled fairly—or, better yet, not taken the case at all—Gore would have won the election. A recount might have led to a Gore victory in Florida. It is also entirely possible that, had the Court acted properly and left the resolution of the election to the Florida courts, Bush would have won anyway. The recount of the 60,000 undervotes might have resulted in Bush's preserving or expanding his lead. The Florida legislature, which was controlled by Republicans, might have stepped in and awarded the state's electoral votes to Bush. And if the dispute had wound up in the House of Representatives, which has the constitutional duty to resolve controversies involving the Electoral College, Bush might have won there, too. The tragedy of the Court's performance in the election of 2000 was not that it led to Bush's victory but the inept and unsavory manner with which the justices exercised their power.

There was only one bright spot in this dismal panorama. John Paul Stevens's dignified, clearheaded, and insistent eloquence honored the Court. Alone among the justices, Stevens was consistent and logical and constitutionally sound in his thinking. From his home in Fort Lauderdale, he composed a peroration that serves as the best epitaph for this sorry chapter in the Court's history: "The [per curiam opinion] by the majority of this Court can only lend credence to the most cynical appraisal of the work of judges throughout the land. It is confidence in the men and women who administer the judicial system that is the true backbone of the rule of law. Time will one day heal the wound to that confidence that will be inflicted by today's decision.

One thing, however, is certain. Although we may never know with complete certainty the identity of the winner of this year's Presidential election, the identity of the loser is pellucidly clear. It is the Nation's confidence in the judge as an impartial guardian of the rule of law." (At the last moment, one of Stevens's clerks prevailed on him, just this once, to give up his favorite word—*pellucidly*—and substitute the more familiar *perfectly*, which is how the famous sentence now reads.)

With one exception, the justices tried to put *Bush v. Gore* behind them and resume business as usual. Three weeks later, Scalia and Ginsburg followed their custom of welcoming the New Year with each other's families. Breyer, characteristically, made a systematic effort to take many of the disappointed liberal law clerks to lunch. In restaurants, often at embarrassingly high decibels, Breyer urged the young lawyers to maintain their faith in the Court and believe that their views might someday return to favor. O'Connor tried to avoid discussing the case. Kennedy pretended the whole matter was no big deal.

David Souter alone was shattered. He was, fundamentally, a very different person from his colleagues. It wasn't just that they had immediate families; their lives off the bench were entirely unlike his. They went to parties and conferences; they gave speeches; they mingled in Washington, where cynicism about everything, including the work of the Supreme Court, was universal. Toughened, or coarsened, by their worldly lives, the other dissenters could shrug and move on, but Souter couldn't. His whole life was being a judge. He came from a tradition where the independence of the judiciary was the foundation of the rule of law. And Souter believed *Bush v. Gore* mocked that tradition. His colleagues' actions were so transparently, so crudely partisan that Souter thought he might not be able to serve with them anymore.

Souter seriously considered resigning. For many months, it was not at all clear whether he would remain as a justice. That the Court met in a city he loathed made the decision even harder. At the urging of a handful of close friends, he decided to stay on, but his attitude toward the Court was never the same. There were times when David Souter thought of *Bush v. Gore* and wept.

PART
THREE

"A PARTICULAR SEXUAL ACT"

When the justices returned following their Christmas break, in January 2001, their docket for the rest of the term finally vindicated Souter's prediction from the previous fall: it was a boring year.

The relief was especially pronounced because the criticism of *Bush v. Gore* left some of the justices shell-shocked. It was one thing to be called wrong, or even reactionary and right-wing—that was routine—but this time critics went after the justices' motives and their integrity. The decision was called a sham, a political fix, a putsch.

The backlash against the decision affected those in the majority in different ways. Rehnquist, who was older than most of his colleagues and more disengaged from contemporary political life, ignored the hubbub. Scalia, who loved a fight, welcomed this one, too. (Notably, Scalia rarely defended *Bush v. Gore* on its own stated terms but rather as a necessary intervention in an out-of-control election—as a tourniquet applied to the body politic. "We had to do something, because countries were laughing at us," Scalia would tell audiences. "*France* was laughing at us.") Thomas found only vindication in the outrage at *Bush v. Gore*.

O'Connor, in contrast, never treasured her role in the decision. She valued her place as the Court's moderate center, and her association with a decision regarded by many as a partisan outrage made her queasy. Like Scalia, O'Connor would rarely defend the decision on its merits. With a nervous, revealing intensity, she would cite the results of the recounts conducted by the news media as supposed proof that *Bush v. Gore* had not mattered as much as its critics claimed. O'Connor did not voice regret for her vote—such soul-searching was definitely not part of the O'Connor style—but neither did she enjoy the memory of the case.

Of the five justices in the majority, Kennedy had the hardest time with the aftermath of *Bush v. Gore*. He had spent most of his adult life as a judge, and he had a special reverence for the profession, "the guild of judges," as he sometimes called it. There would be, it turned out, two Anthony Kennedys on the Supreme Court—the one before December 12, 2000, and the one after—and his transformation was surely one of the most unexpected legacies of this epochal case.

The Justice Kennedy of the post–*Bush v. Gore* era was shaped by one influence in particular—his exposure to foreign law and foreign judges. After 2000, in part to escape the political atmosphere in Washington, Kennedy deepened his commitment to the broader world, and his journeys changed him. Given Kennedy's pivotal role, the Court and the nation would never be the same. The paradox of *Bush v. Gore* is that the justices' gift of the presidency to a conservative sent the Court in its most liberal direction in years.

On the surface, few justices in recent history arrived at the Supreme Court from a more provincial background than Kennedy. When President Reagan nominated him to the Supreme Court in 1987, Kennedy was fifty-one and still lived in the house where he grew up in Sacramento.

But that picture of Anthony Kennedy—of a provincial lawyer tethered to the same small city for his entire life—was misleading. Kennedy's inclinations were hardly those of an insular man. While he was a teenager, his uncle, an oil driller, hired him to work summers on rigs in Canada and Louisiana. Before he graduated from college, Kennedy spent several months studying at the London School of Economics, where he reveled in the range of student opinion and the vehemence of political debate. As a young lawyer, even though his firm in the California capital was small, he developed a robust international practice. Kennedy traveled to Mexico so often on business that he became one of a handful of American lawyers to obtain a license to practice there, where he helped a client establish one of the first maquiladoras—American-owned factories.

Kennedy's father had been a legendary lobbyist in Sacramento, best known for his rousing advocacy (and entertaining) on behalf of the

California liquor industry, among others. Tony Kennedy hung on to the client for his firm, but he cultivated a very different persona around Sacramento—that of a professor rather than a glad-hander. In 1965, when he was only twenty-nine and a few years out of law school himself, Kennedy began teaching constitutional law at McGeorge, the local law school. Kennedy's idea of himself as a teacher, and of law as a transmitter of society's values, was central to his identity.

Kennedy was not even forty years old when Gerald Ford appointed him to the Ninth Circuit. The job of an appeals court judge can be stultifying, especially for a young man, because the principal duties are so sedentary—reading briefs, hearing arguments, and writing opinions. But Kennedy made something more of it, when he accepted an appointment from Chief Justice Burger as supervisor of the territorial courts in the South Pacific, which entailed traveling to Guam, Palau, Saipan, American Samoa, Australia, New Zealand, and Japan. He kept up his teaching, and it was through the law school in Sacramento that Kennedy developed the connection that would transform his judicial career. McGeorge offered a summer program for law students at the University of Salzburg, in Austria, and Kennedy began teaching there in 1987, the year Reagan nominated him to the Supreme Court. Kennedy returned to Salzburg in 1990, and every year thereafter, as soon as the last opinion of the term was handed down, he and his wife, Mary, would pack up their things and head to the idyllic city in the foothills of the Alps.

The Berlin Wall fell a year after Kennedy joined the Court, and the political developments that followed from the collapse of Communism had a profound effect on his approach to interpreting the Constitution. Suddenly, dozens of countries around the world decided to adopt meaningful written constitutions. These aspiring democracies initially consisted of former components and satellites of the Soviet Union, but eventually countries in Asia, the Middle East, and Africa also sought democratic legal expertise. Virtually all of these nations looked to the United States for inspiration—and more specifically, to its Supreme Court.

Kennedy was eager to answer the call, and he began to advise emerging democracies—including Czechoslovakia and Russia—on their constitutional law. In the early nineties, dozens of projects were created to export American legal concepts. Most of the justices participated in some of these exchanges, but Kennedy and O'Connor were by far the most active. In 1990, O'Connor helped create what would become the biggest of these institution-building organizations, the Central European and Eurasian Law Initiative (CEELI) of the American Bar Association. The first meeting of CEELI was going to take place in Salzburg, and since Kennedy was going to be there anyway, O'Connor invited him to come along.

Kennedy enjoyed his summers in the city where many of the most important international judicial conferences took place. The activity was centered in an institution known as the Salzburg Seminar, which was founded in 1947 by three young Harvard graduates who thought that Europe needed a place for the study of American ideals. They raised a few thousand dollars and rented the Schloss Leopoldskron, an eighteenth-century palace that had fallen into disrepair after being seized by the Nazis. The seminar became known as the "Marshall Plan of the mind," and it remained a meeting place for scholars and judges. Since 1971, nine Supreme Court justices have attended sessions at the Schloss, many of them several times. Kennedy participated in four seminars, and even during summers when he was not officially involved, he visited the Schloss frequently to meet with foreign colleagues.

The Schloss Leopoldskron has tight security by Salzburg's relaxed standards, but not because of the jurists. The palace was the setting for several scenes in *The Sound of Music*, the 1965 movie, and has endured more or less constant traffic from fans. The setting for two key romantic scenes, one between Liesl and Rolf (featuring the song "Sixteen Going on Seventeen") and the other between Maria and the Captain ("Something Good"), was a glass gazebo originally situated in the garden. When the crowds became unmanageable, the gazebo was moved to a more central location in Salzburg. (Outside the Schloss, a sign on the wall closest to the street reads, in English, "Trespassers Will Be Prosecuted—Including Tour Groups.") For Kennedy, the Schloss was a second home in Salzburg, one of the few places in the world where a Supreme Court justice could mingle easily with peers.

In Europe, from the moment he took office, George W. Bush was disdained for his unilateralist approach to foreign policy, his contempt for international institutions, and, especially, his cowboy swagger. Starting in 2001, Kennedy could go entire summers without

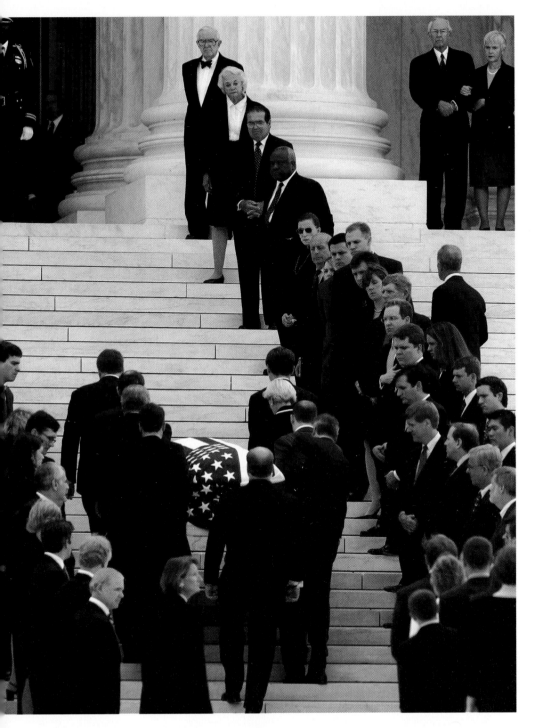

On September 6, 2005, the justices lined up on the steps of the Court to greet the casket of William H. Rehnquist. From the top, John Paul Stevens (in bow tie), Sandra Day O'Connor, Antonin Scalia, Clarence Thomas, Ruth Bader Ginsburg, and Stephen G. Breyer. Anthony M. Kennedy was in China, David H. Souter in New Hampshire. In the upper right corner is John O'Connor, Sandra's ailing husband.

Seven of Rehnquist's former law clerks and one former administrative assistant carried his casket. John G. Roberts Jr., who worked for the then-associate justice in 1980–81, is second in line on the right.

O'Connor weeps as Rehnquist, her friend of more than fifty years, returns to the Court for a final time.

They served together from 1994 to 2005—the longest period without change in the history of the nine-justice Court. Top row, from left: Ginsburg, Souter, Thomas, Breyer. Bottom row: Scalia, Stevens, Rehnquist, O'Connor, Kennedy.

On June 14, 1993, after a tortuous search, President Clinton introduces Ginsburg, his first nominee.

Breyer, Clinton's second nominee to the Court, in 2006.

Stevens, at a speech in Chicago, in 2005.

Souter in 2003.

Thomas at the Ave Maria School of Law in 2004.

Scalia, with a characteristic gesture, in 2006.

Souter, haggard and drained, leaves the Court on December 12, 2000, the day of *Bush v. Gore*, the case that nearly prompted him to resign.

International travel transformed the outlooks of several justices. O'Connor with Chinese president Jiang Zemin in Beijing in 2002. Inset: Kennedy in the Hague in 2004.

A frail Rehnquist rose from his sickbed to administer the oath of office to President Bush on January 20, 2005.

President Bush introduces Roberts as his nominee to replace O'Connor on July 19, 2005. To the side are Roberts's wife, Jane, and daughter, Josephine. His son, Jack, is imitating Spider-Man.

On September 29, 2005, at the White House, Stevens swears in Roberts as the seventeenth chief justice of the United States.

Samuel A. Alito Jr. arrives for the hearing with his wife, Martha-Ann.

Alito at his confirmation hearing on January 11, 2006.

Martha-Ann breaks down in tears at the hearing as Senator Lindsey Graham describes the attacks against her husband.

meeting a Bush admirer, and the subject of *Bush v. Gore* was avoided like a family tragedy. Kennedy was under no illusions about what his international colleagues thought of his president—or of his own decision to put him in office.

One day, after *Bush v. Gore*, Kennedy had lunch with Richard Goldstone, a former justice of the South African Constitutional Court who was in Salzburg to deliver a lecture and, like Kennedy, was eager to meet his foreign counterparts. The two men dined on the second floor of the Schloss, in a room adorned with mirrored panels and gilt sconces that had been reproduced on a soundstage to create the von Trapp ballroom.

"Do you know any of the Russian judges?" Kennedy asked Goldstone. "They are so resilient."

"I've met good and bad. Now the court belongs to the president," he said, referring to Vladimir Putin.

Kennedy mentioned that he was on the board of an American Bar Association group that advised judges and lawyers in China, where he traveled about once a year. "There was a dinner for one of their vice premiers," he said. "I knew that I had to give a gift. We don't have a budget for these things, so I went down to the Supreme Court gift shop, and I found one of these calendars. It was in a nice leather case, and it had some anniversary from American constitutional law for every day of the year. So we're at this dinner, and I present the calendar to him, and he's so pleased, so I just say, 'When's your birthday? Why don't you look it up?' And he says whatever the date was and hands the calendar to the interpreter. So the interpreter just stands there. He looks at me. He looks around. There was this silence. Clearly, he doesn't know what to do. So I say, 'Read it, read it.' And the entry is for *Dennis v. United States*, affirming prison time for eleven American Communists. There was this silence again. My security guy headed to the door. Then the guest of honor just laughed and laughed." Kennedy laughed too, adding, "I am not a world-class diplomat."

These kinds of exchanges went on in Washington as well. Because Rehnquist more or less forbade discussions of Court business at the justices' regular lunches, and because the justices could feign interest in one another's grandchildren for only so long, they started inviting guests. The visitors included Kofi Annan, Condoleezza Rice, Henry Kissinger, the historian David McCullough, the soprano Cathy Malfitano, and Alan Greenspan (the only repeat invitee), but the most frequent guests were foreign judges. Goldstone was one, and so was Aharon Barak, the chief justice of Israel, as well as other lesser-known jurists. In the immediate post–Cold War period, these judicial exchanges may have started as a way of exporting American constitutionalism, but in time the ideas traveled in both directions—with a profound impact on the Court.

The two-way dialogue pushed the Court—and especially Kennedy—to the left. The United States is the most conservative democracy in the world, with a broad national consensus in support of limited government and low taxes. Virtually all other democracies, in Europe and elsewhere, are committed to a more robust public sector, favoring, for example, national health care as well as higher taxes. Accordingly, the judges in other countries tend to be more liberal than their American counterparts. The contrast is especially stark on the death penalty. Not only have virtually all democracies abolished capital punishment, they have tried to ban the practice from their community of nations as well. All countries seeking membership in the European Union must renounce the death penalty. Among many European judges, executions inspire not just opposition but revulsion. Kennedy's voting shaded along with his eyeglasses—out with the seventies-style steel-framed aviators, in with a Euro-chic frameless model.

In the new century, such cosmopolitanism came at the Court from several directions, and a new generation of law clerks brought a new attitude toward homosexuality. In this period, gay rights enjoyed relatively few victories in the mainstream political culture, but the movement completely transformed the world of the legal elite. In major law schools and the big-city firms that employed their graduates (and many former Supreme Court law clerks), the cause of equality for gay people enjoyed close to unanimous support. Schools and firms bragged about their welcoming attitudes toward homosexuals. Significant numbers of gay law students grew up in this environment, accepted it as normal, and went on to clerk at the Supreme Court.

The gay clerks changed the Court, not because of their advocacy but because of their existence. They were, of course, pretty much indistinguishable from their straight colleagues, and that was precisely the point. The justices, who were without exception polite and decent people, treated the gay clerks with civility. When the longtime partner of a senior lawyer on the Court's staff died, the first condolence note to the survivor came from Rehnquist. (The chief also had openly gay people on his immediate staff.) Thomas treated the partners of gay clerks with the same boisterous bonhomie as he did everyone else; the photo on his desk of Stevens's clerk's partner, the snowboarder, was no aberration. O'Connor gave T-shirts with the words "Grand Clerks" to the newborn children of all her law clerks; shortly after 2000, she learned that one of her former clerks, a gay man, was adopting a baby with his partner. In her briskly efficient way, O'Connor poked her head into her current clerks' office, explained the situation, and said, "I should send one of the shirts, right? We think this is a good idea, don't we?" The clerks nodded, and the shirt went in the mail.

This social transformation at the Court occurred against a starkly different legal landscape. In the 1986 case of *Bowers v. Hardwick*, the Court had upheld the conviction of a Georgia man for consensual sodomy with another man. Byron White's opinion for the 5–4 majority was utterly contemptuous of the whole concept of gay rights. "To claim that a right to engage in such conduct is 'deeply rooted in this Nation's history and tradition' or 'implicit in the concept of ordered liberty' is, at best, facetious," White wrote. In his brief, dismissive concurrence, Chief Justice Burger wrote, "To hold that the act of homosexual sodomy is somehow protected as a fundamental right would be to cast aside millennia of moral teaching." For a generation of gay people and their allies, the case remained an open wound.

One Saturday in the spring of 1986, Justice Lewis Powell struck up an unusual conversation with one of his law clerks, Cabell Chinnis Jr., about *Bowers v. Hardwick*. As Chinnis recounted the exchange to Joyce Murdoch and Deb Price, authors of a history of gay rights at the Supreme Court, Powell asked about the prevalence of homosexuality, which one friend-of-the-court brief estimated at 10 percent. Chinnis said that sounded right to him. "I don't believe I've ever met a homosexual," Powell replied. Chinnis said that seemed unlikely. Later the same day, Powell came back to Chinnis and asked, "Why don't homosexuals have sex with women?" "Justice Powell," he replied, "a gay man cannot have an erection to perform intercourse with a woman." The conversation was especially bizarre not just because of its explicit nature but because Chinnis himself was gay (as were several of Powell's previous law clerks). Earlier in the term, Chinnis had introduced Powell to the man he had lived with, but the clerk never knew for sure what Powell understood about his sexuality. The matter turned out to be of more than passing significance because Powell, after a great deal of agonizing, ultimately provided the fifth vote in support of White's opinion in *Bowers*.

Seventeen years later, when the Court weighed whether to overturn *Bowers*, no justice could conceive of asserting that he (or she) had never met a homosexual. But the fact that the justices all knew gay people did not necessarily mean that they were inclined to overrule what was still a fairly recent precedent.

The facts in the new case, *Lawrence v. Texas*, were uncomplicated and very similar to those that gave rise to *Bowers*. On September 17, 1998, Houston police, responding to a report of a weapons disturbance, entered an apartment where John Geddes Lawrence and Tyron Garner were having sex. The two men were arrested for violating the Texas law against "deviate sexual intercourse," which prohibited oral and anal sex. The question for the Court was whether a state could constitutionally prohibit consensual sexual conduct between adults.

Even at the oral argument, it was apparent how much the Court had changed over the years. All Rehnquist could say in support of the Texas law was that "the kind of conduct we're talking about here has been banned for a long time." Even Scalia, who had, like Rehnquist and O'Connor, joined the *Bowers* opinion, sounded defensive. "It's an act committed in private," he said. "The police have not gone around knocking on bedroom doors to see if anyone—I mean—this is not the kind of a crime that the police go around looking for." In questioning Charles A. Rosenthal Jr., the Harris County district attorney, Breyer called the *Bowers* decision "harmful in consequence, wrong in theory, and understating the constitutional value" and asked, "How do you respond to that?"

Rosenthal tried to change the subject.

But Breyer wouldn't give up, saying, "I would like to hear your straight answer."

The worldly Supreme Court audience chuckled at the double entendre, which Breyer himself neither intended nor noticed.

At the conference, only three justices supported the Texas law— Rehnquist, Scalia, and Thomas. O'Connor could not bring herself to repudiate her vote in *Bowers* altogether, but she couldn't bring herself to reaffirm it, either. So she found a characteristic middle ground, voting to overturn Lawrence's conviction on the ground that the prosecution of homosexuals (but not heterosexuals) violated the Equal Protection Clause. That left five votes—Stevens, Kennedy, Souter, Ginsburg, and Breyer—to overturn *Bowers*, and Stevens wisely assigned Kennedy to write the opinion. (Inside the Court, Kennedy was sometimes said to be "clerk-driven"—that is, overly influenced by his law clerks. *Lawrence* demonstrated that the charge was both unfair and unwarranted, because three of Kennedy's four clerks that year were committed conservatives.)

As the Court often saved the most controversial opinions for the last day of the term, everyone knew that the decision in *Lawrence v. Texas* would be announced on June 26, 2003. Justices do not read their full opinions in open court but generally give abbreviated versions for the tourists and other (usually) baffled spectators who happen to be present. But on this day, gay rights supporters from around the country filled the spectator benches, waiting for the result in *Lawrence*. The audience stirred when Rehnquist, impassive as always, said, "The opinion of the Court, number 02–102. *Lawrence versus Texas* will be announced by Justice Kennedy."

Kennedy's voice had an uncharacteristic quaver. He was more worldly than Lewis Powell—Kennedy knew many gay people—but he was also a conservative man by most definitions of that term. A devout and observant Catholic, he needed no instruction in the religious and moral prohibitions on homosexual conduct. He was, simply, a man who had been transformed by the changing world around him.

"We granted certiorari to consider the constitutional claims presented, including the question whether *Bowers v. Hardwick* should be overruled," he said, then quoted a line from that opinion: "The issue as presented is whether the federal Constitution confers a fundamental right upon homosexuals to engage in sodomy." But that framing of the question, Kennedy said, "demeans the claim put forward, just as it would demean a married couple if it were said marriage is simply about the right to have sexual intercourse. The laws involved in *Bowers* and here are, to be sure, statutes that do prohibit a particular sexual act. Their penalties and purposes, though, have more far-reaching consequences, touching upon the most private human conduct, sexual behavior, and in the most private of places, the home. The statutes seek to control a personal relationship that is within the liberty of persons to choose without being punished as criminals." The nation, he went on, "has been shaped by religious beliefs, conceptions of right and acceptable behavior, and respect for the traditional family. For many persons these are not trivial concerns but profound and deep convictions accepted as ethical and moral principles to which they aspire and which thus determine the course of their lives." This was autobiography, for Kennedy's own life had been shaped by those beliefs—but then he said those rules *cannot* prescribe what the Constitution commands for all.

The next part of the opinion—the key part—displayed the influence of Salzburg in Kennedy's jurisprudence. *Bowers* made "sweeping references" to long-standing prohibitions on sodomy in Western civilization. These did not, however, "take account of authorities in an opposite direction," Kennedy said, "including the decision of the European Court of Human Rights in a case called *Dudgeon v. United Kingdom*. That decision, with facts like Bowers and the instant case, held that laws prescribing this sort of conduct are invalid under the European Convention on Human Rights." The pre-Salzburg Kennedy—even the pre–*Bush v. Gore* justice—would never have made such a reference.

As the tension rose in the courtroom, Kennedy finally announced the holding on the case: "The instant case requires us to address whether *Bowers* itself has continuing validity. We conclude the rationale of *Bowers* does not withstand careful analysis, *Bowers* was not correct when it was decided, and it is not correct today. It ought not to remain binding precedent. *Bowers versus Hardwick* should be and now is overruled."

There was no mistaking the significance of Kennedy's opinion. The point was not that the Court was halting sodomy prosecutions, which scarcely took place anymore. Rather, the Court was announcing that gay people could not be branded as criminals simply because of who they were. They were citizens. They were like everyone else. "The petitioners are entitled to respect for their private lives," Kennedy wrote simply. "The State cannot demean their existence or control their destiny by making their private sexual conduct a crime." The people who had devoted their lives to that cause understood precisely what had happened, which was why, to a degree unprecedented in the Court's history, the benches were full of men and women sobbing with joy.

15

"A LAW-PROFESSION CULTURE"

Not everyone was pleased by the ruling in *Lawrence v. Texas*. The case turned out to be a critical moment in the culture wars. Justice Kennedy's opinion was hailed on major editorial pages, in law schools, in big American cities, and in foreign capitals. But those voices, as Justice Scalia was quick to point out, were not the Court's only constituency. In the struggle between elite opinion and popular will, there were no guaranteed winners.

Lawrence cemented the breach between Kennedy and Scalia. Born within a few months of each other and nominated by the same president only a year apart, the former law school contemporaries and jogging partners had been heading in opposite directions for some time, but the post–*Bush v. Gore* Kennedy became unrecognizable to Scalia. Indeed, in his opinion for the Court in *Lawrence*, Kennedy seemingly went out of his way to produce a catalog of everything in modern constitutional law that most repelled Scalia. Like *Roe v. Wade*, *Lawrence v. Texas* was based on the "right to privacy," which Scalia did not believe existed. Kennedy drew at length from *Casey*, the 1992 landmark that he had produced in secret collaboration with O'Connor and Souter, most notably these oft-quoted lines: "These matters, involving the most intimate and personal choices a person may make in a lifetime, choices central to personal dignity and autonomy, are central to the liberty protected by the Fourteenth Amendment. At the heart of liberty is the right to define one's own concept of existence, of meaning, of the universe, and of the mystery of human life." In his dissent in *Lawrence*, Scalia sneered at what he called *Casey*'s "famed sweet-mystery-of-life passage."

Scalia did more than simply ridicule Kennedy's words. *Lawrence* reflected what Scalia, as an originalist, most despised—a Court that shifted according to contemporary trends rather than by the immutable rules set down by the framers. But Scalia made a deeper observation. For all of Kennedy's talk about how the world had changed since 1986, Scalia knew that many Americans—perhaps even most of them—shared his own revulsion for homosexuality. The decision in *Lawrence* did not spring from anything close to unanimous public opinion on the issue; rather it sprang from *one kind* of opinion. "Today's opinion is the product of a Court, which is the product of a law-profession culture, that has largely signed on to the so-called homosexual agenda, by which I mean the agenda promoted by some homosexual activists directed at eliminating the moral opprobrium that has traditionally attached to homosexual conduct," Scalia wrote in his dissent, adding, "The Court has taken sides in the culture war."

Scalia knew that the public—the real public—was on his side on at least some issues, perhaps even most of them, but especially about the clear subtext of the *Lawrence* case—gay marriage. Kennedy, wary of pushing his argument too far, had said pointedly in his majority opinion that the case "does not involve whether the government must give formal recognition to any relationship that homosexual persons seek to enter."

But Scalia shot back with even greater directness: "Do not believe it. . . . This case 'does not involve' the issue of homosexual marriage only if one entertains the belief that principle and logic have nothing to do with the decisions of this Court. Many will hope that, as the Court comfortingly assures us, this is so." True to Scalia's prediction, just five months later, with heavy reliance on the *Lawrence* precedent, the Supreme Judicial Court of Massachusetts held that gay people must be allowed to marry, too.

By that point, Kennedy had decided to press forward on an equally controversial issue—the death penalty.

Although influenced by his summers in Salzburg, Kennedy wasn't even the most ardent internationalist on the Court. Breyer was.

In the way that actors once sought the perfect mid-Atlantic accent, Breyer found the perfect mid-Atlantic life. After graduating from Stanford, he won a Marshall Scholarship to study at Oxford. He returned to the States for Harvard Law School, then moved to

Washington to serve as a law clerk to Justice Arthur J. Goldberg. There he met a young Englishwoman named Joanna Hare, who was then an assistant in the Washington office of the London *Sunday Times*. She came from an aristocratic (and wealthy) British family; her father was John Hare, 1st Viscount Blakenham, a British peer and statesman who served as a leader of the Tory Party in the 1950s and 1960s. The couple married in England, and Joanna Breyer later became a psychologist, treating young patients and their families at the Dana-Farber Cancer Institute in Boston. (Justice Breyer was also fluent in French, a fact that, given the relationship between the Bush administration and France, he did little to advertise.)

At Harvard Law School, on the First Circuit Court of Appeals, where he served from 1980 to 1994, and on the Supreme Court, Breyer eagerly sought the friendship of his counterparts in other countries. He was the first justice in modern times to invoke foreign law as an aid to interpreting the American Constitution. He was cautious at first. In 1999, the Court refused to hear the appeal of a prisoner who argued that spending more than two decades on death row amounted to cruel and unusual punishment, in violation of the Eighth Amendment. Breyer wrote a brief dissent from the denial of certiorari, which was the kind of opinion that had little significance compared with, say, a majority opinion of the Court; such writing was a traditional way for justices to try out new ideas. So in his dissent in *Knight v. Florida*, Breyer quoted legal opinions from Jamaica, India, Zimbabwe, and the European Court of Human Rights to observe that "a growing number of courts outside the United States . . . have held that lengthy delay in administering a lawful death penalty renders ultimate execution inhuman, degrading, or unusually cruel." Breyer carefully noted that these views could not bind American courts, but he thought their observations worthy of note. Still, even this cautious invocation of foreign law drew a swift rejoinder from Clarence Thomas, who said in a brief opinion that the Supreme Court should never "impose foreign moods, fads, or fashions on Americans." With that brief exchange, the battle was on.

It was Kennedy who took the concept to the next level. The issue was one that mattered a great deal to his foreign colleagues. On October 13, 2004, the Court heard argument on whether or not states could execute minors—that is, murderers who committed their crimes before they turned eighteen.

The issue was especially contentious because, as with *Lawrence*, the Court had considered it just a few years earlier. In 1989, Scalia had written in *Stanford v. Kentucky* that states could execute sixteen- and seventeen-year-old offenders. But in 2003, the Missouri Supreme Court had ruled in *Roper v. Simmons* that changes in the law since *Stanford* meant the Constitution now forbade the execution of juvenile offenders.

The emotional temperature of the issues surrounding the death penalty was changing. In his early years on the Court, Rehnquist had crusaded to speed up executions in the United States, and his opinions seethed with frustration at the procedural roadblocks his liberal adversaries—chiefly Brennan and Marshall—had managed to create. In this respect, Bill Clinton was in ideological accord with the chief justice, and in the aftermath of the Oklahoma City bombing, the president signed the Antiterrorism and Effective Death Penalty Act of 1996. The bizarrely named statute was supposed to limit appeals by condemned prisoners, but its impact was muted by larger trends. Crime dropped dramatically during the Clinton years; at the same time, the number of people freed from prisons, often from death row, because of faulty convictions rose. (Many of these exonerations took place because of the use of new DNA technology.) By the time Bush became president, public support for the death penalty, death sentences by juries, and the number of executions were all falling. Executions had peaked in 1999 at ninety-eight and has more or less trended down ever since.

Even without outright opponents of the death penalty like Brennan, Marshall, and (eventually) Blackmun, the Court in the Bush years imposed new limits on executions. In 2002, the Court said judges alone, without the concurrence of jurors, could not impose death sentences; also that year, the justices ruled that the execution of the mentally retarded violated the Eighth Amendment's ban on cruel and unusual punishment. These rulings all came over the vigorous dissents of Rehnquist, Scalia, and Thomas—sometimes joined by Kennedy or O'Connor, who was an especially strong supporter of the death penalty—but the shift on the Court as a whole was unmistakable.

Even in light of these developments, Kennedy's performance at the oral argument of *Roper v. Simmons* was stunning.

"Let's focus on the word 'unusual.' Forget 'cruel' for the moment," Kennedy said to James R. Layton, the local prosecutor in Jefferson City, who was defending the Missouri law. "We've seen very substantial demonstration that world opinion is against this, at least as interpreted by the leaders of the European Union. Does that have a bearing on what's 'unusual'? Suppose it were shown that the United States were one of the very, very few countries that executed juveniles, and that's true. Does that have a bearing on whether or not it's 'unusual'?"

No, said Layton. "The decision as to the Eighth Amendment should not be based on what happens in the rest of the world. It needs to be based on the mores of American society."

Playing his familiar populist card, Scalia jumped in, asking, "Have the countries of the European Union abolished the death penalty by popular vote?" Plainly baffled by this detour into foreign lands, Layton said he didn't know. But Scalia did know—and pointed out that European elites had abolished the death penalty in their countries even though "public opinion polls in a number of the countries support the death penalty."

Kennedy, who saw where Scalia was going, said, "I acknowledged that in my question. I recognize it is the leadership in many of these countries that objects to it. But let us assume that it's an accepted practice in most countries of the world not to execute a juvenile for moral reasons. That has no bearing on whether or not what we're doing is 'unusual'?"

None, said Layton.

Breyer came to Kennedy's aid, pointing out that James Madison and his colleagues drew on foreign sources in writing the Constitution. Surely, said Breyer, there was no reason to think the framers "thought it was totally irrelevant what happened elsewhere in the world to the word 'unusual.'" Abraham Lincoln studied William Blackstone, the great English legal scholar, and "I think he thought that the Founding Fathers studied Blackstone, and all that happened in England was relevant; is there some special reason why what happens abroad would not be relevant here?" (As usual at oral argument, the lawyer was largely a spectator as the justices talked to one another.)

Kennedy turned the question around: "Do we ever take the position that what we do here should influence what people think elsewhere?" Kennedy had spent much of the previous decade trying to influence "what people think" as a missionary for constitutional democracy and the rule of law. But like many other missionaries, Kennedy turned out to be as changed by his journeys as were the people he was trying to convert.

"You thought that Mr. Jefferson thought that what we did here had no bearing on the rest of the world?" Kennedy went on.

Layton said he couldn't speak for Thomas Jefferson.

Ginsburg suggested the Declaration of Independence supplied the answer. "But did he not also say that to lead the world, we would have to show a 'decent respect for the opinions of mankind'?"

All this talk about the international exchange of ideas was more than Scalia could take, so he cut it off with a wisecrack: "What did John Adams think of the French?" The audience laughed.

But Kennedy had made his position clear. The vote in conference was 5–4 to strike down the death penalty for juvenile offenders and to overrule Scalia's fifteen-year-old opinion holding otherwise. Stevens, the senior justice in a majority that also included Souter, Ginsburg, and Breyer, wisely assigned the case to Kennedy, who had shown so much passion about the issue. His opinion turned out to be unlike any in the Court's history. Kennedy began by finding "a national consensus against the death penalty for juveniles," even though twenty states still allowed such executions to take place. But the heart of the opinion—and certainly the most unusual part—was Kennedy's reliance on international evidence to reach his conclusion.

"Our determination that the death penalty is disproportionate punishment for offenders under 18 finds confirmation in the stark reality that the United States is the only country in the world that continues to give official sanction to the juvenile death penalty," he wrote. "This reality does not become controlling, for the task of interpreting the Eighth Amendment remains our responsibility." The evidence from foreign countries may not have been "controlling," but it was obviously highly important to Kennedy and his colleagues in the majority. He noted that the United States had only dismal company in countries that had executed juvenile offenders since 1990: Iran, Pakistan, Saudi Arabia, Yemen, Nigeria, the Democratic Republic of Congo, and China. But since then, even those countries had renounced the practice.

"In sum, it is fair to say that the United States now stands alone in a world that has turned its face against the juvenile death penalty," Kennedy wrote, adding, "The opinion of the world community, while not controlling our outcome, does provide respected and significant

confirmation for our own conclusions." Kennedy ended his opinion in
Roper with one of his orotund, and not entirely comprehensible, per-
orations: "Not the least of the reasons we honor the Constitution,
then, is because we know it to be our own. It does not lessen our fi-
delity to the Constitution or our pride in its origins to acknowledge
that the express affirmation of certain fundamental rights by other nations and peoples simply underscores the centrality of those same
rights within our own heritage of freedom."

It was left to Scalia, once again, to ask what Kennedy's embrace of
foreign sources really meant. "Though the views of our own citizens
are essentially irrelevant to the Court's decision today," he noted with
characteristic asperity, "the views of other countries and the so-called
international community take center stage." But Kennedy had not
put forth any sort of standard by which to determine when the United
States should follow the rest of the world and when it should not.
Scalia went through a long list of areas where American law differed
from others—reliance on juries, the exclusionary rule, separation of
church and state—and he returned, as ever, to his bête noire: "And let
us not forget the Court's abortion jurisprudence, which makes us one
of only six countries that allow abortion on demand until the point of
viability."

With some force, Scalia argued that the Court's grazing among foreign laws was really just an excuse to shape the law "to the justices'
own notion of how the world ought to be." In concluding he warned,
"To invoke alien law when it agrees with one's own thinking, and ignore it otherwise, is not reasoned decisionmaking, but sophistry."

The response to this pointed debate over the influence of foreign
law showed how much Kennedy had strayed from the values of the
contemporary Republican Party. Like O'Connor, Kennedy had come
of age at a time when the GOP stood for low taxes and limited government, but he increasingly saw social issues define his party. As
Kennedy soon learned, hostility to international law—and international institutions like the United Nations—had also become a central tenet of the GOP. In his earnest, even naive way, Kennedy
believed his recognition of foreign law amounted to a corollary to
Bush's evangelism for spreading freedom around the world. "If we are
asking the rest of the world to adopt our idea of freedom, it does seem
to me that there may be some mutuality there, that other nations and
other peoples can define and interpret freedom in a way that's at least
instructive to us," he once said.

In truth, all Kennedy was doing was showing how out of touch he
was with the modern Republican Party. After *Roper*, fifty-four conservatives in the House of Representatives sponsored a resolution crit-
icizing the use of foreign sources by the Supreme Court, and
Representative Steve King, a Republican from Iowa, conducted an investigation of the justices' foreign trips, based on the disclosure forms
that they are required to file. "Between 1998 and 2003, the justices
took a total of ninety-three foreign trips," King said. "And the impli-
cation is that there are at least a couple of justices, chiefly Kennedy
and Breyer, who are more enamored of the 'enlightenment' of the
world than they are bound by our own Constitution."

Every year, one or two justices testified before Congress in support
of the Court's annual budget request, and Kennedy often took on
the assignment. In his testimony after *Roper*, he mentioned in passing that he used the Internet for legal research. This prompted
Tom DeLay, the House majority leader, to tell an interviewer from
Fox News Radio, "We've got Justice Kennedy writing decisions
based upon international law, not the Constitution of the United
States. That's just outrageous, and, not only that, he said in session
that he does his own research on the Internet. That is just incredibly
outrageous." (As DeLay apparently did not know, virtually all legal
research, in U.S. as well as foreign law, is now conducted on the
Internet.)

A few weeks later, near the end of the Court's term, Kennedy gave
a pointed retort to DeLay. For a reunion of Chief Justice Rehnquist's
law clerks, he made a brief video during which he was taped sitting
at his computer. He said that he was doing a little research. He signed
off by saying good-bye in several languages.

The video allowed Kennedy to shrug off DeLay's criticism with a
cheery wink. But there was no mistaking the fact that the Bush presidency was poisoning the atmosphere around the Court, if not inside
it. Ever since his apostasy on abortion in *Casey*, Kennedy had been
anathema to the conservative movement, but his citations to foreign
law tapped into a deep nativism on the right as well. The backlash
against him was fierce. For a time, Souter had been the principal
Republican target, but Kennedy's authorship of high-profile opinions
had made him the public symbol of conservative betrayal.

At a conservative conference in Washington shortly after *Roper*,
Phyllis Schlafly, the veteran antifeminist leader, said Kennedy's decision was "a good ground for impeachment." Michael P. Farris, chair-

man of the Home School Legal Defense Association, said Kennedy "should be the poster boy for impeachment," for citing international law. "If our congressmen and senators do not have the courage to impeach and remove from office Justice Kennedy, they ought to be impeached as well." Given Kennedy's role on the Court in the culture war cases, it wasn't just hyperbole when James Dobson, the founder and director of Focus on the Family, called Kennedy "the most dangerous man in America."

But the right had no monopoly on partisan vitriol aimed at the justices. The left, too, had its favored target. To be sure, Thomas was still widely despised, because of Anita Hill and his voting record on the Court; but because Thomas generally limited his public appearances to friendly audiences, he was rarely visible to his enemies. It was Scalia—brazen, outspoken, gleefully confrontational—who was the conservative whom liberals loved to hate.

The battle with his critics that meant the most to Scalia himself had a peculiar origin. In 1990, Byron White wearied of his assignment as the justice supervising the Court of Appeals for the Fifth Circuit. Based in New Orleans, the Fifth Circuit covers the part of the South where many of the nation's executions are scheduled. The resulting cases produce many emergency applications to the Court, and the circuit justice must administer the flow of paper to his colleagues; White no longer wanted the responsibility for keeping track of it. The job of circuit justice also includes making regular trips to the area for conferences that generally also include parties, receptions, and other social occasions. Once Scalia took up his responsibilities in the Fifth Circuit, some lawyers and judges decided to invite him to enjoy the local sport, hunting.

Scalia made an unlikely hunter. He was born in Trenton, in 1936, and raised in Elmhurst, Queens, as the only child in a thoroughly urban (and urbane) family. His father, a translator and a professor of Romance languages at Brooklyn College, was hardly one for outings in the woods. "My father was a much more scholarly and intellectual person than I am," Scalia once said, as recounted by Margaret Talbot. "He always had a book in front of his face." Scalia received a traditional Catholic school education, with four years of Latin and three years of Greek. He attended Georgetown University, excelled on the debate team, and graduated first in his class. His valedictorian address offered hints of both his literary style and his interests. "Our days were spent in hunting; but our prey was more elusive and more valuable than any forest deer or mountain bear or prairie buffalo," he said. "For we were seekers of the truth." He went on to Harvard Law School, where he made law review, and then, after a brief stop at a law firm in Cleveland, served on the faculties of several leading law schools. He spent the seventies and eighties shuttling between academia and increasingly important jobs in the Justice Department of the Nixon and Ford administrations. Along the way, he and his wife, Maureen, had nine children, one of whom became a priest.

It would be a mistake, however, to regard Scalia as just a bookish man. He was on the rifle team in high school (commuting on the New York subway with a .22 carbine), played the piano, sang in school shows, and fought for his intellectual beliefs with a nearly physical intensity. To his father, unchanging certainty about religion or politics, no matter what the current intellectual fad, was a sign of strength, not weakness. Scalia was only too happy to embrace the verities of Catholic doctrine and reject the moral relativism of the modern world. "For the son of God to be born of a virgin? I mean, really. To believe that he rose from the dead and bodily ascended into heaven. How utterly ridiculous," Scalia said at a meeting of the Knights of Columbus, the Catholic fraternal organization. "God assumed from the beginning that the wise of the world would view Christians as fools, and he has not been disappointed."

Scalia relished the skepticism of critics. "Be fools for Christ," he implored his fellow believers. "Have the courage to suffer the contempt of the sophisticated world." Scalia's mindset, of course, was precisely the opposite of Kennedy's; unlike his colleague, Scalia courted the scorn of global elites.

In this spirit, Scalia embraced the hunt. His trips to the Fifth Circuit ignited a passion for the sport, and in time he turned his chambers into a veritable museum of taxidermy, with his kills mounted and displayed on the walls. For behind his desk, Scalia borrowed a magnificent Gilbert Stuart portrait of George Washington from the Smithsonian. But the painting was overshadowed by the gigantic head of an elk whose nose reached practically across the room as if to make the acquaintance of the first president. And on the small table in front of the sofa, where Scalia entertained visitors, was a smaller but even more provocative display—a wooden duck, a reminder that the justice had become perhaps the best-known duck hunter in the country.

Dick Cheney was the executive branch counterpart to Nino Scalia, an object of loathing and suspicion among their political adversaries. The case before the Supreme Court that brought them together revealed a great deal about contemporary Washington.

A few days after George W. Bush took office, Cheney set up a task force on energy with himself as chair. About five months later, the task force issued a report, then went out of business. Two public interest groups, Judicial Watch, a conservative outfit, and the Sierra Club, the liberal environmental organization, sued the vice president, demanding that he release all of the work papers and communications produced by the task force. Cheney refused, claiming that the executive branch had the right to keep such records confidential.

It was difficult to imagine a controversy with lower stakes. Like most other task force reports in the capital, this one was quickly forgotten, its recommendations largely ignored. The fact that Cheney's group conferred with many energy companies was widely known, completely expected, and entirely proper. Not even the plaintiffs seriously suggested that the task force records would reveal any illegality or impropriety. The case was simply part of Washington trench warfare, a process that often includes minor lawsuits like this one, which became known as *Cheney v. United States District Court.* For two years, the case meandered in deserved obscurity through the legal system.

During this period, Scalia continued his hunting forays through the Southern wilderness. Every December, he went duck hunting in rural Louisiana with Wallace Carline, who ran a company that provided services to oil rigs in the Gulf of Mexico. In 2002, Scalia learned that Carline was an admirer of the vice president, whom Scalia knew from their days together in the Ford administration. At Carline's suggestion, Scalia invited Cheney to join them. Given the complexity of everyone's schedules, the trip could not be arranged until January 2004. By coincidence, three weeks before the trip, the Court granted cert on Cheney's appeal of the case involving the records of his energy task force.

The hunting expedition, which began on January 5, 2004, turned into something of a fiasco. Scalia, along with one of his sons and a son-in-law, bought round-trip air tickets, but Cheney invited them along on Air Force Two for the trip to the small airstrip in the town of Patterson. Residents had never seen anything like Cheney's entourage. The government had already made two reconnaissance trips in November and December, and then the vice president's plane was preceded on arrival day by two Black Hawk air combat helicopters that hovered over the landing area, and followed by a second Air Force jet that carried staff and security aides to the vice president. No photography was allowed as Cheney, Scalia, and about thirteen others got into a line of armored sport utility vehicles.

Carline's compound was usually described as a hunting camp, but it was actually an enormous barge—about 150 feet by 50 feet—that was anchored in the marsh wherever the hunting was best. On top of the barge was a houselike structure with a few small bedrooms, which the group shared in groups of two or three, although Cheney was given his own. Meals were served family style, and hunting was in two- or three-man blinds. (Cheney and Scalia were never in the same one.)

It was raining when Cheney's plane arrived, and it never stopped during the two days the vice president remained. (Scalia and his family stayed for four days.) Counterintuitively, the weather apparently was too wet even for ducks, because few of the targeted greenheads and teals were seen and even fewer killed. Carline said it was the worst duck hunting in thirty-five years.

Later that month, the *Los Angeles Times*, as well as the local *Daily Review* of Morgan City, Louisiana, disclosed the trip, and the Sierra Club asked Scalia to recuse himself from the energy task force case, which was to be argued in April. Curiously, there are no formal rules governing when Supreme Court justices must withdraw from cases. Unlike judges on the lower federal courts (which do have such rules), a Supreme Court justice cannot be replaced in a given case; ties at the Supreme Court amount to an affirmance of the lower court. Because of these unfortunate consequences, the justices are reluctant to drop out. The general rule said justices should withdraw if their "impartiality might reasonably be questioned"—whatever that meant.

The motion to recuse Scalia reflected a trend in Washington to turn disagreements over substantive issues into matters of personal ethics. In the nineties, Republicans pursued Clinton on many frivolous controversies. Later, without control of either house of Congress, Democrats had limited options for payback, but this attack on

Scalia—a kind of petty harassment—was one. There was never any evidence that he and Cheney discussed the case or that Scalia, whose views on the rights of the executive branch were well established, was influenced by the joint outing. In all, the case for Scalia to recuse himself was weak. Cheney had been sued not as an individual but in his official capacity (meaning the case would continue if Cheney left office), and the Supreme Court hears cases against prominent government officials all the time. Most important, by historical standards, the relationship between Scalia and Cheney was hardly unusual; indeed, other executive branch officials and Supreme Court justices have enjoyed much closer friendships.

Breyer, among others, urged Scalia to avoid the controversy, recuse himself, and forget about the whole matter. (This was typical advice from the notoriously conflict-averse Breyer.) Scalia refused. Indeed, after stewing for weeks, he produced an unusual, and unintentionally amusing, public memorandum that was released shortly before the task force case was argued. Scalia's twenty-one-page jeremiad included commonsense observations ("Many Justices have reached this Court precisely because they were friends of the incumbent President"), detailed historical references (several justices played poker with Roosevelt and Truman), and gratuitous attacks on "so-called investigative journalists" for their errors (the *San Antonio Express-News* said the duck-hunting trip lasted nine days).

The memo also included a detailed account of the trip and even Scalia's personal expenses. (His round-trip fare, with an unused half, was still cheaper than buying a one-way ticket, so the ride with Cheney did not save the Scalia clan any money.) Scalia leavened his self-righteousness with a measure of self-pity, noting that he had "becom[e] (as the motion cruelly but accurately states) fodder for late-night comedians." In its brief, the Sierra Club had helpfully supplied examples, like Jay Leno on *The Tonight Show* describing an "embarrassing moment" for Cheney when he visited the White House. "Security made him empty his pockets and out fell Justice Antonin Scalia!"

On balance, Scalia seems to have been correct to remain on the case, which ended with a tangled set of opinions that basically resolved the case in Cheney's favor. (Scalia voted for Cheney's side; Souter and Ginsburg dissented.) With characteristic bravado, Scalia started referring in public to the Cheney controversy as his "proudest" moment as a justice. "The rest took smarts—that took character," he said. It speaks to Scalia's messianic sense of himself that he would choose this insignificant matter—rather than, say, the selection of a president or any number of literally life-or-death controversies.

Scalia's colleagues were used to his dramatics on and off the court, and they collectively greeted the latest controversy with little more than a roll of the eyes. As O'Connor would often say, "That's just Nino." Perhaps Ginsburg put it best in a speech in Hawaii a few months later, when she said a deer killed by Scalia made for delicious venison at their families' traditional New Year's feast. "Justice Scalia," she observed dryly, "has been more successful at deer hunting than he has at duck hunting."

The personal attacks on Kennedy and Scalia illustrated how the polarized ideological environment radiated into the Court itself. The justices remained cordial toward one another, but ideologues outside the Court treated them as if they were just another set of partisans. The fiction that they dwelled outside politics became increasingly difficult to sustain.

The undertow dragging the Court into politics disturbed all the justices, but especially O'Connor. Splitting the difference came naturally to her, but it wasn't possible in every case. During the early years of the Bush presidency, a case was heading to the Court that, to a degree almost unprecedented in history, was directed to a single justice—O'Connor. Her struggle in that case to place the Court in the center of American life—and herself in the center of the Court—became her defining moment.

BEFORE SPEAKING,
SAYING SOMETHING

The problems began with John Ashcroft.

Ashcroft, the former Missouri senator whom Bush named his first attorney general, embodied everything that O'Connor disdained about the modern Republican Party. He was extreme, polarizing, and moralistic—*unattractive*. One of O'Connor's favorite former law clerks was Viet Dinh, who in the course of an extraordinary life fled Vietnam as a boat person and later became a professor of law at Georgetown. When O'Connor heard that Dinh had taken a senior job under Ashcroft, she was appalled. "Working with Ashcroft, he's ruining his career," she told another former clerk.

But O'Connor was wrong. Dinh was actually enhancing his career by associating with Ashcroft, because it was Ashcroft's brand of conservatism, not O'Connor's, that was ascendant in George W. Bush's Washington. O'Connor herself would come to understand this new reality. The story of O'Connor's disillusion with the GOP—and with Bush himself—was the story of her last years on the bench and the final transformation of the Rehnquist Court.

There were early hints that the Bush administration would head in a direction that O'Connor did not expect. The Ashcroft choice was one, and September 11 was another. She and Stephen Breyer were together in India on the day of the attacks, planning to meet with local judges, and they had to struggle for days to secure travel arrangements home. But it was O'Connor's little-noticed reaction to the attacks that showed another way she was slipping away from the Bush orbit.

As with Kennedy, world travel played an important part of O'Connor's ideological journey. Even after O'Connor turned seventy, in 2000, she remained the Court's most indefatigable tourist. (Ginsburg's secretary, who fielded many invitations from the groups that O'Connor had already visited, joked that O'Connor had been so many places that she must have a secret twin sister.)

In her no-nonsense way, O'Connor took advantage of the fact that she was the only celebrity on the Court, showing the country and the world that a woman could serve at the highest level of government. In that respect, her mere presence was sometimes the only message she wanted to impart, but often, especially in later years, O'Connor tried to get across more pointed ideas. She led a delegation of judges to China for the first court-to-court exchange between the United States and the People's Republic, for example. There, in a beautifully appointed room in Beijing, O'Connor sat side by side with President Jiang Zemin, sipping tea out of an elegant porcelain cup and talking about his upcoming trip to President Bush's Crawford, Texas, ranch. As the audience drew to a close, O'Connor leaned over to the Chinese leader and said very slowly and carefully—each had an interpreter— "Mr. President, I cannot leave without reminding you that our country remains deeply concerned about China's treatment of prisoners of conscience." Jiang did not reply.

O'Connor wanted to see the ruins of Ground Zero before they stopped smoldering. On September 28, 2001, when travel to New York was still difficult, O'Connor and her husband kept a long-standing appointment to preside over the groundbreaking of a new building at New York University Law School. (This was her seventh visit to NYU—an institution to which she had no special ties—and she made similar repeat visits to many other law schools around the country.) With the grace of a skilled politician, she began her remarks with reflections on the moment in history. "As the Irishman said, before I speak, I want to say something," she began. "John and I have come to New York City from time to time, as westerners do, especially in the twenty years since I myself have been an East Coast resident. . . . We made a detour early this morning, to go down to the end of the island to get a glimpse, if we could, of the incredible damage done on September the eleventh. I am still tearful from that glimpse." As if on cue, a siren began blaring, the nearly constant background noise of those traumatic days in New York. It wasn't a day for an ordinary speech, and O'Connor did not give one.

"The trauma that our nation suffered will [alter] and has already altered our way of life," O'Connor said, "and it will cause us to reexamine some of our laws pertaining to criminal surveillance, wiretapping, immigration, and so on. It is possible, if not likely, that we will rely more on international rules of law than on our cherished constitutional standards for criminal prosecutions in responding to threats to our national security. As a result, we are likely to experience more restrictions on our personal freedom than has ever been the case in our country. We shall be considering and debating among ourselves all the aspects of our nation's response to terrorism. We wish it were not necessary. We wish we could set the clock back to a time of greater peace and prosperity. But we cannot. We are forced to face the reality of a deadly enemy and of people who are willing to sacrifice everything in order to cause harm to our country. As Margaret Thatcher said, when law ends, tyranny begins."

O'Connor was careful, as she had to be, to avoid taking any specific positions on issues that might come before the Court, but she was showing considerable prescience—and concern. Even in these first few days after the attack, O'Connor was warning about a coming clash between national security and civil liberties. She had not been impressed by the Ashcroft Justice Department and did not fully trust it to provide the appropriate balance. O'Connor's prominent reference to "international rules" was no accident. The Bush administration had already made clear its hostility to international law and institutions, and O'Connor was laying down a subtle marker that she, in notable contrast, had a great deal of faith in the worldwide community of judges and lawyers.

The trip to India where she was stranded with Breyer a few weeks earlier was typical of her travel. O'Connor went abroad not, as Kennedy did, principally to indulge in high-flown rhetoric about the rule of law but rather as a problem solver. She had particular interests in juvenile justice and the role of women in law, and she sought out programs on these subjects. It was no coincidence that she found an ally in Breyer, the Court's leading technocrat. He, too, liked to find practical solutions to problems—how to increase the number of women lawyers, how to provide child care for jurors. Because of their trips, and because they were probably the two least neurotic personalities on the Court, O'Connor and Breyer ultimately became closer than any other pair of justices.

There was an ideological component to O'Connor's travels, too. She often told the story of an earlier trip to India, when she went to hear an argument before that nation's highest court, in New Delhi. The case involved a dispute between Hindus and Muslims over government benefits. But as the argument began, O'Connor was surprised to hear the lawyers on both sides citing precedents from the United States Supreme Court in support of their positions. At one point, the lawyers were debating the meaning of an opinion that O'Connor herself had written about the separation of church and state. As O'Connor said in a speech after she returned, "When life or liberty is at stake, the landmark judgments of the Supreme Court of the United States . . . are studied with as much attention in New Delhi or Strasbourg as they are in Washington, D.C., or the state of Washington, or Springfield, Illinois. This reliance, unfortunately, has not been reciprocal."

O'Connor's alienation from her party did not happen overnight, nor did it ever amount to a complete breach. Her rebellion took place mostly on issues relating to the culture wars—like abortion, church-state relations, and gay rights—but she hardly turned into an across-the-board liberal. On criminal cases, including the death penalty, she remained a hard-liner; on federalism and states' rights, she stayed a firm ally of Rehnquist's. On one issue, fatefully, for the country and within the Court, O'Connor remained poised on dead center—race.

When O'Connor joined the Court in 1981, civil rights still occupied a major part of the justices' agenda. One of her early major opinions for the Court, in 1989, set out her views on the subject—in typically opaque fashion.

Richmond, Virginia, passed a local ordinance requiring businesses contracting with the city to set aside 30 percent of their subcontracts for minority-owned enterprises. After losing a contract for installing stainless steel toilets at the city jail because it lacked the required minority subcontractors, the J. A. Croson Company sued the city, claiming a violation of the Equal Protection Clause. The Court agreed, striking down the set-aside program by a 6–3 vote in *Richmond v. Croson*. O'Connor was assigned to write the opinion.

To do so, O'Connor had to wade into one of the thorniest debates in constitutional law. Five decades earlier, the Roosevelt appointees made sure that the Court vindicated the constitutionality of the New Deal. Henceforth, if Congress or a state legislature approved a statute, the justices weren't going to interfere with the democratic process. But that approach left a major question unanswered. What if a state passed a law that discriminated against a minority group—as, for example, the Southern states did all the time? What if a state said only whites could vote in primaries or serve on juries? Would the Court let those laws stand, too? The justices answered such questions with the most famous footnote in the Court's history. In note 4 of *United States v. Carolene Products*, an otherwise minor case from 1938, Justice Harlan Fiske Stone suggested the Court would treat different kinds of laws in different ways. In cases about economic or property rights, the justices would defer to the political process. But when it came to laws that appeared to be targeted at racial minorities or other "discrete and insular minorities," the Court would apply "more searching judicial scrutiny."

As later justices interpreted the famous footnote, this meant that if a law appeared to discriminate against blacks, the justices would apply what became known as "strict scrutiny" to see if the law was justified. During the civil rights revolution of the 1960s, the Supreme Court repeatedly applied strict scrutiny to all laws that contained racial classifications—all of Jim Crow—and struck them down. As the Court's precedents evolved, it became clear that if the justices were going to examine a law with strict scrutiny, that law was invariably doomed.

The major complication to this doctrine of law emerged in the 1970s, when governments and companies started programs that were supposed to help blacks and other minorities. These affirmative action initiatives included explicitly racial classifications. Should the Court apply strict scrutiny and strike down laws that were supposed to *help* blacks in the same way it invalidated laws that were supposed to *hurt* them? Should the law treat "reverse discrimination" against whites the same way it treated old-fashioned discrimination against blacks? Those were the questions that O'Connor had to answer in the *Croson* case. Specifically, should the Court apply strict scrutiny to the set-aside program that explicitly required a degree of racial balance?

To answer, O'Connor did what came naturally to her. She split the difference. For O'Connor, there was no doubt that the Richmond ordinance contained a racial classification that disadvantaged whites. "The Richmond Plan denies certain citizens the opportunity to compete for a fixed percentage of public contracts based solely upon their race," she wrote. As such, O'Connor decreed, the plan deserved strict scrutiny from the Court: "The standard of review under the Equal Protection Clause is not dependent on the race of those burdened or benefited by a particular classification." This in itself was a major development; it was the first time that the Court applied strict scrutiny to a law that was intended to help blacks.

Historically, strict scrutiny of a law or government program meant automatic invalidation. Was O'Connor ruling out all race-conscious programs, even if they were designed to help disadvantaged minorities? No, not exactly, because here was where O'Connor hedged. Richmond had put its set-aside plan in place without any research on whether minority subcontractors had been discriminated against in that city. The law was based solely on the general sense that there had been a history of discrimination in the field. To O'Connor, that was an inadequate justification, but she raised the possibility that a city might make findings that did justify a racially conscious set-aside plan. "Nothing we say today precludes a state or local entity from taking action to rectify the effects of identified discrimination within its jurisdiction," she wrote. "If the city of Richmond had evidence before it that nonminority contractors were systematically excluding minority businesses from subcontracting opportunities, it could take action to end the discriminatory exclusion."

So the O'Connor position seemed to be that affirmative action was permissible, but only as redress for identifiable discrimination against specific people. Her standard raised as many questions as it settled. What was systematic discrimination? How could it be identified? Did remedies have to go only to the specific victims? Or could the benefits go to a minority community at large? O'Connor never spelled out the answers to all these uncertainties, but she did stick with the same basic ideas in subsequent cases: some affirmative action was permissible—but not too much.

If O'Connor's position on racial issues remained something of a mystery, those of her colleagues did not. Four of them—Rehnquist, Scalia, Kennedy, and Thomas—believed in a "color-blind" Constitution; they thought all laws that drew distinctions based on race, including those that purported to help minorities, should be struck down. Four others—Stevens, Souter, Ginsburg, and Breyer—believed that for the most part government and businesses could give advantages to racial minorities, either to redress prior discrimination or to foster the goal of diversity. More than on any other issue, the Court was divided four-to-four-to-one.

No school in the nation made a greater commitment to affirmative action than the University of Michigan, especially in admissions. Given the vast size of its undergraduate college, Michigan used a statistical test, based primarily on grades and SAT results, for most admissions decisions. Because blacks generally scored lower than whites in both categories, a purely numerical admissions process would have resulted in virtually all-white and Asian classes. Under the program that Michigan adopted, the boosts for minority applicants could be substantial. A minority applicant with a 3.5 grade-point average and a combined SAT score of 1200 would automatically be accepted, and a white candidate with the same scores would likely be rejected. The law school admission process, which involved fewer students, entailed more individualized assessments of applicants but still gave significant advantages to blacks. One year, among applicants with grade-point averages between 3.25 and 3.49 and LSAT scores between 156 and 158, one of fifty-one whites was admitted, and ten of ten blacks were.

Conservative public interest groups like the Center for Individual Rights—a civil rights counterpart to Jay Sekulow's religion-based outfit—had been scouring the country to find the right places to challenge racial preferences. The stark numbers at Michigan made the school an inviting target, as did the availability of sympathetic plaintiffs.

Barbara Grutter was one of nine children of a minister in the Calvinist Christian Reformed Church. When her own children were small, she ran a medical consulting business out of her house, and eventually decided to apply to the University of Michigan Law School, which had a joint program in her field, health care management, and law. She had a 3.8 grade-point average from her undergraduate days at Michigan State and scored 161 on the LSAT. A black student with those grades and scores would certainly have been admitted to the law school, but Grutter was placed on the waiting list and then rejected. Jennifer Gratz, also white, was similarly well qualified for admission to Michigan's undergraduate program and was also placed on the waiting list and then rejected. Both women filed their lawsuits in late 1997, and then began their long march through the federal trial and appellate courts.

From the start, both cases—*Grutter v. Bollinger* and *Gratz v. Bollinger*—were causes célèbres. (Lee C. Bollinger was then president of the University of Michigan.) By some reckonings, the Court was moving in the direction of striking down all racial preferences, and the Michigan cases appeared to be nearly ideal vehicles for supporting that position. O'Connor herself seemed to be inching rightward on the issue, most notably in her opinion for the Court in *Adarand Constructors, Inc. v. Pena*, in 1995. There she reversed a lower court ruling that upheld a federal affirmative action program for minority contractors, but she saw no reason to rule on every affirmative action program in the context of that single case; still, the judicial momentum, as well as the rhetorical energy, seemed to belong to the opponents of such programs. As Scalia put it, in a concurring opinion in *Adarand*, "In the eyes of the government, we are just one race here. It is American." In 1996, the Fifth Circuit struck down the use of affirmative action in admissions at the University of Texas—a prelude, many thought, to the same decision on a nationwide basis by the Supreme Court. The justices denied cert in the Texas case.

At that point, though, an unlikely savior of the Michigan program, and all affirmative action, stepped forward—and he happened to be the most famous Wolverine in the country.

More than most ex-presidents, Gerald R. Ford kept his distance from political controversy after leaving office, but he retained a special interest in the workings of his alma mater. And in 1999, the eighty-six-year-old former varsity football star decided to make a public stand in support of affirmative action at the University of Michigan. He wrote an op-ed piece in the *New York Times* entitled "Inclusive America, Under Attack." There Ford said, "A pair of lawsuits . . . would prohibit [Michigan] and other universities from even considering race as one of many factors weighed by admission counselors." Such a move would condemn "future college students to suffer the cultural and social impoverishment that afflicted my generation."

On September 15, 1999, a month after the article ran, Ford had dinner with James M. Cannon, one of his former White House aides, in Grand Rapids. (The two men were in town to hear a speech at Ford's presidential museum by his only appointee to the Supreme Court, John Paul Stevens.) Ford encouraged Cannon to do what he could to help the university in the lawsuit, and the following day Cannon met with Bollinger in Ann Arbor. Cannon had served on the board of visitors of the U.S. Naval Academy, and he knew how important affirmative action had been to the military, especially its officer corps. Cannon had been told many times that the navy did not want ships full of enlisted men, who tended to be heavily minority, being commanded by all-white groups of officers. Affirmative action wasn't social engineering; it was military necessity—a message that Bollinger wanted to make sure the justices received.

The Michigan tactics in front of the justices came to resemble a political campaign as much as a litigation strategy—which was fitting for a Court that hewed so closely to public opinion on controversial issues. Bollinger and his team knew that the key to winning O'Connor's vote, and thus the case, was mobilizing establishment support for affirmative action. Civil rights groups, even other universities, would be expected to support Michigan's position, but the justices had to know that support for affirmative action transcended what was left of the traditional Democratic Party coalition.

Earlier, when the case was before the district court, Bollinger and Marvin Krislov, the university's general counsel, had persuaded General Motors to submit an amicus curiae, or friend of the court, brief on behalf of the university's program, focusing on the importance of developing a diverse workforce for Michigan's most famous corporate citizen. In the Supreme Court, the university recruited sixty-five of the Fortune 500 to sign a brief in support of its affirmative action program, and it would come to be endorsed by most of the biggest and most respected companies in the country, including Boeing, Coca-Cola, General Electric, and Microsoft. As those companies told the justices in their brief, "Today's global marketplace and the increasing diversity in the American population demand the cross-cultural experience and understanding gained from [an education where students] are exposed to diverse people, ideas, perspectives, and interactions."

But the military was potentially an even greater ally for the university. Active duty officers could not take a stand on such a controversial issue, but the team that Ford set in motion sought out the next best thing—retired military officers. Krislov contacted Joseph Reeder, a Washington lawyer who had been undersecretary of the army in the Clinton administration, and he began recruiting high-profile retirees to sign a brief. The group eventually included H. Norman Schwarzkopf, John Shalikashvili, Hugh Shelton, William J. Crowe, and two dozen others. To write the military brief, the Michigan team recruited Carter Phillips and his colleague Virginia

Seitz, pillars of the Supreme Court bar and thus not at all usual suspects in a civil rights case.

"Based on decades of experience, amici have concluded that a highly qualified, racially diverse officer corps educated and trained to command our nation's racially diverse enlisted ranks is essential to the military's ability to fulfill its principal mission to provide national security," Phillips began his brief. Enlisted military were 21.7 percent African American, while the officer corps was only 8.8 percent black. "The officer corps must continue to be diverse or the cohesiveness essential to the military mission will be critically undermined," he continued.

Then, in the key section of the brief, Phillips showed that the three major service academies—West Point, Annapolis, and Colorado Springs—all practiced race-conscious affirmative action in admissions. (So did the broader ROTC program.) It wasn't enough to say that the military should simply recruit more in minority neighborhoods; the armed services had to extend special treatment—affirmative action—to its minority applicants. In other words, "At present, the military cannot achieve an officer corps that is *both* highly qualified *and* racially diverse unless the service academies and the ROTC use limited race-conscious recruiting and admissions policies."

The implicit question at the heart of the retired officers' brief was, if affirmative action was good enough for the service academies, why wasn't it good enough for the University of Michigan?

And that, precisely, was what Sandra O'Connor was asking herself.

17

THE GREEN BRIEF

The period leading up to the *Grutter* and *Gratz* decisions—the early part of 2003—was not an easy time for O'Connor. Her husband John's condition had continued to deteriorate. He had started to accompany her to work every day, and the justice hired his former secretary to keep an eye on him as he sat on the couch in her office, chatting or reading the newspaper. No one uttered the word *Alzheimer's* at the Court, but the nature of John's problem was increasingly obvious to all.

The justice and her husband would arrive together in time for her exercise class in the morning, stay through their lunch together, and then return home at about two, when she would read briefs. Even then, they never stopped going out at night, to embassy parties, museum openings and the like, just as O'Connor had continued making the rounds fifteen years earlier, when she was weakened by her chemotherapy for breast cancer. In her forthright, determined way, O'Connor did not believe in making concessions to illness, her own or anyone else's.

O'Connor's own health was fine, despite a persistent tremor that she had had for years. For her morning exercise class, she added salsa dancing to step aerobics and Pilates. She still loved the work of the Court and always sought more of it. O'Connor never signed on to Rehnquist's crusade to cut the Court's docket and thus was always urging her clerks to scour the petitions for cases where she could vote for cert. "Find us some good cases!" she would say.

Still, like many older people, O'Connor resisted changes to her routine, especially the one promised by an impending renovation project at the Court. The building had not been upgraded since it opened in

1935, and Rehnquist had prevailed upon Congress to fund a full over-
haul. Each of the justices would have to vacate his or her chambers for
a while, and O'Connor was slated to be the first evacuee, in 2004. A
pack rat who loved her view and her office, especially now that John
was joining her there every day, O'Connor dreaded the prospect of
moving to the Siberia of the Court's second floor.

By now, O'Connor usually had little trouble making up her mind
about how to vote. She assigned one clerk to write a bench memo on
each case to be argued and then invited the other clerks to write counter-
memos if they did not agree with their colleague's recommendation.
This was the year that O'Connor cut back to a five-day schedule—there
were no more crockpot lunches for her clerks on Saturdays—but she still
went over each case with them before oral arguments. She did not agonize. Having laid out her views for her clerks, she had them help her
craft some questions for the lawyers for both sides. She didn't believe in
playing devil's advocate, either. The tilt of her questions at oral argument almost always showed the way she was going to vote.

But *Grutter* and *Gratz* were different. They were not easy cases for
O'Connor. This time, she *did* agonize. In the first place, the stakes were
enormous. Unlike some high-profile cases before the justices, the
Michigan lawsuits had more than symbolic importance. Admissions decisions for thousands of students were at stake, and so, less directly, was
all affirmative action in government and private companies. (In contrast, because there were so few actual prosecutions for sodomy, *Lawrence
v. Texas*, which was argued the same year, had fewer immediate, real-
world consequences.) In addition, O'Connor's favorite route through
any problem—the middle of the road—wasn't readily obvious. Either
universities could consider the race of their applicants or they couldn't;
even O'Connor would have trouble finessing that kind of choice.

In the weeks leading up to the argument, O'Connor sequestered
herself in her office, poring over the briefs of the parties and the amicus briefs as well. Stewing over the Michigan cases at length—a rar-
ity in itself—she would pop out of her office with cryptic and
sometimes contradictory observations. She was thinking out loud.

"I need to be consistent with what I said in *Croson* and *Adarand*."
This suggested a vote for the plaintiffs. (O'Connor thought that a justice being inconsistent was . . . unattractive.)

"Race consciousness is a pernicious thing."

But O'Connor also said:

"What if these schools become all-white? Can we live with that?"

"This isn't government contracting. This is education. And Lewis said that education was different."

"Lewis" was Lewis Powell, O'Connor's mentor on the Court and her predecessor as its swing vote. The key precedent in the area was Powell's opinion from 1978 in *Regents of the University of California v. Bakke*, where the Court struck down a rigid quota system for minorities at the state medical school at Davis. (In each year's class, the university reserved sixteen of one hundred seats for minorities.) In that case, no opinion of the Court commanded a majority, but Powell's came the closest and his view came to be considered the prevailing law on the subject. Powell rejected the quota system at Davis, but he did say that universities could use race as one factor in admissions. His reasoning was somewhat unusual for his time. In the seventies, the main justification offered for affirmative action tended to be that the nation owed a special debt to blacks and other historically disadvantaged groups; because of decades of discrimination, mere equal treatment was not enough to provide them a fair chance.

But Powell justified affirmative action because of what it did for everyone, not just for its immediate beneficiaries. In his view, diversity—a buzzword that came into wide use only after *Bakke*—helped all students of all races. "The nation's future depends upon leaders trained through wide exposure to the ideas and mores of students as diverse as this Nation of many peoples," Powell wrote, so "race or ethnic background may be deemed a 'plus' in a particular applicant's file." (Powell quoted at length from the admissions plan at Harvard College, which stated, in part, that "the race of an applicant may tip the balance in his favor just as geographic origin or a life spent on a farm may tip the balance in other candidates' cases.") In the subsequent twenty-five years, Powell's rationale had become the dominant intellectual justification for affirmative action—not as a handout to the downtrodden but as a net benefit to the society as a whole.

The question in *Grutter* and *Gratz* was whether Powell's ruling should remain on the books. As the justices emerged from behind the red curtain to hear argument on the morning of April 1, 2003, not even O'Connor's clerks knew how she would vote.

The fact that the cases happened to be argued that month was crucially important. Less than two weeks earlier, on March 20, American and allied forces launched their invasion of Iraq. In this initial period, the war looked like a tremendous success, as American troops cut through Iraqi resistance and stormed toward Baghdad. As a result, in the country and at the Court, the military was held in especially high regard. By the morning of the arguments in *Grutter* and *Gratz*, coalition forces had closed to within about forty miles of the Iraqi capital, and there was even more dramatic good news that day for the U.S. military. Army Pfc. Jessica Lynch, who had been kidnapped in Iraq on March 23 and thus become a symbol of American determination, was freed in a raid by Special Operations forces. (Like the war itself, Lynch's story turned out to be more complicated than it originally seemed.) In short, though, the arguments in *Grutter* and *Gratz* took place at a moment when confidence in the American military was soaring.

In specific terms, there were two legal questions at issue. In light of O'Connor's opinion in *Croson*, the Michigan lawyers knew that the Court would apply strict scrutiny to the affirmative action programs. So the first question was whether fostering diversity could ever be a "compelling interest"—that is, the kind of factor that might lead the Court to allow the Michigan programs to withstand the usually fatal strict scrutiny. The second question, which would be reached only if the first one was decided in Michigan's favor, was whether the undergraduate and law school admissions programs were narrowly enough tailored to meet the goal of advancing diversity.

O'Connor didn't make the lawyers wait long for her first question. The argument by Kirk Kolbo, who was representing Grutter in the law school case, had an elegant simplicity. For the university to consider the diversity of its applicants was fine—but only on the basis of experiences or perspectives or geography, not on the basis of race. To Kolbo, the Constitution forbade any consideration of race, as a plus or minus factor for any candidate.

"You say that race can't be a factor at all, is that it?" O'Connor asked. "Is that your position, that it cannot be one of many factors?"

Right, said Kolbo. "Our view, Your Honor, is that race itself should not be a factor among others in choosing students."

"Well, you have some precedents out there that you have to come to grips with"—mostly, she meant *Bakke*—"because the Court obviously has upheld the use of race in making selections or choices in certain contexts," she replied. "But you're speaking in absolutes and it isn't quite that." As usual, O'Connor abhorred absolutes.

But the turning point in the argument began when Ginsburg spoke up. "Mr. Kolbo, may I call your attention . . . to the brief that was filed on behalf of some retired military officers who said that to have an officer corps that includes minority members in any number, there is no way to do it other than to give not an overriding preference but a plus for race," Ginsburg said. Would it really be acceptable to have no minorities in the service academies? Kolbo tried to dodge, saying there was no evidence in the record of this case about the military academies.

But Stevens followed up, saying there was good evidence about the academies: "If the brief is accurate about the regulations, the academies have taken the position . . . they do give [racial] preferences." Souter, too, asked about the policies at the service academies. Again, Kolbo said he didn't know about the policies in Annapolis; this case was about Ann Arbor. But Stevens wouldn't let the subject alone. "Are you serious that you think there's a serious question about that? That we cannot take that green brief as a representation of fact?" (Amicus briefs in the Supreme Court have green covers.) Kennedy jumped in with a question about "the green brief." Amicus briefs are rarely mentioned in Supreme Court oral arguments, but four justices had referred to the military brief in the first several minutes of *Grutter*.

And the justices were just warming up on the subject. The position of the federal government in the Michigan cases had been so controversial that ultimately President Bush himself had to resolve the issue. On the day before the briefs in the case were due, Bush made an announcement, in a speech broadcast on live television, that the administration would oppose the Michigan program. "I strongly support diversity of all kinds, including racial diversity in higher education," he said. "But the method used by the University of Michigan to achieve this important goal is fundamentally flawed. At their core, the Michigan policies amount to a quota system that unfairly rewards or penalizes prospective students based solely on their race." That, he said, was "divisive, unfair, and impossible to square with the Constitution." (Notably, in a television appearance later that week, Colin L. Powell, then the secretary of state and a close friend of several signers of the military brief, declined to endorse the administration position.)

Bush's speech employed rhetoric that pleased his conservative base—and reflected the well-established views of Scalia and

Thomas—but the brief filed by Theodore B. Olson, the solicitor general, took a more nuanced view of the issue. Olson's brief carefully avoided the question of whether a university could ever consider race in admissions—and took no position on whether *Bakke* should be overturned. He said only that the Michigan programs amounted to quotas and should be rejected. That was the position that Olson hoped to express when he stood up to argue in *Grutter*, but he never got the chance.

Before Olson could say anything, Stevens said, "General Olson. Just let me get a question out. You can answer it at your convenience. I'd like you to comment on Carter Phillips's brief. What is your view of the strength of that argument? . . . That's the one about the generals and about the military academies."

"We respect the opinions of those individuals," Olson said, "but the position of the United States is that we do not accept the proposition that black soldiers will only fight for black officers or the reverse." Olson was attacking a straw man, and the justices knew it. The retirees were not saying that blacks would only fight with blacks, they were saying that the military had a strong interest in an integrated officer corps.

Ginsburg went after him next. "But you recognize, General Olson, that here and now, all of the military academies do have race preference programs in admissions?" He did.

"Is that illegal what they're doing . . . a violation of the Constitution?" Ginsburg followed up. This was an exquisitely difficult question. If Olson said yes, he admitted that the federal government was violating the law; if he said no, he looked like a hypocrite. So Olson avoided the issue, saying he had not studied the admissions programs at the academies.

Next it was Souter's turn to wave the green brief, demanding to know how race-neutral recruiting could "respond to the position taken in Mr. Phillips's brief. . . . They simply will not reach a substantial number or be able to attain a substantial number of minority slots in the class." Respectfully, Olson disagreed.

As its lead lawyer in the case, Michigan had hired Maureen Mahoney, and her presence was another reflection of the university's political strategy of tying its cause to the establishment. Before becoming a partner at Latham & Watkins, Mahoney had been a deputy solicitor general under Kenneth Starr and a law clerk to Rehnquist. (During the argument in *Grutter*, the chief slipped once and called her

"Maureen.") A Republican, Mahoney had been nominated to a federal trial judgeship in Virginia during the last months of the George H. W. Bush administration. The Senate never brought Mahoney up for a vote—John Roberts's original nomination to the D.C. Circuit suffered the same fate—so she had the chance, like Roberts, to become one of the leading Supreme Court advocates of her generation. The fact that she came before the Court in *Grutter* bearing impeccable conservative credentials made her all the more appealing as Michigan's messenger.

By the time Mahoney reached the podium, she could tell the Court was leaning her way. No justice had really questioned the first issue before them—whether diversity was a legitimate goal—and the only question appeared to be whether Michigan had gone too far to achieve a worthy end. Mahoney deftly parried Scalia's and Kennedy's attempts to portray the Michigan program as a "quota," but then O'Connor came up with a question that had occurred to her while she was reading *Bakke*.

"Ms. Mahoney, may I shift focus away from this to another point before you're finished that I am concerned about," O'Connor said. "In all programs which this court has upheld in the area of what I'll label affirmative action, there's been a fixed time period within which it would operate, you could see at the end an end to it. There is none in this, is there? How do we deal with that aspect?"

O'Connor was raising one of the more profound questions in American life. When will race no longer matter? The question captured O'Connor's ambivalence on the issue of affirmative action—and her practical, solution-oriented turn of mind. To her, racial preferences were a dubious and extreme remedy at best, and she wanted to make sure they were not enshrined for all time. So how much longer would they be needed?

Mahoney answered with an artful segue: "Well, in *Bakke* itself, Your Honor, there were five votes to allow the University of California, Davis, to use a plan modeled on the Harvard plan. It's been in effect for about 25 years. It has reaped extraordinary benefits for this country's educational system." The answer planted a seed.

Most of the public attention on *Grutter* and *Gratz*—the law school and undergraduate cases—treated the two cases as a single controversy, but there were significant differences between the two admissions programs. To narrow the 3,500 law school applicants to a class of 350, Michigan evaluated each candidate individually, guided by a "focus on academic ability coupled with a flexible assessment of applicants' talents, experiences, and potential to contribute to the learning of those around them." The undergraduate admissions assessment was more strictly numerical, with each student evaluated on a 150-point scale, with students who received more than 100 points guaranteed admission. Points were awarded for high school grade-point average, standardized test scores, and other non-racial factors, but status as a minority also earned applicants an automatic additional 20 points.

As O'Connor prepared to cast her vote in conference, the difference between the two programs loomed large for her. The undergraduate program was not exactly a quota, as Bush had claimed, but its rigidity—the fact that all "underrepresented" minorities were given the exact same number of points—offended O'Connor. In contrast, the law school procedure looked more like the Harvard program that was praised by Powell in *Bakke*. It allowed each applicant to be treated as an individual. Once again, she decided to split the difference—to vote for Gratz and against Grutter. (Breyer voted the same way, affirming the growing ideological as well as personal alliance between him and O'Connor.) The others voted more predictably, Rehnquist, Scalia, Kennedy, and Thomas for both plaintiffs; Stevens, Souter, and Ginsburg for the university. The overall votes were 5–4 for the university in *Grutter*, the law school case; 6–3 for the rejected student in *Gratz*, the undergraduate case.

Grutter would clearly be the more important case, because it would be the one where the five justices outlined when and how race would be permitted to be considered as a factor in university admissions. (The six-justice majority in *Gratz* could say only that the undergraduate program did not meet the new *Grutter* standard.) The central question coming out of the conference was who would write the main opinion.

The decision was up to Stevens, because he was senior among O'Connor, Souter, Ginsburg, and Breyer. (Rehnquist assigned *Gratz* to himself.) Only a week earlier, Stevens had given the majority opinion in the other big case of the term, *Lawrence v. Texas*, to Kennedy. Would Stevens really be selfless enough to hand off *Grutter* as well? He had just turned eighty-three. How many more big opinions could he expect to come his way? Stevens took the weekend to think it over, and, following a conversation with O'Connor, he gave her *Grutter* to write.

Stevens's decision took wisdom and selflessness. O'Connor was clearly the shakiest member of the majority in *Grutter*, and if Stevens had kept the case for himself—as many other justices might have done in similar circumstances—he might ultimately have lost her vote and thus the majority. But Stevens cared more about the issues and less about his own ego; he could sacrifice high-profile assignments more easily than some of his colleagues. Besides, Stevens knew better than most that it took a long time, sometimes decades, for the real winners in Supreme Court jurisprudence to emerge. In 1986, Stevens had written a powerful, if little-noticed, dissenting opinion in *Bowers v. Hardwick*, the case that upheld the homosexual sodomy prosecution in Georgia. (Harry Blackmun's more rhetorically flashy dissent drew most of the attention in that case.) But when it came time for *Bowers* to be overruled in 2003, in *Lawrence*, Kennedy drew heavily on Stevens's seventeen-year-old opinion. So, with the shrewdness of age, Stevens handed the prize *Grutter* assignment—the biggest case since *Bush v. Gore*—to O'Connor.

Even though O'Connor's clerks wrote the first drafts of her opinions, they still had a distinctive style—or antistyle. She would never indulge in a Kennedyesque flourish like "the right to define one's own concept of existence, of meaning, of the universe, and of the mystery of human life"; nor would she, like Scalia, assert that an opposing argument was "really more than one should have to bear." She lined up the facts, usually laid out in some detail, summarized the relevant law, and applied the law to the facts. To O'Connor, the result always mattered more than the rhetoric. She usually began with a crisp statement of the issue at hand. In *Grutter*, it was: "This case requires us to decide whether the use of race as a factor in student admissions by the University of Michigan Law School is unlawful."

O'Connor had a clear model for her opinion in *Grutter*—Powell's statement in *Bakke*. She recounted the Michigan law school's admission procedures in detail, noting the university's broad commitment to diversity of all kinds, not just "racial and ethnic status." O'Connor said that Michigan sought a "critical mass" of minority students, but, significantly, there was "no number, percentage, or range of numbers or percentages that constitute critical mass." Rather, as the lower court in the case held, "the Law School's program was 'virtually identical' to the Harvard admissions program described approvingly by Justice Powell and appended to his *Bakke* opinion." O'Connor then summarized Powell's opinion at length, noting that he "approved the university's use of race to further only one interest: 'the attainment of a diverse student body.' "

As for whether "diversity" was a "compelling state interest," O'Connor said she trusted universities to make that judgment on their own, without guidance from the courts, because "universities occupy a special niche in our constitutional tradition." This observation wasn't just a gesture of deference to educational institutions but also a way of doing what O'Connor often tried to do, which was limit the reach of the Court's opinion. She was taking pains to approve affirmative action at universities, but she was not ruling on the practice in other contexts, like employment or contracting.

O'Connor next turned to the subject that dominated the oral argument—the brief from the retired military officers. She quoted Carter Phillips's brief at length and then, in an extraordinarily rare tribute, simply adopted its words as part of the Court's opinion: "To fulfill its mission, the military 'must be selective in admissions for training and education for the officer corps, *and* it must train and educate a highly qualified, racially diverse officer corps in a racially diverse setting.' " Before submitting his brief, Phillips had worried that the Court might observe (correctly) that there were big differences between a military service academy and a law school, and thus find no relevance of one to the other; but O'Connor did just the opposite. Quoting the brief again, she wrote, "We agree that 'it requires only a small step from this analysis to conclude that our country's other most selective institutions must remain both diverse and selective.' "

In all, considering the oral argument and O'Connor's opinion, the submission from the retired officers may have been the most influential amicus brief in the history of the Court. In notable contrast, O'Connor disdained the Bush administration's brief in the case. She respected Olson, the solicitor general, but she regarded his brief as a political document, the product of an administration from which she was growing more and more estranged.

The draft by O'Connor's clerk did not address her last question to

Mahoney—about when affirmative action would no longer be needed. O'Connor regarded race consciousness as nothing more than a necessary, or at least permissible, evil. She did not want to see it go on forever. But how could she or anyone else fix an ending date?

After twenty-two years on the Court, many of them as the most important vote, O'Connor had an abundance of self-confidence, so she simply made up a time limit. She told a clerk to write an insert: "It has been 25 years since Justice Powell first approved the use of race to further an interest in student body diversity in the context of public higher education. Since that time, the number of minority applicants with high grades and test scores has indeed increased. We expect that 25 years from now, the use of racial preferences will no longer be necessary to further the interest approved today."

The imposition of the time limit was O'Connor at her worst—and her best. To be sure, O'Connor was "legislating from the bench," in the accusatory term that conservatives like Bush used to describe activist judges. From the vague commands of the Constitution, she was extrapolating not just a legal rule but a deadline as well. To originalists like Scalia and Thomas, this was simple judicial arrogance. And one need not be an originalist, or even a conservative, to have qualms about O'Connor's proclamation. By what right does an unelected judge impose such detailed rules on a society? And if the practice will be unconstitutional in twenty-five years, why isn't it illegal now?

"The majority does not and cannot rest its time limitation on any evidence that the gap in credentials between black and white students is shrinking or will be gone in that time frame," Thomas noted in his dissent. "No one can seriously contend, and the Court does not, that the racial gap in academic credentials will disappear in 25 years. Nor is the Court's holding that racial discrimination will be unconstitutional in 25 years made contingent on the gap closing in that time." Moreover, if O'Connor could legislate in this matter on affirmative action, what was to stop her colleagues from establishing codes of behavior in other areas? The answer, of course, was that the only restraints on the judge in such circumstances are his or her conscience and savvy.

And that, ultimately, is the best defense of what O'Connor did. On affirmative action, she picked a result, and reached a compromise, that was broadly acceptable to most Americans. There was no formal limit on her power, but O'Connor's extraordinary political instincts let her exercise her authority in a moderate way. In some basic, almost primal manner, O'Connor understood that twenty-five more years of racial preferences seemed the right amount of time. It is a scary prospect to consider what other justices in the Court's history, including some of her contemporaries, would have done with the power that O'Connor arrogated to herself. Her judicial approach was indefensible in theory and impeccable in practice.

The Michigan cases were something of a rout for the conservatives. Kennedy wrote a separate opinion in *Grutter* saying that he, like Powell in *Bakke*, approved of the use of race in admissions but that the Michigan law school procedure looked too much like a quota for him to approve. Even Rehnquist avoided taking a stand on whether race could ever be considered. Only two justices, Scalia and Thomas, said directly that any use of race in admissions always violated the Constitution.

Thomas, probably the nation's most famous beneficiary of affirmative action, wrote a passionate opinion denouncing the practice. He quoted the words of his hero Frederick Douglass: "What I ask for the negro is not benevolence, not pity, not sympathy, but simply *justice*. The American people have always been anxious to know what they shall do with us. . . . All I ask is, give him a chance to stand on his own legs! Let him alone!" For all its rhetorical power, Thomas's opinion represented only a fringe view—on the Court and in the nation at large.

Among the justices, especially Kennedy and O'Connor, the post–*Bush v. Gore* move to the left continued—and to some extent accelerated—after *Grutter*. Even Rehnquist almost brought what remained of his own federalism revolution to a close; he wrote the opinion in *Nevada v. Hibbs*, which upheld the authority of Congress to pass the Family and Medical Leave Act of 1993, a central accomplishment of the Clinton administration.

Then, in a complex series of cases, the Court struck down state and then federal criminal sentencing guidelines, against the wishes of the Bush administration. By a 6–3 vote, it overturned the Child Pornography Prevention Act, which made it a crime to create or possess "virtual" pornography, which used enhanced computer imaging rather than actual children. Even in several major criminal cases, the Court sided with the defendant and overturned convictions.

After 2000, the majority in *Bush v. Gore*—Rehnquist, O'Connor, Scalia, Kennedy, and Thomas—might have taken full control of the Court, but something close to the opposite took place. Their coalition crumbled. In the 2002 term, only five of the fourteen 5–4 decisions were decided by the bloc that prevailed in *Bush v. Gore*; in the 2003 term, it was nine of nineteen; in the 2004 term, it was four of twenty-two such cases. At first it was the legacy of *Bush v. Gore* that turned O'Connor and Kennedy toward their more liberal colleagues. Later, it was the Bush administration itself.

18

"OUR EXECUTIVE DOESN'T"

The burst of confidence in the military, and in the Bush administration, following the invasion of Iraq in the spring of 2003 was short-lived. A month after the argument in *Grutter*, on an aircraft carrier off the coast of San Diego, the president addressed a cheering crowd underneath a banner that read "Mission Accomplished." But almost from that moment, the fortunes of the American occupation turned. A determined guerrilla insurgency killed more than three thousand American service members. Many thousands more Iraqis died. Elections were held, a constitution was passed, and a new government was established, but the American experience in Iraq turned out to be considerably more difficult than it had initially appeared. And just as the war turned sour, the first cases growing out of the administration's broader war on terrorism reached the Supreme Court. They concerned an idyllic stretch of Caribbean coastline known as Guantánamo Bay.

After American and Cuban forces evicted the Spanish from Cuba in 1898, the United States military remained on forty-five square miles along the southern coast of the island. The American presence became official with a treaty signed by the two nations in 1903, eventually setting an annual rent at $4,085. To this day, the American government offers payment to the Cuban government every year, but during the nearly five decades that Fidel Castro has been in power, his government has accepted it only once.

The war in Afghanistan created an unprecedented level of activity at Guantánamo Bay and gave it international notoriety. On January 10, 2002, the military began moving prisoners there from Afghanistan, and all the armed services, not just the navy, were asked to run

Joint Task Force Guantánamo. In a press conference that same day, Donald Rumsfeld, the secretary of defense, said that the prisoners were "unlawful combatants" who "do not have any rights under the Geneva Convention." Among the rights granted by the Geneva Conventions is the right to an individual hearing to determine the status of each prisoner.

A chorus of international condemnation—from the United Nations, the European Union, and the Organization of American States, among others—cried out against the American government. But within the United States, in the fevered aftermath of the September 11 attacks, the Guantánamo detention and interrogation facility drew little notice and less controversy—at first.

The prisoners at Guantánamo, who eventually numbered about six hundred, were all accused Al Qaeda or Taliban members picked up on battlefields in Afghanistan and neighboring countries—the "worst of the worst," as one American official put it. The notion that such despised and dangerous individuals might be able to challenge their incarceration in an American courtroom initially seemed close to outlandish. They were held in a foreign country; they were virtually incommunicado, limited to a single letter to a family member; they were allowed no visitors. But in early 2002, the family of an Australian national named David Hicks who was being held in Guantánamo reached out to lawyers at the Center for Constitutional Rights in New York, who agreed to file a lawsuit.

It was no coincidence that only the CCR, which stands well to the left of the American Civil Liberties Union in the spectrum of liberal legal interest groups, chose to challenge the American detention policy. In the early stages of the suit, the lawyers in charge could not have differed more from those directing the Michigan effort on affirmative action, with its roster of retired generals, corporate leaders, and a former Republican president. Led by a Minneapolis lawyer named Joseph Margulies, the CCR team sought assistance from several major Washington lawyers and law firms and were turned down by all. Guantánamo seemed nearly a fringe cause.

But as the case moved through the federal courts, and the near hysteria of the September 11 aftermath faded, the claims for the Guantánamo prisoners looked more plausible. The Bush administration had created an unusual legal category for those held on the American base. They were not criminal defendants, subject to the protections of the U.S. Constitution, but neither were they prisoners of war, whose treatment had long been governed by the Geneva Conventions.

Rather, the Guantánamo detainees were labeled "enemy combatants," who could be held and interrogated until the war on terror was over—that is, indefinitely. One reason the military refused to treat the Guantánamo detainees as POWs was because, under the conventions, such prisoners may not be interrogated. And Guantánamo was designed from the start as an interrogation facility where prisoners could be questioned in total isolation, day after day and month after month, without outside interference or knowledge.

Furthermore, the government asserted in response to the CCR lawsuit, the plaintiffs had no right even to file the case. Because the detainees were non-American citizens held in Cuba and that nation had "ultimate sovereignty" over the base, the lawsuit was the equivalent of a foreigner's filing a case from an overseas battlefield—something that American courts never allowed. The lower courts agreed and ultimately dismissed the case, which came to be known as *Rasul v. Bush*. Ironically, Shafiq Rasul himself was among the first prisoners released from Guantánamo, while the case was pending before the Supreme Court; still, his name remained as lead plaintiff. Two related cases, concerning the similarly unlimited detention within the United States of American citizens named Yaser Hamdi and Jose Padilla, worked their way toward the Court at the same time.

After the Supreme Court granted cert in *Rasul*, *Hamdi*, and *Padilla*, in late 2003 and early 2004, the Bush administration began to take the cases more seriously. At last, after two years, it allowed Hamdi and Padilla to meet with their lawyers. Secretary Rumsfeld announced that the military was creating "administrative review boards" to evaluate the status of each prisoner in Guantánamo. The procedures gave the detainees no right to counsel, no right to confront the witnesses against them, and no right of appeal, but they allowed administration lawyers to say the government was at least doing something to assess whether the detainee deserved to remain in custody. The government also asserted that the prisoners had no right even to this meager procedural safeguard; it had been provided "solely as a matter of discretion and does not confer any right or obligation enforceable by law." Mostly, the Bush position remained unchanged—that the war on terror meant that the Guantánamo prisoners deserved no rights, or even a day, in an American courtroom.

The Bush legal team, led by Ted Olson, the solicitor general, brought the same moral certainty to the Supreme Court that the Republican political operation put forth to voters. The issues were straightforward, the choices binary: the United States or the terrorists, right or wrong. Standing up to argue in *Rasul*, Olson laid the same kind of choice before the Court. "Mr. Chief Justice, and may it please the Court: The United States is at war," Olson began with heavy portent. "It is in that context that petitioners ask this Court to assert jurisdiction that is not authorized by Congress, does not arise from the Constitution, has never been exercised by this Court."

But if this kind of talk was intended to intimidate the justices, as it cowed so many others, the tactic did not work. Indeed, it backfired. "Mr. Olson, supposing the war has ended," Stevens jumped in, "could you continue to detain these people on Guantánamo?" Of course we could, Olson said. In other words, the military could detain Rasul and the others whether or not there was a war.

"The existence of the war is really irrelevant to the legal issue," Stevens said.

"It is not irrelevant because it is in this context that that question is raised," Olson replied weakly.

"But your position does not depend on the existence of a war," Stevens insisted, and Olson had to concede it did not. So in just the first moments of the argument, Stevens had shown that the Bush administration was claiming not some temporary accommodation but rather a permanent expansion of its power for all time, in war or peace. And Stevens was showing further that Olson's rhetorical flourish— "The United States is at war"—was nothing more than posturing.

The following week, on April 28, the *Hamdi* and *Padilla* cases were argued, and again the administration put forth its view of unchecked executive authority. Jose Padilla, an American citizen, had been arrested at O'Hare airport in Chicago and held indefinitely on suspicion of ties to Al Qaeda. According to the Justice Department, even though Padilla was an American citizen held on American soil, he had no right to challenge his incarceration, even if he wound up being imprisoned for the rest of his life. Paul Clement, the deputy solicitor general, asserted to the justices that Congress's authorization of the "use of all necessary and appropriate force" following the September 11 attacks justified the unlimited detention of Padilla. In Clement's view, the courts had no right to stop—or even hold a hearing about—Padilla's incarceration, because he was classified as an enemy combatant.

In response, Ginsburg asked a farfetched hypothetical question to test the limits of the government's position. "What inhibits it? If the law is what the executive says it is, whatever is 'necessary and appropriate' in the executive's judgment," she said. "So what is it that would be a check against torture?"

"Well, first of all there are treaty obligations," Clement said, "but the primary check is that just as in every other war, if a U.S. military person commits a war crime, by creating some atrocity on a harmless detained enemy combatant or a prisoner of war, that violates our own conception of what's a war crime and we'll put that U.S. military officer on trial in a court-martial."

But Ginsburg pursued the issue. "Suppose the executive says, 'Mild torture, we think, will help get this information.' It's not a soldier who does something against the code of military justice, but it's an executive command. Some systems do that to get information."

"Well," Clement replied, his voice touched with a hint of indignation, "our executive doesn't."

About eight hours later, on the evening of the arguments in *Hamdi* and *Padilla*, the CBS News program *60 Minutes II* broadcast photographs of U.S. Army personnel documenting physical and sexual abuse of prisoners at Abu Ghraib prison. The photographs, which immediately became symbols of the war, showed U.S. soldiers posing beside naked Iraqi prisoners stacked in a human pyramid, as well as a prisoner who was forced to stand on a box, his head covered by a hood and electric wires apparently attached to his body. (CBS executives had withheld the report for two weeks at the request of Defense Department officials but went ahead with the broadcast when they learned that *The New Yorker* was planning a report on the subject by Seymour Hersh. The magazine story was released on May 1.) As Margulies, the lawyer for Rasul and other Guantánamo detainees, recalled afterwards, "These photos proved to be the most powerful amicus brief of all."

The Abu Ghraib disclosure set off several months of intense public attention to the issue of torture by American personnel in Iraq and Guantánamo. The investigations revealed extensive abuse of prisoners in Iraq by low-level military personnel but, more importantly, considerable support for torture at the highest levels of the Bush administration. While the justices were preparing their opinions in *Rasul,*

Hamdi, and *Padilla* in June 2004, the most sensational document on the subject came to light—the "torture memo." In the summer of 2002, Alberto R. Gonzales, then the White House counsel, had asked the Justice Department to research the question of whether U.S. personnel involved in the war on terror were constrained by the federal law, which bans "cruel, inhuman, or degrading treatment" either inside or outside the United States.

The response came on August 1, 2002, from Jay Bybee and John Yoo, two senior officials who gave a virtually unrecognizably narrow definition of torture, which the law said was "severe physical or mental pain or suffering." To these lawyers, "physical pain amounting to torture must be equivalent in intensity to the pain accompanying serious physical injury, such as organ failure, impairment of bodily function, or even death. For purely mental pain or suffering to amount to torture, . . . it must result in significant psychological harm of significant duration, e.g., lasting for months or even years." What was more, Bybee and Yoo said, the president had inherent authority to overrule the statute and direct any interrogation technique that he believed was necessary. By the time the torture memo was released, Bybee had already been confirmed to a federal appellate judgeship and Yoo had returned to a professorship at the law school of the University of California at Berkeley. Yoo had been a law clerk to Thomas, and several other former Thomas clerks had also played important roles in formulating the Bush administration's legal justifications for the war on terror.

It is too simplistic to say that the disclosures about Abu Ghraib and torture policy determined the outcome of the Supreme Court's rulings in the three terrorism cases, but it is surely true that the news had an impact. In any event, the cases turned into humiliating defeats for the administration. In *Rasul*, the main case, the Court ruled 6–3 that the Guantánamo detainees did have the right to challenge their incarceration in a U.S. district court. In *Hamdi*, the Court again ruled 6–3 that the government could not prevent an American citizen from challenging his or her detention in federal court. In *Padilla*, the Court gave the administration a purely procedural victory, ruling only that the plaintiff should have brought his case in South Carolina instead of New York.

Stevens may have given the *Lawrence* case to Kennedy and *Grutter* to O'Connor, but he wasn't giving the *Rasul* assignment away. As for so many other men of his generation, the defining event of Stevens's youth was his service in World War II. Stevens had been raised in comfortable circumstances; his family built and ran the Stevens Hotel, a block-long Chicago landmark that was later renamed the Chicago Hilton. Stevens graduated from the University of Chicago, Phi Beta Kappa, in 1941 and planned to go to graduate school to study Shakespeare. But on the eve of American involvement in the war, several of his professors were working as talent spotters for the Navy, and they prevailed on him to sign up. Stevens did, on December 6, 1941, allowing him to joke that his enlistment prompted the attack on Pearl Harbor the following day.

Stevens served in the Pacific for four years on the staff of Admiral Chester Nimitz and won a bronze star. He did intelligence work, helping to break Japanese codes, and in later years often spoke of his pride in his service. His intense patriotism prompted the most out-of-character vote of his judicial career, when he sided with the conservatives in the famous flag-burning case of 1989. In his dissent in that case, Stevens said burning the flag was not protected by the First Amendment, because "it is more than a proud symbol of the courage, the determination, and the gifts of nature that transformed 13 fledgling Colonies into a world power. It is a symbol of freedom, of equal opportunity, of religious tolerance, and of goodwill for other peoples who share our aspirations."

Stevens did not presume that his own service as an intelligence officer in World War II gave him the wisdom to second-guess the Bush officials' conduct of intelligence operations at Guantánamo. But his military experience—combined with his quiet self-confidence—made him harder to intimidate on the subject of military necessity. Many of the darkest moments in the history of the Court took place when the justices deferred too much to the purported expertise of the executive branch on matters of national security. During and after World War I, the Court upheld several dubious prosecutions of political dissidents on the ground that their advocacy put the nation in danger.

Most notoriously, during World War II the justices upheld the exclusion of American citizens of Japanese ancestry from the West Coast in *Korematsu v. United States.* (Fred Korematsu himself submitted an amicus brief in support of Rasul.) Stevens knew that history and was determined not to replay it. And the disclosures that took place while the cases were pending—about Abu Ghraib and the torture memo—made the credibility of the administration's representations to the

Court much more suspect. Suddenly, it was the Bush administration itself, not the plaintiffs' leftist lawyers, that looked outside the mainstream of legal and political opinion. For a Court majority determined never to stray too far from what the public believed, that change was crucial.

So, it turned out, was the preposterousness of the administration's key argument in *Rasul*. Olson had maintained that the navy base in Guantánamo was really Cuban soil and to allow a lawsuit there was inviting litigation on a foreign battlefield. But as Stevens put it in his opinion, "By the express terms of its agreements with Cuba, the United States exercises 'complete jurisdiction and control' over the Guantánamo Bay Naval Base, and may continue to exercise such control permanently if it so chooses." The entire *reason* that the military took the detainees to such a remote outpost was because the base offered total freedom from outside interference. Allowing lawyers to visit prisoners in Guantánamo and letting them conduct litigation offered no risk at all of escape or disruption—something that could not be said for many prisons within the United States. Even Scalia's dissent, which was joined by Rehnquist and Thomas, could not work up much passion on the issue.

The reason for Scalia's relative reticence became apparent in *Hamdi*, which was handed down on the same day as *Rasul*. There the repudiation of Bush's position was even more complete, and the author of the majority opinion was O'Connor, that reliable vector for the views of most Americans. Her opinion was scathing, a testament to her growing estrangement from the Bush administration. Her impatience with pious lectures on national security was palpable: "It is during our most challenging and uncertain moments that our Nation's commitment to due process is most severely tested; and it is in those times that we must preserve our commitment at home to the principles for which we fight abroad."

O'Connor had become an evangelist for the cause of judicial independence, and she used *Hamdi* to remind the administration that this Court—her Court—would never become a rubber stamp: "The position that the courts must forgo any examination of the individual case and focus exclusively on the legality of the broader detention scheme cannot be mandated by any reasonable view of separation of powers, as this approach serves only to *condense* power into a single branch of government. We have long since made clear that a state of war is not a blank check for the president when it comes to the rights of the Nation's citizens." If there was any doubt what O'Connor meant, she waved the bloody shirt of one of the worst moments in the Court's history—by citing *Korematsu* itself—to drive home her point.

Remarkably, O'Connor's view was the moderate one on the Court. She said that Hamdi could not be detained without a hearing of some kind but that he did not necessarily have to receive the full protections afforded a criminal defendant. Scalia, of all people, wrote a dissenting opinion (joined by Stevens, an unfamiliar bedfellow) saying that the Bush administration's entire concept of detention of enemy combatants was unconstitutional for American citizens.

Scalia said O'Connor had been too soft on the Bush administration, arguing that Hamdi should be charged with a federal crime—or released immediately. "The proposition that the Executive lacks indefinite wartime detention authority over citizens is consistent with the Founders' general mistrust of military power permanently at the Executive's disposal," Scalia the originalist added. "Whatever the general merits of the view that war silences law or modulates its voice, that view has no place in the interpretation and application of a Constitution designed precisely to confront war and, in a manner that accords with democratic principles, to accommodate it." Only a single justice, Thomas, accepted the administration's position.

Rasul and *Hamdi* were notable also for the fact that on these most crucial cases about the nature of executive and judicial power, the chief justice did not write a majority opinion, dissent, or concurrence. Rehnquist joined Scalia's dissent in *Rasul* and O'Connor's opinion for the Court in *Hamdi*; Rehnquist only wrote the majority opinion in *Padilla*, which resolved that case on procedural grounds.

The relative invisibility of a chief justice on matters of such magnitude would be unusual in any circumstances, but it was especially odd for Rehnquist to remain silent on this particular subject. Since his days in the Justice Department during the Nixon years, and then on the Court, Rehnquist had been an outspoken proponent of executive power versus the other branches of government. Like federalism, it was a signature issue for him. Rehnquist signed on to O'Connor's harsh scolding of Bush, but did he really believe it? His silence was a mystery.

In truth, Rehnquist was a tired old man in the spring of 2004. And he had grown cynical about the work of the Court. Over the years, his opinions had become more terse and cryptic because he had come to think that only the results, not how the justices explained them, really mattered. As Rehnquist told one colleague, who was shocked by the chief's gloom, "Don't worry about the analysis and the principles in the case. Just make sure that the result is a good one this time around—because those principles you announce will be ignored in the next case." The chief didn't write in *Rasul* or *Hamdi* because he didn't think the opinions mattered very much; only the votes did.

Increasingly, Rehnquist didn't have the votes. It was now the Rehnquist Court in name only. Since *Bush v. Gore*, the chief had failed to command a majority in virtually all the important issues before the Court—affirmative action, gay rights, the death penalty, and, now, the legal implications of the war on terror. Even the so-called federalism revolution had dwindled, if not to insignificance, then to modest evolution. The *Lopez* case had suggested that the Court really might cut back on the authority of Congress to pass laws under the Commerce Clause; the Court did no such thing. The Constitution in Exile remained in exile. Thanks to Rehnquist, the Court had limited the ability of Congress to pass laws that allowed the states to be sued in federal court—a real achievement, to be sure, but also, in the history of the Supreme Court, an arcane one. Likewise, there had been a real, but also modest, movement to the right on church-state issues. The Court was clearly set in its ways, and on the issues that mattered most to the public, as well as to the justices themselves, Rehnquist's own views held little sway.

The composition of the Court hadn't changed, either. It had been ten years since Breyer replaced Blackmun—a decade without a new justice—which amounted to the longest period of stability in the history of the nine-justice Court.

In keeping with the collegial spirit of Rehnquist's Court, the spouses of the justices held a surprise party on January 23, 2003, to celebrate the new record for the nine. (There were no changes from 1812 to 1823, but the law provided for only seven justices at that time.) In 2004, Stevens was eighty-four, the oldest among them, but he enjoyed robust health and no affinity for the president who would appoint his replacement. Rehnquist, closing in on eighty himself, was the most likely to leave. He had spoken candidly of his belief that justices should hand their seats to the party of the presidents who appointed them, and George W. Bush's conservative politics reflected his own.

But Rehnquist didn't want to retire. He was a widower who lived in a small town house in suburban Virginia. His three children were long grown. He liked his job and his colleagues. His health was satisfactory, if not robust. With his trademark directness, Rehnquist would point out the grim truth about retirees from the Supreme Court: all they did was die, usually sooner rather than later. He had come to enjoy the administrative side of the job, and he was good at it. If he had lost some interest in the intricacies of Supreme Court doctrine or come to doubt the importance of each word he left behind in the Court's archives, the benefits of the job still outweighed the appeal of retirement. The choice came down to being chief justice of the United States or sitting at home by himself. It wasn't a difficult call.

Besides, Rehnquist had already missed a clear window for Bush to name his successor. By the end of the term in 2004, the presidential campaign was well under way. The Democrats were sure to stall any nomination until after the election, which promised to be close. A traditionalist like Rehnquist would never resign at such a time, unless his health forced his hand. So he retreated, as usual, to his modest summer home in Vermont, where he puttered around, looking for a new book subject. His most recent work, *Centennial Crisis*, a typically lucid and evenhanded study of the disputed presidential election of 1876—his own *Bush v. Gore* legacy—had been published in the spring. He returned to Washington in time for his eightieth birthday on October 1, 2004, and to await the beginning of the new term, on the first Monday, three days later.

There was a problem. Rehnquist had a sore throat that he couldn't shake. The Court heard eleven oral arguments in the first two weeks in October, and by the last one, an immigration case called *Clark v. Martinez* on October 13, the chief's voice had faded to a husky rasp almost unrecognizable from the voice in which he had announced the *Padilla* decision in June. With a three-week break until the next set of arguments, Rehnquist decided to visit a doctor.

The diagnosis did not take long. He had anaplastic thyroid cancer, an especially aggressive and almost invariably fatal form of the disease. (In recent years, Rehnquist had for the most part cut back to a single cigarette a day, but a lifetime of smoking almost certainly contributed to his illness.) On Friday, October 22, he checked into Bethesda Naval Hospital and underwent a tracheotomy, which involved placing a tube through a hole in his throat to help him breathe. The next Monday, October 25, the Office of Public Information at the Court put out a statement that Rehnquist had "thyroid cancer" and was "expected to be back on the Bench when the Court reconvenes on Monday, November 1." (The most common kind of thyroid cancer is generally curable, and the announcement did not say what kind he had.)

But Rehnquist did not even leave the hospital until October 29, and he was clearly in no condition to return to the bench. On November 1, he released a statement that said his original prediction of a return was "too optimistic" and that he would be receiving "radiation and chemotherapy treatments on an outpatient basis." Unlike the first announcement, this one came directly from Rehnquist's chambers, not the public information staff, illustrating how few people at the Court knew anything about his condition. But the length of Rehnquist's absence and the nature of his treatment left the impression, which was correct, that he had the devastating, anaplastic version of the disease. On the morning of November 1, John Paul Stevens, the senior associate justice, presided over the arguments, leaving the center seat conspicuously and ominously vacant.

As the nation voted the following day, Rehnquist's colleagues inferred what the chief justice already knew—that he was dying.

"A GREAT PRIVILEGE, INDEED"

On November 2, 2004, George W. Bush won a narrow victory over John Kerry, and this time the president needed no assistance from the Supreme Court. If Bush had lost, he would have joined Jimmy Carter as the only presidents in American history to serve full terms without having the chance to make an appointment to the Court. But the sudden announcement of Rehnquist's illness on the eve of the election made clear that Bush would soon have such an opportunity. It took less than a day for the political tension surrounding the appointment and confirmation process, which had been long dormant, to explode.

Also on that Election Day, Arlen Specter won his fifth term as a senator from Pennsylvania. A noted curmudgeon, longer on smarts than charm, Specter belonged to a vanishing species in Congress, the moderate Republican. When he was first elected, in 1980, the Senate abounded in such figures, like Robert Packwood, Mark Hatfield, Lowell Weicker, Charles Mathias, and John Heinz, but by 2004 the rightward tilt of the national GOP had pushed the number of moderates almost to insignificance. Specter had moved so far away from the base of his party that he drew a conservative challenger in a Republican primary, who came much closer to beating him than the Democrat did in the general election.

On Wednesday, November 3, Specter held his traditional post–Election Day news conference in Philadelphia. He was asked about possible Supreme Court appointments, an issue that suddenly had special resonance because Specter was finally in line to become chairman of the Senate Judiciary Committee. Repeating a view he had expressed many times, Specter told the reporters he regarded the protection of abortion rights established by *Roe v. Wade* as "inviolate," and he suggested that "nobody can be confirmed today" who didn't share that opinion. After making the statement, Specter didn't give it a second thought.

But Specter was about to learn once more how much his party had changed. Virtually overnight, as news of Specter's statement about *Roe* spread, the conservative groups that had led the primary challenge against Specter, such as Focus on the Family, demanded that he be denied the chairmanship. Protesters chanted outside his office, and telephone calls inundated the Senate switchboards. One Republican senator even added a new option to the automatic phone-answering service in his office: "Press 3 if you're calling about who should be chairman of the Senate Judiciary Committee." On November 17, Specter was forced to implore his Republican Senate colleagues not to withhold the prize for which he had waited so long. Following separate meetings with the Senate leadership and the other Republicans on the Judiciary Committee, Specter was informed he could have the chairmanship—with conditions.

At a press conference the next day, Specter made the terms public. Introduced by Orrin Hatch, who was barred by term limits from continuing as Judiciary chairman, Specter explained the deal. "I have not and would not use a litmus test to deny confirmation to prolife nominees," Specter said in the weary monotone of a Soviet prisoner forced to confess his ideological errors. "I have voted for all of President Bush's judicial nominees in committee and on the floor, and I have no reason to believe that I'll be unable to support any individual President Bush finds worthy of nomination."

Specter had survived to serve as chairman of the committee, but the message to him was unmistakable. Conservatives had waited fourteen years for a Republican president to nominate someone to the Supreme Court, and this time they wanted a true believer. Seven of the nine current justices had been appointed by Republicans—and still the Court continued to disappoint conservatives. The core of the president's party would accept only Supreme Court nominees who embraced the conservative line, especially on *Roe v. Wade*, Arlen Specter notwithstanding. Even before there was a vacancy, much less a nomination, conservative activists like James Dobson and Jay Sekulow, empowered by their critical role in Bush's reelection, were demonstrating precisely what mattered most to them—control of the Supreme Court.

Two months later, the world saw William Rehnquist for the first time since his illness had been announced in the fall. On January 20, 2005, Rehnquist made an unsteady journey down the platform steps in front of the Capitol to administer the oath of office to George W. Bush. With his administrative assistant, Sally Rider, closely monitoring his procession, Rehnquist arrived well after his colleagues and the other guests had taken their places. Chemotherapy had reduced his hair to a few wisps, and the tracheotomy tube, which was still in place, made his voice hard to hear, but the chief had the fortitude to complete his duty. After Bush repeated, "So help me God," an affectation said to have been added to the constitutional oath by George Washington and recited ever since, Rehnquist told the president, "Congratulations." This was a different salute from the ambiguous "Good luck" he offered to Bill Clinton on January 20, 1997, a week after the Court heard arguments in the Paula Jones case. Rehnquist left before Bush's inaugural address, having been present for only thirteen minutes.

No one studied the chief more carefully than the other eight justices. Only Stevens and O'Connor had been allowed to make brief visits to his home. The others had not seen him at all. Rehnquist listened to tapes of the oral arguments, cast his votes by memo, and continued to make assignments from home. In his absence, Stevens presided over the conferences and the oral arguments. Even in good health, Rehnquist preferred to communicate by memo with all but his immediate staff, so the Court functioned normally even though he was not on the premises. Rehnquist had a strong sense of responsibility about his obligations, and he was meticulous about making sure that the Court did not suffer from his illness. He gave no hint if he was thinking of resigning.

As in most other terms, the justices disposed of the easy cases in its first few months. Year in and year out, about 40 percent of the Court's opinions are unanimous, and many more draw just a mild dissent or two. During the first months of Rehnquist's absence, the Court did a pretty good job of avoiding controversy, with the single exception of Kennedy's opinion in *Roper v. Simmons*, which invoked foreign law in striking down the death penalty for juvenile offenders. The case had been argued on the morning of October 13, Rehnquist's last day on the bench, and the decision was handed down on March 1. The chief, silent once more in a major case—one that amounted to yet another demonstration that the Court's center of gravity had moved to the left—joined Scalia's dissent.

O'Connor and Kennedy were the chief beneficiaries of this ideological shift, as they controlled the outcome of more cases and won assignments from Stevens for such opinions as *Lawrence, Grutter,* and *Hamdi.* But in his customary quiet way, David Souter was also swept up in the change, which helped pull him out of his post–*Bush v. Gore* funk.

Souter had minimal financial obligations and a lifestyle that hovered somewhere between modest and ascetic. He had no wife, no children, a venerable family homestead in New Hampshire, and a small apartment in an unfashionable neighborhood in Washington. He worked about seventy hours a week, and his main hobby was jogging. In the annual disclosures that the justices are required to file, Scalia reported being reimbursed in 2003 by universities and bar associations for twenty-one trips, several of them abroad; O'Connor came in second among the justices with nineteen. Souter was last, as usual, with none. He also reported no outside income from speeches or publications and no gifts.

Still, Souter's New England frugality was one factor that kept him on the Court when he thought about resigning after *Bush v. Gore.* Years earlier, he had invested in local bank stocks in his home region, and after a series of takeovers, the value of his shares had soared. By 2003, he reported cash and stock assets of between $5.2 million and $25.5 million, nearly tying with Ginsburg for the highest on the Court. But Souter was also acutely aware that federal judges were entitled to retire with full salary after fifteen years on the bench, a benefit that would become available to him in 2005, when he would be sixty-six. A resignation before that point would forfeit his full pension, so he told friends he thought it would be unwise to forgo that bounty. It was characteristic of his quirky personality that he would worry about his pension when he had little need for it—and almost nothing to spend it on—but Souter's colleagues were used to his eccentricities.

In fact, Souter's gentle charm made him probably the best liked of the justices among his peers, and he returned their affection, which was one reason he stayed on. He was a special favorite of the women justices, who took an almost maternal interest in him, though he was only six years younger than Ginsburg and nine years younger than O'Connor. Ginsburg often invited him to sample her husband Marty's gourmet cooking and to attend events where they could share their love of classical music. She also often noted proudly that she and Souter, unlike the rest of their colleagues, never engaged in caustic or bitter commentary in their dissenting opinions.

O'Connor had a more direct agenda with Souter. She wanted to get him married off. According to her biographer Joan Biskupic, O'Connor boasted about her matchmaking skills, claiming she had once been known as the "Yenta of Paradise Valley," her posh neighborhood in Phoenix. She invited Souter to many of her parties, including one, early in Souter's tenure, that featured "Fajitas and frivolity . . . Dress: Country Western or Effete Eastern." Over the years, practically everyone Souter knew in Washington, including First Lady Barbara Bush, tried to fix him up. None succeeded. One of his fellow justices once prevailed on Souter to take a woman out to dinner, and she reported back that she thought the evening had gone very well—until the end. Souter took her home, told her what a good time he had, then added: "Let's do this again next year."

Washington remained anathema to him, not least because of an incident that took place on April 30, 2004. Souter was taking his nightly jog from his home near the Court to Fort McNair, an old military base on the Potomac, and on his way home, he was assaulted by two men. (The reason for the attack was never determined.) He received a terrible beating, requiring treatment at a local hospital for cuts and bruises, but with typical doggedness still showed up for work the next morning—a Saturday. If any event might have prompted him to flee to New Hampshire for good, this would have been it, but he remained. His fifteenth anniversary came and went without further discussion of retirement.

A clue to the source of Souter's revival on the Court came shortly after the death of Gerald Gunther, the Stanford law professor and biographer of Judge Learned Hand. Gunther and Souter were not close friends, but Kathleen Sullivan, the dean at Stanford, knew that the justice admired Gunther's book, and she decided to invite him to speak at the funeral. (Souter's secretary thought the idea was so unlikely that she laughed when Sullivan called.) But Souter said yes and made what was, in his seventh decade, the second visit of his life to California.

Souter's eulogy praised Gunther and Hand, but it really amounted to a short essay about "what anyone's judging ought to be." Hand had served from 1924 to 1961 on the federal court of appeals in New York, where his views resembled those of the moderate, careful jurisprudence of his friend John Marshall Harlan II, who was Souter's other judicial hero. Souter spoke of "every judge's common obligations: suspicion of easy cases, skepticism about clear-edged categories, modesty in the face of precedent, candor in playing one worthy principle against another, and the nerve to do it in concrete circumstances on an open page." This was autobiography for David Souter, the cautious guardian of the right to privacy, the fierce advocate of strong national government (and unrelenting foe of Rehnquist on federalism), the painstaking, even slow, judicial craftsman.

His eulogy for Gunther also offered a lesson in why Souter joined O'Connor and Kennedy in moving left after 2000. Souter, who recoiled from extremism or "clear-edged categories" of any kind, had a visceral horror of such conservative undertakings as the Constitution in Exile. While centrism was a political philosophy for O'Connor, it was more a matter of temperament for Souter; still, it turned out the two justices were merely taking different paths to a similar jurisprudential destination.

The case that summed up Souter's achievement as a justice was one that was argued and decided during Rehnquist's illness. The issue in *MGM v. Grokster* concerned one of the most vexed issues in copyright law—whether the maker of software that can be used for copyright infringement should be held liable if its product is in fact used that way. Billions of dollars were at stake in the case because virtually all video and audio entertainment can be illegally copied and distributed on software like Grokster. Would ruling for the software maker condemn movie studios to wanton piracy? Would ruling for the studio stifle technological innovation? Before the case was heard, it was widely predicted that the Court would split in the face of those difficult questions and make the law even more complicated than it already was. But Souter managed to unite the Court behind his opinion, which held that software makers could be liable only if they took affirmative steps to encourage infringement. It was a largely apolitical decision that managed to draw support from left and right, creators of entertainment and distributors of it, artists and entrepreneurs—and it was written by a man who worked exclusively with a fountain pen. Souter's opinion showed a sophisticated understanding of the markets for both technology and entertainment—from a man who only in 2003, while presiding over a wedding, learned the name of a singing group that was more than familiar to his colleagues, the Supremes.

Still, for all his popularity on the Court, Souter remained a mystery even to those who knew him best. Part of his appeal was that, peculiar though he was, Souter was comfortable with himself, even capable of having fun with his distinctive place in the Court and American life. It was, for example, a running joke at the Court that outsiders frequently mistook Souter and Breyer for each other. No one could really understand why this happened, because the two bore little resemblance. One day when Souter was making his usual solo drive from Washington to New Hampshire, he stopped for lunch in Massachusetts. A stranger and his wife came up to him and asked, "Aren't you on the Supreme Court?"

Souter said he was.

"You're Justice Breyer, right?" said the man.

Rather than embarrass the fellow, Souter simply nodded and exchanged pleasantries, until he was asked an unexpected question.

"Justice Breyer, what's the best thing about being on the Supreme Court?"

The justice thought for a while, then said, "Well, I'd have to say it's the privilege of serving with David Souter."

During the spring of 2005, when the justices looked for clues about Rehnquist's prognosis, the most important event for the Court involved a case that was never accepted for review. The justices did not write a single opinion in the matter of Terri Schiavo, but no case that year had a greater impact on the Court as an institution.

By the beginning of 2005, Schiavo's story was a familiar one in Florida, if not in the rest of the country. She became suddenly ill on February 25, 1990, and her heart briefly stopped beating, and she went into a deep coma. In 1998, her husband and guardian, Michael Schiavo, went to the state court in Florida, asking that her feeding tube be removed because she was in a persistent vegetative state. Michael said that based on conversations with his wife before she was stricken, he believed she would not have wanted to be kept alive in such circumstances. A judge agreed and ordered the tube removed, but Terri's parents, Robert and Mary Schindler, argued that her condition was not so dire and that she might someday recover. Years of bitter court fights followed.

The struggle over Terri Schiavo was at once a terrible family quarrel and a proxy battle over abortion and the "right to life." It was also, curiously, a recapitulation of the struggle in *Bush v. Gore* in Florida. Throughout the process, the more Democratic-leaning courts in the state found in Michael Schiavo's favor, and the Republican-dominated state legislature, along with Governor Jeb Bush, took the parents' side. In 2003, the state even passed a law authorizing Governor Bush to order Terri's feeding tube to be reinserted—and the state supreme court, the same justices who had ruled twice in Gore's favor, declared that law unconstitutional.

The final crisis in the case was set off when a Florida judge, George Greer, ruled on February 25, 2005, that he would permit no more stays and ordered the tube removed on March 18. In front of the hospice in Pinellas Park where Schiavo was being treated, a series of protests and prayer vigils began under the leadership of Rev. Patrick Mahoney, who was affiliated with a group called the Christian Defense Coalition. (Mahoney was a veteran of the antiabortion movement and many conservative causes; in 1994, he had persuaded Paula Jones to file her sexual harassment lawsuit against Bill Clinton.)

Schiavo's feeding tube was removed on the afternoon of March 18. With their options in Florida exhausted and Terri likely to die in a few days, Schiavo's parents turned to Washington, specifically to Tom DeLay, the majority leader in the House of Representatives. An ardent opponent of abortion rights and a fierce partisan known as the Hammer, DeLay engineered an extraordinary legislative feat with remarkable speed. Congress had gone into recess, but DeLay managed to gather a quorum of 218 representatives on Sunday, March 20, to pass a bill designed to prevent the removal of Schiavo's feeding tube; the Senate did, too. President Bush cut short a vacation at his Crawford, Texas, ranch to fly across the country to sign the bill, which he did at 1:08 a.m. on Monday, March 21. Later that day, Bush said, "It is wise to always err on the side of life."

By its specific terms, the law—known formally as For the Relief of the Parents of Theresa Marie Schiavo Act—instructed the federal district court in Florida to give the case yet another hearing "relating to the withholding or withdrawal of food, fluids, or medical treatment necessary to sustain her life." The law further stated that the district court "shall entertain and determine the suit without delay." So on the very day the law was signed, Judge James D. Whittemore held a hearing in Tampa on the case, and the next day he rejected the Schindlers' attempt to reinsert the feeding tube. The parents appealed to the Eleventh Circuit and then to the U.S. Supreme Court, which on March 24 refused to intervene. By this time, the case had been considered by nineteen judges in six state and federal courts, and between 2001 and 2005 the U.S. Supreme Court had declined to hear the case five times. Terri Schiavo died on March 31.

Her death only increased the rhetorical fervor. On the day of her death, DeLay threatened to impeach the judges who presided over her case, including the Supreme Court justices. "The time will come for the men responsible for this to answer for their behavior," DeLay said. "We will look at an arrogant, out-of-control judiciary that thumbs its nose at Congress and the president."

Four days later, Senator John Cornyn, a Republican from Texas, made an even more incendiary statement. Just weeks earlier, there had been a pair of horrific attacks on judges and their families. In Chicago, a deranged litigant before federal judge Joan Lefkow broke into her home and murdered her husband and mother, and in Atlanta, a defendant in a rape case killed the judge in his trial and two others in the course of an escape attempt. In a speech on the Senate floor, Cornyn suggested the attacks on judges might have taken place because of decisions like *Schiavo.* "I don't know if there is a cause-and-effect connection but we have seen some recent episodes of courthouse violence in this country," Cornyn said. "I wonder whether there may be some connection between the perception in some quarters on some occasions where judges are making political decisions yet are unaccountable to the public, that it builds up and builds up and builds up to the point where some people engage in violence."

The justices watched these developments—the litigation, the frenzied rush to pass a law for Schiavo's purported benefit, the venomous attacks on the judges—with consternation. The assaults on the judges, and Cornyn's ugly reference to them, left a particularly strong impression because, unbeknownst to the public, both O'Connor and Ginsburg had also received recent death threats. One of the messages, which was posted in a Web chat room, said, "Okay commandoes, here is your first patriotic assignment . . . an easy one. Supreme Court Justices Ginsburg and O'Connor have publicly stated that they use [foreign] laws and rulings to decide how to rule on American cases. This is a huge threat to our Republic and Constitutional freedom. . . . If you are what you say you are, and NOT armchair patriots, then those two justices will not live another week." Ginsburg, with her mordant view of human nature, shrugged the whole thing off.

O'Connor did not. To her, the Schiavo case marked only the latest outrage from the extremists who she believed had hijacked her beloved Republican Party. The hiring of John Ashcroft, the politicized response to the affirmative action case, the lawless approach to the war on terror, and the accelerating disaster of the war in Iraq all appalled O'Connor. (As someone who prized order, O'Connor used a favorite epithet, "a mess," to describe the war. This judgment was especially painful for her because her only close friend serving in the administration was Donald Rumsfeld, the architect of the war.) But in O'Connor's list of grievances against Republicans in general and Bush in particular, the Schiavo case was the worst.

O'Connor's radar for the political center worked flawlessly in the Schiavo controversy. Though members of Congress in both parties thought they were doing the public's bidding by scrambling to pass the Schiavo bill, polls revealed widespread revulsion at the way Washington intervened in the family tragedy. Around 70 percent of the public disapproved of Bush's and Congress's handling of the Schiavo matter. According to polls, most people objected to the Schiavo legislation for the same reason majorities generally supported women's right to choose abortion—that the decision was one for individuals and families, not the government.

This view appealed to O'Connor's libertarian streak, but the core of her outrage had a different source. To O'Connor, the real danger was the idea that, with this law, Congress was trying to dictate to the courts how they should rule. In other words, worse than telling a family what to do was telling judges what to do.

The subject had long been a theme of her foreign travels. She saw Ukrainian lawyers trained by her CEELI initiative lead the Orange Revolution of 2004, where that nation's Supreme Court voided a corrupt national election. She mourned the loss of judicial independence in Zimbabwe, where the regime of Robert Mugabe sent thugs into its Supreme Court, ignored the court's rulings, and forced some justices off the bench. She frequently mentioned that in Russia presidential guards had killed the chief judge's pet cat. In a little-noticed speech in 2003, at the Arab Judicial Forum in Bahrain, O'Connor had implored nascent democracies to embrace the cause of judicial independence. "It is the kernel of the rule of law, giving the citizenry confidence that the laws will be fairly and equally applied," she said. "Judicial independence allows judges to make decisions that may be contrary to the interests of other branches of government. Presidents, ministers, and legislators at times rush to find convenient solutions to the exigencies of the day. An independent judiciary is uniquely positioned to reflect on the impact of those solutions on rights and liberty, and must act to ensure that those values are not subverted."

With Schiavo, O'Connor saw the threat to judicial independence not in some far-off capitol but in the one across First Street from her own office. Bush and his allies were undermining the separation of powers in the war on terror, ignoring the rule of law in Guantánamo, and undermining judges in Florida—and O'Connor wasn't going to watch in silence as it happened. Later in 2005, she took her indignation on the road, giving fiery speeches on the subject of judicial independence.

O'Connor's foes weren't backing down either. On April 7, Tom DeLay told a conservative conference in Washington entitled "Confronting the Judicial War on Faith" that "judicial independence does not equal judicial supremacy." Speakers at that conference advocated "mass impeachment," stripping the courts of jurisdiction to hear certain cases, and using Congress's budgetary authority to punish offending judges. O'Connor fired right back at him, noting in a speech to an appellate lawyers' association that "this was after the Terri Schiavo case, when the federal courts applied Congress's one-time-only statute as it was written, but, alas, perhaps not how the congressman wished it was written," O'Connor said.

"It gets worse," O'Connor went on. "In all the federal courts, death threats have become increasingly common." Taking aim at Senator Cornyn, she said, "It doesn't help when a high-profile senator, after noting that decisions he sees as activist cause him 'great distress,' suggests there may be 'a cause-and-effect connection' between such activism and the 'recent episodes of courthouse violence in this country.' "

The threats were not an abstract issue for O'Connor. In this very month, April 2005, just weeks after the malicious comments in the chat room, each of the justices was sent homemade cookies containing lethal doses of rat poison. The packages were intercepted before they reached the justices' chambers; the woman who sent them, Barbara Joan March, of Bridgeport, Connecticut, also sent poison to several executive branch officials. (The next year, March was sentenced to fifteen years in prison.) At the time of the Cornyn and DeLay remarks, the episode left O'Connor feeling that the judiciary was under siege.

In her final year on the Court, O'Connor advocated vigorously for the system that made possible all that she had done. Only an independent Supreme Court kept the government tethered to the core values of the Constitution. To O'Connor, the fight for judicial independence had never been more important, because she and her cause now had powerful adversaries—the political party she had once loved and the president she had once installed in office.

For all the challenges she faced, it was still a great time in O'Connor's life. She was a healthy seventy-five-year-old woman working in a job that she adored, one that had given her the chance to be the most important woman in American history. She reviled the current administration, but she had the world's best platform to speak out against its abuses. She was more influential than ever, the critical vote on issue after issue, and she reveled in that responsibility. In Breyer, O'Connor had found a true friend and ally—her first since Powell left the bench many years earlier.

But as the months passed in 2005, O'Connor did not have the chance to savor her good fortune. After a period of some stability, her husband's health was again declining. John did not take well to her move to the second-floor chambers. Worse, he began to exhibit one of the most heartbreaking symptoms of Alzheimer's disease, a penchant to wander. If he was not watched at all times, John simply left her chambers. Several times Court personnel tracked him down just before he got outside, where he could have been lost, injured, or worse. Even with all the resources available to a Supreme Court justice, the situation was becoming unmanageable.

John's comments on election night in 2000 about Justice O'Connor's wish to resign had leaked to the press soon after the decision in *Bush v. Gore*, so speculation about her retirement had been incessant. O'Connor enjoyed public attention and sought publicity, but only on her own terms. Aware that reporters would ask her friends and colleagues if they knew about her plans, she never discussed the subject with them. O'Connor said little even to her three sons about what she should do. But by the end of the Court's term in June 2005, there really wasn't much to debate. She had not outsourced her boys' upbringing, she said, and she was not going to outsource John's care either.

A few days before the end of the term, O'Connor asked to see Rehnquist in his chambers. More than on any other subject, the justices respected each other's privacy on the question of retirement, but the issue couldn't wait anymore. So, more than fifty years after they met at Stanford, the two old friends sat opposite each other and talked about their future.

"Bill, I think John needs me. I think I need to go, but I don't want to leave the Court with two vacancies," she said.

The chief said he couldn't know how his disease would progress, but he was stable at the moment and his doctors had hope. He had returned to the bench on March 21, 2005, after five months away, and he had presided for the last weeks of the term with his tracheotomy tube still in place. "I think I can make it another year," Rehnquist said. "I'm not going to resign." O'Connor was willing to stay one more year and in some ways wanted to remain on the Court. But the chief's desire to hang on for another term meant that it would be two years until she could retire, and she didn't think John could wait that long for her. Rehnquist had forced her hand and thus delivered O'Connor's seat—the crucial one on the Court—to George W. Bush.

The final day of the term was Monday, June 27, and the courtroom was packed in anticipation of news of a possible retirement—Rehnquist's. But the chief merely closed the Court's term with best wishes for a good summer, and the thought of a Supreme Court vacancy seemed to pass from the Washington agenda for another year.

Three days later, however, around lunchtime on Thursday, Pamela Talkin, the marshal of the Court, called Harriet E. Miers, the White House counsel, to arrange for hand delivery of a letter the following morning. (Miers had recently been promoted from deputy chief of staff to succeed Alberto Gonzales as White House counsel.) Talkin did not say which justice would be sending it. The next morning, Friday, July 1, just before nine, Talkin called Miers and said the letter, which was from O'Connor, was on its way.

The news of O'Connor's resignation hit official Washington like thunder. The expected replacement of Rehnquist would have been momentous—there had, after all, been forty-three presidents but only sixteen chief justices. But a Bush appointee in that seat would not change the balance of power on the Court in any dramatic way. The loss of O'Connor, in contrast, would. The conservative counterrevolution, thwarted for so long, often by O'Connor herself, might finally have a chance to succeed.

Few people paid attention to the text of the letter that had been delivered to the president, but O'Connor had crafted the message with care:

> Dear President Bush,
>   This is to inform you of my decision to retire, . . . effective upon the nomination and confirmation of my successor. It has been a great privilege, indeed, to have served as a member of the court for 24 Terms. I will leave it with enormous respect for the integrity of the court and its role under our constitutional structure.
>
>   Sincerely,
>   Sandra Day O'Connor

It was, in O'Connor's polite way, a direct shot at Bush and a plea for the cause that obsessed her in her final days on the bench. She was determined to protect the Court's "role under our constitutional structure" precisely against the incursions that she thought Bush and his allies were attempting to make.

But few people noticed. O'Connor discovered quickly that retirement brought fulsome tributes but also immediate irrelevance. One moment she was the swing vote on the Supreme Court and the next, it seemed, she was a display piece in a museum. She had lost her job, and the political party that was her home had lost her. Worst of all, she was losing her husband. In those first days after her announcement, she didn't answer the phone too often. She sat in her office and cried.

PART
FOUR

" 'G' IS FOR GOD"

The planning for this moment—the opportunity for George W. Bush to nominate a justice to the Supreme Court—had begun shortly after Election Day in 2000. At the time, with Florida still undecided, it was not even clear that Bush would become president, but his team wanted to be ready with a nominee as soon as there was a vacancy. The transformation of the Court would be a central priority of the new administration, if Bush had the chance.

When he began his campaign for president, Bush did not devote a great deal of attention to the subject of the Court. As governor of Texas, he appointed judges with backgrounds much like his own; they were conservatives, but mostly in the corporate rather than the social and evangelical wing of the Republican Party. During the 2000 campaign, Bush sent signals that he would operate much the same way in the White House. In a debate with Al Gore, he was asked whether voters should assume all his judicial appointments would be prolife. "Voters should assume that I have no litmus test on that issue or any other issue," Bush replied blandly. "The voters will know I'll put competent judges on the bench."

But five years later, when Bush finally had the chance to make an appointment to the Court, he had a very different agenda for his nominees. Inside the White House, "moderation" had gone from a goal to an epithet. The messianic nature of his presidency—Bush's conception of his time in office as a moment of dramatic change for the world—affected his judicial nominations as much as it did his decisions on the Middle East. Through a combination of the staff he selected, the political strategy underlying his reelection, and his own personal evolution, Bush now sought transformative appointees, justices who would move the Court sharply and immediately to the right.

Only a few days after the 2000 election was resolved, Bush announced that he would be taking Alberto Gonzales, formerly his chief counsel in Austin, with him to Washington as White House counsel. Gonzales, whom Bush had recently placed on the Texas Supreme Court, chose just one of his local deputies, Stuart Bowen, to go with him. For the remainder of the White House legal staff—the people who would select and vet the candidates for the Supreme Court and other judgeships—the two Texans tapped into the conservative network that had been created two decades earlier for just this opportunity. Conservatives may have represented a lonely minority on law school campuses in the 1980s, but by the new century they constituted a powerful force in Washington. Nothing mattered more to them than taking control of the federal judiciary, especially the Supreme Court.

The young lawyers on the White House staff had a great deal in common. Virtually all of them were members of the Federalist Society. Many had worked on the various Republican investigations of the Clinton administration during the previous eight years. (Brett M. Kavanaugh was the principal author of the Starr report, Christopher Bartolomucci was an investigator in Senator Alfonse D'Amato's investigation of Whitewater, and Bradford Berenson became a familiar media commentator on the investigations.) Several others, like Bowen himself and Timothy Flanigan, who ultimately became Gonzales's deputy, joined up after working for Bush on the recount litigation in Florida. Most had clerked for conservative justices on the Court. (Kennedy clerks like Kavanaugh and Berenson predominated, because the justice tended to hire law clerks who were more conservative than he was.)

Before the inauguration, the early arrivals on the staff—like Kavanaugh, Berenson, and Helgi Walker, a former Thomas clerk— established themselves in office space reserved for the transition in a downtown Washington building. Among their first assignments was to write what were called "candidate memos"—that is, profiles of prospective appointees to the Court. Nearly fifty, Flanigan was the oldest of the lawyers on the staff and the only one who had served in the first Bush administration, as a high-ranking Justice Department official. He had a basic familiarity with the well-known Republican appointees to the courts of appeals, so he farmed out the writing of about a dozen of the profiles to the junior lawyers. Without contacting the candidates and working only from material in the public domain, they set out to analyze the judges' suitability for the Court and their chances for confirmation. Some of the memos ran to almost a hundred pages. Their subjects became known as the "short list."

After Bush took office in January 2001, the counsel's operation moved to the Old Executive Office Building, next door to the White House. The lawyers soon turned their attention to the end of the Court's term in June, a traditional time for justices to announce their retirement; an annual office pool on resignations was set up, with the winner awarded dinner at the AV Ristorante, a run-down Italian restaurant that served as an unofficial clubhouse for conservative lawyers in Washington. (The place was a favorite of Scalia's until it closed in 2007.) Each year, throughout Bush's first term, the betting focused on Rehnquist and O'Connor, but the killjoys who chose no resignations always wound up with the free pizza.

As the years passed without an opening on the Court, the lawyers rotated to other jobs, but one thing rarely changed—the short list. What was especially striking about the list was that it was compiled with little involvement from Gonzales—and none at all from Bush. The president had essentially delegated the matter of Supreme Court appointments to Gonzales, and he turned it over to his young aides. Bush, of course, would make any final decision, but the all-important culling was done almost entirely by some of the most conservative lawyers in the capital. Their priorities were straightforward—movement conservatives only; no "squishes."

Gonzales and Flanigan provided minimal guidance. Bush wanted someone with judicial experience and a proven ideological track record. As was often the case in the Bush White House, the president was eager to avoid what he regarded as the mistakes of his predecessors. Bush didn't want any Clinton-style agonizing or a long public search featuring abundant news leaks. When a vacancy came, the decision should be quick. Nor did Bush want a process like the one that led his father to nominate David Souter—where outsiders like

Warren Rudman, then a New Hampshire senator, intervened at the last minute to push his protégé into the mix. That disorderly rush produced a nominee whose views turned out to be a surprise, at least to conservatives. George W. Bush didn't want any surprises.

In public, the president invariably relied on the same catchphrases when describing his favored judicial philosophy. "I believe in strict constructionists—judges who strictly interpret the Constitution and will not use the bench to write social policy," he said. Or, as he put it on other occasions, he favored judges who would "interpret the law, not legislate from the bench." Of course, all judges, even the most liberal, believe they are interpreting the law, so Bush's summary really amounted to a coded reference to the outlines of a judicial philosophy. When Bush said judges were "legislating from the bench," he meant overturning laws on individual-rights grounds, most notably restrictions on abortion rights. Bush was also talking about judges who prohibited public displays of religious observance. The president—and especially Vice President Cheney—also felt strongly that judges should not interfere with what they felt were the prerogatives of the executive branch in the conduct of foreign policy or military affairs.

As for a more detailed philosophy, like whether Bush supported the Constitution in Exile—and a return to a 1930s conception of the role of the federal government—no one really knew. During the 2000 campaign, Bush said in passing that he would look for judges in the mold of Scalia and Thomas, but he never repeated that promise, because downplaying it served his political purposes. The vow pleased his conservative base, but most voters ignored it. Still, the Scalia and Thomas remark ended up being the most important guidance the White House lawyers received. Unlike their boss, the young conservatives on Bush's staff had thought through precisely what stamp they wanted to place on the federal judiciary—and a network of Scalia and Thomas acolytes was precisely what they had in mind.

The closest Bush came to spelling out what he wanted came every six weeks or so, when he met his judicial selection team, which usually included the vice president, Gonzales, and about a half dozen Justice Department and White House officials. Bush had a businessman's contempt for lawyers generally, and he viewed the process of choosing judges with impatience. Like most other presidents in recent years, Bush deferred to senators of his party on the selection of trial court judgeships, and he always wanted to know what home-state Republicans thought of appeals court candidates as well. All he

needed to know was that a judicial candidate was a "good conservative." He rarely asked questions about candidates' judicial philosophy
and never gave any sign that he had read their judicial opinions.

But Bush did have another priority for his judges—diversity. Early
in his presidency, when the political divisions in the country were not
as toxic as they would become, Bush pressed for women and minorities on the bench. Given the ideological inclinations of the lawyers on
his staff, it wasn't the easiest assignment, but they did initially find a
diverse group of judges to send to the Senate. In fact, the nomination
of Bush's first group of judges would be a little-noticed turning point
in Bush's administration.

Gathered in the East Room on May 9, 2001, the eleven nominees
"looked like America," as the Clinton-era phrase had it. There were
two African Americans, including Roger Gregory, whom Clinton
himself made a recess appointment to the Fourth Circuit after Senator
Jesse Helms blocked a full-fledged appointment, and Barrington
Parker Jr., a Clinton appointee to the district court whom Bush was
promoting to the Second Circuit. There were also three women—
Edith Brown Clement, Deborah Cook, and Priscilla Owen—and a
Hispanic, Miguel Estrada, a brilliant Honduran immigrant who was
tapped for the D.C. Circuit. "A president has few greater responsibilities than that of nominating men and women to the courts of the
United States," Bush said. "He owes it to the Constitution and to the
country to choose with care. I have done so."

Two weeks later, however, Senator James Jeffords, a Vermont
Republican, created a political upheaval by shifting his alliance to the
Democratic Party, thus transferring control of the evenly divided
body away from the GOP. Suddenly, less than a year into Bush's presidency, the Democrats were running the agenda in the Senate. As far
as Bush's judicial nominations were concerned, the change meant that
Patrick Leahy, a committed liberal, also from Vermont, would take
over from Orrin Hatch, the Utah conservative, as chairman of the
Judiciary Committee. Under Hatch, all eleven of Bush's nominees
could have been assured prompt hearings and all but certain confirmation. But Leahy decided to slow down the process, especially for
some of the more controversial nominees, including Owen and
Estrada.

A justice of the Texas Supreme Court, Owen had staked out a position on the far right that had sometimes put her in conflict with
Alberto Gonzales himself. Estrada had glittering credentials—

Harvard Law School, followed by an acclaimed career as a federal prosecutor, an assistant to the solicitor general, and a top corporate
lawyer—but he also had a prickly personality and a reluctance to
share many of his views about constitutional law with the committee.
Because Estrada was tapped for the august D.C. Circuit, where he
would be a likely choice as first Hispanic on the Supreme Court,
Democrats let his nomination linger in limbo.

In short, after the Democratic takeover of the Senate, the atmosphere around Bush's judicial nominations soured. Republicans, especially those in the White House, thought their gestures of goodwill,
like the nominations of Gregory and Parker, had counted for nothing.
Democrats thought Bush, with just a few exceptions, was choosing
conservative extremists. Positions hardened on both sides. Owen's
nomination was stalled for years. After a similar delay, Estrada with-
drew his name in frustration. The others on Bush's original list of
eleven nominees eventually did win confirmation, including the president's choice to fill another vacancy on the D.C. Circuit, John G.
Roberts Jr.

John Roberts was not genetically engineered to be a justice of the
Supreme Court, but it often seemed that way. His career trajectory
was so smooth, his progress so steady, his reputation so exalted, his
personality so winning, that he seemed at times preternaturally favored for that ultimate destination.

Roberts was born in Buffalo on January 27, 1955, and raised in
Indiana, where his father was an executive in the steel industry. Young
John was captain of his high school football team and the best student
in his high school class. In 1976, he graduated from Harvard College
summa cum laude; three years later, he received his degree magna
cum laude from Harvard Law School, where he was managing editor
of the *Law Review*. His colleagues on the *Review* included Justice
Ginsburg's daughter, Jane. Both the college and the law school still
bore the scars of the politically tumultuous 1960s, but Roberts managed to excel without making enemies, a skill that would serve him
well. His first judicial clerkship was with Henry J. Friendly, a legendary judge on the Second Circuit whose chambers in New York
were a frequent destination for especially cerebral graduates of
Harvard Law. Friendly came out of the moderate Republican tradition

that included such judges as Learned Hand and John Marshall Harlan II, who were Souter's great inspirations on the bench.

Roberts decided his future was in Washington, not New York, and he moved to the capital just in time to join in the Reagan revolution. He arrived in William Rehnquist's chambers as a law clerk in the summer of 1980, when the young associate justice was a relative outsider on a Supreme Court that was still dominated by the liberal William Brennan. But conservatives were ascending, and Roberts thrived. After his clerkship, he spent four years in the office of Reagan's White House counsel, where he earned a reputation for brilliance and good humor. His plainspoken memos, preserved in the Reagan Presidential Library, display wit, common sense, and conservative politics in equal measure. For example, regarding a proposal by Chief Justice Warren Burger to lighten the workload of the Supreme Court by the creation of a new intermediate appeals court above the existing circuit courts, Roberts made this tart observation: "While some of the tales of woe emanating from the Court are enough to bring tears to the eyes, it is true that only Supreme Court justices and schoolchildren are expected to and do take the entire summer off."

With perfect timing, Roberts left the Reagan White House shortly before the administration nearly imploded in the Iran-Contra scandal, and he established himself as a successful appellate litigator at the distinguished Washington firm of Hogan & Hartson. With the election of the first President Bush in 1988, Roberts returned to government, this time as the principal deputy to Solicitor General Kenneth Starr. Roberts's easy manner, combined with his vast intellect, made him a favorite of the justices, and he ultimately came to argue thirty-nine cases, far more than any other nominee in the Court's recent history. Such was Roberts's reputation that in 1992, at only thirty-seven, in what would be the last year of the 41st presidency, he was nominated to the D.C. Circuit.

Then, for the first time in his life, Roberts came up against something he couldn't overcome. The Democrats who controlled the Senate sensed victory in November and essentially shut down the confirmation process. Even then, Roberts looked like Supreme Court material, so the Democrats were especially pleased to block his promising judicial career. With Bush's defeat in 1992, Roberts returned to Hogan & Hartson and, in all likelihood, a career of gilded obscurity in corporate law.

Roberts's failure to win confirmation to the D.C. Circuit in 1992 turned out to be a lucky break. For the next eight years, he developed perhaps the best Supreme Court practice in the United States, mostly representing large corporations in business disputes with one another or with the government. Almost every year, Roberts had several arguments before the justices, and he also filed a steady stream of cert petitions and amicus briefs. (Not incidentally, he also made approximately a million dollars a year.) Roberts generally steered clear of the political controversies of the Clinton years, declining to participate in any investigations of the White House and refusing even to become a prominent talking head about impeachment. His contribution to Bush's legal strategy in the Florida recount was important but low profile. A natural reticence and skill at avoiding enemies kept him largely out of public view. Still, among his former colleagues in Republican politics and law, Roberts retained a golden aura, even without having established a public record of partisanship. Miguel Estrada used to advise young lawyers coming out of the solicitor general's office, "Go work for John G. Roberts. The 'G' is for God."

If Roberts had been confirmed in 1992, of course, he would have amassed an extensive paper trail of controversial decisions on the D.C. Circuit by the time George W. Bush took office in 2001. Instead, Roberts had only enhanced his reputation by excelling as an advocate. Again, once Democrats established control of the Judiciary Committee in the middle of the year, they tried to stall Roberts's second nomination as they did his first nine years earlier. But the Republicans retook control of the Senate in 2002, and Hatch promptly moved Roberts through the process early the following year. On May 8, 2003, he was confirmed by the full Senate on a voice vote, without opposition. Before Roberts had even taken his seat as a federal appeals court judge, his friends in the White House counsel's office started compiling the dossier that put him on the short list for the Supreme Court.

In 2000, Bush had campaigned as a "compassionate conservative" and "a uniter, not a divider," pledging to surmount the partisanship that had consumed Washington during the Clinton years. But in the 2004 race, Bush shifted to more ideological priorities, hoping to motivate a conservative base, mostly evangelical Christians, that had felt slighted during the earlier contest. The issues that mattered most to them were all on the Supreme Court's agenda, and so the Court played a more central role in Bush's second campaign.

Indeed, the president's courtship of evangelicals led to a curious moment in the campaign. During Bush's second debate with John Kerry, the president answered a question about possible Supreme Court appointments by attacking the *Dred Scott* decision, which he characterized as "where judges years ago said that the Constitution allowed slavery because of personal property rights. That's a personal opinion; that's not what the Constitution says." Decided in 1857, the *Dred Scott* case has been obsolete for decades because it was overruled by the passage of the Thirteenth and Fourteenth Amendments after the Civil War. Though many observers in the mainstream media were puzzled by Bush's invocation of the ancient and irrelevant precedent, it served an important purpose. Within the antiabortion movement, *Roe v. Wade* is often described as the *Dred Scott* of modern times—a monstrous case that deserves reversal. In coded language, Bush used the debate to signal his agreement with that view.

So the conservative base came into 2005 expecting payback, in the form of thoroughly acceptable judicial appointments. Just after the election, those activists first made their presence felt by punishing Arlen Specter for his comments about *Roe v. Wade*. In the months that followed, they pushed the Senate to confirm many of Bush's long-stalled judicial nominees. (Priscilla Owen, the Texas justice, had still not received a vote four years after she was named in Bush's initial group of eleven nominees.) During Bush's first term, Democrats had used Senate rules to force Republicans to muster sixty votes, rather than just a majority, on Bush's more controversial judicial nominees. These Democratic tactics amounted to filibusters against the would-be judges, and conservative activists like Jay Sekulow began pressing the Senate to ban the use of filibusters to stop judicial nominations.

In the spring of 2005, the Senate nearly imploded over the issue of judicial confirmations. The filibuster rule amounted to the principal difference between the rules of the House of Representatives and the Senate; in the House, a simple majority could essentially force through any legislation it supported, while the Senate required a three-fifths majority, or sixty votes. With only fifty-five Republicans in the Senate, the filibuster rule meant that the minority Democrats could delay or even stop any law or nomination, if they could stay united. The filibuster rule was designed to push senators toward compromises and bipartisanship. Conservatives, including many

Republican senators, began arguing for a change in the Senate rules, so that a simple majority could bring nominations to a vote. The proposed change in the venerable Senate procedures was so great that the proposal was nicknamed the Nuclear Option. For his part, Bush implicitly endorsed the change in his State of the Union address, insisting, to huge applause in the chamber, "Every judicial nominee deserves an up or down vote."

At the last minute, though, with the Senate at the nuclear brink, a compromise put off the conflagration, at least for the time being. A bipartisan group of fourteen moderate Senators, meeting in Senator John McCain's office on May 23, 2005, brokered a deal where some of Bush's long-delayed nominees (like Owen) would finally get their up or down votes and thus be confirmed. In return, the Republicans in the group agreed not to change the Senate's rules—yet. Under the deal, the so-called Gang of 14 announced jointly that "nominees should only be filibustered under extraordinary circumstances," a term that was carefully left undefined.

The ultimate battle had been postponed, but the political message was unmistakable—that the confirmation of very conservative judges was a central concern of the Republican Party. The compromise essentially left the moderates of both parties in charge of determining whether a filibuster could ever be mounted; since these senators generally disdained filibusters, and even the Democrats among them cared less about thwarting Bush's judicial agenda, the compromise amounted to a victory for the conservatives.

Five weeks later, O'Connor announced her retirement. By that point, it was clear that Arlen Specter and other old-timers were reading an obsolete script for modern confirmation battles. In 1987, Robert Bork was defeated because he was too conservative for a Democratic Senate, and Specter still believed that the current Senate might vote down a nominee who was too conservative. In truth, the bigger risk for a George W. Bush nominee was if he or she was not conservative enough. To put it another way, Bork couldn't be confirmed *because* he opposed *Roe v. Wade*; in 2005, a nominee couldn't be selected *unless* he or she opposed *Roe v. Wade*.

O'Connor submitted her resignation on Friday, July 1, just before the Fourth of July holiday weekend. By the beginning of the next workweek, the conservative base started making demands about her replacement. The first: anyone except Alberto Gonzales.

From the moment Gonzales had come to Washington from Austin, it had been more or less assumed that Bush would appoint him to the Supreme Court. His story could hardly be more inspiring. The second of eight children of a construction worker and a homemaker, the grandson of Mexican immigrants, Gonzales was raised in a Texas town whose name matched his family's circumstances—Humble. He enlisted in the air force out of high school, graduated from Rice University, and earned a degree from Harvard Law School in 1982. Gonzales became a partner in the prominent Houston law firm of Vinson & Elkins, where he worked until Governor Bush named him his general counsel in 1994. Three years later, Bush appointed him secretary of state, and in 1999 he named Gonzales a justice of the Texas Supreme Court. Gonzales served for less than two years, because Bush took him to Washington as his first White House counsel. After his reelection, the president named Gonzales the nation's eightieth attorney general and first Hispanic to hold the job. Gonzales was only fifty years old in 2005, the perfect age to begin a long career as a justice. He would, of course, have been the first Hispanic, a major milestone for an ethnic group that Bush had spent much of his political career courting. In addition, on a personal level, Bush adored Gonzales, who was by 2005 one of his closest friends in the government.

The clear political and personal logic for a Gonzales appointment meant that leading conservatives felt they had to move swiftly to forestall his nomination. The attacks began early the next week, in the pages of the *Washington Times*, a sort of house organ of the conservative movement (owned by the Reverend Sun Myung Moon). Then, Phyllis Schlafly, founder of Eagle Forum, a conservative activist group, said, "I don't see any paper trail that convinces me he is somebody who is a strong constitutionalist." Similarly unsupported comments came from Paul Weyrich, chairman of the Free Congress Foundation, a founding father of the New Right. The *National Review* published an editorial entitled "No to Justice Gonzales." Robert Novak, the conservative columnist, wrote of "deep and broad opposition [to Gonzales] from the president's own political base."

In fact, the "base" was a couch—in the living room of the Capitol Hill town house belonging to a former congressional staffer named Manuel Miranda. A year earlier, Miranda had been forced out of his job as a staffer for Bill Frist, majority leader of the Senate, when it was revealed that he had been reading the e-mails of Democratic staffers on the Judiciary Committee. So Miranda set up shop at home, founding what he called, rather grandly, the Third Branch Conference, which mostly amounted to himself, his laptop, and cordless phone. But Miranda knew almost everyone in the conservative legal movement, and his blast e-mails and conference calls became a key conduit of anti-Gonzales information.

Just two hours after O'Connor's retirement became public on the morning of July 1, Miranda scheduled a conference call with his allies, telling them he was "urging that the nomination not be Alberto Gonzales." After the long weekend, Miranda elaborated on his reasons, saying that Gonzales "is not a movement conservative. He has not written prolifically on many issues. And so, there is no paper trail. And, we don't know what he really thinks on many, many issues. That is something that conservatives on this nomination cannot tolerate. Justice David H. Souter did not have a paper trail. Justice Anthony M. Kennedy had a paper trail, but not on the particular issues that conservatives wished to see. So, it's really no more Souters and no more Kennedys. And that does not add up to an appointment for Gonzales." Miranda wasn't much more than a glorified blogger, but his passion and his contacts whipped his views into something like the conservative conventional wisdom. He helped popularize the devastating quip " 'Gonzales' is Spanish for 'Souter.' "

By this time, bigger guns than Miranda were taking up the anti-Gonzales cause. A delegation of conservative lawyers, led by former attorney general Edwin Meese III and C. Boyden Gray, White House counsel to the first President Bush, met with Andrew Card, the president's chief of staff, to warn against a Gonzales appointment. The onslaught was so immediate and intense that Bush himself, who was on a state visit to Denmark on July 6, felt compelled to respond. "I don't like it when a friend gets criticized. I'm loyal to my friends. And all of a sudden this fellow, who is a good public servant and a really fine person, is under fire," Bush said. "And so, do I like it? No, I don't like it at all."

Inside the White House, the young Federalists in the counsel's office—conservative firebrands themselves—watched the attacks on

Gonzales with astonishment. They knew that he had been among the administration's true believers, "a hundred percenter," in the movement argot. Gonzales had taken the most aggressive position among Bush's allies on the legal basis for the war on terror, dismissing the protections of the Geneva Conventions as "quaint." He had reversed decades of precedent by refusing to submit Bush's judicial nominees to the scrutiny of the American Bar Association, because he thought the ABA was too liberal. He had joined with Vice President Cheney in asserting a new and expansive view of executive power and concurred fully with the refusal to turn over the documents in the energy task force lawsuit. He had negotiated the government's position in the *Grutter* and *Gratz* affirmative action cases (albeit with a slightly more sympathetic view than Dick Cheney and Ted Olsen) and had supervised the selection of the judicial nominees who had so outraged the Democrats that they were moved to filibuster. Gonzales had proved his conservative bona fides many times over. What do these people want? the young lawyers in the White House asked in bewilderment. He hired us, didn't he? What did Gonzales do to deserve this kind of treatment?

The answer was straightforward. In 2000, during his brief career on the Texas Supreme Court, Gonzales had participated in a series of cases known as *In re Jane Doe*. Bush, then governor, had signed a law that required minors to obtain the consent of their parents if they wanted an abortion. As required by United States Supreme Court precedent, the law contained an exception that allowed some girls—abuse victims, for example—to proceed with the permission of a judge rather than a parent. Interpreting this so-called judicial bypass provision, Gonzales joined a 6–3 majority on the court in allowing a seventeen-year-old to go to a judge rather than her parents. The conclusion obviously troubled Gonzales, but he felt compelled to follow the law. "While the ramifications of such a law may . . . be personally troubling to me as a parent, it is my obligation as a judge to impartially apply the laws of this state without imposing my moral view on the decisions of the Legislature," he wrote.

The conclusions of the Texas court in the abortion case were narrow. None of the judges, including Gonzales, addressed whether *Roe* should be affirmed or overturned. The opinions didn't interpret the U.S. Constitution at all. The only issue was how one specific Texas law applied to one girl. But those caveats counted for nothing. Gonzales's career—including four years of loyal service in George W. Bush's

White House—also counted for nothing. Fairly or not, accurately or not, the decisions branded Gonzales as unreliable on abortion, and that was enough for conservatives to veto him as a nominee to the Supreme Court. Such was the power of movement conservatives—and such was the importance of abortion to them—that Bush had no choice but to eliminate his good friend from consideration. The president never wavered in his admiration for Gonzales and never passed up an opportunity to say kind things about him. But he also never seriously considered him for a seat on the Supreme Court.

RETIRING THE TROPHY

I n the sticky heat of a summer evening, Theodore Olson surveyed with evident and understandable satisfaction the guests assembled in his spacious backyard. For years, Ted and Barbara Olson, the first couple of the conservative legal world, had dreamed of a night like this one. A Californian who came east to be an assistant attorney general under Reagan, Ted went on to argue *Bush v. Gore* and, as a reward, to serve four years as Bush's solicitor general. His wife, a former Republican Senate staffer, had been a vitriolic and telegenic critic of the Clintons and the author of best-selling books attacking their morals, politics, and marriage. The Olsons' wedding in 1996 had drawn such conservative luminaries as Clarence Thomas, Robert Bork, and the couple's close friend Kenneth Starr. If Hillary Clinton's vast right-wing conspiracy had a headquarters, it was their estate in Great Falls, Virginia. Together the Olsons had dreamed of a true conservative majority on the Supreme Court, and now the moment had come. And the likely next justice was among the guests that night.

With the moment of triumph so close, there was a note of poignancy to the evening, because Barbara was not there to share in the celebration. She had been a passenger on the plane that crashed into the Pentagon on September 11, 2001. Her courageous phone calls to her husband in the moments before she died provided important clues to what happened on that terrible day. Still, there was little doubt that she would have approved Ted's raiding their famous wine cellar for this special occasion.

It was a more polished crowd than one would find at, say, the Colorado Springs headquarters of Focus on the Family. The partygoers eschewed the rhetoric associated with the likes of Jay Sekulow or Manuel Miranda. But for all the differences in class and temperament in the conservative movement, the agenda for the Supreme Court was remarkably consistent across the board. Reverse *Roe*. Expand executive power. Speed executions. Welcome religion into the public sphere. Return the Constitution from its exile since the New Deal. All of these goals seemed increasingly within reach.

The ostensible reason for the party was to salute David Leitch, who was leaving his position as deputy White House counsel to become general counsel to the Ford Motor Company. The gathering was modest—perhaps twenty-five people—and it served as a reminder of what a small world the Washington conservative legal elite was. Leitch himself had an almost comic number of connections to the likely nominees. He had been a law clerk for J. Harvie Wilkinson III, had worked for Michael Luttig in the first Bush Justice Department, had become Roberts's protégé at Hogan & Hartson, and had then served as Gonzales's deputy in the White House.

The candidates assembled that night began with Olson himself. He had a place on the short list, but no one, including Olson, thought he had much chance. He had never been a judge, his political activities had made him a Democratic target, and besides, at sixty-four he was probably too old.

Al Gonzales was there, receiving commiseration for the abuse he was taking from the movement conservatives—some of whom were also among Olson's guests. Gonzales was technically still a possibility, but the conservative assault had taken its toll. He, too, looked like a very long shot.

Harvie Wilkinson, the courtly former chief judge of the Fourth Circuit, remained in the running. He was telling stories to his fellow guests in the same soft Virginia accent as that of his mentor, Lewis Powell. The O'Connor seat was vacant, but everyone knew Rehnquist probably wouldn't last much longer, so many in the White House were planning for this first nominee to move up to chief justice. That was good for Wilkinson because he had the patrician charm of a Southern politician, a valuable skill for the more public duties of a chief. Still, Wilkinson was already sixty years old and, worse, he had the dreaded taint of moderation about him.

There were no such worries about Michael Luttig, whom no one ever called a moderate. Although Luttig was invited, he didn't make it to Olson's party, and his nonappearance reflected a problem with his candidacy: he was awkward and unsocial. Still, if anyone was the favorite for the job at this point, it was Luttig, Wilkinson's colleague on the Fourth Circuit. Luttig was just fifty years old, the perfect age, a former Scalia clerk and a judge since 1991, with a network of former law clerks pressing hard for his appointment. Luttig still lived in Vienna, Virginia, a Washington suburb, and he remained well wired in the capital. He had been a groomsman at Roberts's wedding.

Like Olson, Luttig had suffered a random tragedy. In 1994, his parents were the victims of a carjacking in their driveway in Tyler, Texas. His father was killed, and his mother survived only by playing dead. During the trial of his father's killers, Luttig moved his chambers to Tyler and testified for the prosecution in the penalty phase. In 2002, Napoleon Beazley was executed for the murder.

John Roberts was there, too, of course, hanging back as was his custom, smiling at other people's jokes, taking in the scene. In the sticky heat, Olson was wearing a Hawaiian shirt and shorts, but Roberts never removed his blazer and tie.

Anticipating that Rehnquist would resign, Bush's advisers had prepared intensively for the end of the Court's term in June. In May, all of the leading candidates were invited to Washington for interviews with senior administration officials. Luttig, Roberts, Wilkinson, and two others—Samuel A. Alito Jr., the veteran judge on the Third Circuit, and Edith Brown Clement, a much newer appointee to the Fifth Circuit—were questioned by a panel that included Gonzales, Andrew Card, Karl Rove, the president's political adviser, Cheney, and Lewis Libby, the vice president's chief of staff.

Clement was a surprise, because she had only joined the appeals court bench in 2001, after a decade as a federal trial judge in New Orleans. The presence of such an obscure figure in the final group—she had not written a single opinion of note—illustrated a problem with Bush's stated goal of diversity when it came to Supreme Court appointments. Several Republican women appointed to the federal bench—like Edith Jones on the Fifth Circuit, the just-confirmed Janice Rogers Brown on the D.C. Circuit, and Priscilla Owen, also on the Fifth—were incendiary figures, likely to ignite filibusters among Democrats. Others could be dismissed as closet moderates. Joy Clement, as she was known, had charm in abundance and was well regarded for her conservative speeches on the after-dinner circuit. But she clearly lacked the stature of her competitors.

Bush remained largely detached from the process until he returned from Europe in the second week in July. He had taken the candidate memos with him to study, but he prided himself on his ability to size people up in person. His aides spoke often of his "intuitive" style of managing, which relied more on gut reactions than detailed research. (After first meeting President Vladimir Putin of Russia, Bush said, "I looked the man in the eye. . . . I was able to get a sense of his soul.") On July 14 and 15, several of the candidates were ushered in to see the president through the East Wing of the White House to make sure that they were not seen by the reporters who monitored the west gate. Wilkinson, Clement, Alito, Luttig, and Roberts all spent about an hour with the president. Their conversations, though, were little more than chitchat. Bush asked them all about their families, several about their exercise routines, and Wilkinson about Yale, where the president had been his contemporary. There was little discussion of judicial philosophy, and none at all of individual cases. (Recalling his interview with Bush, Luttig later complained to a friend, "It was totally nonsubstantive"—and thus revealed why he didn't get the job.)

Still, this was a time of big ambitions, even grandiosity, at the White House. When it came to appointments, Bush's advisers liked to brag, "We only hit home runs." In the first summer of his second term, Bush still had a sense that his presidency would bring dramatic changes to the country and the world. Right after his reelection, he had said, "I earned capital in the campaign, political capital, and now I intend to spend it. It is my style." In his second inaugural address, Bush had announced, "It is the policy of the United States to seek and support the growth of democratic movements and institutions in every nation and culture, with the ultimate goal of ending tyranny in our world." In the domestic sphere, Bush had committed himself to transforming the most venerable and sprawling of all federal programs, Social Security. The appointment of a Supreme Court justice, in Bush's view, had to represent a similarly large gesture.

That doomed Wilkinson. Bush's aides condemned the Virginian by calling him "a cautious choice." At that moment, the Bush presidency was not about caution. The president liked Clement a great deal, but he was troubled by her lack of a substantial judicial record. In addition, an estranged former law clerk of Clement's was threatening to go public with purported tales of racially and religiously insensitive comments by the judge; the controversy might be disruptive, because there was so little else to say about her. Alito struck Bush as solid, but he had few passionate supporters (or detractors) in the White House or Washington generally. (Alito, who lived outside Newark, was not invited to the Olson soirée.)

In the end, the choice came down to Roberts or Luttig. Roberts had been teaching a summer class in London, and he came back to Washington for his interview with Bush on July 15, then returned overseas. He was blessed with supporters in the right places. Leitch revered Roberts, as did William Kelley, a professor at Notre Dame Law School who was Harriet Miers's successor as deputy White House counsel. Brett Kavanaugh, who was now Bush's staff secretary, and Christopher Bartolomucci and Bradford Berenson, who had left the White House, all weighed in heavily on Roberts's behalf. Most important, Bush immediately took to Roberts in their interview. The president had radar for anyone who put on airs, and Roberts's Midwestern reserve played well with Bush. The fact that Roberts had just adopted two young children especially impressed the president.

Still, Luttig was the conservative's dream choice—probably smarter than his mentor Scalia, twenty years younger, and very likely more conservative. He had been a hero to the movement since 1991, when as a Justice Department official he had steered Thomas through his agonizing confirmation hearings. Luttig's long history of writing conservative judicial opinions made him the opposite of a stealth nominee; he was a guarantee. Much more than Roberts, Luttig had paid his dues to the cause.

Luttig had one important ally on the White House staff—who was also a Roberts skeptic, if not an outright detractor. Harriet Miers had been White House counsel for only a few months, replacing Gonzales when he was named attorney general. She did not come out of the Washington legal establishment that seemed so enamored of John Roberts. All she heard about Roberts was . . . Trust us, trust us, he's a real conservative. But that wasn't enough for Miers. She was a lawyer who believed in facts, not opinions. Her favorite candidate was Sam Alito, who had written dozens of judicial opinions that left no doubt in Miers's mind that he belonged on the Supreme Court. As for Roberts, Miers wanted the same level of proof that he was a Bush conservative.

Miers was so skeptical of Roberts that she summoned Leonard Leo, the executive vice president of the Federalist Society, to make the case for him. Leo, along with Boyden Gray, Jay Sekulow, and Ed Meese, served as the principal emissaries between the White House and the conservative movement on Supreme Court nominations. Even among that quartet, Leo was known as the monitor of the various nominees' ideological purity. Miers wanted Leo to convince her that Roberts was a true conservative. Leo assembled a selection of Roberts's writings from the Reagan White House and his decisions from the D.C. Circuit and walked Miers through them, but she still had her doubts. "Well," Miers said, signaling the direction the search was going, "I hope you're right."

Miers had worked in the White House, largely in obscurity, throughout the first term. She came to Washington from her law practice in Dallas to be Bush's staff secretary, an important but largely ministerial job that involves controlling the paper flow in and out of the Oval Office. The job suited her meticulous temperament and deep loyalty to Bush. The only substantive responsibility was examining the recommendations that came to the president and determining whether they comported with his ideology and record. To do her job, Miers felt she almost had to know Bush so well that she had, in essence, to become him.

No one was better suited to this self-denying task than Miers. For one thing, no one worked harder. Her red Mercedes (with Bush bumper stickers going back to his gubernatorial races) was often the first one in the White House parking lot in the morning and the last one out at night. After two years as staff secretary, she moved on to be deputy chief of staff for policy, another job where she had to test initiatives from the cabinet departments for their loyalty to the Bush program. Miers had few known views of her own but a fierce allegiance to the president, both personally and politically. Her question about John Roberts was: What has he ever done to pay his dues to the cause?

Dick Cheney had similar questions. The vice president was the only figure in the White House who was touting Scalia as a possible replacement for Rehnquist, whose departure seemed imminent. As became clear in their duck-hunting expedition, Cheney and Scalia had been friends since the Ford years. (The lawyers on the White House staff regarded a possible Scalia promotion as an unnecessary additional confirmation fight for a man who, at age sixty-nine, probably would not serve for very long anyway.) Cheney was also the guardian of ideological purity at the White House and, like Miers, he needed some proof that Roberts was actually as conservative as his backers promised he would be.

Their doubts may have been overcome in any case, but then a fortuitous coincidence sealed Roberts's nomination. On July 15, 2005, the day of his interview with Bush, the D.C. Circuit upheld the administration's plans for the use of military tribunals for the prisoners held at the navy base at Guantánamo Bay, Cuba. In 2004, of course, O'Connor's scathing rebuke to the administration in the *Hamdi* case had mandated that the detainees receive some sort of due process of law. In *Hamdan v. Rumsfeld*, Roberts joined a three-judge panel that approved the Bush plan that had been developed in response to O'Connor's scolding. In that case, it was clear that the administration's procedures did not comport with the Geneva Conventions, which required that all prisoners receive trials "by a regularly constituted court affording all the judicial guarantees which are recognized as indispensable by civilized peoples." But Roberts and his colleagues said the Bush administration did not have to comply with the international treaty, because the "Geneva Convention cannot be judicially enforced."

No issue mattered more to Cheney (and to Bush and, thus, to Miers) than preserving the power of the president, especially with regard to what the president called the global war on terror. International obligations, and especially the Geneva Conventions, drew sneers in this White House. The vice president believed that since the Nixon years the executive branch had steadily ceded authority to Congress, the courts, and even international institutions, and he made it his mission to arrest that decline. (It was the principle at issue in the energy task force/duck-hunting case in the Supreme Court.) As important as abortion was to the outside conservative groups, the issue of executive power—and stopping the meddling of liberal judges—was to Cheney. With *Hamdan*, Roberts had proved himself worthy. Cheney and Miers were on board.

The next Monday, Roberts was told to return from London once more; Bush's decision was near. The following morning, Tuesday, July 19, rumors swept Washington that the choice would be Clement, who had met with Bush over lunch on Saturday. (Sekulow, who fancied himself a White House insider but was merely a useful instrument to those in power, spent the morning saying Clement was a done deal.) In fact, at 12:35, Bush left a meeting with the Australian prime minister to call Roberts and offer him the job. Roberts's wife and two children joined him and the president at the White House for dinner at 7:00, and at 9:00, in the East Room, on live television, Bush introduced Roberts to the nation. The contrast with the last announcement of a Supreme Court nominee was stark. In 1994, during the news graveyard of Friday afternoon, Clinton had made a rushed and grumpy disclosure of Breyer's name, without even having the nominee by his side. Bush was showcasing Roberts in prime time.

With his two children scampering nearby, his son, Jack, in short pants acting out Spiderman moves, Roberts spoke as the best Supreme Court advocates always do—without notes. "Thank you, Mr. President," he said. "Thank you very much. It is both an honor and very humbling to be nominated to serve on the Supreme Court. Before I became a judge, my law practice consisted largely of arguing cases before the Court. That experience left me with a profound appreciation for the role of the Court in our constitutional democracy and a deep regard for the Court as an institution. I always got a lump in my throat whenever I walked up those marble steps to argue a case before the Court, and I don't think it was just from the nerves. I am very grateful for the confidence the president has shown in nominating me, and I look forward to the next step in the process before the United States Senate." He concluded by thanking his family and acknowledging his children, "who remind me every day why it's so important for us to work to preserve the institutions of our democracy."

Any doubts about Roberts's confirmation, to the extent there ever were any, vanished that evening. His obvious intelligence, abundant qualifications, and even his wholesome good looks would have made sustained opposition difficult. Within a day of the Roberts choice, Republicans in the Gang of 14 were saying that his nomination did not constitute the "extraordinary circumstances" justifying a filibuster. More important, the Democrats in the gang quickly agreed. As Senator Joseph Lieberman said, "This is a credible nominee and not one that, as far as we know now, has a record that could in any sense be described as extremist." With fifty-five Republicans in the Senate and a filibuster effectively off the table, Roberts could expect to cruise to confirmation. His hearings were set to begin on Tuesday, September 6, the day after Labor Day.

Rehnquist had surprised almost everyone by not resigning on the last day of the term in June. His voice had been raspy and his tracheotomy tube still in place, but his good humor that day suggested he might be holding his disease at bay. His stated hope to O'Connor that he wanted to serve one more year appeared plausible, if not exactly realistic.

But the chief's health had declined over the summer. Anaplastic thyroid carcinoma is an especially virulent cancer; it is rare for patients to live longer than a year after diagnosis, and Rehnquist by summer had passed the eight-month mark. His mind never failed, and he was delighted to learn that Roberts, his former law clerk, had been nominated to serve with him. Only four former Supreme Court law clerks had gone on to become justices: Byron White (clerk for Chief Justice Fred Vinson), Rehnquist himself (for Robert Jackson), Stevens (for Wiley Rutledge), and Breyer (for Arthur Goldberg). Roberts would have been the first to serve alongside his one-time boss.

During the summer, although Rehnquist was twice taken to the hospital with breathing problems, his dry humor remained intact. When asked on his final visit to the emergency room who his primary care physician was, the chief muttered, "My dentist." On Monday, August 29, he told a visitor to his home that he still planned to participate when the Court opened in October, but at that point there was nothing more his doctors could do for him. He died with his three children beside him in his town house in Arlington on the night of Saturday, September 3.

Earlier in the week of Rehnquist's death, starting on August 29, Hurricane Katrina nearly demolished New Orleans and the surrounding area. The stumbling federal response to the crisis transformed the Bush presidency, including the selection of Supreme Court justices.

The president didn't make it to the general vicinity of the damage until September 2, when he received a briefing at the airport in Mobile, Alabama. There, on that morning, Bush uttered one of the defining phrases of his presidency—"Brownie, you're doing a heck of a job"—to the hapless director of the Federal Emergency Management Agency, Michael Brown. Even in the first few days after Katrina, it was clear that the White House needed any distraction from the calamity.

In normal circumstances, Bush might have taken some time to study his options following Rehnquist's death on the Saturday of a holiday weekend. Cheney, as well as some others in the conservative movement, had been urging him to consider promoting Scalia, and the idea at least seemed worthy of some consideration. But Roberts's nomination in July had been a total success, and now the administration—rather desperately—needed another. As almost always throughout his presidency, Bush defined success as pleasing his base.

Over the summer, conservatives embraced Roberts, who was little known outside Washington when he was nominated. During that time, reporters obtained access to about 75,000 pages of documents from Roberts's days as a young lawyer in the Reagan White House. His memos showed him to be an enthusiastic and sometimes caustic conservative who, for example, dismissed "the purported gender gap" between men and women in income and asserted that proposals to address the problem were "staggeringly pernicious" and "anti-capitalist." Reflecting the views of his bosses, Roberts supported school prayer and opposed affirmative action. In response to a proposal by a Democratic congressman to hold a "conference on power-sharing" to iron out the duties of each branch of government, Roberts said, "There already has, of course, been a 'Conference on Power Sharing.' It took place in Philadelphia's Constitution Hall in 1787, and someone should tell [Congressman] Levitas about it and the 'report' it issued."

In the mainstream news media, which were still largely working off an obsolete model of the confirmation process, these memos were generally treated as problems for Roberts's nomination (although manageable ones, to be sure). The governing idea behind the news coverage was that Roberts, like Bork, risked defeat if he was seen as too conservative. But the truth was precisely the reverse—that the only threat to a Bush nominee to the Supreme Court was if he or she was seen as not conservative enough. As Manuel Miranda wrote in the online *Wall Street Journal* about Roberts's Reagan-era memos, "One sentiment is widely shared among conservatives: What a relief. Judge Roberts's writing as a young lawyer show him to be a solid constitutionalist."

Bush needed good news so badly that he acted with a degree of haste that was nearly disrespectful to Rehnquist. At 8:01 a.m. on September 5, Labor Day, less than forty-eight hours after Rehnquist died, Bush summoned the news media to the Oval Office to announce that he was nominating Roberts to be the seventeenth chief justice of the United States. "For the past two months, members of the United States Senate and the American people have learned about the career and character of Judge Roberts," Bush said. "They like what they see. He's a gentleman. He's a man of integrity and fairness."

The continuing fallout from the hurricane meant that Roberts's hearings received relatively little attention, especially since the outcome was a foregone conclusion. (They began slightly later than originally planned because Roberts was now being considered for chief, not associate, justice.) In his opening statement, on September 12, Roberts said, "A certain humility should characterize the judicial role. Judges and justices are servants of the law, not the other way around. Judges are like umpires. Umpires don't make the rules; they apply them. The role of an umpire and a judge is critical. They make sure everybody plays by the rules. But it is a limited role. Nobody ever went to a ball game to see the umpire." Roberts was right about the motivations of baseball fans, if not Supreme Court justices. In truth, unlike umpires, Supreme Court justices *do* make the rules, and their job amounts to far more than a mechanical process of applying them.

As to how Roberts himself would apply the vague commands of the Constitution, he was careful not to commit himself. Under questioning from Arlen Specter, Roberts said that *Roe* was "settled as a precedent of the court, entitled to respect under principles of stare decisis," but he also pointed out that the justices sometimes reversed their own precedents. Roberts wouldn't say how he would vote on *Roe*. Like all other nominees, Roberts dodged making commitments, but his winning manner and broad erudition were manifest. He remembered the names of old cases with ease and summarized the arguments on a wide variety of constitutional controversies. He quoted the Federalist papers from memory. Senator Dick Durbin, an Illinois Democrat, spoke for many when he said Roberts "retired the trophy" for outstanding performance by a judicial nominee. On September 22, he was confirmed by the Judiciary Committee by a vote of 13–5. A week later, he was confirmed by the full Senate by a vote of 78–22.

Shortly after Bush nominated Roberts for chief justice, the White House announced that the president would refrain from announcing his choice for the O'Connor seat until the new chief was confirmed. Administration officials reasoned wisely that there was no reason to give political opponents several extra months to attack a second choice for the Court. But even though the White House wasn't making any names public as possible replacements for O'Connor during that period, Bush's aides were weighing their options.

With the exception of the Roberts nomination, the summer brought only dismal news for the Bush administration. Earlier in 2005, Iraqis had staged their first free elections since the war, and the voters' purple-ink-stained fingers became symbols of a hopeful emerging democracy. But in the months that followed, chaos reigned, and dozens of American troops continued to die in Iraq each month. Also during this period, Bush's plan for including private accounts in the Social Security system crashed, scorned even by most Republicans. Finally, the overall federal response to Hurricane Katrina was widely viewed as indifferent at best and incompetent at worst. Bush's approval ratings plunged—from around 60 percent favorable at the time of his reelection to about the same percentage unfavorable less than a year later. It was in this context that the president made his second appointment to the Supreme Court.

Once again Bush considered naming a woman to the Court. After O'Connor's resignation, he had been pressured on the subject from some unusual sources. While on a trip to South Africa, Laura Bush said on NBC's *Today* show, "I would really like him to name another woman." Later that day, Bush appeared startled that his usually circumspect wife had made such a direct appeal through the press. "I can't wait to hear her advice—in person—when she gets back," he said in the Oval Office. O'Connor herself signaled that she felt more freedom in her public comments now that she was a lame duck. Returning to a judicial conference in Spokane after a day of flyfishing, she was informed that Roberts would be named to replace her. "That's fabulous!" she said, calling Roberts a "brilliant legal mind, a straight shooter, articulate. He's good in every way, except he's not a woman."

But what woman? Bush had already considered various possibilities earlier in the summer, and he had not come up with a perfect choice. The president had been explicitly warned by Harry Reid, the Democratic leader in the Senate, that the women judges most beloved by conservative activists—Janice Rogers Brown, Edith Jones, and Priscilla Owen—would likely meet a filibuster. Bush didn't shy from confrontations, but he saw no reason to prompt an unnecessary clash either. Wouldn't it be better to propose a justice who shared his own views—which were essentially indistinguishable from those of his party's most conservative members—but who would also have an easy time getting confirmed? Was there anyone who fit that description?

As Bush was talking about the issue with his aides, he remembered something else that Reid had said earlier in the summer. Reid, too, wanted to avoid an unnecessary battle over the Supreme Court. In addition to proffering his Democratic blacklist, the senator raised an interesting possibility. He said he had met with Harriet Miers shortly before Roberts was nominated and he had been very impressed. Reid said Bush should consider his own White House counsel as a nominee to the Supreme Court.

Bush was intrigued. No one was more loyal to him and his agenda than Harriet. And the Democratic leader was suggesting that she could be confirmed without a fight.

"I KNOW HER HEART"

The nomination of Harriet Miers to the Supreme Court quickly devolved into political black comedy. The caricature of Miers that emerged during her brief journey across the national consciousness—that of a luckless spinster manifestly unqualified to serve on the Court—contains a measure of truth, but her defeat actually stood for something of larger significance. Miers holds a unique place in the history of the Supreme Court as the only nominee to withdraw her name from consideration by the Senate even though she probably would have been confirmed. Why would anyone do such a thing? Because Miers had been vetoed by the most conservative elements of the Republican Party.

Shortly after O'Connor announced her resignation in July of 2005, Andrew Card, Bush's chief of staff, had asked Miers whether she wanted to be considered for the vacancy, and she declined. As a result, Miers administered the White House operation for selecting the next justice. She was well suited for the job, because it called for meticulousness and discretion and thus resembled her earlier work in the White House, as staff secretary and then deputy chief of staff. In her new post as White House counsel, Miers had run the search, supervising her associate counsels' updates of the candidate memos and then bringing in the finalists for interviews. She also consulted with members of the Senate, leading Harry Reid to become a fan. Once Bush chose Roberts, Miers coordinated the White House end of the confirmation process—juggling the requests for information from senators, managing the preparation of the mammoth background questionnaire that Supreme Court nominees must complete, and arranging for the "murder boards" where Roberts trained for his testimony before the Judiciary Committee. This complex process went as smoothly as Roberts's own performance, so the easy confirmation of the new chief justice cast a favorable glow on Miers as well as Roberts himself.

Bush did not focus as much on the second vacancy as he did on the first. He spent almost the whole month of August 2005 on vacation at his ranch in Crawford, Texas. When he returned to Washington, he immediately became preoccupied with trying to address the humanitarian and political aftermath of Hurricane Katrina. By mid-September, the Roberts process was wrapping up, and Bush still had no nominee for the O'Connor seat—and hadn't thought much about it, either.

Miers had returned to her role of running the search. Prodded by the unusual public nudge from his wife, Bush said he wanted to nominate a woman for the O'Connor seat, so that was how Miers focused her efforts. During one two-and-a-half-hour session with representatives of conservative activist groups, Miers went through a list of all female Republican appointees to the federal courts of appeals, weighing their suitability for a nomination. Some were appealing but intellectually undistinguished (Edith Brown Clement), others were too politically inflammatory to get through the Senate (Janice Rogers Brown and Edith Jones), others were dismissed as too moderate (Consuelo M. Callahan of the Ninth Circuit). Because women judges, like women generally, tend to be more liberal than their male counterparts—and because Democrats like Clinton appointed more women to the bench than Republicans—the female Republican pool was not large. No candidate stood out, either to Miers or to her superiors.

Still, Miers's competence in handling this process impressed Bush, who had a history of turning the leader of a search into its target. (In 2000, of course, Dick Cheney had led the vice presidential selection process that led to his own designation.) Unhappy with the available options, Bush mentioned Miers as a candidate to Card. He, in turn, told Bill Kelley, Miers's deputy, to look into the possibility. Miers learned of Card's interest, and this time she didn't rule out a nomination, though neither she nor Kelley took it very seriously. Kelley set to work on a memo about his boss's qualifications.

O'Connor and Miers were born fifteen years apart—in 1930 and 1945, respectively—and they both grew up in the Southwest at a

time when women lawyers were considered an exotic and often un-
welcome species. But the differences between them reflected both the
swiftly changing fortunes of women in the post–World War II era and
more fundamental contrasts in character. O'Connor grew up on a
ranch, and Miers was raised in a big city, Dallas. O'Connor was
wealthy, Miers wasn't. Her father ran a struggling real estate business
before he had a stroke when she was a freshman at Southern Methodist
University, and she won a scholarship and worked to make it through
SMU and its law school. When O'Connor came out of Stanford Law
in 1952, she received no better offer than a secretary's job at a law
firm. When Miers graduated in 1970, she also found a frosty reception but managed to land a prestigious clerkship with a federal judge
who introduced her to the law firm where she would spend the next
twenty-four years of her life, Locke, Lidell & Sapp.

Once O'Connor settled in Phoenix, she lived in a happy frenzy, juggling legal work, a growing family, and a passion for politics and raucous fun. Miers found a different route to success—narrow focus and
dogged effort. By relentless hard work she overcame the customary
condescension shown to women lawyers. She was the first woman
lawyer at her firm, and its first woman president. Like most big-firm
litigators, she tended to represent corporations in lawsuits that settled
before trial; companies like Disney and Microsoft, two of her major
clients, generally preferred the certainty of a resolution to the risk of
a court verdict. Miers's long hours left little time for diversion. When
she was deposed in a lawsuit in 1989, the opposing lawyer asked if she
had read a particular book. "I probably can shorten this line of questioning," Miers said, "if you just asked me when's the last time I read
a whole book."

Miers's existence outside the firm amounted to an extension of her
life in it. She belonged to the Democratic Party when virtually all of
the state's power brokers did; she contributed $1,000 to Al Gore's
campaign for president in 1988. She worked her way up the hierarchy
in the state bar association, a traditional route for advancement in the
profession, until she became the first woman president of the Texas
bar in 1992. The previous year, she had quit after serving a single
two-year term as a member of the Dallas City Council. She felt ill
suited for running for office, because she was far more interested in
corporate work than in politics. She didn't litigate constitutional issues or, it would seem, based on the available evidence, give them
much thought either.

Like many other single-minded careerists who had focused on their professional life to the exclusion of most everything else, Miers appears to have undergone a spiritual crisis of sorts. For many years, she had an on-and-off romantic relationship with Nathan Hecht, a combative conservative who was a justice on the Texas Supreme Court. Miers was raised a Catholic, but Hecht invited her to join him at Valley View Christian, one of the biggest evangelical churches in Dallas. She did—and it changed her life. As her minister recalled, "Her purpose for life changed. She has a servant's mentality, and I think that is a tribute to her personal faith. Jesus told his disciples that he didn't come to be served but to serve. Harriet epitomizes that."

Not long after Miers's religious conversion, George W. Bush, who was then running for his first term as governor, ran into some trouble involving a fishing club in east Texas. The caretaker said he had been unjustly fired, and he was suing the members, including Bush. The future governor hired Miers as his lawyer, and she deftly (and quietly) won the case. The up-and-coming politician kept her on as his personal attorney, and Miers embraced George W. Bush with the same born-again passion that she brought to her new church.

On September 21, 2005, Bush held a meeting with a bipartisan group of senators about his plans for filling O'Connor's seat. To some extent, such "consultations" with senators were a sham; the Bush White House zealously guarded its prerogatives, and no presidential power was more important than the right to select Supreme Court justices. At the meeting, Arlen Specter set his colleagues' eyes rolling with a preposterous suggestion—that Bush wait until 2006 to nominate anyone, so as to see how Roberts was faring as chief justice, and then to appoint someone who would preserve the Court's balance. But Bush and his supporters wanted *change* on the Court, not *balance*, and they ignored Specter's idea. Harry Reid then again mentioned Miers as a possible candidate.

The idea still made sense to the president—the appointment of, in effect, his own ideological clone who would attract no opposition from the Democrats in the Senate. That night Bush summoned Miers to the Oval Office and formally asked her whether she wanted to be considered. This time, she said yes.

Miers's presence as an official candidate for the seat complicated the search process, which was now accelerating as Roberts's confirmation grew nearer. (The Judiciary Committee approved Roberts on September 22.) Miers was not asked to bring in any other candidates for interviews with Bush. Only a handful of staffers, including Card, Rove, and Kelley, knew that Miers was a candidate, and they all honored Bush's wish for a selection process without leaks. On the day that the committee approved Roberts, Kelley called Leonard Leo of the Federalist Society and told him that Miers had become a serious candidate. They met the next day for breakfast at the Ritz-Carlton in Tysons Corner, and Leo said that Miers's lack of a record would present a problem for conservative groups. "This would be a heavy lift," he said. But Leo's message never penetrated the upper levels of the White House. (During the following week, Leo tried to sound out his colleagues in the conservative movement about a Miers nomination, but no one would take the idea seriously. They didn't approve or disapprove so much as dismiss her appointment as a possibility.) Every White House is an echo chamber of sorts, and leaks often serve the useful purpose of flushing out problems. But since there were no leaks about Miers, no one in the White House knew what the reaction to her nomination would be.

All of the top officials who were considering Miers's appointment—Bush, Cheney, Card, Rove, and Miers herself—had relatively little idea what Supreme Court justices actually do all day. ("All we do is read and write," Breyer liked to say. "I used to tell my son if you're really good at doing homework, you get to do homework for the rest of your life.") Everyone in Bush's inner circle came out of the corporate world, where they believed that good judgment and instincts mattered more than reflective analysis. The same was true for corporate lawyers. Bush would never have dreamed of asking prospective members of his cabinet for writing samples, and he didn't require them of Miers either. For the president, it was not a problem that Miers had no writing to offer.

Talking only to a handful of insiders—and again to Miers on September 28 and 29—Bush grew more and more convinced that she was a good choice. Their last conversations had to do less with whether she belonged on the Supreme Court and more with whom the White House might recruit as knowledgeable surrogates to speak on her behalf. At this point, the search remained leak-free. Remarkably, the first time any news accounts mentioned Miers was just before Roberts was confirmed on September 29, and even then her name appeared only at the end of a long list of possibilities. But when Miers agreed to be considered on September 21, the search process essentially stopped.

Only over the weekend of October 1–2 did the White House begin notifying outsiders that Miers might be the choice. Like the president, Karl Rove played a less active role in the selection of the second justice. Heavily involved in trying to handle the fallout from Katrina, he was facing an additional problem. During September, the prosecutor Patrick Fitzgerald's criminal investigation into the leak of CIA official Valerie Wilson's name had reached a critical stage; Rove faced the real possibility of being indicted.

So it was not until Sunday, October 2, that Rove fully engaged with the nomination process. His first call—which revealed whose opinion really mattered—was to James Dobson, the founder and leader of Focus on the Family, to tout Miers's credentials. Rove assured Dobson that Miers was an evangelical Christian and a strict constructionist. Rove said further that her friend Nathan Hecht of the Texas Supreme Court could vouch for Miers's soundness on social issues. In fact, Hecht himself would be speaking on a conference call for evangelical leaders the following day. Rove's stroking of Dobson made political sense, because Bush's political adviser knew, even if the mainstream media did not, that it was evangelical leaders like Dobson, not Senate Democrats, who had the power to make or break Bush's nominees.

That Sunday afternoon, Bush formally offered the appointment to Miers. She accepted, and the White House press office spent the evening working in secrecy to produce the biographical material and talking points that would accompany the announcement.

On Monday, October 3, at Bush's now customary 8:01 a.m., the president and Miers stood side by side in the Oval Office. "This morning, I'm proud to announce that I am nominating Harriet Ellan Miers to serve as associate justice of the Supreme Court. For the past five years, Harriet Miers has served in critical roles in our nation's government, including one of the most important legal positions in the country, White House counsel. She has devoted her life to the rule of law and the cause of justice," he said. "I've known Harriet for more than a decade. I know her heart, I know her character. I know that Harriet's mother is proud of her today, and I know her father would be proud of her, too. I'm confident that Harriet Miers will add to the wisdom and character of our judiciary when she is confirmed as the 110th justice of the Supreme Court."

Miers, unlike Roberts, chose to read her brief remarks: "From my early days as a clerk in the federal district court, and throughout almost three decades of legal practice, bar service, and community service, I have always had a great respect and admiration for the genius that inspired our Constitution and our system of government. My respect and admiration have only grown over these past five years that you have allowed me to serve the American people as a representative of the executive branch." Then Miers tried to define her judicial philosophy, which she clearly had not developed in her legal career. "The wisdom of those who drafted our Constitution and conceived our nation as functioning with three strong and independent branches have proven truly remarkable," she began, ungrammatically. "It is the responsibility of every generation to be true to the founders' vision of the proper role of the courts in our society." By citing the "founders' vision," Miers was positioning herself as an originalist, like Scalia. "If confirmed," she went on, "I recognize that I will have a tremendous responsibility to keep our judicial system strong, and to help ensure that the courts meet their obligations to strictly apply the laws and the Constitution." Likewise, the use of the word *strictly* was meant to identify her with strict constructionists, like Rehnquist.

But Miers's tentative advocacy for herself was already late. By the time her announcement ceremony concluded at 8:14 a.m., the assault on her had already begun.

At 8:12, Manny Miranda sent out an e-mail to his colleagues in the conservative movement. "The president has made possibly the most unqualified choice since Abe Fortas, who had been the president's lawyer," Miranda wrote. "The nomination of a nominee with no judicial record is a significant failure for the advisors that the White House gathered around it." At 8:51, David Frum, a former speechwriter in the Bush White House, offered a similar dismissal of Miers, based on firsthand knowledge. "Harriet Miers is a taut, nervous, anxious personality," Frum wrote on his blog for the *National Review*. "I am not saying that Harriet Miers is *not* a legal conservative. I am not saying that she is *not* steely. I am saying only that there is no good reason to believe either of these things."

Later that day, as Rove had promised, Nathan Hecht, as well as another Texas judge, Ed Kinkeade of the federal district court, convened
a conference call for conservative leaders, to make an affirmative case
for Miers. The call was organized for members of the Arlington
Group, an alliance of about sixty "pro-family" groups, and its members included such well-known figures as Gary Bauer of the American
Values group, Richard Land of the Southern Baptist Convention, and
James Dobson, the national chairman of the group. (The Arlington
Group had been a leading advocate for placing constitutional amendments against gay marriage on state ballots in 2004, a strategy that
was widely credited with increasing conservative turnout and aiding
the Bush campaign.) Dobson presided over the call, saying Rove had
suggested that Hecht and Kinkeade could vouch for Miers's conservative bona fides. This, of course, led to the key question about her candidacy.

"Do you believe she would vote to overturn *Roe v. Wade?*"

"Absolutely," said Kinkeade.

"I agree with that," said Hecht.

The electronically assembled conservatives were mollified—for the
moment.

News of the conference calls quickly leaked. The press attention
spooked Kinkeade from further campaigning for Miers's confirmation. Hecht was energized by it.

In the next week or so, Hecht gave more than 120 interviews on
Miers's behalf and proved to be a mixed blessing as an advocate.
Hecht had served on the Texas court since 1988 and established himself as the most extreme right-wing voice on an already conservative
court. He spoke often about Miers's devout faith and her decision, late
in life, to become baptized in his evangelical church. But his message
was compromised somewhat by his ambiguous status in her life.
Hecht's stream-of-consciousness ramblings to reporters somehow provided both too little information—and too much. "We are good, close
friends," Hecht told the *Los Angeles Times.* "And we have been for all
these years. We go to dinner. We go to the movies two or three times
a year. We talk. And that's the best way to describe it. We are not dat-
ing. We are not seeing each other romantically. Not currently."
Hecht's vigorous and lonely advocacy raised the possibility that the

only one the White House could find to endorse Miers was her boyfriend. (Hecht apparently had a complicated social life. He was also the sometime boyfriend of Priscilla Owen, his former colleague on the Texas Supreme Court, who had recently been confirmed to the Fifth Circuit and was a favorite of conservatives for the nomination that went to Miers.)

The absence of pro-Miers surrogates reflected the nature of her work for Bush, both in Texas and in Washington, as well as her personality. In Austin, Bush gave her the part-time job of supervising the state's troubled lottery system, but her real work for him consisted of private legal counseling—not the kind of activity that produces a body of public accomplishments. Similarly, as staff secretary and then deputy chief of staff at the White House, Miers operated as a coordinator and traffic cop more than as an initiator of ideas. No one could testify to her views on constitutional law, because she had never been called on to have any. Even when Miers filled out her questionnaire for the Senate, listing the significant cases she had litigated, most of the trials were business disputes that settled. She had never argued a case in the United States Supreme Court or even in the Texas Supreme Court.

It quickly became apparent that the White House had no backup plan for pushing Miers's nomination. Rove and the others figured that Hecht's word would calm any conservative uncertainty, and Bush counted on the Republicans who controlled the Senate to fall into line, just as they had on every other issue for the past four-and-a-half years. Crucially, though, Bush failed to see that Iraq and Katrina had crippled his influence in Congress. The nomination of Miers reflected Bush's arrogance, his sense that vouching for his personal lawyer would be all that was necessary to bring the Senate along. The president had miscalculated his own remaining clout—and the importance of the Supreme Court to his more ardent supporters. On this issue above all, a "Trust me" from George W. Bush would simply not be enough.

Although the right tried to phrase its complaints about Miers as a matter of qualifications rather than of ideology, its sleight of hand amounted to little more than a pretense. In recent years, the Supreme Court had been populated exclusively with experienced appellate judges (despite Clinton's hapless attempt to break the trend), but in the broader sweep of history Miers's qualifications were hardly unusual. Lewis Powell had never worked in government and had, like Miers, served prominently in local and national bar associations; William Rehnquist had a routine civil practice in Phoenix, followed by his tenure as an assistant attorney general, heading the Office of Legal Counsel; Byron White spent even less time as deputy attorney general following an unremarkable career as a private lawyer in Denver. For the movement conservatives, the problem with Miers was not her lack of qualifications but their own lack of certainty that she would follow their agenda on the Court.

Still, Miers's rocky debut on the national scene did not immediately doom her nomination. Harry Reid welcomed the choice, as did some Republican senators, like John Cornyn of Texas. On the Wednesday after she was nominated, Miers paid her first courtesy call on her home-state senator, and Cornyn embraced her publicly, playing a populist card on her behalf. She filled a "very real and important gap" on a Supreme Court dominated by Ivy Leaguers and Beltway intellectuals, he said after she left his office; he asked conservatives to "reserve judgment" and said that Miers had "ample qualifications" and was an "engaging person." With few exceptions, senators did what came naturally: they refrained from making commitments one way or the other.

But the conservative rebellion was just starting. Ken Mehlman, the chairman of the Republican National Committee, and his predecessor, Ed Gillespie, attended a pair of gatherings of conservative activists in Washington, and both ran into a torrent of complaints about Miers. "For the president to say 'Trust me,' it's what he needs to say and has to say, but it doesn't calm the waters," said Grover Norquist, the head of Americans for Tax Reform and the host of one of the meetings. "I told Mehlman that I had had five 'trust-mes' in my long history here," Paul Weyrich, the host of the other luncheon, remarked, referring to the nominations of Stevens, O'Connor, Kennedy, and Souter as the others. "And I said, 'I'm sorry, but the president saying he knows her heart is insufficient.' " When Gillespie told his group that there was a "whiff of sexism and a whiff of elitism" about the complaints, he was nearly shouted down with demands that he apologize for the slur. Mehlman replied by citing Bush's decade-long friendship with Miers: "What's different about this trust-me moment as opposed to the other ones is this president's knowledge of this nominee."

This conservative outcry against Miers in October was nearly identical to the one against the possible nomination of Alberto Gonzales in July. As with Gonzales, Miers's critics on the right could not point to any unacceptable positions that she had taken; also as with Gonzales, White House officials watched with astonishment a colleague they knew to be one of the most fervent conservatives on the staff portrayed as a closet liberal.

Facts played little part in the assault on Miers. The public statements about her, like those of her friend Nathan Hecht, suggested that she held views precisely in line with those who were most outraged by her nomination. The record of her single campaign for the Dallas City Council, while sparse, bore out Hecht's summary of her views. In response to a questionnaire from Texans United for Life, Miers had said she would support a constitutional amendment to overturn *Roe v. Wade*, that she supported denying public funds to pro-choice groups, and that she would use her office "to promote the pro-life cause." It was not enough. The conservative movement against Miers fed on itself and grew.

For the most part, Democrats simply chortled, relishing the intramural quarrel on the other side of the aisle. They made sure that reporters saw the fawning notes that Miers had written to Bush during his years as governor. "Hopefully, Jenna and Barbara recognize that their parents are 'cool'—as do the rest of us," she wrote in one. "Keep up the great work. Texas is blessed!" And "You are the best governor ever—deserving of great respect!" And "You and Laura are the greatest!"

Democratic senators raised questions about cronyism, which were especially resonant in the aftermath of Katrina. But notably, not a single Democratic senator announced his or her intention to vote against Miers. As the right-wing attacks on her grew more frenzied, some Democrats began to think that perhaps Miers really was a secret moderate and thus the best they could hope for as a Bush nominee.

Specter set the start of Miers's hearings for November 7, and as the date grew closer the chairman of the Judiciary Committee made it clear that he was unimpressed with Miers. Unlike most of his fellow Republicans, the dyspeptic Specter cared more about her qualifications than about her ideology. He noted publicly that she would need a "crash course" on constitutional law, which was not something that anyone could have said about John Roberts. On October 19, Specter and Patrick Leahy, the ranking Democrat on the committee, sent Miers a nasty letter complaining about several of her answers on her questionnaire. They wanted more detail on "the nature and objectives" of all organizations to which she had belonged and "any and all communications, including those about which there have been recent press reports, in which friends and supporters of yours, among others, were said to have been asked by the White House to assure certain individuals of your views." In other words, they wanted to know about Hecht's promises that she would vote to overrule *Roe*. The senators gave Miers until October 26 to complete her answers.

Through the second and into the third week of October, Miers continued to meet privately with senators and to prepare for her public testimony. Neither the meetings nor the rehearsals went especially well. Miers lacked Roberts's charm as well as his deep knowledge of constitutional law—which allowed him to summarize the state of the law at length without letting on much about his own views—and she did little in person to help her cause.

Still, despite the predictions of her increasingly desperate enemies, Miers likely would have handled the hearings with relative ease. Congressional hearings almost always reflect better on the witness than on the senators, who generally come across (with some reason) as pompous and uninformed. Hostile cross-examination from conservatives would almost certainly have evoked sympathy for the nominee. Miers's personal story of triumph over adversity, like Thomas's fourteen years earlier, would have counted for a great deal with the public. The forty-four Democrats in the Senate, figuring that Miers was the best they could do (and already sixty years old), would probably have voted overwhelmingly to confirm. Even perfunctory lobbying by Bush would have produced a substantial number of Republican votes. By mid-October, Miers's confirmation looked likely—if she could get to a vote.

That was why her enemies in the conservative movement were determined to prevent that vote from ever taking place. On October 21, the syndicated columnist Charles Krauthammer, a conservative opposed to Miers, wrote, "We need an exit strategy from this debacle. I have it." Senators should ask for "privileged documents from Miers's White House tenure," and the president should refuse to turn them over. The request could create a conflict "of simple constitutional prerogatives: The Senate cannot confirm her unless it has this information. And the White House cannot allow release of this information lest it jeopardize executive privilege. Hence the perfectly honorable way to solve the conundrum: Miers withdraws out of respect for both the Senate and the executive's prerogatives."

The idea was breathtakingly cynical—a more or less open fraud—but it served the conservatives' purpose. Republicans had been complaining for years that Democratic filibusters were denying Bush's judicial nominees "up-or-down votes"; the president even used that phrase in his State of the Union address in 2005. Yet the exact same people who were complaining about the denial of votes to Bush's other judicial nominees were mobilizing to deny just such a vote to the White House counsel, who helped select most of the other would-be judges. But to the conservatives, nothing mattered—not consistency, not fairness, not the fate of an otherwise allied figure—except getting guaranteed control of the Supreme Court. The "Krauthammer solution," as it became known, was put into effect.

One person who could have stopped the railroading of the nominee was Miers herself. In 1987, Robert Bork refused to withdraw even when it became clear that he would lose in the Senate, and the recorded vote went forward, a 58–42 defeat. In this case, it was by no means clear that Miers would lose. But at a fundamental level, Miers always acted more as Bush's attorney than as an independent actor. A lawyer always puts a client's interests ahead of his or her own, and Bush's priority was pleasing his most conservative supporters, particularly when it came to the Supreme Court. Miers would not force Bush to disappoint his base, even at great personal cost. She would withdraw as a nominee.

At 8:30 p.m. on Wednesday, October 26, twenty-three days after Miers was nominated, she called Bush to tell him that she would drop out. For the moment, the decision remained their secret, and later that evening the White House even submitted the answers to the senators' follow-up questions. But the next morning, they executed the Krauthammer solution. Miers wrote a letter to Bush saying that senators were planning on asking about her service in the White House. "I have steadfastly maintained that the independence of the Executive Branch be preserved. . . . Protection of the prerogatives of the Executive Branch and continued pursuit of my confirmation are in tension. I have decided that seeking my confirmation should yield." In a statement issued the same day, Bush "reluctantly accepted" Miers's withdrawal.

The next day, Friday, October 28, Lewis "Scooter" Libby, the vice president's chief of staff, was indicted in the CIA leak investigation for perjury and obstruction of justice, ending perhaps the worst week of the Bush presidency. The Miers debacle and the Libby charges took place while the Gulf Coast remained in extremis and the Iraq disaster continued. Facing similar crises, other presidents had found refuge in moderation, in bipartisanship, in gestures of conciliation to political adversaries.

But George W. Bush did not conduct that kind of presidency. Over the weekend, Harriet Miers, ever loyal even in the face of public humiliation, accompanied the president to Camp David to help choose a replacement for herself. Their goal remained unchanged—to select the most conservative possible Supreme Court justice, one who would be welcomed by James Dobson, the Arlington Group, Ed Meese, Jay Sekulow, Manny Miranda, and the rest of the president's base. By 8:01 on Monday morning, they had their man.

DINNER AT THE
JUST DESSERTS CAFÉ

The weekend at Camp David was mainly for relaxation, at least for the president. Bush had already made up his mind. Notwithstanding the distraction of the Libby indictment, both Bush and Andrew Card found time to call Judge Samuel A. Alito Jr. in his chambers in Newark. Again the conversations were cursory, but they reflected Bush's more or less instantaneous decision. He had liked Alito more than Luttig (the only other candidate considered), so Alito it would be. As for Laura Bush's preference for a woman, the Miers fiasco convinced the president that choosing a reliable conservative mattered more.

In a curious way, the nomination of Alito amounted to Miers's revenge. Miers had been the lone skeptic about Roberts's conservative credentials, only to have her own nomination implode because she could not convince the true believers of her own. So the seat went to Miers's favorite candidate from the beginning, the one who everyone agreed represented a guaranteed conservative voice. For Alito, Karl Rove would not need to organize plaintive conference calls to his friends in the conservative movement; they were already on board. As Manny Miranda wrote in his first blast e-mail on Monday morning, October 31, just minutes after Bush and Alito stood together in the White House, "As with Chief Judge John Roberts, the President has hit a grand slam with this nomination."

That was not Sandra O'Connor's view. Shortly after she announced her departure from the Court, the president held a private dinner for her at the White House, where O'Connor was invited to prepare the guest list of about fifty people. After Bush's toast, O'Connor offered a perfunctory thank-you. And as she was leaving, she sighed to the wife of a current justice, "Well, that wasn't so bad."

O'Connor had learned not to be shocked by anything Bush did, but the Alito nomination felt like a direct affront. O'Connor had been vaguely insulted by the Miers selection, as well. Regarding Miers, O'Connor asked acidly why Bush couldn't find anyone with more stature than his own lawyer. In fairness, Miers probably had about as much stature as O'Connor herself did in 1981 as an obscure judge on a midlevel appeals court in Arizona. But by 2005, O'Connor had long since become accustomed to her status as the most powerful woman, and one of the most admired, in America.

Alito was a different story altogether. To a great extent, the judicial careers of Alito and O'Connor had been defined by the same case—where they had been on opposite sides.

Like John Roberts, Alito had been nominated for a federal appeals court judgeship during the first Bush administration. Unlike Roberts, Alito had been confirmed, taking his seat on the Third Circuit in 1990. The backgrounds of the two men were similar. Alito came from more modest circumstances—his father was a civil servant in New Jersey state government—but young Sam, like the future chief justice, had an Ivy League education, with Princeton followed by Yale Law. Then, like Roberts, Alito had been a star among the cadre of conservative young lawyers who accompanied Ronald Reagan to Washington. Alito spent four years in the solicitor general's office, two more with the Office of Legal Counsel, and then, in 1987, became the U.S. attorney in his home state of New Jersey. Alito had just turned forty in 1990 when he received his lifetime appointment to the federal bench.

A year later, Alito had a chance to help his fellow judicial conservatives usher *Roe v. Wade* to its demise. The new judge participated in the epochal *Casey* lawsuit as part of the three-judge panel that reviewed the law. The Third Circuit panel upheld the law's restrictions on abortion, such as its new rules on parental consent and waiting periods, almost in their entirety, but two of the three judges thought one provision about spousal notification went too far. Noting that "the number of different situations in which women may reasonably fear dire consequences from notifying their husbands is potentially limitless," the majority ruled that part of the law violated women's rights.

Alito disagreed. He wrote his own opinion saying that he would have approved the Pennsylvania law in full and thus offered states a road map to restricting abortions as much as possible without outlawing the practice altogether. Since Pennsylvania wanted to limit the number of abortions, Alito said the requirement that wives notify their husbands of their plans was a reasonable means to that objective. Alito wrote in the same bland way that he spoke, and he observed, "The Pennsylvania legislature could have rationally believed that some married women are initially inclined to obtain an abortion without their husbands' knowledge because of perceived problems—such as economic constraints, future plans, or the husbands' previously expressed opposition—that may be obviated by discussion prior to the abortion."

The following year, the troika of O'Connor, Kennedy, and Souter saved *Roe* in their joint opinion in this case. (In the small world of conservative legal politics, John Roberts, then the deputy solicitor general, signed a brief at the time, which urged the justices to overrule *Roe* once and for all.) In drafting the portion of the *Casey* opinion striking down spousal notification, O'Connor had excoriated Alito's logic, approach, and conclusions. Famously, O'Connor had called Alito's view "repugnant to our present understanding of marriage and of the nature of the rights secured by the Constitution. Women do not lose their constitutionally protected liberty when they marry."

Now that very judge was getting a promotion to O'Connor's own seat—and largely *because* Alito had proved his conservative bona fides in that very case. As one White House lawyer said of the new nominee, "He was on the bench for fifteen years, and he never got a case wrong."

O'Connor had announced her resignation in July of 2005 with every expectation that her replacement would be on the bench when the Court returned on the first Monday in October. Yet by Halloween, Bush was only then nominating another purported successor, with hearings and votes to follow over the next several months. O'Connor had genuinely hoped to be gone from the Court, but her protracted leave-taking did yield one side benefit—the chance to serve with John Roberts.

O'Connor loved Roberts. More than most of the justices, O'Connor cared about how the public regarded the Supreme Court, and she thought that Roberts's good looks and charisma projected exactly the right image. Once, during one of the first arguments before the Roberts Court, a lightbulb exploded on the ceiling, prompting the court police to reach for their sidearms. "It's is a trick they play on new chief justices all the time," Roberts quipped, calming the courtroom. O'Connor told that story for weeks, as an example of Roberts's charm. She even wrote a fawning, faintly embarrassing story about Roberts for *Time* magazine. ("The stars must have been aligned that January morning in 1955 when John G. Roberts Jr. was born in Buffalo, N.Y., because almost everything thereafter led him straight to the Supreme Court of the U.S.") But O'Connor was hardly, as some thought, a starstruck schoolgirl. At a meeting to plan a conference she was hosting, someone wondered if the chief justice might be asked to attend. With icy confidence, O'Connor said, "I'll take care of John Roberts."

For all of O'Connor's fondness for Roberts, his appointment did not restrain the move to the left that characterized her jurisprudence and thus the Court's. Indeed, as Rehnquist and O'Connor prepared to leave, there was a quality of a Prague Spring in the Court's decisions—a last gasp of liberalism before a likely surge to the right. At the end of his tenure, Rehnquist was never more beloved, but also never more irrelevant.

Take, for example, the chief's vaunted federalism revolution. After the justices struck down the federal law prohibiting the possession of guns near schools in *Lopez*, Rehnquist had apparently revived the Commerce Clause as a meaningful check on Congress's authority to pass laws. The decision raised the possibility that the Court would really stop Congress from regulating local activity, something legislators had been doing without interference since the New Deal. In 2005, however, the justices took up a challenge to a California law that allowed state residents, with a doctor's prescription, to cultivate and use marijuana. A woman named Angel McClary Raich challenged the federal law prohibiting possession of marijuana, arguing that Congress, under the Commerce Clause, could not prohibit the purely private, noncommercial transactions covered by the law.

In *Gonzales v. Raich*, six justices, including Kennedy and Scalia, said that Congress could indeed prohibit private, doctor-authorized pot farming. Stevens, writing almost as if the Court had never issued the *Lopez* opinion, gave nearly unlimited scope to congressional power under the Commerce Clause. Relying on the same New Deal cases that Rehnquist had scorned in *Lopez*, Stevens wrote that Congress may regulate "purely intrastate activity that is not itself 'commercial' " if to do so is necessary to regulate interstate commodity markets. The federal government can regulate the activity of one individual if, when aggregated together with those of all similarly situated people, that person's activity will have a "substantial effect" on interstate commerce. "That the regulation ensnares some purely intrastate activity"—such as the personal possession of marijuana for medical use—"is of no moment," Stevens explained.

Because nearly every kind of private economic activity, no matter how minor, could impact interstate commerce if aggregated nationwide, Stevens's decision meant that Congress could regulate virtually everything. The pre-1995 status quo had returned. Again, Stevens's patience during his long tenure had paid off with a thoroughgoing vindication of his views. Rehnquist could only join a forlorn protest in dissent.

It wasn't just the conservative federalism revolution that sputtered in 2005; that year Kennedy invoked foreign law to strike down the death penalty for juvenile offenders. And these decisions followed the Court's rejection of the administration's position on Guantánamo Bay and O'Connor's endorsement of affirmative action at the University of Michigan Law School. But it was perhaps the most controversial pair of cases from 2005 that underlined which remaining justice had the most to lose from O'Connor's departure from the Court.

On the morning that O'Connor resigned, Stephen Breyer heard the news on National Public Radio. The two had become so close that it hurt Breyer's feelings a little that she gave him no advance notice. Typically, O'Connor just attributed her secrecy to common sense; she didn't want to place any of her colleagues in an awkward position if they were asked about her plans. But her alliance with Breyer had only grown stronger over time. In some cases it was hard to tell which one of them represented the Court's swing vote.

Few justices took to the work of the Supreme Court with greater ease or enthusiasm than Breyer. His intelligence had never been in doubt, but when Clinton appointed him in 1994, Breyer had little experience in the grist of Supreme Court work—constitutional law. He was a problem solver, a technocrat, an antitrust and administrative law expert, the author of the federal sentencing guidelines. He was not someone who had given much thought to the majestic generalities of the Constitution. But in 2005, he did something that no justice had attempted in several generations—to write his own manifesto on the meaning of the Constitution. Characteristically, Breyer's book, *Active Liberty*, was hardly an airy philosophical treatise but a practical book by a practical man. "Our constitutional history," he wrote, "has been a quest for workable government, workable democratic government, workable democratic government protective of individual personal liberty." No word better suited Breyer's approach than *workable*.

In part, Breyer wrote *Active Liberty* to challenge Scalia's doctrine of originalism. Like many other critics of Scalia, Breyer pointed out there was no way of knowing precisely what the framers meant by such phrases as *freedom of speech* or *due process of law*, much less how they would have applied those terms today. Scalia and Thomas's approach, Breyer wrote has, "a tendency to undermine the Constitution's efforts to create a framework for democratic government—a government that, while protecting basic individual liberties, permits citizens to govern themselves, and to govern themselves effectively." That was what Breyer meant by "active liberty"—a Constitution that not only protected citizens from government coercion but affirmatively gave power to citizens themselves to participate. Government existed to give everyone an equal chance to join in the political process.

Breyer had the opportunity to put that theory into action in the two Ten Commandments cases of 2005. There, civil liberties advocates challenged, as violations of the Establishment Clause of the First Amendment, two public displays of the commandments, one in a pair of Kentucky courthouses, the other on the grounds of the Texas state capitol. Four justices (Stevens, O'Connor, Souter, and Ginsburg) rejected both states' displays as violations of the Constitution's separation of church and state; four others (Rehnquist, Scalia, Kennedy, and Thomas) approved both states' displays. Only Breyer, the swing vote in both cases, saw a difference between the two: he rejected the display in the Kentucky courthouses and upheld the one in the Texas park.

Breyer's seemingly inconsistent positions drew some ridicule, but they illustrated his pragmatic, and almost overtly political, approach to judging. In his opinion concurring in the judgment in the Texas case, *Van Orden v. Perry*, Breyer noted that there was "no single mechanical formula that can accurately draw the constitutional line in every case," and he proceeded to compare the history of the displays. The Texas commandments, which are carved into a granite monument, had been donated to the state by the Fraternal Order of Eagles, a private civic (and primarily secular) organization, in 1961. (The commandments were originally posted in many places around the country to generate publicity for Cecil B. DeMille's 1956 movie, *The Ten Commandments*.) Most important, Breyer argued, no one had complained about the structure, which was situated for decades among sixteen other monuments and twenty-one historical markers. Indeed, the plaintiff in the case was actually a homeless person who spent more time lingering in the park, reading the inscriptions, than most other people. "Those forty years suggest more strongly than can any set of formulaic tests that few individuals, whatever their system of beliefs, are likely to have understood the monument as amounting, in any significantly detrimental way, to a government effort to favor a particular religious sect," Breyer wrote.

By contrast, the displays in the Kentucky case, *McCreary County v. American Civil Liberties Union*, had been placed on the walls of small courthouses by local officials, accompanied in one case by a Christian minister, in 1999 and had immediately become objects of controversy. In his opinion in the Texas case, Breyer wrote, "The short (and stormy) history of the [Kentucky] courthouse commandments' displays demonstrates the substantially religious objectives of those who mounted them." (For example, the display noted that the posted commandments came from the "King James Version.")

Breyer's controlling opinions in the cases told politicians to stop erecting provocative religious monuments, with the understanding that old ones could stay. As a political compromise, if not constitutional jurisprudence, it made total sense. O'Connor did not join Breyer in both cases; she actually voted to his left, arguing that both displays should be removed. But Breyer's split-the-difference approach reflected her influence. So, too, did Breyer's wish to diffuse conflict; few people might have known the Ten Commandments were in the Austin park before the lawsuit, but a Court-ordered removal would surely have turned into an ugly drama. As Breyer put it, removing uncontroversial displays like the one in Texas could "create the very kind of religiously based divisiveness that the Establishment Clause seeks to avoid."

Visitors to Breyer's chambers at the Court might assume that the rows of venerable leather-bound books in the shelves behind his desk came from his wife's aristocratic family in Great Britain. Their home in Cambridge is full of heirlooms from the stately home of the 1st Viscount Blakenham. But the books were collected by Breyer's late uncle Leo Roberts, an eccentric philosopher and freelance academic who haunted used-book sales. Young Stephen and his uncle would sometimes rise at dawn to get first crack at the sales, where they rarely paid more than a dollar a book. And there were ultimately thousands of books, which Breyer, with just the exceptions in his chambers, donated to the University of Massachusetts in Boston after Roberts died.

Breyer's demeanor, as well as his jurisprudence, reflected both his patrician in-laws and his own Jewish parents. He sometimes lapsed into what sounded like an English accent, and one of his daughters became, of all things, an Episcopal priest. But Breyer's reluctance to stir up religious animosity was strictly urban pol in origin. From his parents and their experience in San Francisco politics, he learned the dangers of religious conflict, even in the United States, and he saw the Constitution as the vehicle to keep ecumenical passions in check. A natural conciliator, Breyer liked nothing less than picking unnecessary fights.

And that spirit, in 2005, gave Breyer something close to control of the Court. Of all the justices, he cast the fewest dissenting votes that term, ten, just behind O'Connor's eleven. He brokered an extraordinary compromise in a series of complex cases reviewing the federal sentencing guidelines that he, as an appeals court judge, had played a major role in creating. After years of hotly contested cases on the subject, the result was that the guidelines would be advisory rather than mandatory, which was what Breyer had sought all along. He controlled the outcome of the Ten Commandments cases, voted with Kennedy on the juvenile death penalty, and even joined an unusual majority in the most enjoyable case of the year. In May, the Court ruled 5–4 that states could not permit in-state wineries to ship to consumers while prohibiting out-of-state producers from doing the same thing. The pro-wine majority consisted of Kennedy, the author of the opinion, Scalia, Souter, Ginsburg, and Breyer—who all happened to be the leading wine aficionados on the Court. Breyer later called the group "the rosy-cheeked caucus."

This long run of success was why Breyer despaired at the other big case that came down at the end of the same term. In 1998, Pfizer had announced plans to build a research facility in New London, Connecticut; the city intended to spruce up the surrounding neighborhood. As part of the development, New London used its power of eminent domain to take the homes of several residents and turn them over to private developers for a shopping center or perhaps a parking lot. Susette Kelo and several of her neighbors sued, claiming that the city was violating the Fifth Amendment, which says that "private property [shall not] be taken for public use, without just compensation." A city could take land for a highway, school, or hospital, the plaintiffs claimed, but the transfer of private property from one private entity to another did not amount to a public use.

When *Kelo v. City of New London* was argued back in February 2005, the case drew relatively little attention. Even to the justices, the matter seemed to be a fairly esoteric dispute over a familiar part of the Constitution. The Court had found previously that government could use eminent domain powers to transfer land to private parties—to railroads, for example—and the question here was simply whether an urban redevelopment plan qualified as a public use. It hardly seemed the stuff of high drama, and at the end of the term, Stevens wrote a straightforward opinion for a five-justice majority (including Kennedy, Souter, Ginsburg, and Breyer) approving what the city had done. Stevens styled his opinion as an exercise in judicial restraint, as he deferred to the local elected officials about what constituted a public use. "Just as we decline to second-guess the City's considered judgments about the efficacy of its development plan, we also decline to second-guess the City's determinations as to what lands it needs to acquire in order to effectuate the project," he wrote.

But the justices, especially Stevens, had misjudged the emotional resonance of the subject. By raising the possibility that a city could simply transfer a private home to another private owner, the case tapped into powerful fears of unchecked government. O'Connor understood better than any of her colleagues how the public would see the case and wrote in her dissent, "Under the banner of economic development, all private property is now vulnerable to being taken and transferred to another private owner, so long as it might be up-graded—*i.e.*, given to an owner who will use it in a way that the leg-islature deems more beneficial to the public." (The case was one of the few where O'Connor and Breyer parted company.) In any event, the *Kelo* decision set off a noisy backlash.

Overnight, it was as if the Terri Schiavo chorus had reconvened. Rather than as a victory for judicial restraint, the conservative move-ment treated *Kelo* as a triumph of big government. Tom DeLay called it "a horrible decision," adding, "This Congress is not going to just sit by—idly sit by—and let an unaccountable judiciary make these kinds of decisions without taking our responsibility and our duty given to us by the Constitution to be a check on the judiciary." DeLay in the House and John Cornyn in the Senate pushed measures to deny federal funds to any local project that would use eminent domain to force people to sell their property to make way for a profit-making venture. Ever alert for the chance to make a public splash, Jay Sekulow claimed implausibly that the *Kelo* decision might lead to government seizures of church land—and added the case to his bill of particulars against the Supreme Court.

The animosity toward the Court reached frenzied proportions. A conservative activist, Logan Darrow Clements, wrote to the govern-ment of Souter's hometown in New Hampshire asking that the town take over the justice's farm and turn it into the "Lost Liberty Hotel," featuring the "Just Desserts Café." "The justification for such an em-inent domain action is that our hotel will better serve the public in-terest as it will bring in economic development and higher tax revenue to Weare," wrote Clements. The following year, the matter even came up for a vote in Weare, with the town voting 1,167 to 493 to leave the Souter farm alone. (Even if Souter had lost the vote, it was unlikely that his home would have been taken.) In more serious re-sponses to the case, several states tightened requirements on the use of eminent domain. (In a way, these actions vindicated Stevens, who wrote that while the Constitution allowed such uses of eminent do-main, states were, of course, free to restrict the practice.)

Breyer despaired at the drubbing the Court was taking. He took every opportunity to point out that the decision did not *order* any lo-cal government to buy land but merely *permitted* the practice under limited circumstances. The complaints should have gone to the ini-tiators of such seizures, not the justices. In truth, the controversy was stoked by conservatives precisely because it took place at the same time as the confirmation fights. The cause united social and economic conservatives against a "liberal" Supreme Court. As Sean Rushton, the executive director of the Committee for Justice—Boyden Gray's organization, dedicated to pushing Bush's judicial nominees—said of the *Kelo* decision, "It's so bad, it's good."

When Roberts began his first term, with O'Connor still on the bench, the Court enjoyed a docket full of relatively uncontroversial cases. In addition, the new chief justice made a point of pushing his colleagues toward narrow decisions that could command unanimous support. In a speech at Georgetown, he made the case for this judicial minimalism, asserting, "The broader the agreement among the justices, the more likely it is a decision on the narrowest possible grounds." For a time, the justices indulged the chief's wishes, and the percentage of unanimous cases ticked upward. In conference, Roberts let discussions linger for longer than Rehnquist had, and the additional conversation encouraged the justices to absorb the views of their colleagues and write opinions accordingly. Roberts's buoyant good nature, and the end to the grim vigil over Rehnquist's health, immediately made the Court a cheerier place.

Roberts also proved himself a skillful judicial craftsman. His first important opinion touched on gay rights, academic freedom, and the power of the military—and still produced a unanimous Court. The case also revealed the deep cleavages in the legal profession between the liberal faculties of leading law schools and the conservative majorities in Congress. After the fights early in the Clinton administration over gays in the military, most leading law schools banned military recruiters on campus because the armed services refused to hire openly gay people and thus violated the schools' nondiscrimination policies. (Many of the faculty votes for the bans were unanimous, suggesting an extraordinary level of political conformism.) Enraged at these snubs to the military, conservatives in Congress responded by passing the Solomon Amendment, which cut off all federal funds to universities that did not allow equal access to recruiters from the armed forces. At many universities, the amendment put tens of millions of dollars in federal medical research money at risk, so law school faculty members sued, arguing that the law violated their rights to free speech under the First Amendment.

In an opinion by Roberts, the Court unanimously upheld the Solomon Amendment and rejected the claim by the law professors. In short, Roberts said that he who pays the piper calls the tune. "Congress is free to attach reasonable and unambiguous conditions to federal financial assistance that educational institutions are not obligated to accept," he wrote. The case had nothing to do with free speech, he continued, arguing that the Solomon Amendment "neither limits what law schools may say nor requires them to say anything. . . . As a general matter, the Solomon Amendment regulates conduct, not speech." In this way, Roberts diffused a potentially incendiary controversy.

The same was true for his first encounter with abortion. In 2003, New Hampshire passed a law prohibiting physicians from performing an abortion on a minor without giving one of her parents at least forty-eight hours' notice. Physicians could dispense with the notification requirement if they could certify that the abortion was "necessary to prevent the minor's death." The main issue in the case was whether the state also had to establish an exception to the notice requirement if the minor's health was at risk. For decades, the Court had insisted on "health" exceptions in abortion laws, and for just as long, abortion opponents had argued that such exceptions were so broad that they amounted to no restriction at all. The case concerned a fairly narrow corner of the law, but there is no such thing as an unimportant abortion ruling at the Supreme Court, and the case seemed likely to offer the first clues as to how the Roberts Court would deal with the most fraught topic on its agenda.

But Roberts, with the unanimous agreement of his colleagues, managed to avoid a major confrontation. The lower courts had invalidated the entire New Hampshire law when they could have just evaluated the contested portion; the justices thus resolved the case on procedural grounds, sending it back for further review (and, perhaps, some sort of compromise settlement). This kind of opinion—avoiding a hot controversy if at all possible—was a classic O'Connor strategy, and it was fitting that Roberts assigned her the opinion.

Ayotte v. Planned Parenthood of Northern New England would be the final majority opinion of Sandra O'Connor's quarter century as a justice—and an apt summary of her extraordinary influence on the Court and the nation. "We do not revisit our abortion precedents today," she began, but she did take the time to offer a summary of that law. "We have long upheld state parental involvement statutes like the Act before us, and we cast no doubt on those holdings today," she wrote. As for laws regulating abortions themselves, O'Connor said that they were to be tested under the "undue burden standard." She went on, "New Hampshire does not dispute, and our precedents hold, that a State may not restrict access to abortions that are 'necessary, in appropriate medical judgment, for preservation of the life or health of the mother.'" The internal quotation came from the *Casey* decision, which was in turn quoting *Roe v. Wade*.

The dry legal language obscured that this brief opinion amounted to a story of remarkable personal triumph for O'Connor. Like most other Americans, O'Connor believed in parental notification laws. Like most others, she also believed that not all abortions should be banned. And she thought, again like most of her fellow citizens, that abortion restrictions should not risk "the life or health of the mother." When she joined the Court in 1981, not one other justice believed that abortion laws should be tested under an "undue burden standard," but O'Connor had invented that test and over time persuaded a majority of her colleagues to agree with her. She had single-handedly remade the law in the most controversial area of Supreme Court jurisprudence. And she had done it in a way that both reflected and satisfied the wishes of most Americans. No other woman in United States history, and very few men, made such an enormous impact on their country.

O'Connor read *Ayotte* from the bench on January 18, 2006. By that point, though, the longevity of her influence seemed ever more open to question.

"I AM AND ALWAYS
HAVE BEEN . . ."

The lawyers in the Bush White House who researched possible nominees to the Supreme Court operated according to strict rules. Because they did not want the nature of their inquiries to be widely known—and because they had so many people to investigate—they examined only the public record. For sitting judges, they looked primarily at their published opinions and also ran the candidates' names through databases like Nexis and Google. The small group of associate counsels did not, however, have the time or resources to search through the National Archives, so it was journalists who discovered the key document about Samuel Alito, two weeks after Bush announced his selection.

Alito had joined the staff of the solicitor general as a career lawyer in 1981, but he quickly established himself as an enthusiastic supporter of the Reagan administration. In time, he sought to move up to a position as deputy assistant attorney general in the Office of Legal Counsel, the official constitutional adviser to the president and the unofficial ideological command center during the Reagan years. The job was a political appointment, so Alito had to be vetted by the White House. The application letter that Alito wrote for the job, the document found in the archives, proved to be an easy-to-decipher Rosetta Stone about his political and judicial philosophy.

Alito's letter of November 15, 1985, began, "I am and always have been a conservative," and removed any mystery about the kind of justice he would be. But the treatment of Alito's letter in his confirmation hearings illustrated other truths about the contemporary confirmation process, the difference between Democrats and Republicans, and the future of the Court.

When Roberts testified at his own hearing, he was asked about his authorship of the brief advocating the reversal of *Roe v. Wade*. The future chief justice parried the inquiry, noting that he was then a lawyer representing a client, President George H. W. Bush, whose opposition to *Roe* was a matter of public record. Roberts asserted that the position in the brief did not necessarily reflect his own views about *Roe*, which he declined to reveal. Alito, in contrast, had written in his 1985 application that "it has been an honor and a source of personal satisfaction to me to serve in the office of the Solicitor General during President Reagan's administration and to help to advance legal positions in which I personally believe very strongly. I am particularly proud of my contributions in recent cases in which the government has argued in the Supreme Court that racial and ethnic quotas should not be allowed and that the Constitution does not protect a right to an abortion."

So there was no mystery about Alito's personal beliefs. Indeed, the letter showed that his judicial philosophy, at least in 1985, was well to the right of where, say, even Rehnquist was in 2005. Alito had also written, "In college, I developed a deep interest in constitutional law, motivated in large part by disagreement with Warren Court decisions, particularly in the areas of criminal procedure, the Establishment Clause, and reapportionment." The major Warren Court decisions in these subjects were those creating the *Miranda* warning, banning government-sponsored prayer in schools, and calling for one person, one vote in legislative districting. Even conservatives like Rehnquist came to terms with these rulings, but such was Alito's passion for the conservative cause in the Reagan years that he apparently found them too liberal. As a lower court judge for the past fifteen years, Alito had no right to overturn these precedents, but he gave every indication that he would if he could.

Despite Alito's potentially extreme views, simple arithmetic made his confirmation nearly a foregone conclusion. As soon as he was nominated, it became clear that he would survive the most important test for any Bush nominee to the Court—what might be called the Republican primary, that is, the approval of the conservative base.

The full Senate, by comparison, would be easy for Alito. There were fifty-five Republicans, and all but a handful—Lincoln Chafee of

Rhode Island, and Susan Collins and Olympia Snowe of Maine—
would be certain to vote for a true conservative like him. (A moderate in other circumstances, Arlen Specter could not oppose a Bush
nominee to the Supreme Court and keep his beloved chairmanship of
the Judiciary Committee.) From the moment of Alito's nomination,
the only hope for Democrats to stop his confirmation would be to establish and hold a filibuster of forty or more senators.

No Supreme Court nominee in history who had the support of a
majority of senators had ever been stopped by a filibuster. (In 1968,
there was a filibuster against Lyndon Johnson's nomination of Abe
Fortas to be chief justice, but it was not clear that Fortas had the votes
to be confirmed.) So a Democratic filibuster against Alito was unlikely, and if one had been attempted, it might have led to the elim-
ination of the tactic for good. In advance of the debate, Bill Frist, the
majority leader, was clearly itching for a fight so that he could invoke
the "nuclear option" and do away with filibusters on judicial nominees once and for all. Such a move would have ingratiated Frist with
the Republican base, whose support the Tennessee senator was then
courting for a possible presidential run in 2008. (He later declined to
run.) In short, the odds were always stacked against a Democratic attempt to stop Alito's confirmation; there were simply too many votes
on the other side.

Still, the reaction to his nomination among Democrats showed just
how much times had changed since the Bork hearings. It was only a
year since Specter thought the conventional wisdom was that nobody
could be confirmed unless he or she supported *Roe v. Wade*. Samuel Alito
and the Republican Senate were about to provide a specific refutation.

The Democratic Party had a base, too, and the pro–abortion rights
position was just as important to these activists as the opposing view
was to the conservatives. When it came to judicial nominations, the
liberal position was embodied by People for the American Way, a
well-funded, politically savvy advocacy group founded by Norman
Lear, the television producer, and led by Ralph G. Neas, an architect
of Bork's defeat in 1987. PFAW had a membership list of 750,000 activists, and as soon as Alito was nominated, Neas set out to mobilize
them against a man he called the embodiment of "the radical right le-

gal movement." Certain that Alito would lead the fight to overturn *Roe* and a host of other civil rights rulings, Neas insisted that he had to be stopped.

Neas's protest drew a tepid response. Unlike Miers, Alito had a network of friends and former law clerks (some of them Democrats) who knew him well and were only too happy to give public testimonials in his behalf. In addition, Alito's impeccable credentials—from his sterling academic record to fifteen years on the federal appellate bench—made it impossible for anyone to oppose him on the ground of his qualifications. (The American Bar Association screening panel unanimously found Alito "well-qualified.") The only reason to vote against him—and it was the focus of PFAW's effort—was that he was simply too conservative and would vote to overturn *Roe v. Wade*. But on this point the difference between the parties was manifest.

The Democratic base did not control its members the way the conservatives controlled the GOP. Moderate Democrats tended toward the center and so were unwilling to take up a filibuster. Alito's handlers in the White House immediately sent him to meet with members of the Gang of 14, and the visits had the desired effect. Moderate Democrats like Ben Nelson of Nebraska responded to Alito neutrally to positively, and Republicans like Mike DeWine of Ohio and Lindsey Graham of South Carolina said they would invoke the nuclear option if the Democrats tried to filibuster. As DeWine observed accurately, "This nominee should not have shocked anyone. George Bush won the election." By the time Alito's public testimony began on January 9, 2006, the possibility of a filibuster had faded; his confirmation appeared all but assured.

"During the previous weeks, an old story about a lawyer who argued a case before the Supreme Court has come to my mind, and I thought I might begin this afternoon by sharing that story," Alito said when he first addressed the senators. "The story goes as follows. This was a lawyer who had never argued a case before the Court before. And when the argument began, one of the justices said, 'How did you get here?' meaning how had his case worked its way up through the court system. But the lawyer was rather nervous and he took the question literally and he said—and this was some years ago—he said, 'I came here on the Baltimore and Ohio Railroad.' This story has come to my mind in recent weeks because I have often asked myself, 'How in the world did I get here?' " This leaden tale, which was greeted with mystified stares, turned out to be a fair augury of the testimony that followed. Alito was a dreadful witness in his own behalf—charmless, evasive, and unpersuasive.

In response to questions about his 1985 job application, Alito essentially dismissed the document. "When someone becomes a judge, you really have to put aside the things that you did as a lawyer at prior points in your legal career and think about legal issues the way a judge thinks about legal issues," he said. As for his current feelings about *Roe*, "I would approach that question the way I approach every legal issue that I approach as a judge, and that is to approach it with an open mind and to go through the whole judicial process, which is designed, and I believe strongly in it, to achieve good results, to achieve good decision making." Alito repeatedly declined to express a view about whether *Roe* should be overturned. Thus, under the peculiar standards of contemporary political discourse, all eighteen members of the Senate Judiciary Committee were expected to—and did—take a stand on *Roe* during their campaigns; but the only people who actually have a say on *Roe*, future justices, were allowed to refuse to answer.

Alito's hearing came shortly after the *New York Times* disclosed that the Bush administration engaged in extensive warrantless wiretapping of phone calls to or from outside the United States. Going back to the Reagan years, Alito's record suggested that he took an expansive view of executive power, though, characteristically, he declined to say much on the subject during the hearings. He did disown one sentence in the 1985 job application, when he said, "I believe very strongly in the supremacy of the elected branches of government." That was a "very inapt phrase," Alito asserted, because he actually believed in three *equal* branches. In almost his only substantive answer, Alito added, "I don't think that we should look to foreign law to interpret our own Constitution"—evidence of how much Kennedy's crusade on the subject had alienated conservatives. (Roberts had expressed a similar sentiment in his hearings.)

Bad as Alito's performance was, that of his Democratic inquisitors was worse. Joseph Biden of Delaware resembled a parody of a bloviating politician, talking for twenty-four of the thirty minutes alloted for his initial questions. Ted Kennedy, the Massachusetts veteran of nineteen Supreme Court confirmation hearings, peppered Alito with a long series of manifestly unfair questions about his participation in a case involving the Vanguard mutual funds, in which the judge had invested. (Alito recognized his error and promptly recused himself in a case of such minor significance that it could not have affected his own portfolio.) Kennedy did annoy Alito by asking him about his membership in a group called Concerned Alumni of Princeton, which had conducted distasteful protests about coeducation and affirmative action at the college. But Alito's role in the group was minor, and he diffused the issue by saying he was merely supporting the return of ROTC to the Princeton campus. Other Democratic senators made halfhearted attempts to engage the nominee on such varied issues as separations of powers, the environment, and law enforcement. Alito dodged with impunity.

In a crowning absurdity, on the third and next-to-last day of Alito's testimony, Lindsey Graham decided to make a theatrical rush to the nominee's defense. Graham mocked Kennedy's line of attack and asked if Alito was a "closet bigot," then expressed sorrow that Alito's family "had to sit here and listen to this." A moment later, Alito's wife, Martha-Ann, burst into tears and rushed from the committee room. Her reaction was certainly peculiar, since it came during Graham's ostentatiously sympathetic questioning. Even though there was no reason to think she staged an onset of the vapors, the day's news focused on her tears, much to the nominee's benefit. Any momentum in the Democrats' direction disappeared.

The final vote in the committee, held on January 24, went along party lines, 10–8 for Alito's confirmation. Senator John Kerry called for a filibuster against Alito, but he did so while on his trip to Davos, Switzerland, signaling a somewhat less than intense focus on the Supreme Court vote. (In a deft bit of mockery, Republicans assailed Kerry for politicking from a ski resort.) Few of Kerry's colleagues joined his call to arms. When the time came for a vote on the Senate floor, on January 31, Alito's opponents mustered forty-two votes against him—more than the forty needed for a filibuster. But many of the senators voting no made clear that they would not support a filibuster, so the fifty-eight votes in Alito's favor amounted to a comfortable margin of victory.

Alito joined the Court almost four months to the day after Roberts, and the two of them struggled to keep up with the sudden onslaught of cert petitions and oral arguments. Their distinct coping mechanisms reflected the modest but real differences between them. Roberts immediately endeared himself to the loyal and long-serving Supreme Court staff by keeping on Rehnquist's secretaries and some of his law clerks; he brought others with him from the D.C. Circuit. In recent years, some of the conservative justices on the Court had begun hiring slightly older law clerks who had both completed the customary appellate clerkships and spent some time in the Bush Justice Department. Alito took this practice to an extreme, hiring as his first clerk Adam Ciongoli, a thirty-seven-year-old senior vice president of Time Warner who had recently completed a two-year stint as one of John Ashcroft's closest aides. It is easy to overstate the importance of law clerks, but the appointment of Ciongoli, who had clerked for Alito a decade earlier on the Third Circuit, suggested a closer than usual tie between the new justice and the administration. In any event, the fortuitous absence of blockbuster cases in the first few months of the Roberts Court allowed the justices to become acclimated to their new surroundings.

Curiously, the person most affected by the two appointments appeared to be Scalia, who had just turned seventy. In public, Scalia had joked about the possibility of becoming chief justice, but the recognition that his career had reached a final plateau seems to have encouraged him to shed his inhibitions. For all his theatrics in oral arguments and the panache of his dissenting opinions, Scalia simply did not love the job as much as his colleagues did. As far back as 1996, he had written to Harry Blackmun, "I am more discouraged this year than I have been at the end of any of my previous nine terms up here. I am beginning to repeat myself, and don't see much use in it anymore." Ten years later, Scalia was still repeating himself, and he was bored.

It should have been a glorious time for Scalia, with two new likeminded justices joining the Court. But as Scalia contemplated his twentieth anniversary on the bench, his legacy looked modest. Although his famous dissents often produced admiring chuckles among his readers, the dissents only rarely become law. In two decades on a generally conservative Court, his number of important majority opinions was almost shockingly small; asked at a public forum his favorite of his opinions—a common question for the justices in such settings—he came up with an esoteric case interpreting the Confrontation Clause of the Sixth Amendment.

Nor did Scalia have much influence on his colleagues. Most famously, from the beginning of his tenure, Scalia had actively repelled O'Connor, pushing her toward her moderate, swing role. He had a similar effect on Kennedy. Even Thomas had long since passed Scalia, en route to a kind of nineteenth-century conservatism.

And the two new justices, though they almost always voted with Scalia in their early days on the bench, seemed to be cutting independent paths. In his confirmation hearing, Roberts issued a nearly Breyer-style denunciation of Scalia's originalism, saying, "I think the framers, when they used broad language like 'liberty,' like 'due process,' like 'unreasonable' with respect to search and seizures, they were crafting a document that they intended to apply in a meaningful way down the ages." Moreover, Roberts's much-advertised minimalism clashed with Scalia's more sweeping approach to writing opinions. As part of his "textualism," Scalia shunned any reference to the legislative history of laws, preferring to interpret only the actual words of a statute rather than the congressional debates leading to a law's passage. But in one of his very first opinions, Alito did cite legislative history, and Scalia, as he always did, dissociated himself from the reference.

Outside of the Court, Scalia's frustration manifested itself in juvenile petulance. Few on the Court traveled as much as he did, and no one more enjoyed mixing it up with critical audiences. These confrontations did not always bring out the best in the justice. He called those who did not share his originalist approach "idiots"; he invited those disappointed with the result of *Bush v. Gore* to "get over it"; he called the international constitutional courts in Europe "the mullahs of the West." In one episode, on March 26, 2006, at a church in Boston, a reporter shouted a question to him about his religious beliefs. "You know what I say to those people?" he replied, and then flicked his fingers under his chin at the questioner. "That's Sicilian," he explained. The next day, the *Boston Herald* wrote that Scalia had made an "obscene" gesture. Two days later, Scalia wrote a letter to the editor of the paper that read in part:

> It has come to my attention that your newspaper published a story on Monday stating that I made an obscene gesture— inside Holy Cross Cathedral, no less. The story is false, and I ask that you publish this letter in full to set the record straight.

Your reporter, an up-and-coming "gotcha" star named
Laurel J. Sweet, asked me (oh-so-sweetly) what I said to those
people who objected to my taking part in such public religious
ceremonies as the Red Mass I had just attended. I responded,
jocularly, with a gesture that consisted of fanning the fingers of
my right hand under my chin. Seeing that she did not
understand, I said "That's Sicilian," and explained its
meaning—which was that I could not care less.

That this is in fact the import of the gesture was nicely
explained and exemplified in a book that was very popular
some years ago, Luigi Barzini's The Italians: "The extended
fingers of one hand moving slowly back and forth under the
raised chin means: 'I couldn't care less. It's no business of mine.
Count me out.' . . . How could your reporter leap to the
conclusion (contrary to my explanation) that the gesture was
obscene? Alas, the explanation is evident in the following line
from her article: " 'That's Sicilian,' the Italian jurist said,
interpreting for the 'Sopranos' challenged." From watching too
many episodes of the Sopranos, your staff seems to have
acquired the belief that any Sicilian gesture is obscene—
especially when made by an "Italian jurist." (I am, by the way,
an American jurist.)

To be sure, there was something endearing about Scalia's unique mix
of élan and erudition. He was a justly popular public speaker. But
over two decades, Scalia failed to charm his most important audience,
his colleagues, and his moxie never translated into influence.

In Roberts and Alito's first year, there turned out to be only one
blockbuster case—the appeal of the fortuitously timed decision that
convinced Dick Cheney to support Roberts for chief justice. Once
again, the justices would turn to the prisoners of Guantánamo Bay.

Few cases had a more unlikely journey to the Supreme Court than
Hamdan v. Rumsfeld. The primary instigators of the lawsuit were a
small group of military lawyers who, at great risk to their careers,
agreed to represent the detainees at Guantánamo. These lawyers, led
by Will Gunn of the Air Force and Charles Swift of the Navy, proved
to be dogged, if overmatched, in repeatedly challenging the actions of

their superiors in the Department of Defense. For help, they turned to a thirty-three-year-old law professor at Georgetown, Neal Katyal, who had served briefly in the Clinton Justice Department after finishing a clerkship with Breyer. With minimal assistance and vastly more experienced adversaries, Katyal constructed a legal assault on the Bush administration's legal position that changed constitutional history.

In 2004, when the justices had first contemplated the case of the prisoners in Cuba, the Bush administration had argued that the case should have been thrown out forthwith, that the detainees were simply outside the reach of the American legal system, with no rights even to bring a case. The justices had rejected this claim in a pair of opinions that included O'Connor's tart reminder that "a state of war is not a blank check for the President." In response, the administration had unilaterally set up a system for allowing the detainees to challenge their incarcerations in abbreviated trials known as commissions. It was this system that the military lawyers, later joined by Katyal, were challenging. For their client, Katyal and his colleagues chose perhaps the least threatening prisoner taken from the battlefields of Afghanistan, Salim Ahmed Hamdan, who was accused of being Osama bin Laden's driver but not a terrorist or even a fighter.

The young professor had one important advantage in the argument on Tuesday morning, March 28—the extremism of the claims made by the Bush administration. (Katyal was making his first argument before the justices; his adversary, Paul Clement, the solicitor general, was making his thirty-fourth.) Clement argued that in authorizing a response to the attacks of September 11, Congress had implicitly suspended the writ of habeas corpus, something that had been done only four previous times in American history. It was a claim that nearly sent Souter flying over the bench.

"Isn't there a pretty good argument that a suspension of the writ by Congress is just about the most stupendously significant act that the Congress of the United States can take?" he asked. "And, therefore, we ought to be at least a little slow to accept your argument that it can be done from pure inadvertence?"

Well, Clement replied, if we're only talking about people outside the territory of the United States . . .

"Now wait a minute," Souter shot back. "The writ is the writ!"

But in a Supreme Court without O'Connor, *Hamdan* would be a breathless wait to see which way Anthony Kennedy was going to vote. Scalia, Thomas, and Alito were likely allies of the administration; Stevens, Souter, Breyer, and Ginsburg would go the other way. (Roberts could not participate because he had already ruled in the case, on the Bush side, in the D.C. Circuit.)

The case tapped into Kennedy's deep interest in international law. Indeed, in just a few weeks Kennedy would be leaving for Salzburg and then, in 2006, for a round-the-world tour: Washington to Hawaii, for a speech before the American Bar Association; to Malaysia, to meet with the sultan, who was also a judge; on to Dubai for a conference of four hundred judges; and then to the Old Bailey, in London, where he would observe a murder trial; and finally back to Washington. The heart of the Bush administration's argument before the Court in *Hamdan* was that the Geneva Conventions—the treaty that is at the core of international law and that the United States had long ago signed—did not apply to the prisoners at Guantánamo.

"Well, let me put it this way," Kennedy said to Katyal. "If we were to find that the Geneva Convention or other settled principles of international law were controlling here, why couldn't we just remand to the D.C. Circuit and let it figure that out?"

That might work, Katyal said.

"Well, suppose we told the D.C. Circuit that the Geneva Convention or some other body of international law controls . . . ?"

Kennedy was tipping his hand. At conference, he joined the four liberals in striking down the Bush plans for Guantánamo—again. Stevens's opinion for the Court, issued on June 29, the last day of the term, amounted to an even more thorough rebuke to the administration than the Court had issued two years earlier. The Pentagon could *not* write procedures for the military commissions unilaterally; Congress had to approve them as well. The Pentagon could *not* ignore the Geneva Conventions; the procedures had to comport with the treaty. The courts would *not* sit out the dispute, as Clement had urged, until detainees had actually been convicted and sentenced. The administration would have to start complying with the Constitution right away. Writing in his usual restrained style, Stevens made clear that he and his colleagues regarded the Bush position as something close to lawless. The Geneva Convention "is applicable here," he wrote, and "requires that Hamdan be tried by a 'regularly constituted court affording all the judicial guarantees which are recognized as indispensable by civilized peoples.' "

The dissenters replied with rhetoric that reflected the Republican political campaigns of 2002, 2004, and 2006. Thomas said the decision would "sorely hamper the President's ability to confront and defeat a new and deadly enemy," and suggested that it undermined the nation's ability to "preven[t] future attacks." Joined by Kennedy, Souter, and Ginsburg, Breyer issued an unusually pointed and eloquent reply in a concurring opinion in which he quoted the famous words of his departed ally, O'Connor: "The Court's conclusion ultimately rests upon a single ground: Congress has not issued the Executive a 'blank check.' "

As both sides in *Hamdan* recognized, the case was crucial, and not just because the detainees in Guantánamo Bay faced the possibility of execution by their American captors. The lawsuit was about defining the meaning of the Constitution in an age of terror—and with a changing Supreme Court. "Where, as here, no emergency prevents consultation with Congress, judicial insistence upon that consultation does not weaken our Nation's ability to deal with danger," Breyer wrote. "To the contrary, that insistence strengthens the Nation's ability to determine—through democratic means—how best to do so. The Constitution places its faith in those democratic means. Our Court today simply does the same."

PHANATICS?

For many years, the Court had a tradition of holding a welcoming dinner for each new member, with the former junior justice acting as host. The practice fell into disuse in recent years because there had been so little turnover among the justices. Still, during the summer of 2006, Breyer said he wanted to revive the custom and have a dinner for Alito. The permanent staff members of the Court, with their usual reverence for tradition, took to the assignment with gusto—and even staged a full rehearsal dinner, just to make sure that the evening would be flawless.

On Friday, October 6, a small ensemble from the Marine Corps band greeted the justices and their spouses in the Great Hall of the Court. It was on occasions like this one that the Court most felt like a family. Sandra and John O'Connor were there, as were the widows of Thurgood Marshall and Potter Stewart. At last, just before dessert, Breyer rose to give a toast.

"Sam, we are here to welcome you," Breyer said, "and we are very happy to have this dinner for you. But I have to warn you about something. Everyone here tonight is very nice to you. But they'll turn on you. They'll dissent from your opinions. They won't sign on to your dissents. It's a tough group."

In the flickering light of the candelabras, the guests exchanged puzzled looks.

"What you need here is a friend," Breyer went on. "You need someone who will stand by you—really stand by you, not like these people around the table."

At that moment, the door to the dining room swung open and a giant beast with green fur, purple eyelashes, and a Philadelphia

Phillies jersey burst into the room. The Phillie Phanatic, mascot of Alito's beloved baseball team, lumbered over to Alito, gave him a prolonged embrace, and then left the room, leaving raucous laughter in its wake.

The welcoming dinner for Alito showed how the comradely spirit of the Rehnquist Court had survived the transition to a new chief. Roberts displayed the same genial manner with his new colleagues that he had before the Judiciary Committee. Courteous, even deferential, Roberts controlled the mechanics of the Court in the same even-handed way that had made Rehnquist so popular among the justices. In conference, as before, everyone still had the chance to speak once before anyone spoke twice—and they did so at somewhat greater length than Rehnquist had permitted. Roberts also parceled out opinion-writing duties in the same fair-minded way that Rehnquist had, distributing the "dogs" and significant cases in roughly even numbers. In his annual message on the judiciary, the chief justice issued a passionate call to Congress to grant long-delayed pay increases for federal trial and appellate judges—a cause important to both liberal and conservative members of the Court. In speeches, Roberts repeated his pleas for judicial minimalism—narrow decisions endorsed by clear majorities (or, better yet, unanimous agreement) of the justices.

But the good cheer—and the promises of incremental change—masked the truth about the Roberts Court on the only thing that mattered, the substance of its decisions. George W. Bush's second term has been marked by a series of political calamities for the president and his party—on the Iraq war, Hurricane Katrina, Social Security and immigration reform, and the midterm elections, to name a few. But one major and enduring project went according to plan: the transformation of the Supreme Court. Quickly, almost instantly by the usual stately pace of the justices, the Court in 2006 and 2007 became a dramatically more conservative institution.

Outsiders recognized the change before the justices acknowledged it.

The first clear indication came from the lawyers in the Court's first major school desegregation case in many years. In Louisville, schools had been segregated by law before *Brown v. Board of Education* in 1954; and even after the Court struck down the doctrine of separate but equal, Kentucky officials, like so many around the nation, avoided complying with *Brown* and maintained separate schools for black and white students into the 1970s. But when the community finally decided to comply with the law, Louisville faced a familiar problem. Its neighborhoods were so segregated that placing students only in schools close to their homes would scarcely change the racial balance. As a result, the school board eventually came up with a plan in the mideighties that considered a variety of issues in assigning children to schools. Student choice was the major factor, as was the presence of siblings in a school, but race counted as well. Louisville managed enrollment so that each school had no less than 15 percent and no more than 50 percent black students. A group of parents challenged the plan in court, asserting that the school board had no right to use race in school assignments. In a related case, a similar plan in Seattle was attacked as well.

At one level, the two school cases looked easy. As lower courts had noted, the plans comported with the rules O'Connor had set down in the *Grutter v. Bollinger* case just three years earlier. Like the University of Michigan Law School, the Louisville and Seattle school boards decided that they wanted to foster diversity in their communities. And, like Michigan, the schools included race as one factor among several in selecting students. But the Supreme Court of 2006 and 2007 was not the Supreme Court of 2003. And the lawyers for the Louisville parents put the challenge to the justices in the most direct way. The same month that Alito was confirmed, the parents asked the justices to grant certiorari in their case. To the lawyers in the new case, the question presented was straightforward, and chilling for O'Connor's legacy: "Should *Grutter v. Bollinger* . . . be overturned?" Certiorari was granted.

Like all former justices, of course, O'Connor could only watch what the Court would do to the precedents she had laid down. Her retirement had turned out to be nothing like what she expected. O'Connor had left the Court to be with her husband, but during the long delay, his illness took a cruel toll on John O'Connor. Alzheimer's disease follows an unpredictable path, and John deteriorated much faster than anyone had expected. By 2007, he no longer knew his wife. He was moved to an assisted-living facility in Phoenix, near the O'Connors' sons. In a sad irony, Justice O'Connor had not wanted to resign, but had done so to take care of John, and then suddenly there was nothing she could do for him.

O'Connor responded in a characteristic manner—not with self-pity or despair but rather with almost frenzied work and activity. In her first fall away from the Court, she threw herself into the cause that had obsessed her since the Terri Schiavo case. In September 2006, she sponsored, organized, and hosted a conference at Georgetown University Law Center on judicial independence. Many speakers at the conference targeted the Republicans who had been challenging judges on such issues as abortion, criminal sentencing, and the influence of foreign courts throughout the Bush years. O'Connor's self-confidence was intact. At a planning meeting for the Georgetown event, several people wondered whether the new chief justice might attend. "You just leave John Roberts to me," O'Connor promised, and the new chief dutifully paid homage.

At the same time O'Connor was planning the judicial independence conference, she agreed to serve as a member of the Iraq Study Group, the panel of eminences, cochaired by James A. Baker III and Lee H. Hamilton, charged with plotting a new course for the war. Even though she had no direct experience in the military or diplomatic matters, O'Connor knew how to ask questions, and she played a key role in examining some of the hundred or so witnesses the ISG consulted over almost six months. O'Connor's impatience and brisk efficiency became a source of amusement to her nine fellow members. When the photographer Annie Leibovitz came to one ISG meeting to take a group portrait for *Men's Vogue*, O'Connor refused to participate in such silliness. "That's not what I'm here for," she growled, and her colleagues sheepishly followed her lead. Years earlier, O'Connor had sat for a Leibovitz portrait and found the experience tedious. Baker and Hamilton did eventually sit for Leibovitz.

The ISG report, which was released on December 6, 2006, began by asserting, "The situation in Iraq is grave and deteriorating." O'Connor and her colleagues called for a new, largely diplomatic approach, leading to a gradual withdrawal of American military forces. President Bush ignored most of the group's recommendations and instead ordered a "surge" of tens of thousands more American troops.

As with so much of the Bush presidency, O'Connor was appalled but not surprised by his rejection of the core of the ISG plan. Still, she was fatalistic, resigned to her limited role in events. At the news conference announcing the ISG's findings, she noted that, like her duties at the Court, her role on the commission had concluded. "It really is out of our hands, having done what we did," O'Connor said. "It's up to you, frankly."

At the Court, suddenly, it was up to Anthony Kennedy. Even more than O'Connor had over the previous decade, Kennedy now controlled the outcome of case after case. During the Rehnquist years, O'Connor and Kennedy had had idiosyncratic enough views that it wasn't always clear whose vote would turn out to be dispositive. But the Roberts Court had four outspoken conservatives—Roberts, Scalia, Thomas, and Alito—and four liberals, at least by contemporary standards—Stevens, Souter, Ginsburg, and Breyer. Kennedy, always, was in the middle. And he loved it.

Kennedy had long had the most difficult judicial philosophy on the Court to describe. It was centered on his perception of the judge—and of himself—as a figure of drama and wisdom, more than any specific ideology. Kennedy believed that, at home and abroad, the rule of law was protected by enlightened individuals as much as by any identifiable approach to the law. In his two decades on the Court, Kennedy had come to have a usually predictable, if intellectually incoherent, collection of views. He believed what he believed, but it was hard to say why.

This was especially true on abortion. He had been the key figure in the *Casey* decision of 1992 and the author of the passages affirming the result in *Roe v. Wade*. (The opinion was jointly written with O'Connor and Souter, but only Kennedy's portion was written in his distinctive purple prose.) "The liberty of the woman is at stake in a sense unique to the human condition and so unique to the law," he wrote. "Her suffering is too intimate and personal for the State to insist, without more, upon its own vision of the woman's role, however dominant that vision has been in the course of our history and our culture. The destiny of the woman must be shaped to a large extent on her own conception of her spiritual imperatives and her place in society."

Eight years after *Casey*, in 2000, Kennedy had changed his mind—dramatically. In *Stenberg v. Carhart*, Breyer had painstakingly demonstrated that Nebraska's ban on so-called partial birth abortion had done just what Kennedy said a state could not do. But Kennedy wrote a theatrical dissent, asserting that "the political processes of the State are not to be foreclosed from enacting laws to promote the life of the unborn and to ensure respect for all human life and its potential."

Adopting the language of the antiabortion movement, Kennedy called the doctors who performed the procedure "abortionists" and claimed that "medical procedures must be governed by moral principles having their foundation in the intrinsic value of human life, including life of the unborn." Kennedy's hymn to women's autonomy in 1992 turned into a paean to the life of the unborn in 2000.

After Bush's election, Congress and the president bet that Kennedy's view—not Breyer's—would ultimately hold sway at the Court. Congress passed a federal law that was nearly identical to the Nebraska statute struck down by Breyer's opinion. Like the one from Nebraska, the federal law banned the "partial birth" procedure, and it did not contain an exception that permitted the procedure to protect the health of the mother. Every appeals court that evaluated the new law found it unconstitutional, relying on Breyer's *Stenberg* opinion and the absence of a health exception. But it was the new Roberts Court that heard the appeal of those decisions early in the 2006 term. The result gave a hint of what was to come.

Alito's replacement of O'Connor flipped the result in the case, to a 5–4 ratification of the federal abortion law. Roberts assigned the case to Kennedy, who essentially turned his *Stenberg* dissent into a majority opinion—the sweetest kind of vindication that a Supreme Court justice can enjoy. The Court in the new case, *Gonzales v. Carhart*, did not formally overrule *Stenberg* but did so effectively. Breyer's opinion—and the requirement that abortion prohibitions contain exceptions to protect the health of the woman—were now obsolete. As always, Kennedy had to turn the attention on himself; in his view, his ruling was not simply a ratification of an act of Congress but rather his gift to women as well. "While we find no reliable data to measure the phenomenon," Kennedy wrote, "it seems unexceptionable to conclude some women come to regret their choice to abort the infant life they once created and sustained." Small wonder that Kennedy found no such data, because, notwithstanding the claims of the antiabortion movement, no scientifically respectable support existed for this patronizing notion. Notably, too, foreign law (which had often pushed Kennedy to the left) was generally more restrictive of abortion rights than that of the United States, so on this subject, unlike gay rights or the death penalty, Kennedy mostly received reinforcement from his colleagues abroad.

Given Kennedy's and Alito's well-known views on abortion, no student of the Court could be surprised at the result in the case. Still, the expansiveness of Kennedy's opinion (with its dismissive acknowl-edgments of the *Roe* and *Casey* precedents) left the four liberals on the Court shocked. And the year had just started.

In his confirmation hearing, Roberts had suggested the Court could increase the number of cases it heard, but the justices' schedule in the fall of 2006 set them on pace to issue embarrassingly few opinions. Fearing criticism for their languid ways, the justices quickly filled their calendar for the set of arguments that began in January 2007. The year would still yield only sixty-eight decisions, a record low for the Court in modern times, but the back-loaded schedule made for a hectic spring. Indeed, the decisions came so fast that it took a while for even the justices themselves to recognize what was going on.

Ginsburg saw it first. Shy, awkward, isolated from her colleagues in her second-floor chambers, Ginsburg had never been a center of influ-ence at the Court. She lacked Stevens's seniority, Breyer's bonhomie, Scalia's bombast, or O'Connor's and Kennedy's swing-justice status. (Ginsburg had a particular aversion to Kennedy's intellectual mean-derings.) As it happened, two of the justices Ginsburg liked most— Rehnquist and O'Connor—left in quick succession, so she began the term lonelier than usual. But more than the others, Ginsburg was free of illusions about the supposedly apolitical nature of judging and made a clear-eyed assessment of the motives and consequences of her colleagues' actions.

What Ginsburg saw was that the conservatives were taking over, and moving swiftly to consolidate their gains. The arguments hadn't changed; the personnel had. Over the past few years, O'Connor had moved left so swiftly that she probably passed Breyer in that direc-tion, and Rehnquist had become an institutionalist, committed to the stability of the Court more than to ideological change. (For example, the old chief, as he was now referred to, never embraced the *Miranda* decision, but he came to accept it.) Roberts and Alito were different, as the spring of 2007 quickly illustrated. As Ginsburg observed wryly in her dissent in the abortion case, the only reason for the result was that the Court "is differently composed than it was when we last con-sidered a restrictive abortion regulation."

As a minor consolation, the abortion case gave Ginsburg the chance to float her own distinctive view of the constitutional basis for abortion rights. Even before she became a judge, Ginsburg had not cared for Blackmun's privacy rationale in *Roe v. Wade*. Rather, as she wrote in her dissent in *Gonzales v. Carhart*, "legal challenges to undue restrictions on abortion procedures do not seek to vindicate some generalized notion of privacy; rather, they center on a woman's autonomy to determine her life's course, and thus to enjoy equal citizenship stature." Ginsburg believed abortion rights protected women's equality, not their privacy, and she persuaded all of her fellow dissenters— Stevens, Souter, and Breyer—to sign on with her. But as the spring wore on, these four justices increasingly were speaking only to each other.

For years, Ginsburg had prided herself on her restraint in writing dissents, citing O'Connor and Souter as her fellow exemplars of politesse. In speeches and in private, she said she thought Scalia-style posturing and invective distracted the Court from its work. But on April 18, she read her fiery dissent in the abortion case from the bench, and on May 29, she denounced her colleagues in *Ledbetter v. Goodyear Tire & Rubber Company*, a case that seemed almost designed to infuriate her. While still a law school professor, Ginsburg had represented women in equal pay cases under Title VII, which bans discrimination in the workplace. That law requires individuals to file their cases within 180 days of "the alleged unlawful employment practice." For years, the courts said that if a woman sued within 180 days of her last offending paycheck, she received compensation for the entire period she had suffered from discrimination. But in *Ledbetter*, the five conservatives ruled that plaintiffs could be paid for discrimination only within the six-month statute of limitations.

"The Court does not comprehend, or is indifferent to, the insidious way in which women can be the victims of pay discrimination," she said. As Ginsburg knew better than anyone who had ever served on the Court, the majority's ruling ignored the realities of actual litigation. She said that women can't possibly know within 180 days that they are being paid less than men. "Ledbetter's initial readiness to give her employer the benefit of the doubt should not preclude her from later seeking redress for the continuing payment to her of a salary depressed because of her sex," Ginsburg continued. She concluded by imploring Congress to amend Title VII to make clear that the majority's interpretation was wrong. Her current colleagues, Ginsburg suggested, were beyond help.

In his two years as chief, Roberts made his public goals clear. Decide more cases; achieve more unanimity; write narrower opinions—judicial minimalism. In 2007, Roberts failed on each one. Only 25 percent of the decisions were unanimous, down from 45 percent in his first year. (About a third of the opinions were unanimous in the Rehnquist years.) Even more striking, 33 percent of the cases in 2006 and 2007 were decided by votes of 5–4—a level of division unprecedented in the Court's recent history.

So was Roberts's second year a failure? To the contrary. The new chief's stated goals dealt with procedural niceties. The president who nominated him (and those who pushed Bush to appoint him) cared above all about the substance of the Court's decisions, and the changes were dramatic in precisely the way Roberts's sponsors sought. As the spring of 2007 wore on, the pace of conservative change accelerated. The Court invalidated some of the restrictions on political advertising in the McCain-Feingold campaign finance bill, less than four years after the Court had approved practically the same rules. In a key church-state ruling, the Court made it much harder for citizens to challenge government activity that endorsed or supported religious activity. In a curious case from Alaska, the Court reduced the free-speech rights of students by approving the suspension of a high school senior who unfurled a banner that said, BONG HiTS 4 JESUS. All of these cases were 5–4, with Kennedy joining the conservatives.

Like Ginsburg, Souter generally declined to denounce his colleagues in his opinions, but one of the last cases in June undermined his restraint. In this case, the same majority rejected an appeal by a prisoner who had filed his case in advance of a deadline set by a federal district judge. Because the judge had misread the law and given the prisoner too much time to file—three extra days—the Court said that the case had to be thrown out. The dissenting opinion by the usually mild-mannered Souter (joined again by Stevens, Ginsburg, and Breyer) reflected true anguish. "It is intolerable for the judicial system to treat people this way, and there is not even a technical justification for condoning this bait and switch," he wrote.

In several of these cases—on abortion, campaign finance, and church-state relations—the rulings of the majority directly contradicted Court precedents, but Roberts and his colleagues did not come out and say that the old cases had been overruled. This frustrated Scalia and Thomas, who wanted to see the Court make more explicit denunciations of its past. In a concurring opinion in the campaign finance case, Scalia chided Roberts for failing to administer the coup de grâce to the earlier ruling. "This faux judicial restraint is judicial obfuscation."

Scalia had a point. Roberts had engaged in the pretense of minimalism—that is, of respecting the Court's precedents—without actually doing so. Leaving cases like Breyer's *Stenberg* opinion on the books without actually following their holdings amounted to a kind of sophistry, and Scalia, to his credit, believed in candor in opinion-writing. But Roberts coolly turned such complaints aside. The labels on the opinions may have been misleading, but their contents were not. By the spring of 2007, the Court was a more conservative institution, and so, it followed, were the rules of American life.

The Court puts off its most contentious cases for the last weeks—and the toughest of all for the last day. That final day of a term always offers an unvarnished picture of the justices. By that point, they are tired and grumpy. In the headlong rush to finish, they have spent entirely too much time with each other and their law clerks and too little on the obligations of everyday life. At the stroke of ten on June 28, 2007, as the justices emerged from behind the velvet curtains, it was clear that a majority needed haircuts.

Samuel Alito, in the junior justice's chair on the audience's far right, stared blankly into the middle distance. He had been an appeals court judge for fifteen years before becoming a justice, but the unique burdens of the high court weighed on him as they did on all newcomers. Pasty-faced, phlegmatic, conservative in demeanor as well as conviction, Alito fought sleep from the moment he sat down.

The tiny Ginsburg was all but swallowed up in the next chair toward the middle, her head barely visible above the bench. Immaculate as ever, unlike her weary colleagues, she stared in evident fury straight ahead of her. The term had been a disaster, and she had no intention of pretending otherwise.

In the best of circumstances, David Souter loathed ceremonial occasions like this one. In a venerable custom, before many oral arguments, the Court still allows lawyers to be sworn in as members of the

Supreme Court bar in person. The proceeding usually takes about ten minutes and concludes with the chief justice welcoming the new group. Unlike his colleagues, Souter never cracks a smile at what he regards as a total waste of time. So, too, on this day, Souter seethed at having to sit through a pointless ritual at the end of another unhappy year.

Scalia looked fine, his eyebrows dancing in satisfaction at the year's accomplishments. He hadn't won every case, and his colleagues had not gone as far or as fast as he would have preferred, but it had still been the best term for Scalia in a long, long time.

Roberts, in the center seat, showed the first traces of gray in his hair, but his face was as unlined as when he'd carried Rehnquist's casket into the building twenty-two months earlier. His confidence had deepened. It was his Court, and everyone knew it.

Stevens, to the chief's right, looked the same as ever, two months after his eighty-seventh birthday. (At the time, his older brother, William, was still practicing law part-time in Florida in his ninety-first year.) With his bow tie, unfashionably large tortoise-shell glasses, and inscrutable expression, John Stevens gave nothing more away than he did at the bridge table in Fort Lauderdale, where he would soon be going.

Kennedy's studied earnestness could not conceal his joy. No justice in history had had a term like his; in the twenty-four cases decided by votes of 5–4, Kennedy was in the majority in every single one. And he had two more majority opinions, and a crucial concurrence, to announce. After an early-morning workout on the elliptical trainer, this seventy-year-old man glowed.

The last two seats on the bench enjoy the dubious privilege of immediate proximity to the press section. On this day, Nina Totenberg of NPR sat closest to the justices, and Clarence Thomas swung so far back in his chair that Stephen Breyer blocked her view of him—and his of her. Before Alito's arrival, Thomas had spent more than eleven years at the other side of the courtroom from the reporters, an arrangement much more to his liking. Thomas's chair was adjusted to allow him to lean back much farther than his colleagues, and he, unlike Alito, didn't look like he was trying to keep his eyes open. Even by Thomas's own peculiar standards, this had been an extraordinary year. Over an entire Court term, Thomas had sat through one hundred and four oral arguments and not asked a single question.

At the end of the bench, Breyer twitched, leaning forward and then back, his hand straying from the thick stack of papers before him to his bald head and back. Breyer always fidgeted more than his colleagues, but he looked on this day as if he wanted to jump out of his skin. This epochal term on the Court had changed Breyer more than anyone. He had lost cases before, of course, but he had always responded with energy and hope—as when he rallied the liberal clerks out of their despair after *Bush v. Gore*. Now, the conservative onslaught had darkened Breyer's naturally sunny temperament. Desperate for productive work throughout this dismal spring, he had thrown himself into lobbying Congress for the pay raises for judges. At least on the other side of First Street, Breyer had a chance of winning.

Three cases remained. Kennedy announced the first, when the Court didn't even offer the pretense of minimalism and overruled a ninety-six-year-old precedent. Since the case, known as *Dr. Miles*, in 1911, the Court had held that antitrust law forbade manufacturers from setting minimum prices for their products. The idea was that minimum prices discouraged competition and raised costs for consumers. Henceforth, according to Kennedy and the four conservatives, minimum prices would sometimes be allowed.

As always, Kennedy gave a longer summary of his opinion that the others tended to do, and Breyer, two seats to his right, rolled his eyes in irritation. "Justice Stevens, Justice Souter, Justice Ginsburg, and I have filed a dissenting opinion," Breyer began, in his singsong voice. "I want here to emphasize one point: stare decisis." That was his theme for the day and for the year: that the conservatives were abandoning the rule of precedent without justification.

In the next case, it was Kennedy again, this time siding with the four liberals. They struck down a death sentence for a Texas man who suffered from mental illness. This case reflected true judicial minimalism, because the Court set down no new rules and simply ordered the lower court to give the man a new hearing. Thomas, the Court's most reliable supporter of executions, wrote a dissent for Roberts, Scalia, and Alito, but he declined to speak from the bench.

Then, finally, it came down to the last case of the year, the combined appeals on the Louisville and Seattle school desegregation cases, and Roberts announced he would deliver the opinion himself. Few justices in history have taken to opinion-writing as quickly as Roberts. The new chief is good-natured, to be sure, but he is also intensely competitive, and he writes his opinions as he did his briefs when he was a litigator—with crystalline logic, pungent rhetoric, and vivid examples. Once more the Court was limiting a precedent rather than overturning it outright—now it was O'Connor's *Grutter* opinion—but the message was the same as in the other cases. The conservative majority had arrived.

Like any warrior, Roberts took the high ground, and at the Supreme Court, there is no rampart more protected than *Brown v. Board of Education*, the unanimous landmark decision of 1954 where Chief Justice Earl Warren forbade official segregation in public schools. To Roberts, any plan that assigned even a single student for a single year to a school based on his race violated *Brown*. "Before *Brown*, schoolchildren were told where they could and could not go to school based on the color of their skin. The school districts in these cases have not carried the heavy burden of demonstrating that we should allow this once again—even for very different reasons," the chief justice read in his flat midwestern accent. "The way to stop discrimination on the basis of race is to stop discriminating on the basis of race."

Breyer then spoke for twenty-seven minutes, one of the longest spoken protests in the Court's history, summarizing a dissenting opinion that he called "twice as long as any other I have written." Kennedy agreed with the result in the Louisville and Seattle cases, but not with all of Roberts's opinion. In a vague and confusing concurring opinion of his own, Kennedy suggested that some race-conscious plans might be permissible, but not those in these two cities. Many big-city schools were in fact already moving away from the explicit race-consciousness of Louisville and Seattle, concentrating more on raising test scores than mixing races. Thus, the practical effect of the day's decisions was left rather mysterious and may turn out to be modest.

But Breyer wrote at such length, and spoke with such passion, because of something more than the immediate stakes. In part, he (joined again by all three liberals) was simply offended at the hijacking of *Brown* by the conservatives. "The lesson of history is not that efforts to continue racial segregation are constitutionally indistinguishable from efforts to achieve racial integration," he said. "And it is a cruel distortion of history to compare Topeka, Kansas, in the

1950s, to Louisville and Seattle in the modern day." In part, too, Breyer saw planted in Roberts's opinion the end of all affirmative action—in employment, in business, and in government, as well as in education. The "color-blind" Constitution, long favored by Scalia and Thomas and now apparently by Roberts and Alito, would end it all. (In a brief dissent that was more bewildered than angry, Stevens made the remarkable assertion, "It is my firm conviction that no Member of the Court that I joined in 1975 would have agreed with today's decision.")

But Breyer, most fundamentally, was talking in his long opinion about the Court. For the second time that day, he asked, "What has happened to stare decisis?" He listed *Grutter* and six more cases that now appeared to be dead letters. "The plurality's logic writes these cases out of the law," he said, and then added words that did not appear in the published version of his dissenting opinion: "It is not often in law that so few have so quickly changed so much."

At this direct slap, Alito roused himself and stared across the bench at Breyer. Roberts didn't change expression, but the muscles in his jaw twitched. Above all, Breyer was taking a stand against the agenda that was born in the Reagan years, nurtured by the Federalist Society, championed by the right wing of the Republican Party, and propelled by the nominations of Roberts and Alito. Expand executive power. End racial preferences intended to assist African Americans. Speed executions. Welcome religion into the public sphere. And, above all, reverse *Roe v. Wade* and allow states to ban abortion. As Breyer knew better than anyone, the two new justices, plus Scalia, Thomas, and (usually) Kennedy, put all those goals tantalizingly within reach.

As soon as Breyer finished, Roberts, graceful as always, closed the year by paying tribute to Harry Fenwick, the Court's food preparation specialist, who would be retiring two days later after thirty-eight years of service. "Thanks for everything, Harry," Roberts said. Then the chief justice declared a recess until the first Monday in October.

THE STEPS—CLOSED

On the day that President Bush nominated John Roberts to the Supreme Court, the future chief justice reflected upon the great symbol at the heart of Cass Gilbert's design—the steps. "I always got a lump in my throat whenever I walked up those marble steps to argue a case before the Court," Roberts said, "and I don't think it was just from the nerves." Over the years, countless Americans have shared Roberts's sense of awe as they entered Gilbert's temple of justice. Soon, however, no one else will. The steps will be closed to the public as an entranceway to the Court.

Rehnquist made the renovation of the Supreme Court building a priority during his final years as chief justice. Like many government building projects, a fairly modest restoration metastasized into an over-budget, much-delayed shambles, which may (or may not) be completed around 2009. And like much else in Washington after September 11, 2001, the design decisions about the renovation were made with obsessive attention to the issue of security. Most notably, the public entrance up the front steps—the defining feature of Gilbert's concept for the structure—was deemed an undue risk. So a new entrance will be gouged into the side of the steps, near the base of the building. Visitors will still be allowed to depart down the front steps, and watch Gilbert's vision recede behind them.

Whether the closing of the steps turns out to be a metaphor for deeper change at the Court will be determined in part by the justices but even more by the American people. More than any other influence, the Court has always reflected the political currents driving the broader society. In the early days of the Republic, when regional conflict predominated, that tension could be seen on the Court. Presidents felt obligated to replace, say, a California justice with another from the same state. (Later, of course, it passed almost without notice that the Court for many years had two justices, Rehnquist and O'Connor, from the relatively unpopulated state of Arizona.) In the nineteenth and twentieth centuries, the great tide of European immigration put religion near the center of politics, and the tradition of a "Catholic seat" and a "Jewish seat" arose. The fact that President Clinton drew little comment by appointing two Jews to the Court proved the passing of this era. Likewise, there is little significance that there are now five Catholic justices. The most important liberal in the Court's history, William Brennan, was Catholic, too.

Today, the fundamental divisions in American society are not regional or religious but ideological. Roberts, Scalia, Kennedy, Thomas, and Alito were not appointed because they are Catholic but because they are conservative. The base of the Republican Party—from James Dobson and Jay Sekulow among the evangelicals to Ted Olson and Leonard Leo among the Federalists—recognized that they could use their influence to shape the Court. They organized more, mobilized more, and *cared* more about the Court than their liberal counterparts. And when their candidate won the presidency, these conservatives demanded more—a pair of justices who were precisely to their liking (and the ejection of one nominee, Harriet Miers, who was not). With admirable candor, and even greater passion, conservatives have invested in the Court to advance their goals for the country.

In public at least, Roberts himself purports to have a different view of the Court than his conservative sponsors. "Judges are like umpires," he said at his confirmation hearing. "Umpires don't make the rules; they apply them." Elsewhere, Roberts has often said, "Judges are not politicians." None of this is true. Supreme Court justices are nothing at all like baseball umpires. It is folly to pretend that the awesome work of interpreting the Constitution, and thus defining the rights and obligations of American citizenship, is akin to performing the rote, almost mindless task of calling balls and strikes. When it comes to the core of the Court's work, determining the contemporary meaning of the Constitution, it is ideology, not craft or skill, that controls the outcome of cases. As Richard A. Posner, the great conservative judge and law professor, has written, "It is rarely possible to say with a straight face of a Supreme Court constitutional decision that it was decided correctly or incorrectly." Constitutional cases, Posner wrote, "can be decided only on the basis of a political judgment, and a political judgment cannot be called right or wrong by reference to legal norms."

For this reason, Breyer's wan longing for stare decisis will stir few hearts. Breyer and his liberal colleagues (joined on this occasion by Kennedy) did not care about stare decisis when they voted in *Lawrence v. Texas* to overturn the Court's barely seventeen-year-old decision in *Bowers v. Hardwick*. Rather, they believed that the time had come to recognize that it was an abomination to allow criminal punishment of consensual homosexual sex and voted accordingly. On that occasion, as so often, ideology trumped precedent. It is, of course, possible to overstate the flexibility in the meaning of the Constitution. Honorable judges always tether their views to the words of the document, its history, and the precedents, so the justices' freedom to interpret is vast but not absolute.

Still, when it comes to the incendiary political issues that end up in the Supreme Court, what matters is not the quality of the arguments but the identity of the justices. There is, for example, no meaningful difference between Scalia and Ginsburg in intelligence, competence, or ethics. What separates them is judicial philosophy—ideology—and that means everything on the Supreme Court. Future justices will all likely be similarly qualified to meet the basic requirements of the job. It is their ideologies that will shape the Court and thus the nation.

So one factor—and one factor only—will determine the future of the Supreme Court: the outcomes of presidential elections. Presidents pick justices to extend their legacies; by this standard, George W. Bush chose wisely. The days when justices surprised the presidents who appointed them are over; the last two purported surprises, Souter and Kennedy, were anything but. Souter's record pegged him as a moderate; Kennedy was nominated because the more conservative Robert Bork was rejected by the Senate. All of the subsequently appointed justices—Thomas, Ginsburg, Breyer, Roberts, and Alito—have turned out precisely as might have been expected by the presidents who appointed them. That will almost certainly be true, too, of the replacements for the three justices most likely to depart in the near future—Stevens, Souter, and Ginsburg.

This is as it should be. Cass Gilbert's steps represent at some level a magnificent illusion—that the Supreme Court operates at a higher plane than the mortals who toil on the ground. But the Court is a product of a democracy and represents, with sometimes chilling precision, the best and worst of the people. We can expect nothing more, and nothing less, than the Court we deserve.

ACKNOWLEDGMENTS

This book was much improved by the attentive and skillful editing of Phyllis Grann. At Doubleday, I am grateful also to Karyn Marcus, Todd Doughty, Roslyn Schloss, Rebecca Holland, Michael Collica, Bette Alexander, and the boss, Stephen Rubin. Once again, my agent, Esther Newberg, has steered me the right way. My thanks as well to John Q. Barrett of the St. John's School of Law and to Tom Goldstein of the Akin, Gump firm for their helpful comments on the manuscript, and to Dan Kaufman for fact-checking assistance.

I am privileged to work at *The New Yorker*, where David Remnick has been a generous editor and a loyal friend. I am fortunate to work with Dorothy Wickenden, Emily Eakin, and Jeffrey Frank. I am lucky, too, in my CNN colleagues, and I thank Jon Klein and Bill Mears for their support of this venture.

Covering the World Cup had absolutely nothing to do with writing about the Supreme Court, but that experience, with my son Adam, was the highlight of this book's creation. Talking with my daughter Ellen is always a part of my continuing education, about law, politics, and everything else. My days with their mother, Amy McIntosh, are nothing less than the highlight of my life.

NOTES

This book is based principally on my interviews with the justices and more than seventy-five of their law clerks. The interviews were on a not-for-attribution basis—that is, I could use the information provided but without quoting directly or identifying the source.

I have also steeped myself in the vast literature about the Court. In addition to the works cited below and in the bibliography, I have benefited from the day-to-day coverage of the Supreme Court press corps, especially that of Linda Greenhouse, Lyle Denniston, Chuck Lane, Dahlia Lithwick, Tony Mauro, David Savage, and Nina Totenberg. My thanks also to the Public Information Office of the Court, its excellent website, www.supremecourtus.gov, and Kathy Arberg, Patricia McCabe, and Ed Turner. Like all contemporary students of the Court, I benefited from my immersion in Justice Blackmun's papers at the Library of Congress. My discussion of the *Casey* abortion decision drew heavily from this priceless trove.

Fortunately, the Court's opinions are now widely available online. I relied on Cornell University's http://supct.law.cornell.edu/supct/index.html. For transcripts and recordings of the Court's oral arguments, Professor Jerry Goldman of Northwestern University created www.oyez.org, which I found indispensable. Among blogs, I looked often at the authoritative www.scotusblog.com, the encyclopedic http://howappealing.law.com, and the irresistible, if much diminished http://underneaththeirrobes.blogs.com. I am grateful, too, to Dr. Robert Browning and his colleagues at the C-Span archive in West Lafayette, Indiana, for the opportunity to study their many treasures.

PROLOGUE

1 **The architect Cass Gilbert:** Paul Byard, "Supreme Court Architecture," lecture, Supreme Court Historical Society, U.S. Supreme Court, March 24, 1999; Fred J. and Suzy Maroon, *Supreme Court*, chs. 1–2; William H. Rehnquist, *Supreme Court*, pp. 100–2; Leo Pfeffer, *Honorable Court*, p. 69.

CHAPTER 1: THE FEDERALIST WAR OF IDEAS

13 **They called themselves the Federalist Society:** George W. Hicks, "The Conservative Influence of the Federalist Society on the Harvard Law School Student Body," *Harvard Journal of Law and Public Policy* 29 (2006), p. 648.

15 **some conservatives started questioning that wisdom:** For an extensive and critical examination of the Constitution-in-exile movement, see Cass R. Sunstein, *Radicals in Robes*, and Jeffrey Rosen, "The Unregulated Offensive," *New York Times Magazine*, April 17, 2005.

15 **a speech at Yale in 1982:** Hicks, "Conservative Influence," p. 649.

19 **"object to as much as the last one":** Ethan Bronner, *Battle for Justice*, p. 312.

21 **Sununu promised that the president:** Jane Mayer and Jill Abramson, *Strange Justice*, p. 13.

CHAPTER 2: GOOD VERSUS EVIL

25 **"They'll both bite":** Mayer and Abramson, *Strange Justice*, p. 16.

28 **Minnesota Twins:** Linda Greenhouse, *Becoming Justice Blackmun*, p. 63.

29 **William O. Douglas, then the senior associate justice:** Bob Woodward and Scott Armstrong, *The Brethren*, p. 170.

29 **Stewart responded eagerly:** J. Anthony Lukas, "The *Playboy* Interview: Bob Woodward," *Playboy*, Feb. 1989.

29 **"right on target!":** Joan Biskupic, *Sandra Day O'Connor*, p. 158.

31 **top hat as a gift:** Greenhouse, *Becoming Justice Blackmun*, p. 56.

31 **"just like a clown":** John W. Dean, "The Rehnquist Choice," p. 86.

32 **"Voices outside the room":** Bonnie Goldstein, "Rehnquist's Skeletons," *Slate*, Jan. 16, 2007, www.slate.com/id/2157684.

33 **Rehnquist had tentatively planned:** Mayer and Abramson, *Strange Justice*, pp. 349–50.

33 **the *Post* decided not to pursue the issue:** Ibid., p. 350.

CHAPTER 3: QUESTIONS PRESENTED

38 **bagpipes provided accompaniment:** Biskupic, *Sandra Day O'Connor*, pp. 31–32, 51.

39 **she voted to end criminal prohibitions:** Ibid., p. 58.

40 **a young Justice Department aide named Kenneth Starr:** David J. Garrow, "The Unlikely Center," *New Republic*, Feb. 28, 2006.

40 **audacious litigation tactics:** Edward Lazarus, *Closed Chambers*, pp. 459–86; Greenhouse, *Becoming Justice Blackmun*, pp. 199–206.

41 **he simply kept *Planned Parenthood v. Casey* off the list of cert petitions:** There is some dispute about how hard Rehnquist tried to delay the *Casey* argument. Blackmun clearly thought the chief was trying to run out the clock before the election. See David J. Garrow, "Dissenting Opinion," *New York Times Book Review*, April 19, 1998.

43 **never managed to catch up:** David J. Garrow, "Justice Souter Emerges," *New York Times Magazine*, Sept. 25, 1994.

44 **"close approach to solitude":** Garrow, "The Unlikely Center."

CHAPTER 4: COLLISION COURSE

53 **helped spark the Civil War:** David G. Savage, "The Rescue of *Roe v. Wade*," *Los Angeles Times*, Dec. 13, 1992.

53 **"decisions we do not like":** Lazarus, *Closed Chambers*, p. 471.

54 **"Wow! Pretty extreme!":** Greenhouse, *Becoming Justice Blackmun*, p. 203.

54 **a letter from a nun:** Savage, "The Rescue of *Roe v. Wade*."

55 **"correctness and legitimacy":** Greenhouse, *Becoming Justice Blackmun*, p. 204.

55 **unlikely jogging partners:** Savage, "The Rescue of *Roe v. Wade*."

56 **" 'what I think it ought to mean!' ":** Margaret Talbot, "Supreme Confidence," *New Yorker*, March 28, 2005, p. 42.

56 **correct for all time:** Mark Tushnet, *A Court Divided: The Rehnquist Court and the Future of Constitutional Law*, p. 215.

57 **He needed to "brood":** Terry Carter, "Crossing the Rubicon," *California Lawyer*, Oct. 1992.

CHAPTER 5: BIG HEART

64 **Cuomo faxed Clinton:** George Stephanopoulos, *All Too Human: A Political Education*, pp. 167–68.

67 **the Guinier nomination blew up:** John F. Harris, *The Survivor: Bill Clinton in the White House*, p. 60.

69 **less sympathy than some judges:** See http://www.oyez.org/oyez/resource/legal_entity/107/biography.

71 **"answer will be nothing but yes":** Stephanopoulos, *All Too Human*, pp. 170–71. See also Henry J. Abraham, *Justice, Presidents, and Senators*, pp. 315–20.

72 **Ruth Bader Ginsburg had been to women's rights:** Roger K. Newman, "President Clinton's Supreme Court Appointments," lecture, Hofstra University, Nov. 11, 2005.

73 **he was the only person:** David Remnick, "Negative Capability," *The New Yorker*, Nov. 27, 1995, p. 44.

CHAPTER 6: EXILES RETURN?

76 **witty speech Breyer had given:** Newman, "President Clinton's Supreme Court Appointments."

77 **"how awful you are?":** Ibid.

79 **Clinton asked his staff to leave him alone:** Ibid.

79 **His distinguished service on the judiciary continued:** See Morris Sheppard Arnold, "A Tribute to Richard S. Arnold," *Arkansas Law Review* 58 (2005): 481, 482.

82 **libertarian magazine:** Douglas H. Ginsburg, "Delegation Running Riot," *Regulation* 18, no. 1 (1995).

CHAPTER 7: WHAT SHALL BE ORTHODOX

87 **"no other gods before me":** See discussion in Noah Feldman, *Divided by God*, pp. 151ff.

89 **His law firm declared bankruptcy:** Tony Mauro, "Jay Sekulow's Golden Ticket," *Legal Times*, Oct. 31, 2005.

93 **"Wrong table":** Jeanne Cummings, "In Judge Battle, Mr. Sekulow Plays a Delicate Role," *Wall Street Journal*, May 17, 2005.

96 **various civic groups:** Biskupic, *Sandra Day O'Connor*, pp. 282–86.

CHAPTER 8: WRITING SEPARATELY

102 **Thomas required the new ones:** Kevin Merida and Michael Fletcher, *Supreme Discomfort: The Divided Soul of Clarence Thomas*, p. 163.

102 **still bedridden most of the time:** Tony Mauro, "Decade after Confirmation, Thomas Becoming a Force on High Court," *Legal Times*, Aug. 20, 2001.

104 **his mother was struggling:** Ibid., p. 39.

104 **"condo on wheels":** Merida and Fletcher, *Supreme Discomfort*, p. 340.

105 **"universally untrustworthy":** Diane Brady, "Supreme Court Justice Clarence Thomas Speaks," *BusinessWeek*, March 12, 2007.

111 **would not appear on television morning news shows:** David D. Kirkpatrick with Linda Greenhouse, "Memoir Deal Reported for Justice Thomas," *New York Times*, Jan. 10, 2003.

111 **$42,200 in gifts:** Richard A. Serrano and David G. Savage, "Justice Thomas Reports Wealth of Gifts," *Los Angeles Times*, Dec. 31, 2004.

CHAPTER 9: CARDS TO THE LEFT

117 **Clinton always said he had no memory:** Of course, it is possible that both Jones and Clinton were lying and that a consensual sexual encounter took place. See Jeffrey Toobin, *A Vast Conspiracy: The Real Story of the Sex Scandal That Nearly Brought Down a President*, p. 158.

123 **In 1975, as Jeffrey Rosen first reported:** Jeffrey Rosen, "Rehnquist the Great?" *Atlantic Monthly*, April 2005.

CHAPTER 10: THE YEAR OF THE ROUT

125 **the riches he extracted:** On Sekulow's financial arrangements, see Mauro, "Jay Sekulow's Golden Ticket."

132 **an anonymous informant slipped:** On the history of "partial birth" legislation, see Chris Black, "The Partial-Birth Fraud," *American Prospect*, Fall 2001.

CHAPTER 11: TO THE BRINK

142 **a dozen roses for him:** Biskupic, *Sandra Day O'Connor*, pp. 167–68.

143 **Stoessel's party:** See Jeffrey Toobin, *Too Close to Call: The Thirty-Six-Day Battle to Decide the 2000 Election*, pp. 248–49; Evan Thomas and Michael Isikoff, "The Truth Behind the Pillars," *Newsweek*, Dec. 25, 2000; Jess Bravin et al., "For Some Justices, the Bush-Gore Case Has a Personal Angle," *Wall Street Journal*, Dec. 20, 2000; Biskupic, *Sandra Day O'Connor*, pp. 308–9.

143 **"Pool hustler":** Biskupic, *Sandra Day O'Connor*, pp. 31, 293.

CHAPTER 12: OVER THE BRINK

156 **many clerks think they are more important:** For a realistic and moderate view of the role of law clerks, see Emily Bazelon and Dahlia Lithwick, "Endangered Elitist Species," *Slate*, posted June 13, 2006, http://www.slate.com/id/2143628/, which discusses Todd C. Peppers, *Courtiers of the Marble Palace*, and Artemus Ward and David L. Weiden, *Sorcerers' Apprentices*.

164 **"Please make sure":** For details of the actions of the Bush and Gore teams in connection with *Bush v. Gore*, see Toobin, *Too Close to Call*, chs. 15–16.

CHAPTER 13: PERFECTLY CLEAR

167 **a Ginsburg clerk:** David Margolick et al., "The Path to Florida," *Vanity Fair*, Oct. 2004; Toobin, *Too Close to Call*, chs. 15–16.

172 **how votes are counted after the election:** See, e.g., Jack Balkin, "*Bush v. Gore* and the Boundary between Law and Politics," *Yale Law Journal* 110 (2001): 1407.

172 **as innumerable commentators subsequently pointed out:** For a recent case, *Bush v. Gore* has already generated a vast literature. See, e.g., Bruce

Ackerman, ed., *Bush v. Gore: The Question of Legitimacy*, New Haven: Yale University Press, 2002; E. J. Dionne Jr. and William Kristol, eds., *Bush v. Gore: The Court Cases and the Commentary*, Washington: Brookings Institution Press, 2001; Richard A. Posner, *Breaking the Deadlock*, Princeton: Princeton University Press, 2001; Cass R. Sunstein and Richard A. Epstein, eds., *The Vote: Bush, Gore & the Supreme Court*, Chicago: University of Chicago Press, 2001.

175 **The journalists' confusion was understandable:** In fairness, I should disclose that I was one of those reporters trying to translate the opinion on live television.

176 **The recount of the 60,000 undervotes:** After the election, the most comprehensive examination of the ballots in Florida was led by eight news organizations, including the *New York Times* and the *Washington Post*, and conducted by the National Opinion Research Center. See http://www.norc.org/fl/voting.asp. The "media recount," as it became known, examined all 175,010 ballots in the state that were undervotes or overvotes and thus not counted in the final tally. Under all of the contemplated scenarios, if a full statewide recount had been conducted, the media recount showed that Gore would have won Florida; if the Court had allowed the recount to proceed in just the disputed counties, according to this recount, Bush would have won. As with the official election results, the margins between the candidates in the media recount were tiny, just a few hundred votes; moreover, this recount did not review the already counted ballots, nor could it capture the uncertainties of vote counting in the real world. In short, it is fair to say that there is no way of knowing with certainty whether Bush or Gore would have won if the Court had allowed the recount to proceed.

CHAPTER 14: "A PARTICULAR SEXUAL ACT"

184 **where a Supreme Court justice could mingle:** Anne-Marie Slaughter, *A New World Order*, ch. 2.

187 **an unusual conversation with one of his law clerks:** John C. Jeffries Jr., *Justice Lewis F. Powell Jr.* See also Joyce Murdoch and Deb Price, *Courting Justice: Gay Men and Lesbians v. the Supreme Court*, pp. 272–75.

CHAPTER 15: "A LAW-PROFESSION CULTURE"

199 **"He always had a book in front of his face":** Talbot, "Supreme Confidence."

202 **Black Hawk air combat helicopters:** David G. Savage and Richard A. Serrano, "Scalia Was Cheney Hunt Trip Guest; Ethics Concern Grows," *Los Angeles Times*, Feb. 5, 2004; Adam Nossiter, Associated Press Wire, Feb. 5, 2004.

CHAPTER 16: BEFORE SPEAKING, SAYING SOMETHING

208 **O'Connor was assigned to write the opinion:** See Biskupic, *Sandra Day O'Connor*, pp. 205–8; David G. Savage, *Turning Right: The Making of the Rehnquist Supreme Court*, pp. 239–43; Lazarus, *Closed Chambers*, pp. 291–99.

211 **grade-point averages:** Nicholas Lemann, "The Empathy Defense," *New Yorker*, Dec. 18, 2000, p. 46.

211 **Barbara Grutter was one of nine children:** Ibid., p. 48.

CHAPTER 17: THE GREEN BRIEF

227 **four of twenty-two such cases:** See generally David Cole, "The Liberal Legacy of *Bush v. Gore*," *Georgetown Law Journal* 94 (2006): 1427.

CHAPTER 18: "OUR EXECUTIVE DOESN'T"

229 **the lawyers in charge could not have differed more:** For a detailed account of the lawsuit from the plaintiff's perspective, see Joseph Margulies, *Guantánamo and the Abuse of Presidential Power*.

232 **"These photos proved to be the most powerful":** Ibid., pp. 152–53. There is no evidence that Clement knew anything about the torture.

234 **later renamed the Chicago Hilton:** On Stevens's connection to the hotel, see Charles Lane, "Justice on a Small Scale," *Washington Post*, June 5, 2005.

237 **the Court did no such thing:** See Simon Lazarus, "Federalism RIP?" *DePaul Law Review* 56 (2006): 1, 30–35.

CHAPTER 19: "A GREAT PRIVILEGE, INDEED"

242 **This was a different salute:** Linda Greenhouse, "The Inauguration: Ailing Chief Justice Makes Good His Promise," *New York Times*, Jan. 21, 2005.

244 **"Fajitas and frivolity":** Biskupic, *Sandra Day O'Connor*, p. 249.

CHAPTER 20: "'G' IS FOR GOD"

268 **Miranda wasn't much more than a glorified blogger:** See Michael Crowley, "Miranda Rights," *New Republic*, July 25, 2005; Alexander Bolton, "Fall and Rise of Miranda," *Hill*, Nov. 9, 2005.

CHAPTER 21: RETIRING THE TROPHY

277 **Cheney and Miers were on board:** Peter Baker, "Unraveling the Twists and Turns of the Path to a Nominee," *Washington Post*, July 25, 2005.

283 **he remembered something else that Reid:** Elsa Walsh, "Minority Retort," *New Yorker*, Aug. 8 and 15, 2005, p. 42.

CHAPTER 22: "I KNOW HER HEART"

286 **the law firm where she would spend:** J. Michael Kennedy et al., "Few Clues to Miers' Convictions," *Los Angeles Times*, Oct. 6, 2005.

287 **"Harriet epitomizes that":** Ibid.

289 **Hecht himself would be speaking:** John Fund, "Judgment Call," Opinionjournal.com, Oct. 17, 2005.

291 **"I agree with that":** Ibid.

293 **an "engaging person":** Dana Milbank, "The Sales Calls Begin on Capitol Hill, but Some Aren't Buying," *Washington Post*, Oct. 6, 2005.

293 **"this president's knowledge of this nominee":** Peter Baker and Dan Balz, "Conservatives Confront Bush Aides," *Washington Post*, Oct. 6, 2005.

CHAPTER 23: DINNER AT THE JUST DESSERTS CAFÉ

307 **DeLay in the House and John Cornyn in the Senate:** Mike Allen and Charles Babington, "House Votes to Undercut High Court on Property," *Washington Post*, July 1, 2005.

CHAPTER 24: "I AM AND ALWAYS HAVE BEEN . . ."

311 **he sought to move up to a position:** Jo Becker and Dale Russakoff, "Proving His Mettle in the Reagan Years," *Washington Post*, Jan. 9, 2006.

314 **Neas insisted that he had to be stopped:** Lois Romano and Juliet Eilperin, "Republicans Were Masters in the Race to Paint Alito," *Washington Post*, Feb. 2, 2006.

320 **Katyal constructed a legal assault:** See Nina Totenberg, profile of Neal Katyal, National Public Radio, http://www.npr.org/templates/story/story.php?storyId=575135.

CHAPTER 25: PHANATICS?

325 **"Should *Grutter v. Bollinger* . . . be overturned?":** By a public initiative passed on November 7, 2006, Michigan voters overturned the university affirmative action program which the Supreme Court had approved in *Grutter*. The conservative leader Ward Connerly led the fight to end preferential treatment for minority students. The initiative itself, known as Proposal 2, has also been challenged in the courts.

331 **unprecedented in the Court's recent history:** All statistics come from the authoritative compilation at Scotusblog. See http://www.scotusblog.com/movable type/archives/MemoOT06.pdf.

333 **Thomas had not asked a single question:** According to a study of the year's oral argument transcripts by Michael Doyle of the McClatchy Newspapers, Breyer spoke the most words, 34,937, followed by Scalia with 30,087. Alito

was second-to-last with 5,674, and Thomas last with zero. See http://www. mcclatchydc.com/201/story/16193.html.

EPILOGUE: THE STEPS—CLOSED

338 "It is rarely possible to say": Richard A. Posner, "The Supreme Court 2004 Term—Foreword: A Political Court," 119 *Harvard Law Review* 31 (2005).

BIBLIOGRAPHY

Abraham, Henry J. *Justices, Presidents, and Senators*. Rev. ed. New York: Rowman and Littlefield, 1999.

Amar, Akhil Reed. *America's Constitution: A Biography*. New York: Random House, 2005.

Atkinson, David N. *Leaving the Bench: Supreme Court Justices at the End*. Lawrence: University Press of Kansas, 1999.

Biskupic, Joan. *Sandra Day O'Connor: How the First Woman on the Supreme Court Became Its Most Influential Justice*. New York: Ecco Books, 2005.

Bork, Robert H. *The Tempting of America: The Political Seduction of the Law*. New York: Free Press, 1990.

Breyer, Stephen. *Active Liberty: Interpreting Our Democratic Constitution*. New York: Alfred A. Knopf, 2005.

Bronner, Ethan. *Battle for Justice: How the Bork Nomination Shook America*. New York: W. W. Norton, 1989.

Clinton, Bill. *My Life*. New York: Alfred A. Knopf, 2004.

Dean, John W. *The Rehnquist Choice: The Untold Story of the Nixon Appointment That Redefined the Supreme Court*. New York: Free Press, 2001.

Feldman, Noah. *Divided by God: America's Church-State Problem—and What We Should Do about It*. New York: Farrar, Straus and Giroux, 2005.

Foskett, Ken. *Judging Thomas: The Life and Times of Clarence Thomas*. New York: Harper Perennial, 2005.

Garbus, Martin. *Courting Disaster: The Supreme Court and the Unmaking of American Law*. New York: Times Books, 2002.

Greenburg, Jan Crawford. *Supreme Conflict*. New York: Penguin Books, 2007.

Greenhouse, Linda. *Becoming Justice Blackmun: Harry Blackmun's Supreme Court Journey*. New York: Times Books, 2005.

Gunther, Gerald. *Learned Hand: The Man and the Judge.* New York: Alfred A. Knopf, 1994.

Harris, John F. *The Survivor: Bill Clinton in the White House.* New York: Random House, 2005.

Harris, Richard. *Decision.* New York: E. P. Dutton, 1971.

Jeffries, John C. Jr. *Justice Lewis F. Powell Jr.* New York: Fordham University Press, 2001.

Klarman, Michael J. *From Jim Crow to Civil Rights: The Supreme Court and the Struggle for Racial Equality.* New York: Oxford University Press, 2004.

Kramer, Larry D. *The People Themselves: Popular Constitutionalism and Judicial Review.* New York: Oxford University Press, 2004.

Lazarus, Edward. *Closed Chambers: The Rise, Fall, and Future of the Modern Supreme Court.* New York: Penguin Books, 1999.

Margulies, Joseph. *Guantánamo and the Abuse of Presidential Power.* New York: Simon and Schuster, 2006.

Maroon, Suzy, and Fred J. Maroon. *The Supreme Court of the United States.* New York: Thomasson-Grant and Lickle, 1996.

Mayer, Jane, and Jill Abramson. *Strange Justice: The Selling of Clarence Thomas.* Boston: Houghton Mifflin, 1994.

McElroy, Lisa Tucker. *John G. Roberts, Jr.* Minneapolis: Lerner Publications, 2007.

Merida, Kevin, and Michael Fletcher. *Supreme Discomfort: The Divided Soul of Clarence Thomas.* New York: Doubleday, 2007.

Murdoch, Joyce, and Deb Price. *Courting Justice: Gay Men and Lesbians v. the Supreme Court.* New York: Basic Books, 2001.

Murphy, Bruce Allen. *Wild Bill: The Legend and Life of William O. Douglas.* New York: Random House, 2003.

O'Brien, David M. *Storm Center: The Supreme Court in American Politics.* 6th ed. New York: W. W. Norton, 2003.

Peppers, Todd C. *Courtiers of the Marble Palace: The Rise and Influence of the Supreme Court Law Clerk.* Stanford: Stanford University Press, 2006.

Pfeffer, Leo. *This Honorable Court.* Boston: Beacon Press, 1965.

Posner, Richard A. *Not a Suicide Pact: The Constitution in a Time of National Emergency.* New York: Oxford University Press, 2006.

Rehnquist, William H. *The Supreme Court: How It Was, How It Is.* New York: William Morrow, 1987.

Rosen, Jeffrey S. *The Most Democratic Branch: How the Courts Serve America.* New York: Oxford University Press, 2006.

———. *The Supreme Court.* New York: Times Books, 2007.

Savage, David G. *Turning Right: The Making of the Rehnquist Supreme Court.* New York: John Wiley and Sons, 1993.

Scalia, Antonin. *A Matter of Interpretation: Federal Courts and the Law.* Princeton: Princeton University Press, 1997.

Schwartz, Bernard. *A History of the Supreme Court.* New York: Oxford University Press, 1993.

Simon, James F. *The Center Holds: The Power Struggle Inside the Rehnquist Court.* New York: Simon and Schuster, 1995.

Slaughter, Anne-Marie. *A New World Order.* Princeton: Princeton University Press, 2004.

Starr, Kenneth W. *First among Equals: The Supreme Court in American Life.* New York: Warner Books, 2002.

Stephanopoulos, George. *All Too Human: A Political Education.* Boston: Little, Brown, 1999.

Stohr, Greg. *A Black and White Case: How Affirmative Action Survived Its Greatest Legal Challenge.* Princeton: Bloomberg Press, 2004.

Stone, Geoffrey R. *Perilous Times: Free Speech in Wartime.* New York: W. W. Norton, 2004.

Sunstein, Cass R. *One Case at a Time: Judicial Minimalism on the Supreme Court.* Cambridge: Harvard University Press, 1999.

———. *Radicals in Robes: Why Extreme Right-Wing Courts Are Wrong for America.* New York: Basic Books, 2005.

Toobin, Jeffrey. *Too Close to Call: The Thirty-Six-Day Battle to Decide the 2000 Election.* New York: Random House, 2001.

Tribe, Laurence H. *God Save This Honorable Court: How the Choice of Supreme Court Justices Shapes Our History.* New York: Random House, 1985.

Tushnet, Mark. *A Court Divided: The Rehnquist Court and the Future of Constitutional Law.* New York: W. W. Norton, 2005.

Ward, Artemus, and David L. Weiden. *Sorcerers' Apprentices: 100 Years of Law Clerks at the United States Supreme Court.* New York: New York University Press, 2006.

Woodward, Bob, and Scott Armstrong. *The Brethren: Inside the Supreme Court.* New York: Simon and Schuster, 1979.

Yarbrough, Tinsley E. *David Hackett Souter: Traditional Republican on the Rehnquist Court.* New York: Oxford University Press, 2005.

PHOTO CREDITS

Grateful acknowledgment is given to the following for the photos in this book:

Page 1.   Mark Wilson/Getty Images
Page 2.   Win McNamee/Getty Images
Page 3, top.   Jason Reed/Reuters/Corbis
Page 3, bottom left.   Jeffrey Markowitz/Corbis Sygma
Page 3, bottom right.   Frank Franklin II/AP/Wide World Photos
Page 4, top left.   Aynsley Floyd/AP/Wide World Photos
Page 4, top right.   J. Scott Applewhite/AP/Wide World Photos
Page 4, bottom left.   Paul Sancya/AP/Wide World Photos
Page 4, bottom right.   Peter A. Smith
Page 5, top.   Kenneth Lambert/AP/Wide World Photos
Page 5, bottom.   Liu Jiansheng/AP/Wide World Photos
Page 5, bottom right.   Michael Kooren/REUTERS
Page 6.   Jason Reed/Reuters/Corbis
Page 7, top.   Kevin Lamarque/Reuters/Corbis
Page 7, bottom.   Ron Edmonds/AP/Wide World Photos
Page 8, top left.   Charles Dharapak/AP/Wide World Photos
Page 8, top right.   Dennis Cook/AP/Wide World Photos
Page 8, bottom.   Joe Raedle/Getty Images

INDEX

ABA (American Bar Association), 184,
185, 269, 314
abortion rights, 12, 13, 75, 260, 326,
329–30, 331
Arizona legalization efforts on, 39–40
as central judicial issue, 36, 62, 241,
265, 266, 270, 277, 312
foreign laws on, 197
as fundamental right, 46–47, 56
maternal health considered in, 49–50,
133, 134, 135, 309, 310
physicians' assessment linked to, 49–50
privacy rights argument on, 15–16, 45,
49, 71
religious opposition to, 20, 53, 88
trimester analysis applied to, 49, 50, 58
abortion rights, limitation of, 3, 7, 336
gag rule as, 43
judicial bypass of parental consent
requirement as, 269–70
on late-term procedures, 132–36,
327–29
parental notification requirement as,
309–10
risk information mandated as, 16–17
as sex discrimination, 71
spousal notification as, 37–38, 52, 54,
58–59, 132, 299–300
twenty-four-hour waiting period as, 37,
50, 199
undue burden standard applied to,
50–51, 58, 310
Abramson, Jill, 33
Abu Ghraib prison, 232, 233, 234
ACLJ (American Center for Law and
Justice), 92, 125–26
ACLU (American Civil Liberties Union),
40, 41, 69, 92, 125, 229, 304

Active Liberty (Breyer), 303
Adarand Construction, Inc. v. Pena, 212, 216
affirmative action. *See* racial preferences
Afghanistan, U.S. detainees from, 228–29
See also Guantánamo Bay, U.S. detainees
held at
African Americans
affirmative action programs for; *see* racial
preferences
in military service, 214
airports, religious proselytizing at, 90–91
Albert Gore, Jr. v. Katherine Harris, 157–68,
160
See also Bush v. Gore
Alito, Martha-Ann, 316
Alito, Samuel A., Jr., 318, 319, 325, 332,
333
on abortion rulings, 16–17, 37–38, 52,
58, 59, 299–300, 312, 315, 328
background of, 299, 311, 314
conservative credentials of, 298, 311,
312, 314, 327
death penalty supported by, 334
on Guantánamo detainees, 321, 322
law clerks hired by, 317
on race case, 336
as Supreme Court candidate, 273, 274,
275, 298, 299, 311–16
welcoming dinner for, 323–24
Al Qaeda, 229, 231
American Bar Association (ABA), 184,
185, 269, 314
American Center for Law and Justice
(ACLJ), 92, 125–26
American Civil Liberties Union (ACLU),
40, 41, 69, 92, 125, 229, 304
American Enterprise Institute, 110
American Medical Association, 135

ABOUT THE AUTHOR

Jeffrey Toobin is a staff writer at *The New Yorker*, senior legal analyst at CNN, and the author of such bestsellers as *Too Close to Call: The Thirty-Six-Day Battle to Decide the 2000 Election*, *A Vast Conspiracy: The Real Story of the Sex Scandal That Nearly Brought Down a President*, and *The Run of His Life: The People v. O. J. Simpson*.